Pattern Recognition in Soft Computing Paradigm

Fuzzy Logic Systems Institute (FLSI) Soft Computing Series

Series Editor: Takeshi Yamakawa *(Fuzzy Logic Systems Institute, Japan)*

Published

Vol. 1: Advanced Signal Processing Technology by Soft Computing
edited by Charles Hsu (Trident Systems Inc., USA)

Forthcoming

Vol. 3: What Should be Computed to Understand and Model Brain Function? — From Robotics, Soft Computing, Biology and Neuroscience to Cognitive Philosophy
edited by Tadashi Kitamura (Kyushu Institute of Technology, Japan)

Vol. 4: Practical Applications of Soft Computing in Engineering
edited by Sung-Bae Cho (Yonsei University, Korea)

Vol. 5: A New Paradigm of Knowledge Engineering by Soft Computing
edited by Liya Ding (National University of Singapore)

 Soft Computing Series — Volume 2

Pattern Recognition in Soft Computing Paradigm

Editor

Nikhil R Pal
Indian Statistical Institute

Fuzzy Logic
Systems Institute
(FLSI)

World Scientific
Singapore • New Jersey • London • Hong Kong

Published by
World Scientific Publishing Co. Pte. Ltd.
P O Box 128, Farrer Road, Singapore 912805
USA office: Suite 1B, 1060 Main Street, River Edge, NJ 07661
UK office: 57 Shelton Street, Covent Garden, London WC2H 9HE

British Library Cataloguing-in-Publication Data
A catalogue record for this book is available from the British Library.

PATTERN RECOGNITION IN SOFT COMPUTING PARADIGM
FLSI Soft Computing Series — Volume 2

Copyright © 2001 by World Scientific Publishing Co. Pte. Ltd.

All rights reserved. This book, or parts thereof, may not be reproduced in any form or by any means, electronic or mechanical, including photocopying, recording or any information storage and retrieval system now known or to be invented, without written permission from the Publisher.

For photocopying of material in this volume, please pay a copying fee through the Copyright Clearance Center, Inc., 222 Rosewood Drive, Danvers, MA 01923, USA. In this case permission to photocopy is not required from the publisher.

ISBN 981-02-4491-6

Printed in Singapore by Uto-Print

To
my mother, the source of all my inspiration

Series Editor's Preface

The IIZUKA conference originated from the Workshop on Fuzzy Systems Application in 1988 at a small city, Iizuka, which is located in the center of Fukuoka prefecture in the most southern island, Kyushu, of Japan, and was very famous for coal mining until forty years ago. Iizuka city is now renewed to be a science research park. The first IIZUKA conference was held in 1990 and from then onward this conference has been held every two years. The series of these conferences played important role in the modern artificial intelligence. The workshop in 1988 proposed the fusion of fuzzy concept and neuro-science and by this proposal the research on neuro-fuzzy systems and fuzzy neural systems has been encouraged to produce significant results. The conference in 1990 was dedicated to the special topics, chaos, and nonlinear dynamical systems came into the interests of researchers in the field of fuzzy systems. The fusion of fuzzy, neural and chaotic systems was familiar to the conference participants in 1992. This new paradigm of information processing including genetic algorithms and fractals is spread over the world as "Soft Computing".

Fuzzy Logic Systems Institute (FLSI) was established, under the supervision of Ministry of Education, Science and Sports (MOMBUSHOU) and International Trade and Industry (MITI), in 1989 for the purpose of proposing brand-new technologies, collaborating with companies and universities, giving university students education of soft computing, etc.

FLSI is the major organization promoting so called IIZUKA Conference, so that this series of books edited from IIZUKA Conference is named as FLSI Soft Computing Series.

The Soft Computing Series covers a variety of topics in Soft Computing and will propose the emergence of a post-digital intelligent systems.

                                        Takeshi Yamakawa, Ph.D.
                                        Chairman, IIZUKA 2000
                                        Chairman, Fuzzy Logic Systems Institute

Volume Editor's Preface

Pattern recognition (PR) consists of three important tasks: feature analysis, clustering and classification. We view image analysis also a pattern recognition task. Success of a clustering algorithm or of a classifier heavily depends on the set of features used to represent the objects of interest. Any set of nominated features may or may not be necessary (or sufficient) for a given problem. There may be features that have derogatory effects; some may be redundant, while others may be indifferent. Choice of a good set of features depends on the task as well as the tools used. Hence, feature analysis is one of the most important steps of designing any successful PR system. A distinguishing feature of this volume is that it deals with all three aspects of PR, namely feature analysis, clustering and classifier design. It also encompasses image processing methodologies to image retrieval with subjective information. The other interesting part of the volume is that it covers all three major facets of soft computing : fuzzy logic, neural networks and evolutionary computing.

Based on the papers presented in IIZUKA'98 conference, a small set of papers was short-listed for the edited volume. Authors of the short-listed papers were then requested to submit enhanced versions of their papers for the book. All submitted chapters went through a rigorous review process and based on the review results we have selected only fourteen chapters covering various facets of pattern recognition in a soft computing paradigm.

The first five chapters provide an adequate representation of feature analysis including dimensionality reduction and data visualization and their applications. Chapter 6 is on fuzzy clustering while chapters 7 through 11 are on classifier design using soft computing approaches. The last three chapters of the book deal with image analysis in soft computing paradigm.

Chapter 1 is on feature extraction and multivariate data projection. The author does an excellent job of reviewing various relevant methods - supervised and unsupervised, linear and non-linear. Utility of some such methods in different applications is assessed. The author also discusses different advanced mapping techniques and interactive visualization techniques which can be used for navigation through data.

Chapter 2 also deals with feature analysis using the Self-Organizing Map (SOM). Authors explains how SOM can be used for visualization and novelty detection in a high dimensional data. They also present some interesting methods for enhancing the visualization capability of SOM based methods. Some applications to industrial processes are presented. Tools discussed in Chapters 1 and 2 can be used for knowledge discovery from the jungle of data.

Analysis of the ocean surface is very important for the study of climatic changes, resources management etc. The author presents an interesting system based on a hierarchy of self-organizing maps for clustering and differentiation of oceanic water in Chapter 3. Unlike the radiative transfer model, the unsupervised neural network used in this method does not make any assumption about how spectra are distributed and interwined together. This makes the approach attractive and promising.

In Chapter 4, a modified version of multiplayer feed-forward neural network is used for feature selection. The network has a "fractal connection structure". The feature subset selection algorithm is based on evaluation of features according to their contribution to correct classification rate estimated using samples not used for training. Specifically, a feature is removed and performance of the net on a test set is evaluated. The feature having the least influence is treated as the most irrelevant feature and so on.

Chapter 5 deals with character recognition problem in a soft computing paradigm. A set of fuzzy features is defined and extracted from the Hough transform of the character images. Genetic algorithm is used for feature selection and finally the selected fuzzy features are used to train a multiplayer network producing fuzzy output label vectors. Authors used a two-state Markov chain to model degraded documents for simulation studies.

Most clustering algorithms require users to specify the number of clusters. Authors of Chapter 6 propose a new clustering method which decides on the number of clusters using Genetic Algorithms. It is assumed that each cluster follows normal distribution. Authors use the density function values to compute the fuzzy membership of each data point to different clusters. They investigated two coding schemes, graph structured coding and linear structured coding. The former can produce better solutions at the cost of more iterations while the later requires less number of generations.

A new classification method is proposed in Chapter 7 using the associatron neural network model. The associatorn model is altered to have three level stable outputs. Some applications including diagnosis of liver disease are demonstrated.

A system for analyzing hand shape changes using Generalized Radial Basis Function (GRBF) network has been developed in Chapter 8. The network can recognize a limited number of 3D – hand shapes and shape changes. The "structural learning" algorithm used by the authors automatically determines the number of nodes required in the hidden layer for the given task.

Chapter 9 deals with non-linear discriminat analysis using feed-forward neural networks and use it for medical diagnosis problems. The parameters of the network are estimated using the maximum likelihood principle. The goodness of the obtained network is evaluated using the statistic deviance which follows a chi-square distribution. Authors also considered Akaike's information criterion in this regard. Statistical tools are used for network pruning and selection of a "best" subset of predictor variables.

Measurement of a feature for decision making usually involves some cost and time, and both of these could be high for applications like medical diagnosis. In Chapter 10, authors demonstrate that measurement of all attributes are not necessary when classifying a pattern by a trained network. Unlike feature analysis where a fixed subset of features is always used, here for different inputs the number of features used could be different. The proposed scheme is based on interval arithmetic in which each unmeasured feature is represented by an interval containing its possible values. Authors try to minimize the number of attributes to be measured without degradation of classification performance.

Chapter 11 deals with extraction of fuzzy rules from numerical data for pattern classification. The approach is of exploratory nature. For each feature, a set of fuzzy feature values is generated by a fuzzy partitioning of the concerned domain and then a "descriptor-pattern" table is constructed which is used for discovering rules. A rule minimization scheme is then used to retain a small set of rules which is refined through tuning of membership functions using genetic algorithms. Unlike most classifiers, the proposed method can detect ambiguous data and declare them as unclassified and it can also deal with fuzzy test data.

Genetic programming is used in Chapter 12 to develop a framework for automated generation of texture filters. The 2D texture filtering framework is based on 2D-lookup which enables one to represent a large number of texture filters easily. The genetic programming based evolution is driven by the user specified goals. Authors demonstrated their algorithm for several applications including fault detection.

Texture image segmentation is an important facet of many applications. Consequently, extraction of good texture features is important. Chapter 13 proposes an interesting approach for extraction of texture features and their application to texture segmentation. A gray level image is first segmented into several binary images using several threshold and then topological features are computed from all these binary images. Using these features a pyramid linking method with band-pass filter neural networks is used to develop a texture segmentation algorithm.

Chapter 14 presents a system for image retrieval that can deal with each user's subjectivity and perception. The prototype system developed allows users to retrieve images using various adjectives to describe the characteristics of the desired images. The system has the capability to identify the correlation between the features of the images and the user's description through interactive learning.

These fourteen chapters will provide the readers a wide spectrum of theories and applications of soft computing in pattern recognition.

Before I conclude, I would like to express my sincere thanks to Prof. Yamakawa, the Series Editor, for inviting me to work on this volume. I also like to thank the referees for their valuable time and effort. Thanks also due to the authors who have always extended their cooperation to complete this volume. Last, but not the least, I am thankful to my wife who has helped me in different ways to complete this book.

Nikhil R. Pal
Indian Statistical Institute
Calcutta
June, 2000

Contents

Series Editor's Preface v

Volume Editor's Preface vii

Chapter 1   Dimensionality Reduction Techniques for Interactive
            Visualization, Exploratory Data Analysis, and Classification 1
            A. König

Chapter 2   The Self-Organizing Map as a Tool in Knowledge Engineering 38
            J. Himberg, J. Ahola, E. Alhoniemi, J. Vesanto and O. Simula

Chapter 3   Classification of Oceanic Water Types Using Self-organizing
            Feature Maps 66
            E. J. Ainsworth

Chapter 4   Feature Selection by Artificial Neural Network for
            Pattern Classification 95
            B. Chakraborty

Chapter 5   MLP Based Character Recognition using Fuzzy Features and
            a Genetic Algorithm for Feature Selection 110
            S. Sural and P. K. Das

Chapter 6   A New Clustering with Estimation of Cluster Number Based
            on Genetic Algorithms 142
            K. Imai, N. Kamiura and Y. Hata

Chapter 7   Associative Classification Method 163
            A. Kanagawa and H. Takahashi

Chapter 8   Recgonition of Shapes and Shape Changes in 3D-Objects
            by GRBF Network: A Structural Learning Algorithm to
            Explore Small-Sized Networks 181
            M. Okamoto, M. Hirakawa, N. Kinoshita, T. Katsuki,
            T. Miyazaki, and M. Ishibashi

Chapter 9 Non-Linear Discriminant Analysis Using Feed-Forward
          Neural Networks 196
          T. Koshimizu and M. Tsujitani

Chapter 10 Minimizing the Measurement Cost in the Classification
           of New Samples by Neural-Network-Based Classifiers 225
           H. Ishibuchi and M. Nii

Chapter 11 Extraction of Fuzzy Rules from Numerical Data for Classifiers ... 249
           N. R. Pal and A. Sarkar

Chapter 12 Genetic Programming Based Texture Filtering Framework 275
           M. Koppen and B. Nickolay

Chapter 13 A Texture Image Segmentation Method Using Neural
           Networks and Binary Features 305
           J. Zhang and S. Oe

Chapter 14 Image Retrieval System Based on Subjective Information 330
           K. Yoshida, T. Kato and T. Yanaru

About the Authors 351

Keyword Index 387

Chapter 1
Dimensionality Reduction Techniques for Interactive Visualization, Exploratory Data Analysis, and Classification

Andreas König
Dresden University of Technology

Abstract

In this contribution, from three decades of research in various disciplines, algorithms for dimensionality reduction, serving for feature extraction and multivariate data projection are briefly reviewed and compared in an unifying approach. The applicability of the reviewed dimensionality reduction methods for data compression or discriminance analysis in classification systems is assessed. Techniques for ensuing interactive data visualization, data navigation and visual exploratory data analysis are presented. Advanced mapping algorithms and hierarchical concepts are introduced that in conjunction with interactive visualization techniques explicitly support the remarkable human perceptive and associative capabilities for visual exploratory data analysis. The benefit of the visualization approach for systematic recognition system design is pointed out.

Keywords : data structure analysis, visual exploratory data analysis, topology preserving mapping, distance preserving mapping, Gestalt theory, multivariate projection, multivariate classification, discriminance analysis, data compression

1.1 Introduction

Dimensionality reducing mappings for feature extraction, multivariate data projection, visualization, and interactive analysis have been a topic of interest for more than three decades [26], [27]. Especially the pioneering work of Sammon is giving inspiration for todays information processing systems. Already in his work, dimensionality reduction was combined with the issues of interactive visual data analysis, classification, and interactive visual classifier design [27]. Recently, there is strong renewed interest in this topic incented by, e.g. data mining, data warehouse, and knowledge discovery applications. To cope with todays flood of data from rapidly growing databases and related computational resources, especially to discover salient structures and interesting correlations in data, advanced methods of machine learning, pattern recognition, data analysis and visualization are required. The remarkable ability of human observers to perceive clusters and correlations, and thus structure in data, is of great interest and can be well exploited by effective systems for data projection and interactive visualization.

This paper will give a focused survey of interdisciplinary activities in pattern recognition and neural networks, starting three decades in the past until today. In the following section, dimensionality reduction techniques will be reviewed in an unifying approach. Then, techniques and benefits of interactive visualization will be presented. The last section before the conclusions is dedicated to advanced ideas and mapping techniques for visualization and analysis.

1.2 Feature Extraction and Multivariate Data Projection

To escape the *curse of dimensionality* [7], i.e. the exponential increase of required samples with growing dimensionality of pattern space, dimensionality reduction techniques are applied. In pattern recognition, for feature vectors $\mathbf{v} = [v_1, v_2, \ldots, v_o]^T$ *feature extraction* and *feature selection* [8] are defined as a transformation $J(A) = max_A J(\mathcal{A}(\mathbf{v}))$ and $J(X) = max_\chi J(\chi)$, respectively. While in selection, according to a chosen criterion J, the best features are retained and the remaining ones are discarded, in extraction all features are retained and are subject to transformation A. In both cases a mapping $\Phi : R^o \to R^d$ optimizing a criterion J with $d < o$ and $\mathbf{y} = [y_1, y_2, \ldots, y_d]^T$ is determined. Here $\mathbf{y} = \mathcal{A}(\mathbf{v})$ can be a linear or non-linear mapping as transformation and employ unsupervised well as a supervised information. Especially in image processing, the step from iconic to symbolic representation by means of heuristic procedures is often denoted as *feature computation* though this could also be included in the definition of feature extraction. Feature computation and extraction or selection can be cascaded for ensuing *classification*, that carries out a partitioning of the final feature space. This feature space should be optimum with regard to both constraints compactness and discriminance and thus, the achievable dimensionality is application dependent and for the sake of discriminance should not be fixed in advance. *Feature visualization* in contrast requires a dimensionality reduction to a two or three-dimensional representation (cf. e.g., [28], [29], [21]). Fig. 1.1 gives a taxonomy of state-of-the-art dimensionality reduction methods in an unified presentation. The methods given in

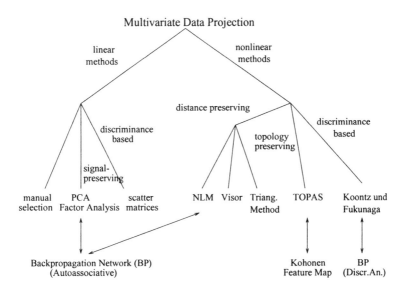

Fig. 1.1 Taxonomy of Projection Methods.

the taxonomy have all been implemented and assessed in this work [18], [16]. Recently emerging relevant techniques will be pointed out throughout the discussion. Though emphasis of this contribution is on unsupervised mapping procedures also relevant supervised mapping techniques are covered [7], [20]. Further, interesting mapping and display techniques dedicated to data classification [4], [5] should at least be mentioned here in the broader context of the topic. Complementing the definitions given above, the terms of feature computation, extraction, selection, and ranking are summarized introducing the term of *feature analysis* [25].

1.2.1 Benchmark data

For demonstration of method properties, several data sets will be used in the following. First, an artificial data set, denoted as *Cube*-data will be used for unsupervised mappings to demonstrate structure preservation properties. A cube with 50 points on eight edges of two opposite sides was generated. The 3D-cube was rotated by $45°$ with regard to the coordinate axes. Points of respective edges were numbered consecutively from 1 to 8. Further, the well known *Iris data* (cf. e.g. [32]) was used for demonstration of supervised and unsupervised mapping techniques. Especially for demonstration of visualization techniques, for the sake of clarity, this data set was predominantly employed. Another example from mechatronics [31] was used in the following. The 24-dimensional data was generated from Fourier spectra obtained from the compressor of a turbine jet engine. Four operation regions were defined as classes. Five data sets, denoted as $Mech_1$ to $Mech_5$, with 375 samples each were drawn from a compressor set-up. The objective of the underlying research was the development of a *Stall-Margin-Indicator* for optimum jet engine operation. An additional data set comes from an X-ray inspection of ball grid array packages in electronics manufacturing. Here, 10 dimensional feature vectors were computed and 3 classes had to be distinguished [14].

1.2.2 Unsupervised linear mapping techniques

A mapping can most simply be achieved by explicit selection of two (or three) salient components or factors. However, context knowledge is required for such a selection, e.g. supervised automatic feature selection methods [8], [11] can be employed to find salient features for visualization. As an alternative to selection, the simultaneous display of multiple linked pairwise plots of the data set is proposed in some tool kits. However, the combinatorial explosion ($\frac{M(M-1)}{2}$ plots for M-dimensional data) limits practical application of this approach. This is demonstrated in Fig. 1.2 for Iris data with (y,x) is (1,2), (1,3), (1,4), (2,3), (2,4), and (3,4), respectively. A mapping can also be achieved by the first two (three) principal components of *Principal Component Analysis* (PCA) [7] If the PCA assumption of Gaussian distribution is met and most variance is presented by the first two principal components, then suitable plots can be achieved by this linear method [28]. Fig. 1.3 gives an example for $Mech_1$. The crite-

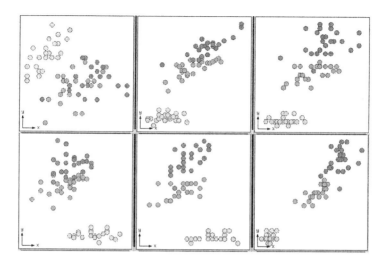

Fig. 1.2 Multiple pairwise plots for Iris data.

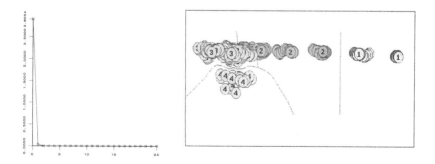

Fig. 1.3 Scree plot and two first principal components plot for Mech$_1$.

rion for the PCA mapping is *signal preservation*, i.e. least error distortion when the signal is reconstructed from the selected principal components and not structure preservation or discriminance gain. Thus, neither for ensuing classification nor for visualization the best results can in general be expected from PCA (cf. e.g., [27], p.602). Further, if the data set size is not adequate with regard to data dimension, accuracy as well as numerical problems might result. As a rule of thumb, for each position in the covariance matrix one pattern is required for an acceptable estimation. However, for data such as Mech$_1$ PCA would be good, maybe even first choice (cf. scree plot in Fig. 1.3). An interesting alternative, not implemented here, are PCA neural networks as summarized and proposed by Oja [24].

1.2.3 Neural network based unsupervised mapping techniques

Backpropagation networks (BP) have been applied in autoassociative mode and a bottleneck topology to achieve mappings comparable to PCA [24]. With a five layer topology a nonlinear, *signal preserving* mapping is computed from the input to the middle layer (cf. Fig. 1.4 a)). However, thus

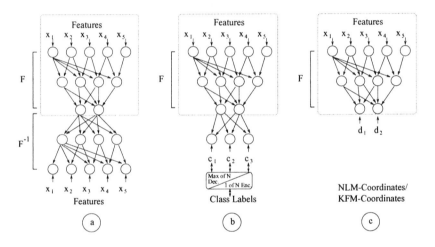

Fig. 1.4 Topologies of BP-networks for feature extraction and data projection.

achieved projections are hard to interpret and strongly depend on other network parameters, e.g. the number of hidden layer neurons.

The most promising mapping methods in terms of structure preservation use the criteria of either topology or distance preservation for the nonlinear mapping process. Kohonen's Self-Organzing Map (SOM) [19] is perhaps the most popular method for data visualization. During training, the SOM unfolds in pattern space and creates a topology preserving mapping of the multivariate data on the fixed neuron grid (or cube for 3D-SOM). Though this mapping, as given in Fig. 1.5, is interesting concerning neighborhood relations, no information is given on intra/inter-cluster distance. Researchers working on exploratory data analysis thus complemented the SOM with

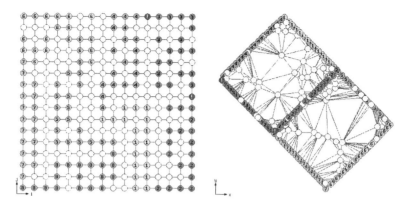

Fig. 1.5 SOM trained with *Cube*-data: grid (left) and Visor-projection (right).

this distance information by a method denoted as *Unified-Distance-Matrix* (U-matrix) [30]. The U-matrix method exploits the third dimension to plot

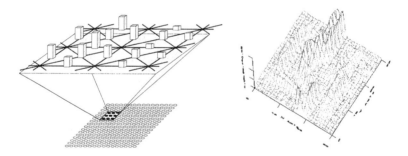

Fig. 1.6 U-Matrix principle (left) and plot for *Cube*-data (right).

interneuron distance information as a landscape or grey-value shading on the SOM-grid, i.e. a mountain range implicates a large distance between clusters. Kohonen proposed distance preserving mappings, e.g. Sammon's *Non-Linear-Mapping* (NLM) [26], as a means to include distance information in SOM visualization by mapping SOM weight vectors (cf. Fig. 1.8 right). In addition to the missing distance information, several other practical problems will be met using SOM displays. First, due to the quantization carried out by SOM along with the topology preserving mapping the SOM is not suited for identifying the position of individual data vectors in the map visualization. All data vectors falling in the Voronoi cell of a certain

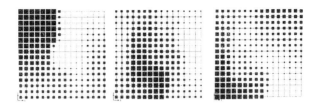

Fig. 1.7 SOM component planes for *Cube*-data.

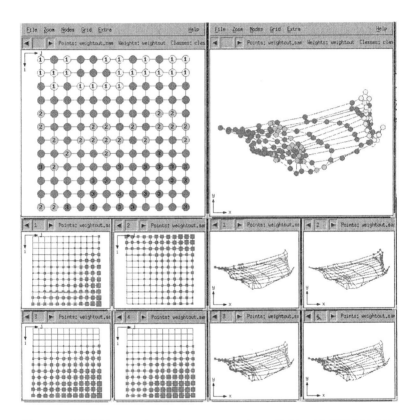

Fig. 1.8 SOM Iris mapping and component planes (left), with NLM (right).

SOM weight vector are represented by the same point on the SOM-grid. Second, SOM interpolation properties cause the placement of weight vectors in pattern space regions actually void of data vectors. Third, if the training data possesses not only a high absolute dimension but also a high *intrinsic dimension* [7] larger than two (or three) dimensions, the SOM starts to fold and twist in the attempt to establish a mapping to the plane of the neuron grid. This can lead to the scattered representation of an intrinsically high-dimensional cluster all over the map and consequently to misinterpretations by human observers. Using 3D-SOM increases the range of applicability, but as soon as problems with intrinsic dimension larger or equal to four are met, the same arguments hold again. The *Growing-Cells* of Fritzke [2] offer a remedy to the second SOM problem, as they dynamically allocate neurons only in regions of significant pattern density. However, no improvement is evident from the method for the other two issues.

1.2.4 *Nonlinear unsupervised mapping techniques*

The NLM of Sammon [26] in contrast is a distance preserving nonlinear mapping. Interpoint distances d_{Xij}, and thus implicitly the data structure, shall be preserved in the mapping according to the cost function $E(m)$:

$$E(m) = \frac{1}{c} \sum_{j=1}^{N} \sum_{i=1}^{j} \frac{(d_{Xij} - d_{Yij}(m))^2}{d_{Xij}} \quad (1)$$

Here $d_{Yij}(m) = \sqrt{\sum_{q=1}^{d} (y_{iq}(m) - y_{jq}(m))^2}$ denotes the distance of the respective data points in the visualization plane and $d_{Xij} = \sqrt{\sum_{q=1}^{M} (v_{iq} - v_{jq})^2}$ in the original data space and $c = \sum_{j=1}^{N} \sum_{i=1}^{j} d_{Xij}$. Based on a gradient descent approach, the new coordinates of the N pivot vectors in the visualization plane $\mathbf{y}_i$ are determined by:

$$y_{iq}(m+1) = y_{iq}(m) - \text{MF} * \Delta y_{iq}(m) \quad (2)$$

with

$$\Delta y_{iq}(m) = \frac{\partial E(m)}{\partial y_{iq}(m)} \bigg/ \left| \frac{\partial^2 E(m)}{\partial y_{iq}(m)^2} \right| \quad \text{and } 0 < MF \leq 1. \quad (3)$$

It is well known today, that the NLM achieves a fair projection of the data, but if it is supposed to be used for feature extraction in a pattern recognition application, after the NLM computation, only the training set is mapped. There remains the open issue of mapping individual points or a complete test set without the entire recomputation of the NLM. One solution to the problem is the training of a neural network with the mapping computed for the training data (cf. e.g. [22]). However, achieving convergence and an acceptable error bound can be quite involved. As suggested in [26], the process can be simplified by a hierarchical approach. First a data reduction step, e.g. SOM clustering or alternatives [6], takes place for the training data, the cluster centers are mapped by NLM (cf. Fig. 1.8 (right)), and finally a neural network, e.g. a backpropagation network, is trained with the mapping data.

In prior work [10], an interesting alternative has been developed. The NLM is computed as described above for the N patterns of the training data. Then, a *NLM recall* algorithm is applied for individual patterns or a test set of M patterns. This algorithm uses the complete mapping of the training set as a reference, i.e. both high-dimensional data and mapped data of the training set is required in recall. All distances d_{Xij} of the new pattern j to the training set patterns i, with $i \in [1, N]$ are computed. Then, based on a random initialization the respective distances d_{Yij} are computed, and the standard gradient approach is applied only for the pivot point coordinates of the new pattern j. Duration of the gradient procedure can again be determined by step limit or error threshold, respectively. Fig. 1.9 shows an application example for Iris training and test data. The approach is viable, though it is heuristic and neglects the mutual

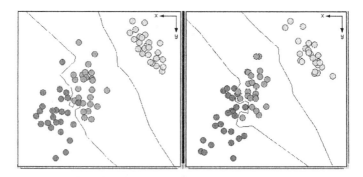

Fig. 1.9 Sammon Train (left) and Recall Mapping (right) for Iris data.

distance information between patterns of the test set. However, as the NLM cannot satisfy all distance constraints in the mapping anyway, the approach provides competitive results, requires no tedious parameter settings, and the computational complexity is *iterations* $\times M \times N$, which is especially advantageous for $N \ll M$. It can be used in a classification system the same way as standard PCA or a trained neural network. Results, however, with regard to compression and discriminance are generally slightly better than PCA. To obtain a fair assessment of mapping abilities with regard to dimensionality reduction and achievable discriminance, for several data sets, quality measures q_o and q_s, which compute overlap and separability in pattern space, respectively, based on efficient nearest neighbor techniques [9], [11], have been applied. Table 1.1 gives the obtained results.

Table 1.1 Assessment of unsupervised mapping techniques

Method	Dim	Train	q_o	q_s	Test	q_o	q_s
Original	4	Iris	0.95503	0.90666	Iris	0.91683	0.88000
PCA	2	Iris	0.91329	0.86667	Iris	0.91970	0.89333
NLM	2	Iris	0.94250	0.89333	Iris	0.93128	0.89333
BP	2	Iris	0.93008	0.90666	Iris	0.91630	0.90667
Original	24	$Mech_1$	1.00000	0.98933	$Mech_2$	0.99799	0.96308
PCA	2	$Mech_1$	0.98959	0.97067	$Mech_2$	0.94889	0.91384
NLM	2	$Mech_1$	0.97898	0.94400	$Mech_2$	0.95730	0.91384
BP	2	$Mech_1$	0.97861	0.94400	$Mech_2$	0.93619	0.89538

It was shown that for large data sets the computational effort of NLM is considerable and that the gradient procedure does not always achieve an accurate projection (cf. e.g. [3]). These facts were well known to researchers in the field, and as in general all distances could not be perfectly preserved by the mapping anyway, Lee, Slaggle and Blum [21] developed a fast distance preserving mapping, that focuses on the exact preservation of only a limited number of $2N - 3$ distances, neglecting all remaining ones. For this mapping, the *Minimal-Spanning-Tree* (MST) of the data distance graph is computed, the MST is traversed and points are mapped by a triangulation method, based on the previously mapped MST-neighbors serving as pivot point P1, P2, and P3 (s. Fig. 1.10). This algorithm achieves a fast and quite accurate projection. However, due to the MST based mapping, for closed, circular data structures problems occur. The same authors also introduced the idea of a global reference point as an alternative to the second nearest neighbor (P2 in Fig. 1.10), to be used in the triangulation step. This modification allows to focus the mapping, and thus supports the idea of a *region of interest* (ROI). As the choice of the reference point determines, where a majority of the perfectly preserved

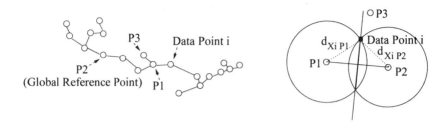

Fig. 1.10 Minimal Spanning Tree and triangulation mapping principle.

distances are situated in the mapping, the ROI clearly is defined by the reference point.

However, in spite of the appealing heuristic idea, MST computation and traversal itself still has $O(N^2)$ complexity. Thus, in prior work, an even faster mapping algorithm has been developed [9]. This alternative mapping, denoted as *Visor* mapping, also uses a triangulation mapping step, however with fixed global pivot points, that are heuristically chosen from the data set. Based on centroid computation, three data points are selected as pivot points from the data set, that meet the constraints of maximum distance from the centroid as well as maximum mutual distance. This algorithm has $O(N)$ complexity and thus provides data projections with a very short response time. As shown by prior investigations with a mapping quality measure, achievable mapping quality is similar to the NLM [9] (s.Fig 1.11). Storing the pivot points of the mapping step, as for

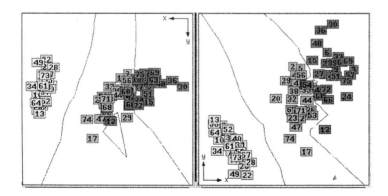

Fig. 1.11 2D projections of Iris data by Visor (left) and NLM (right).

NLM, a recall mode is also feasible for Visor. A Visor recall algorithm just inputs the pivot points and carries out the standard triangulation step for single patterns or complete test sets.

In comparison to other mapping techniques, distance preserving mappings are esteemed as the most convenient, powerful and practical option for fast mapping and visualization [9], [21].

1.2.5 Linear supervised mapping technique

Similar to PCA, a linear discriminant analysis method, denoted as scatter matrices (STM) was introduced in [7]. The linear mapping tries to increase interclass and decrease intraclass distance while also dimension reduction is an objective. In the simple parametric case, a Gaussian assumption is made and the intraclass scattermatrix is computed by:

$$\mathbf{S_w} = \frac{1}{N} \sum_{i=1}^{L} \sum_{j=1}^{N_i} (\mathbf{v}_j^{\omega_i} - \mu^{\omega_i})(\mathbf{v}_j^{\omega_i} - \mu^{\omega_i})^T \qquad (4)$$

Here $\mathbf{v}_j^{\omega_i}$ denotes a feature vector of class ω_i, $\mu^{\omega_i} = \frac{1}{N_i} \sum_{j=1}^{N_i} \mathbf{v}_j^{\omega_i}$ the centroid of class ω_i, and N_i the number of vectors in class ω_i with $N = \sum_{i=1}^{L} N_i$. The interclass scattermatrix is computed by:

$$\mathbf{S_b} = \sum_{i=1}^{L} \frac{N_i}{N} (\mu^{\omega_i} - \mu)(\mu^{\omega_i} - \mu)^T \qquad (5)$$

It characterizes the scatter of the class specific centroids with regard to the centroid $\mu = \frac{1}{N} \sum_{j=1}^{N} \mathbf{v}_j = \sum_{i=1}^{L} \frac{N_i}{N} \mu^{\omega_i}$ of the complete sample set. One possible quality measure for separability is given by $J_s = Tr(\mathbf{S_w}^{-1} \mathbf{S_b})$ [7]. This measure attains large values if interclass scatter becomes large and if intraclass scatter becomes small. As variance for PCA, most discriminance is related to those m eigenvectors of $(\mathbf{S_w}^{-1} \mathbf{S_b})$ associated with the largest m eigenvalues. This approach works well if the Gaussian assumption is met, however for nonparametric or even multimodal data, results may be unsatisfying. [7] proposed an advanced technique that computes interclass scatter based on k-nearest-neighbor technique. The resulting nonparametric scattermatrix $\mathcal{S}_\mathbf{b}$ is given by:

$$\mathcal{S}_b = \frac{1}{N} \sum_{i=1}^{L} \sum_{j=1}^{N_i} g_j (\mathbf{v}_j^{\omega_i} - \mu_{jNN}^{\neq \omega_i})(\mathbf{v}_j^{\omega_i} - \mu_{jNN}^{\neq \omega_i})^T \qquad (6)$$

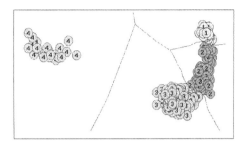

Fig. 1.12 STM Mapping of Mech$_1$ by the first two eigenvectors.

where $\mu_{j_{NN}}^{\neq \omega_i} = \frac{1}{k}\sum_{l=1}^{k} \mathbf{v}_{l_{NN}}^{\neq \omega_i}$ denotes the mean vector of the k-nearest neighbors of $\mathbf{v}_j^{\omega_i}$, which origin from different class regions. Obviously, vectors located off the class borders in the center of class regions bring high values, though they provide little information on class regions border and shape. Thus, a weighting factor reduces the influence of vectors with growing distance from the class borders:

$$g_j = \frac{min\{d^\zeta(\mathbf{v}_j^{\omega_i}, \mu_{j_{NN}}^{\omega_i}), d^\zeta(\mathbf{v}_j^{\omega_i}, \mu_{j_{NN}}^{\neq\omega_i})\}}{d^\zeta(\mathbf{v}_j^{\omega_i}, \mu_{j_{NN}}^{\omega_i}) + d^\zeta(\mathbf{v}_j^{\omega_i}, \mu_{j_{NN}}^{\neq\omega_i})}. \quad (7)$$

Control parameter $\zeta \in [0, \infty[$ determines the weight decay of feature vectors with increasing distance to the class border. The number k of regarded nearest neighbors, as well as ζ have to be specified.

The parametric intraclass scattermatrix $\mathbf{S_w}$ is retained. As a first step data is decorrelated with regard to $\mathbf{S_w}$, i.e. $\mathbf{S_w}$ in space $\mathbf{Y}$ will be $\mathbf{S_w} - \mathbf{I}$. For this aim eigenvectors ψ_i^w and eigenvalues λ_i^w of intraclass scattermatrix $\mathbf{S_w}$ are computed. Pattern data is transformed by $\mathbf{y}_j = (\mathbf{\Psi}_{1...M}^w (\Lambda^w)^{-\frac{1}{2}})^T \mathbf{v}_j$ retaining data dimension. As in $\mathbf{Y}$ $\mathbf{S_w} = \mathbf{I}$ holds, $Tr(\mathbf{S_w}^{-1}\mathcal{S_b}) = Tr(\mathcal{S_b})$. Consequently, $\mathcal{S_b}$ is computed in $\mathbf{Y}$ and its eigenvalues λ_i^b and vectors ψ_i^b are determined. To achieve a dimensionality reducing projection in $\mathbf{Y}^*$ the m eigenvectors $\mathbf{\Psi}_{1...m}^b$ corresponding to the m largest eigenvalues are chosen. The dimensionality reducing projection finally is given by:

$$\mathbf{y}^*_j = (\mathbf{\Psi}_{1..m}^b)^T \mathbf{y}_j = (\mathbf{\Psi}_{1..m}^b)^T (\mathbf{\Psi}^w (\Lambda^w)^{-\frac{1}{2}})^T \mathbf{v}_j. \quad (8)$$

This approach has been implemented and one result obtained for Mech$_1$ is shown in Fig. 1.12 A quantitative assessment can be found in Table 1.2. The mapping works well with default parameters $k = 5$ and $\zeta = 2$. In contrast to selection schemes, where features are discarded, potentially all features can contribute in projection space **Y** to classification. Experiments showed, that especially nonparametric STM is a salient method for classification systems. However, as PCA, STM is affected by small ratios of pattern number vs. pattern dimension.

1.2.6 Nonlinear supervised mapping technique

In [20] a mapping related to Kruskal's work and Sammon's NLM was introduced by Koontz and Fukunaga, denoted in the following as KFM. They introduced an additional term $\delta(\omega_i,\omega_j)d_{Ypj}{}^2$ in the cost function, e.g. Sammon's stress, dedicated to separability, which implies supervised information, i.e. class affiliation, for each pattern vector. During mapping both the constraints of distance preservation and separability of class regions are pursued. The priority of the respective constraints is controlled by parameter $\hat{\lambda}$. Thus, in our implementation the stress was defined as:

$$E(m) = \frac{1}{c}\sum_{j=1}^{N}\sum_{i=1}^{j}\frac{\delta(\omega_i,\omega_j)d_{Yij}{}^2 + \hat{\lambda}\left(d_{Xij} - d_{Yij}(m)\right)^2}{d_{Xij}} \quad (9)$$

where c, $d_{Yij}(m)$, and d_{Xij} are the same terms as for NLM and

$$\delta(\omega_i,\omega_j) = \begin{cases} \hat{\alpha} & : \omega_i = \omega_j \\ 0 & : \omega_i \neq \omega_j \end{cases} \quad (10)$$

with $\hat{\alpha} = 1$. Also, new coordinates of a projection point are computed by $y_{iq}(m+1) = y_{iq}(m) - \text{MF} * \Delta y_{iq}(m)$ with $\Delta y_{iq}(m) = \frac{\partial E(m)}{\partial y_{iq}(m)} \bigg/ \left|\frac{\partial^2 E(m)}{\partial y_{iq}(m)^2}\right|$ as for NLM. Due to the modified cost function, the partial derivations differ however and are given by

$$\frac{\partial E(m)}{\partial y_{iq}(m)} = \frac{2}{c}\sum_{\substack{j=1 \\ j\neq i}}^{N}\left[\frac{\delta(\omega_i,\omega_j)}{d_{Xij}} - \hat{\lambda}\left(\frac{1}{d_{Yij}} - \frac{1}{d_{Xij}}\right)\right](y_{iq} - y_{jq}) \quad (11)$$

$$\frac{\partial^2 E(m)}{\partial y_{iq}(m)^2} = \frac{2}{c}\sum_{\substack{j=1 \\ j\neq i}}^{N}\left[\frac{\delta(\omega_i,\omega_j)}{d_{Xij}} - \hat{\lambda}\left(\frac{1}{d_{Yij}} - \frac{1}{d_{Xij}} - \frac{(y_{iq}-y_{jq})^2}{d_{Yij}{}^3}\right)\right] \quad (12)$$

In the original algorithm of Koontz and Fukunaga parameter $\hat{\lambda}$ affects only the term of distance preservation. Modifying $\hat{\alpha}$ in $\delta(\omega_i,\omega_j)$ to $\hat{\alpha} = 1 - \hat{\lambda}$

gives a normed variant of the algorithm that allows to control the mapping from pure structure preservation $\hat{\lambda} = 1.0$ (NLM), over balanced objective pursuit with $\hat{\lambda} = 0.5$, to pure separability achievement $\hat{\lambda} = 0.0$. Fig. 1.13 illustrates the mapping results for Iris data and Mech$_1$ with $\hat{\lambda} = 0.3$ after hundred iterations. The significant discriminance capability of the mapping leads to linear separability in projection space. A recall procedure, as in

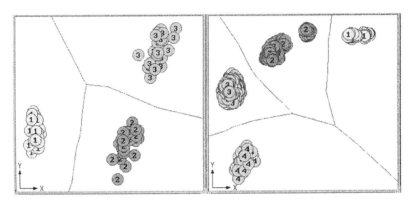

Fig. 1.13 KFM mapping results for Iris data and Mech$_1$.

the case of the NLM obviously is not directly feasible for the KFM, as the required class information is not available. Koontz and Fukunaga presented a non-iterative, yet not uncritical method based on a distance function and a pivot point approach for placement [20].

An interesting alternative is already given in Fig. 1.4 c), where the KFM mapping is used to train a neural network. This approach, though it is not straight forward to achieve network convergence and good approximation of the KFM, allows to project to an arbitrary dimension and to map single points or test sets. An example is given in Fig. 1.14 for a 4-9-5-2 BP network trained 200 epochs with KFM mapping data. It should be noted here, that the transformation within a multilayer backpropagation network, as given in Fig. 1.4 b), basically achieves a similar mapping. By reducing the second hidden layer size to the desired target dimension and training the network with the training set, a comparable mapping is achieved. However, the KFM's property of structure preservation is not explicitly available in the backpropagation network. Fig. 1.15 shows some results achieved, training a 4-5-2-3 network 100 epochs with Mech$_1$ and recalling it with Mech$_2$, Mech$_3$, and Mech$_4$. Table 1.2 gives quantitative assessment results

Dimensionality Reduction Techniques for Interactive ... 17

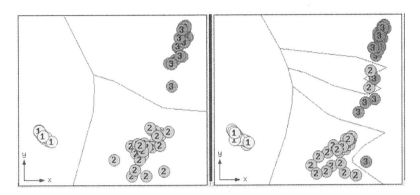

Fig. 1.14 BP network trained with KFM: Recall of training (left) and test set (right).

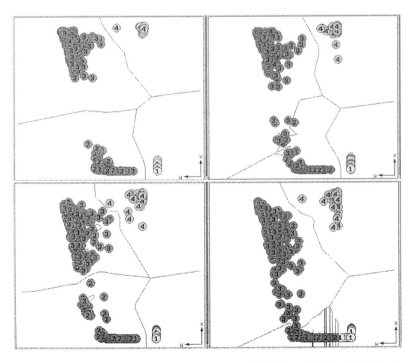

Fig. 1.15 BP network for discriminance analysis with $Mech_1$ to $Mech_4$ (clockwise from top left).

for the supervised mappings. Thus, the KFM mapping is more predictable

Table 1.2 Assessment of supervised mapping techniques

Method	Dim	Train	q_o	q_s	Test	q_o	q_s
Original	4	Iris	0.95503	0.90666	Iris	0.91683	0.88000
STM	2	Iris	0.98224	0.94666	Iris	0.95788	0.90666
BP	2	Iris	0.97536	1.00000	Iris	0.95295	0.94667
KFM/BP	2	Iris	1.00000	1.00000	Iris	0.94023	0.92000
Original	24	$Mech_1$	1.00000	0.98933	$Mech_2$	0.99799	0.96308
STM	2	$Mech_1$	0.99908	0.99200	$Mech_2$	0.98716	0.97536
BP	2	$Mech_1$	0.99988	0.99733	$Mech_2$	0.99373	0.99385

and finer to control. Both BP networks as well as radial-basis-function networks can serve to learn the KFM, as well as the NLM mapping.

Though these kinds of mappings, affiliated to discriminance analysis, are very powerful to separate and shape clusters, in the case of significant class regions' overlap for test data sets related errors remain (cf. Fig. 1.14). Also, using a backpropagation network as a classifier, the step of discriminance analysis should not be necessary, as it was proven that any mapping can be represented by the network. However, finding the appropriate configuration can be tedious, and therefore a hierarchical network approach can be beneficial. One example for this situation is given in Table 1.3, where for all data sets but $Mech_4$ an improvement could be achieved.

Table 1.3 Classification results for simple and hierarchical neural classifier

Method	Net Topology	$Mech_1$	$Mech_2$	$Mech_3$	$Mech_4$	$Mech_5$
Simple-BP	24/9/2/4	100%	97,53%	97,33%	93,33%	98,46%
Hierarch.-BP	24/9/2–2/5/4	100%	98,2%	97,60%	92,50%	98,80%

1.3 Interactive Data Visualisation and Explorative Analysis

After data projection, which carries out a dimensionality reduction of the multivariate data to dimension two or three by one of the methods discussed above, visualization of the resulting feature space is the next step. Though the option of a three-dimensional display is tempting, and in cases of high *intrinsic dimension* even may be of practical benefit, in the following the consideration will be limited to two-dimensional representations and displays. The main reason is, that the additional degree of freedom given by three-dimensional representations on todays 2D-displays will impose more complex interaction on the user. Thus, in addition to computational aspects, 2D representations are easier to assess, to handle, and to interpret. However, with the advent of 3D-displays in computing devices, this situation could be subject to change.

After achieving a mapping of acceptable quality, visualization of this data seems to be a trivial matter. Typically, a 2D scatter plot will be found in tools and in research reports. Category or class information typically is imposed using individual markers, e.g. box, cross, or circle. However, such

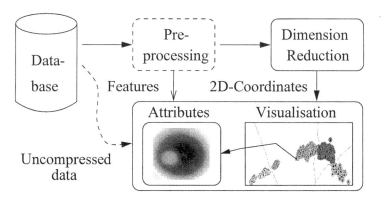

Fig. 1.16 Block diagram of the multivariate data visualization and analysis system.

a static display misses out all the benefits that could be included by employing enhanced user interaction and CAD like functionality. Further, data analysis features could be added as well as a connection to the application database could be established to achieve a transparent and intuitive man-machine-interface (MMI) for the domain of pattern recognition [27] or soft computing in general. For this aim, in the presented work, the concept of the WeightWatcher (WW), was developed, which was implemented first on SUN workstation and then on PC as part of the QuickCog system [11], [16]. Initially, WW was devised to serve for visual analysis of neural networks. But the intriguing approach was soon broadened to serve for visualization and analysis of arbitrary multivariate data sets to make optimum exploitation of the remarkable human perceptive and associative capabilities. Fig 1.16 gives a block diagram of the developed multivariate data visualization and analysis system, incorporating WW.

1.3.1 *Generalized component planes and mesh displays*

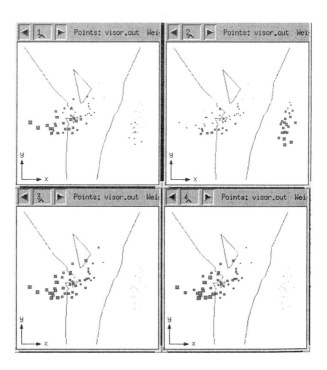

Fig. 1.17 Component planes for Iris data with sketch of class borders.

The salient SOM visualization techniques, which in part have already been shown in Fig. 1.5, 1.6, and 1.7, were abstracted to other mapping techniques, e.g. NLM, LSB or Visor. Fig. 1.17 shows the resulting projections and generalized component planes for Iris data by Visor with a sketch of the class borders. In component planes, the value of one selected feature is displayed at the respective projection point coordinates for all feature vectors. The feature value can be encoded, similar to Hinton diagrams, by a square area, leading to differently scaled, uniformly coloured squares in the component plane. Alternatively, uniformly scaled circles with varying intensity and colour can be applied for value encoding. The latter approach is to be preferred for signed value representation. Additionally, using size coding, class affiliation can be displayed by using class dependent colours, while feature value is coded by the respective area. Examples are given in Fig. 1.18. Including a sketch of the class borders in the visualization

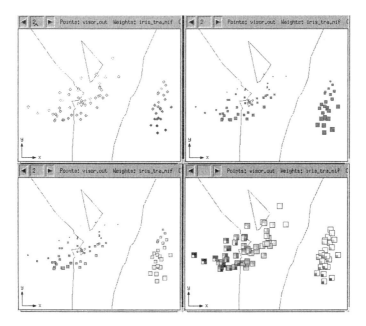

Fig. 1.18 Component planes for Iris data with: grey-value coded (top, left), size coded (top, right), size coded with class affiliation (bottom, left), and *Weight Icons* (bottom, right).

allows the visual assessment of feature saliency. Significant features can be identified by unique ranges of feature values assumed in the individual class regions. The saliency of a feature decreases proportional to the overlap of value ranges met in different class regions. In the visualization, this can be observed by the presence of identically sized squares in different class regions. Using this assessment criterion, for Iris data feature 1 and 2 can easily be discarded as non salient features (s. Fig. 1.17). All component planes, or selected permutations, can be displayed in parallel to interactively discover correlations in the data. Of course, with increasing data dimensionality, this approach becomes more and more cumbersome. One interesting alternative is the joint visualization of all features at the respective projection point. This can be achieved in orthogonal or radial representation. In the first case, denoted as *Weight Icons*, features are aligned in an image like block and the individual feature value is contiguously displayed as grey value (s. Fig. 1.18, (bottom, right)). In the second case, denoted here as *Snow Flakes*, a circle is evenly divided in segments by the number of features and the radius for each segment is defined by the normalized feature value (cf. [13]). Both representations provide a texture like pattern in the visualization, so that correlations and structure in data can be observed according to texture similarity.

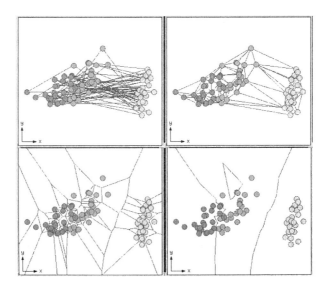

Fig. 1.19 WW mesh variants for Iris data: sequential threading (top, left), Delaunay grid (top, right), Voronoi tesselation (bottom, left), and class specific Voronoi tesselation (bottom, right).

WW offers numerous visualization aids as, e.g. fixed raster display for SOM and arbitrary raster display for NLM vector and component planes (cf. Fig. 1.8). Several mesh drawings are supported. The SOM lattice was already demonstrated in the previous section. For other mappings, which do not not have the fixed neighborhood of SOM, the resulting mesh threads the projection points according to their occurrence in the data set. Further, Delaunay grid, Voronoi tesselation [19], and class specific Voronoi

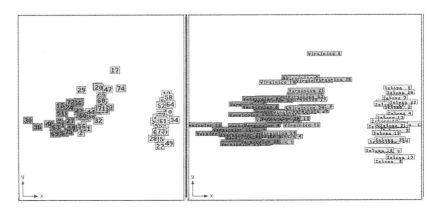

Fig. 1.20 WW attribute plot for Iris data: pattern index (left) and text attributes, e.g. class, feature, or object names (right).

tesselation are provided (cf. Fig .1.19). For two-dimensional data, the class specific Voronoi tesselation gives the actual class borders according to a nearest neighbor consideration. For higher dimensional data, a rough but viable approximation of the actual class borders is provided by this approach. An additional attribute display complements the projection points by class labels, pattern index with regard to sample set, or textual description in the plot. This is illustrated in Fig. 1.20. The information of class affiliation is retained by the field colour for pattern index or text attribute display. Though the information carried by the fields of each projection point is salient, the required size can be detrimental, as contiguous fields can occlude the view on their neighbors. Fig. 1.21 shows three variants of WW display, that give a general view of the data set, neglecting details in the fields for the sake of an overview. Especially the display mode employing coloured class specific Voronoi tesselations (cf. Fig. 1.21) is very helpful to discover enclosures in different class regions, e.g. outliers. As not only the individual projection point but the whole corresponding Voronoi cell is coloured in this mode, while projection points are displayed as tiny

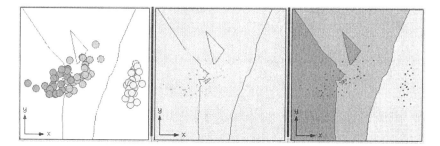

Fig. 1.21 WW display modes: reduced size fields (left/middle) and coloured class specific Voronoi tesselations (right).

dots, a very good insight in the data structure and distribution is given. Additionally, a stacking mechanism has been implemented in WW, that puts each selected field at the bottom of the stack, thus exposing occluded vectors. To identify the presence of identical vectors, which especially in case of different class affiliations can be a severe problem for neural network learning, a graphical feature has been included in WW. Identical vectors are marked by a field with a hexagonal shape. Thus, stacking through the vectors hidden under a hexagonal field, the number, pattern indices, and class affiliations can speedily be identified. This has proven to be useful and time conserving for trouble shooting in pattern recognition system design.

1.3.2 *Interactive navigation and exploratory analysis*

These described mechanisms alleviate the first insight in the data structure. However, especially for very large data sets with considerable local density variations, analysis on a single scale will not be feasible. Therefore, navigation in the projection is supported by zoom and pan functions and an additional overview or navigation window. The navigation window shows the complete data set in a representation similar to Fig. 1.21 (middle). In addition the current zoom level is visible in the navigation window (cf. Fig. 1.22 (left)) by the size of a rectangle that corresponds to the part of the projection currently visible in the main WW display. The current position of the main WW display can also easily be identified in the navigation window. (Fig. 1.23 gives an even better example based on a data set from visual inspection in industrial manufacturing, which shows considerable density variations.) This feature allows to interactively explore

Fig. 1.22 WW navigation: navigation window (left) and local WW display (right).

the data from global to local aspects. According to the local density of the data, the zoom factor can be chosen, so that appropriate details and corresponding attributes are visible. The focus of interest can conveniently be shifted across scales by zooming in or out and in the same scale by shifting the navigation window. This approach can saliently be combined with advanced hierarchical mapping and visualization schemes (cf. 1.3.4).

1.3.3 *Mapping quality and attribute display*

The achieved mappings of NLM, LSB or Visor provide mappings that give a fair impression of the underlying global data structure. However, with growing intrinsic dimensionality, mapping faults occur and lead to distortions and twists in the 2D-representation. For accurate interpretation of displays WW provides an *Actual local neighborhood display* (ALND) demonstrated in Fig. 1.23. For this technique, the k-nearest neighbors of the selected pattern are computed. Currently, the computed k-nearest neighbors are threaded by a red line in the order of their actual neighborhood position in feature space. So, if the projection is corrupt and has local twists, the ALND discloses the mapping error and provides the correct neighborhood for analysis and valid conclusion drawing. For instance, the nearest neighbor list can be traversed in ascending or descending order. For each neighbor currently in the focus of interest, further attributes can be displayed and compared with the other threaded vectors. In concept, the attributes can comprise all steps of processing, from the original data vectors, e.g. images, to symbolic feature vectors. Fig. 1.24 gives an example for the X-ray inspection task [14], where images have been invoked from the sample set database for analysis and comparison. Summarizing,

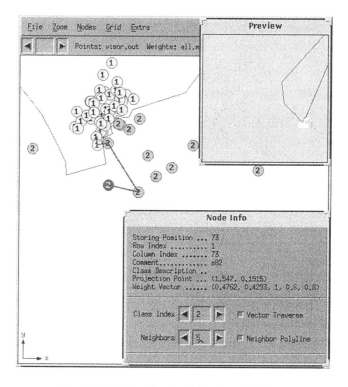

Fig. 1.23 Actual local neighborhood display.

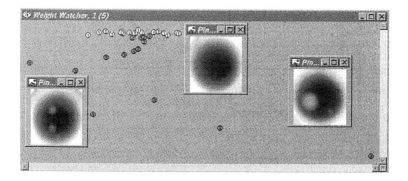

Fig. 1.24 WW database invokation example for X-ray inspection task.

with the technique of the ALND the user can find, traverse, and analyse the actual k-nearest neighbors of selected points (data entries) of interest.

Thus, mapping faults can be identified in feature space regions, where a reliable mapping is mandatory, and largely be overcome by this interactive feature. Alternatively, it is feasible to compute local mapping errors, e.g. the measure q_m introduced in prior work [9], for each projection point and display these in the fields of the projection point. Thus, mapping reliability becomes overt all over the mapping. However, computation of mapping error can be quite involved, so that in case of the fast mapping techniques it will take longer than the actual mapping step. Therefore, the ALND should be preferred for practical work.

Though navigation considerably alleviates access and analysis, finding certain vectors or attributes can be tedious. Thus, search functions are currently implemented that direct navigation to search hits, according to simple and in the future more complex search cues (cf. [13]).

1.3.4 *Hierarchical mapping and interactive visualization*

Some of the mapping problems described above could be ruled out by more advanced hierarchical mapping schemes that closely integrate mapping and visualization. The basic idea is depicted in Fig. 1.25, where a global mapping of the complete data set is achieved by a very fast technique, as e.g. the Visor algorithm. Naturally, local mapping faults may be encountered but the overall obtained structure fairly represents the data set and thus can serve for the first preview and ensuing navigation. In case of low quality demand imposed on the mapping, as in the current implementation, a zoom step just will scale the available mapping information and display the chosen section in the main WW window. In the hierarchical approach, the ROI and scale information optionally can serve to control a high quality mapper, employing a mapping principle with a computational complexity, that is practically not feasible for the complete data set. The high quality mapper would select the subset of patterns from the database, that is comprised in the current ROI (white rectangle in the navigation window). Only this subset of points is subject to the computationally burdensome mapping step by the high quality mapper. Thus, a very focused analysis can be conducted and a balanced approach with regard to mapping reliability and response time of the system is provided. It is straightforward, of course, to use the proposed method over several levels of hierarchy.

Besides general database mining and data analysis tasks, another practical exploitation of the visualization and analysis context described here

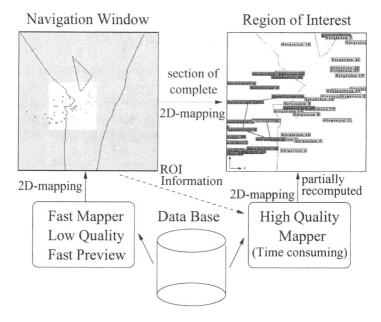

Fig. 1.25 Improving mapping quality by a hierarchical approach.

lies in the fast and transparent design of recognition systems [11]. The following advantages are provided by the approach:

(1) Clustering and structure in the data can be observed
(2) The discriminance of the computed feature set can be assessed by imposing classification labels on the data representation
(3) Assessment of feature computation alternatives is feasible
(4) Open-loop parameter optimization for feature computation is feasible
(5) Interactive selection of significant features can be carried out by evaluation of component planes in the *WeightWatcher*
(6) Outliers can be easily identified and eliminated from the sample set
(7) For data analysis tasks, heretofore unlabeled data can manually or semi-automatically be labeled in the *WeightWatcher* according to the human observation of data structure in the projection
(8) Last not least, classification errors can be spatially identified in the projection for trouble shooting and analysis (cf. Fig. 1.26)

Fig. 1.24 and Fig. 1.26 show an example for training and test data of the X-ray BGA inspection task. Erroneously classified patterns are em-

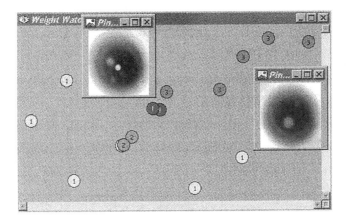

Fig. 1.26 WW database invokation example for test data of X-ray inspection task.

phasized in the mapping of Fig. 1.26 (exclamation mark in red field) and attributes, as e.g. the underlying original images, can be invoked and compared with neighbors in the mapping. These options are extensively used in the QuickCog PC-system [11], [16], considerably simplifying the process of recognition system design, validation, optimization, and especially trouble shooting.

1.4 Advanced Projection Methods

In general, none of the surveyed projection techniques will lead to a satisfying result with regard to global and local mapping quality as well as the often unavoidable mapping error caused by high intrinsic dimensionality. Thus, recent techniques, as e.g. [1], employ hierarchical mapping and visualization approaches. Three main directions of approach can be distinguished. The first bases on hierarchical clustering and mapping of the data, using standard clustering techniques, e.g. c-means, or as in our own investigations more sophisticated techniques, e.g. employing principles or laws of Gestalt theory such as the *law of proximity* [32]. The second uses interactive techniques, based on ROI selection, reference point selection, and ROI-based hierarchical mapping as given in 1.3.4. The third bases on a global to local shift of the mapping stress, implemented by a limited or shrinking neighborhood during the mapping process. An unfolding of the folded manifold of the data can be achieved this way. In the following, two mappings employing the latter concept are presented

1.4.1 An experimental topology preserving mapping

In prior work an experimental mapping (*TOpology Preserving mApping of sample Sets*, TOPAS) has been developed as a first step to achieve mappings of high quality and reliability. To assess topology preservation in addition to distance presevation, the measure q_m was developed [9], [10]. It bases on an assessment of rank order in space **X** and **Y**, respectively. Similar to ALND, the n-nearest-neighbors NN_{ji} $(i = 1, \ldots, n)$ are computed and their rank order is assessed according to a simple credit assignment scheme:

3 credits,	if	NN_{ji} in **X** $= NN_{ji}$ in **Y**		
2 credits,	if	NN_{ji} in **X** $= NN_{jl}$ in **Y**	$l = 1, \ldots, n$	$j \neq i$
1 credit,	if	NN_{ji} in **X** $= NN_{jt}$ in **Y**	$t = n, \ldots, m$	$n < m$
0 credit	else			

So for each point, a local topology measure q_{m_i} and a global measure $q_m = \frac{1}{3n \times N} \sum_{i=1}^{N} q_{m_i}$ can be computed. The measure implements a graceful degradation for increasing topological faults and returns $q_m = 1.0$ for perfect topology preservation. A quantitative comparison of mapping methods

Table 1.4   Mapping quality q_m for NLM and Visor with (n=4, m=10)

Data set	NLM		Visor	
	q_m	$E(m)$	q_m	$E(m)$
$Iristrain$	0.6667	0.0098	0.6711	0.0093
$Mech_1$	0.4527	0.0933	0.4207	0.1628

can be carried out by q_m and distance error $E(m)$ (cf. Table 1.4).

The TOPAS mapper was devised, using the measure $q_{m_i}^*$, ($n = N$, only the first row of the credit assignment scheme is activated) as a cost function for the mapping. TOPAS is based on rank order evaluation Ξ^X in the original space and Ξ^Y in the mapping space for the current data vector p and the remaining $N - 1$ data vectors with $i \neq p$. If the respective rank positions in **X**- and **Y**-space are not identical, a correction is required to obtain the proper rank order. To achieve gradual corrections of the points

$\mathbf{y}_i$ in the visualization plane with regard to $\mathbf{y}_p$ in the iterative mapping process, as for NLM, distance information is used in the adaptation rule:

$$y_{ij}(m+1) = y_{ij}(m) + \alpha_p(m, \Xi^Y(\mathbf{y}_i)) \frac{[y_{ij} - y_{pj}]}{d_{Y_{i,p}}} \qquad (13)$$

with $d_{Y_{i,p}} = \sqrt{\sum_{j=1}^d [y_{ij} - y_{pj}]^2}$. Similar to SOM, $\alpha_p(m, \Xi^Y(\mathbf{y}_i))$ denotes time and position dependent learning rate. The temporal factor decays with time. In addition, the regarded neighborhood shrinks as in SOM, so that the mapping focuses more and more on close neighbors. Fig. 1.27 shows some achieved results of TOPAS in comparison to NLM . Obviously, TOPAS

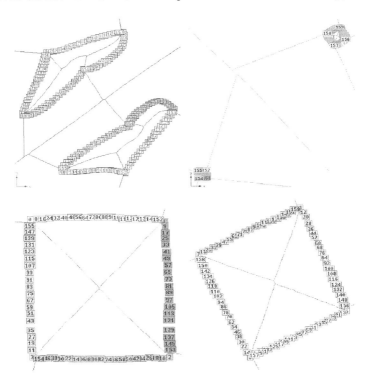

Fig. 1.27 NLM and TOPAS mapping of *Cube*.

provides a much better structure preservation than NLM. However, besides a scaling problem associated with the current learning rule, the complexity of $O(N^3)$ is a disadvantage of this algorithm.

1.4.2 An enhancement of Sammon's NLM

The salient features of TOPAS can be easily integrated in an *Enhanced NLM* (ENLM). Extending Sammon's *Magic Factor* MF, the basic NLM adaptation rule is enhanced to

$$y_{iq}(m+1) = y_{iq}(m) - \alpha_t(m) \times \Delta y_{iq}(m, \alpha_n(d_{X_{ij}}, \sigma(m))) \quad (14)$$

by a time and position dependent learn rate. For the neigborhood function $\alpha_n(d_{X_{ij}}, \sigma(m))$, a Gaussian function with decaying $\sigma(m)$ is chosen, so that after achieving a global arrangement, long distances d_{Xij} are more and more neglected in the mapping and a better fine tuning of local data structures is achieved. Fig. 1.28 shows some achieved results for *Cube* data. In the top left, the result of an NLM mapping with 200 iterations and $\alpha_t(m=0) = 0.8$ is given. In the top right position the result of an corresponding ENLM mapping with a Gaussian neighborhood and exponential decay of the learnrate is given. Neighborhood linearly decays from width 40 to 0.3 in 180 steps and remains constant for another 20 steps. The learnrate exponentially decays from 0.8 to 0.6 in 180 steps and then remains constant. The remaining two results at the bottom of Fig. 1.28 were obtained with

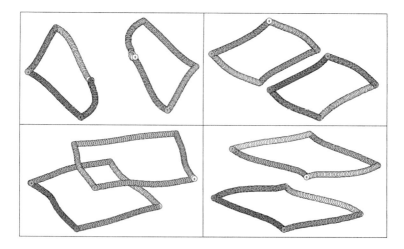

Fig. 1.28 NLM and three ENLM mappings of *Cube* (clockwise from top to bottom).

fixed learnrate of $\alpha_t(m=0) = 0.8$ and 100 steps. The Gaussian neighborhood width was linearly decreased from 30 to 0.5 in 70 steps. Obviously, varying random initialization leads to slightly different results.

All achieved results had a better structure preservation than the basic NLM. Though, the TOPAS structure was perfectly straight, a scaling problem could be observed. The ENLM in contrast provides good local structure preservation, as well as a good global proportion of the achieved mapping. Additionally, the computational overhead is only slightly beyond NLM.

It should be mentioned here, that Niemann and Weiss [23] already introduced a factor $d_{X_{ri}}^p$ in the Sammon stress for control from local ($p < 0$, with $p = -1$ corresponds to standard NLM), balanced ($p = 0$), to global mapping ($p > 0$). However, as p is fixed either, long range or short range distances are preferred in the mapping. In the ENLM in contrast, a coarse to fine tuning process takes place during mapping iterations.

The idea of the reference point introduced in [21] can be incorporated both in TOPAS and ENLM by adding an additional weighting factor in the correction rule, e.g. with a linear decay proportional to $d_{X_{ri}}$:

$$g_r(d_{X_{ri}}) = 1 - \frac{d_{X_{ri}} - d_{X_{ri\,min}}}{d_{X_{ri\,max}}} \qquad (15)$$

By this factor, computed for each data vector before the actual mapping step, emphasis is on accurately preserving distances (rank order) close to the reference point, while accuracy of distance preservation may decay with growing displacement $d_{X_{ri}}$ from the reference point. Experiments and investigations with TOPAS showed, that the local mapping quality can be increased at the cost of the global mapping quality [10]. From results achieved

Table 1.5 Mapping quality of *Iristrain* data with reference point $i = 59$.

Mapping quality with reference vector	Mapping quality without reference vector
q_{m_i} (n=4, m=10) 0.417	q_{m_i} (n=4, m=10) 0.250
q_m (n=4, m=10) 0.651	q_m (n=4, m=10) 0.758

in prior investigation this is demonstrated in Table 1.5 for *Iristrain* data and the chosen reference point 59. The mapping quality in the local neighborhood of the reference vector could be increased by about 66.6% for the chosen linear weighting function. The local improvement resulted in deterioration of the global measure q_m. However, for selective local unfolding, e.g. to achieve a good partial projection of an intrinsically high-dimensional data structure, a different weighting term would be required. In ongoing extensions of ENLM, this is currently investigated.

1.5 Conclusions and Future Work

A review and a brief assessment of dimensionality reduction techniques for feature extraction and multivariate data projection, as well as of interactive visualization techniques was given. Advanced mapping techniques were introduced in conjunction with improved visualization techniques and tools. The presented work based on the experience gathered with the *Public-Domain* VIP-tool-package [18] (UNIX/SUN) that incorporates the mapping methods covered in the taxonomy and the WW. In 1998 the **QuickCog**-System on PC (Windows'95, NT) became available (cf. [16], [17]), both as free version for unfunded research and also as commercial tool, which comprises most of the described mappers and the WW as part of an environment for image/signal processing and rapid recognition system design. All methods will be integrated in **QuickCog** to be instantly amenable for applications, ranging from widespread pattern recognition applications, medical data analysis to database navigation tasks [15].

Recently, incented by the increasing commercial attention and interest, further research approaches to multivariate data visualization, not covered by this survey, are reported (cf. e.g., [1]). A balanced comparison of the described techniques and the newly introduced methods with regard to computational complexity and mapping speed, mapping quality and reliability, as well as transparence and user convenience of ensuing visualization techniques based on the same artificial and real-world data sets are aspired as one part of future work.

The valuable contribution of numerous students [11], [17], [18] to the implementation of the described methods is gratefully acknowledged.

References

[1] Christopher M. Bishop, Michael E. Tipping, "A Hierarchical Latent Variable Model for Data Visualisation", IEEE Transactions on Pattern Analysis and Machine Intelligence, Vol. 20, pp. 281-293, 1998.

[2] Bernd Fritzke, "Growing Cell Structures – A Self-Organizing Network for Unsupervised and Supervised Learning", Neural Networks, Vol. 7, pp. 1441-1460, 1994.

[3] Witold Dzwinel, "How to make Sammon's Mapping useful for Multidimensional Data Structure Analysis", Pattern Recognition, Vol. 27, pp. 949-959, 1995.

[4] Keinosuke Fukunaga, David R. Olsen, "A Two-Dimensional Display for the Classification of Multivariate Data", IEEE Transaction on Computers, Vol. 20, pp. 917-923, 1971.

[5] Keinosuke Fukunaga, James M. Mantock, "A Nonparametric Two-Dimensional Display for Classification", IEEE Transactions on Pattern Analysis and Machine Intelligence, Vol. 4, pp. 427-436, 1982.

[6] Keinosuke Fukunaga, James M. Mantock, "Nonparametric Data Reduction'", IEEE Transactions on Pattern Analysis and Machine Intelligence, Vol. 6, pp. 115-118, 1984.

[7] Keinosuke Fukunaga "Introduction to Statistical Pattern Recognition", ACADEMIC PRESS, INC. Harcourt Brace Jovanovich, Publishers, 1990.

[8] Joseph Kittler, "Feature Selection and Extraction", Handbook of Pattern Recognition and Image Processing, ACADEMIC PRESS, INC., Tzai. Y. Young King Sun-Fu Publishers, pp. 59-83, 1986.

[9] Andreas König, Olaf Bulmahn, Manfred Glesner, "Systematic Methods for Multivariate Data Visualization and Numerical Assessment of Class Separability and Overlap in Automated Visual Industrial Quality Control", Proceedings of the 5th British Machine Vision Conference BMVC'94, pp. 195-204, 1994.

[10] Andreas König "Neural Structures for Visual Surface Inspection of Objects in an Industrial Environment", Doctoral Thesis at TU Darmstadt D 17, http://www.iee.et.tu-dresden.de/~koeniga, 1995.

[11] Andreas König, Michael Eberhardt, Robert Wenzel, "A Transparent and Flexible Development Environment for Rapid Design of Cognitive Systems", Proceedings of the International EUROMICRO Conference, Workshop CI, pp. 655-662, 1998.

[12] Andreas König, "A Survey of Methods for Multivariate Data Projection, Visualisation and Interactive Analysis", Proceedings of the 5th International Conference on Soft Computing and Information/Intelligent Systems IIZUKA'98, Vol. 1, pp. 55-59, 1998.

[13] Andreas König, Friedrich E. Blutner, Michael Eberhardt, Robert Wenzel, "An Acoustic Database Navigator for the Interactive Analysis of Psychoacoustic Sound Archives", Proceedings of the 5th International Conference on Soft Computing and Information/Intelligent Systems IIZUKA'98, Vol. 1, pp. 60-63, 1998.

[14] Andreas König, Andreas Herenz, Klaus Wolter "Application of Neural Networks for Automated X-Ray Image Inspection in Electronics Manufacturing", Proceedings of the International Work-Conference on Biological and Artificial Neural Networks IWANN'99, Vol. 2, pp. 588-595, 1999.

[15] Andreas König, Friedrich E. Blutner, Michael Eberhardt, Robert Wenzel, "Design and Application of an Acoustic Database Navigator for the Interactive Analysis of Psychoacoustic Sound Archives and Sound Engineering", Advanced Signal Processing Technology by Soft Computing, Edited Books from IIZUKA'98, FLSI Soft Computing Series, Charles Hsu (Ed.), Vol. 5, 1999.

[16] Andreas König, Michael Eberhardt, Robert Wenzel, "QuickCog - Cognitive Systems Design Environment", QuickCog home page: http://www.iee.et.tu-dresden.de/~ koeniga/QuickCog.html, 1999.

[17] Andreas König, Michael Eberhardt, Robert Wenzel, "QuickCog Self-Learning Recognition Systems – Exploiting machine learning techniques for transparent and fast industrial recognition system design", Image Processing Europe, PennWell, Vol. 5, pp. 10-19, 1999.

[18] Andreas König, et al., "VIP – Visualization Package for Multivariate Data Analysis and Classification", http://www.iee.et.tu-dresden.de/~ koeniga, 1998.

[19] Teuvo Kohonen, "Self-Organization and Associative Memory," Springer-Verlag, 1989.

[20] Warren L.G. Koontz, Keinosuke Fukunaga, "A Nonlinear Feature Extraction Algorithm Using Distance Transformation", IEEE Trans. on Computers, Vol. 21, pp. 56-63, 1972.

[21] R.C.T. Lee, J.R. Slaggle, H. Blum, "A Triangulation Method for the Sequential Mapping of Points from N-Space to Two-Space", IEEE Transactions on Computers, Vol.26, pp. 288-292, 1977.

[22] Jianchang Mao, Anil K. Jain, "Artificial Neural Networks for Feature Extraction and Multivariate Data Projection", IEEE Transactions on Neural Networks, Vol. 6, pp. 296-317, 1995.

[23] H. Niemann, J. Weiss, "A fast Converging Algorithm for Nonlinear Mapping of High-Dimensional Data to a Plane", IEEE Transactions on Computers, Vol. 28, pp. 142-147, 1979.

[24] Erkki Oja, "Data Compression, Feature Extraction, and Autoassociation in Feedforward Neural Networks", Proceedings of the 1rst International Conference on Artificial Neural Networks ICANN'91, Vol. 1, pp. 737-742, 1991.

[25] Nikhil R. Pal, "Soft Computing for Feature Analysis'", Fuzzy Sets and Systems, Elsevier, Vol. 103, pp. 201-221, 1999.

[26] John W. Sammon, "A Nonlinear Mapping for Data Structure Analysis", IEEE Transaction on Computers, Vol. 18, pp. 401-409, 1969.

[27] John W. Sammon, "Interactive Pattern Analysis and Classification", IEEE Transactions on Computers, Vol. 19, pp. 594-616, 1970.

[28] Wojciech Siedlecki, Kinga Siedlecka, Jack Sklansky, "An Overview of Mapping Techniques for Exploratory Pattern Analysis", Pattern Recognition, Vol. 21, pp. 411-429, 1988.

[29] Wojciech Siedlecki, Kinga Siedlecka, Jack Sklansky, "Experiments on Mapping Techniques for Exploratory Pattern Analysis", Pattern Recognition, Vol. 21, pp. 431-438, 1988.

[30] Alfred Ultsch, H.P. Siemon, "Exploratory Data Analysis: Using Kohonen Networks on Transputers", Internal report Nr. 329, University of Dortmund, 1989.

[31] Hu Wang, D.K. Hennecke, Andreas König, Peter Windirsch, Manfred Glesner, "Method for Estimating Various Operating States in a Single Stage Axial Compressor", AIAA Journal of Propulsion and Power, Vol. 11, pp. 385-387, 1995.

[32] Charles T. Zahn, "Graph-Theoretical Methods for Detecting and Describing Gestalt Clusters", IEEE Transactions on Computers, Vol. 20, pp. 68-86, 1971.

Chapter 2
The Self-Organizing Map as a Tool in Knowledge Engineering

Johan Himberg, Jussi Ahola, Esa Alhoniemi,
Juha Vesanto, and Olli Simula
Helsinki University of Technology

Abstract

The Self-Organizing Map (SOM) is one of the most popular neural network methods. It is a powerful tool in visualization and analysis of high-dimensional data in various engineering applications. The SOM maps the data on a two-dimensional grid which may be used as a base for various kinds of visual approaches for clustering, correlation and novelty detection. In this chapter, we present novel methods that enhance the SOM based visualization in correlation hunting and novelty detection. These methods are applied to two industrial case studies: analysis of hot rolling of steel and continuous pulp process. A research software for fast development of SOM based tools is briefly described.

Keywords : explorative data analysis, self-organizing map, visualization of multidimensional data, correlation detection, clustering, novelty detection, process analysis, hot rolling of steel, continuous pulp process

2.1 Introduction

Traditionally, modeling and control of industrial processes is based on analytic system models. The models may be built using knowledge based on physical phenomena and assumptions of the system behavior. However, many practical systems, e.g., industrial processes, are so complex that global models cannot be defined. In such cases, system modeling must be based on experimental data obtained by various measurements.

Modern automation systems produce large amounts of measurement data. However, interpretation of this data and the correlations between measurements and other system parameters is often difficult. In many practical situations, even minor knowledge about the characteristic behavior of the system might be useful. For this purpose, easy visualization of the data is of great help. The measurements need to be converted into some simple and comprehensive display which would reduce the dimensionality of measurements and simultaneously preserve the most important metric relationships between the data.

Artificial neural networks have successfully been used to build system models directly based on process data. They provide means to analyze the system or process without explicit physical model. The Self-Organizing Map (SOM) [12] is one of the most popular neural network models. Due to its unsupervised learning and topology preserving properties it has proven to be especially suitable in analysis of complex systems. The SOM algorithm implements a nonlinear topology preserving mapping from a high-dimensional input data space onto a two-dimensional network or grid of neurons. The network roughly approximates the probability density function of the data and, thus, inherently clusters the data. Various visualization alternatives of the SOM are useful, e.g., in searching for correlations between measurements and in investigating the cluster structure of the data.

SOM based data exploration has been applied in various engineering applications such as pattern recognition, text and image analysis, financial data analysis, process monitoring and modeling as well as control and fault diagnosis [15; 19]. In addition, the SOM has been used in analysis and monitoring of telecommunications systems. Applications include equalizer structures for discrete-signal detection and adaptive resource allocation in telecommunications networks.

The ordered signal mapping property of the SOM algorithm has proven to be powerful in analysis of complex industrial systems and processes. The SOM allows easy visualization of system parameters and their correlations, cluster structure of the data, monitoring of operation state, and novelty detection. The SOM based approach has, for instance, been utilized to determine the reasons for situations where the output quality of an industrial process is not satisfactory. The case studies presented in this chapter include analysis of pulping and steel rolling processes.

The SOM can be used in many different ways for data visualization and exploration. In this chapter, we present SOM based tools for data exploration in practical industrial applications. Novel methods to enhance the SOM based visualization in correlation detection, cluster analysis, and operation monitoring as well as novelty detection will be discussed.

2.2 Data analysis using the Self-Organizing Map

Our approach to data analysis is explorative and will concentrate on visualization based approaches. The main idea is to provide an overall picture of the data and create tools that help the analyst to *see* what the data are like and get ideas for further, perhaps more quantitative descriptions of the data.

2.2.1 The Self-Organizing Map

A SOM is formed of units located on a regular low-dimensional grid (usually 1D or 2D to enable visualization). The lattice of the grid can be hexagonal or rectangular. The former is often used because it is more pleasing to the eye.

Each unit i of the SOM is represented by an n-dimensional prototype vector $\mathbf{m}_i = [m_{i1}, \ldots, m_{in}]$, where n is equal to the dimension of the input space. On each training step, a data sample $\mathbf{x}$ is selected and the prototype vector $\mathbf{m}_c$ closest to it, the winner unit, is found from the map. The prototype vectors of the winner unit and its neighbors on the grid are moved towards the sample vector:

$$\mathbf{m}_i := \mathbf{m}_i + \alpha(t) h_{ci}(t) (\mathbf{x} - \mathbf{m}_i), \tag{1}$$

where $\alpha(t)$ is the learning rate and $h_{ci}(t)$ is a neighborhood kernel centered on the winner unit c. Both learning rate and neighborhood kernel radius decrease monotonically with time. During the iterative training, the SOM behaves like a flexible net that folds onto the "cloud" formed by input data.

2.2.2 Data analysis scheme

Using the SOM in data analysis is only one part of a multi-staged process. The map — as any method — is a fruitful tool only if the input data really describe the essential phenomena and is not governed by completely erroneous data. The phases of a basic explorative data analysis process using the SOM can be sketched as follows:

Data acquisition may be real time measurement collection (on-line) or database query (off-line) which is usually the case when an exploratory analysis is made.

Data preprocessing, selection and segmentation are usually elaborate tasks involving a lot of *a priori* knowledge. Erroneous raw data have to be removed. Proper data scaling and representational transformations (e.g., symbolic to numerical values) have to be considered. Clearly inhomogeneous data sets may have to be divided to disjoint subsets according to some criteria in order to avoid problems which would come up if a global model was applied.

Feature extraction is the phase where preprocessed and segmented data are transformed into feature data vectors. It is important to realize that the objective in our case is to interpret the data and extract knowledge from it and from relations in it — not to make black-box classification or regression. Therefore, the feature variables have to describe the important phenomena in the data in such a way that they are clear in the analysis. It is evident that this and the previous stages cannot be properly done without knowledge of application domain.

Training of the SOM is performed according to the Sec. 2.2.1. The training parameters need to be determined. Fortunately, the basic SOM algorithm seems to be rather robust in this sense, and by following certain basic guidelines (see, e.g., [12]) satisfactory results are usually obtained. However, one delicate issue is the scaling of the feature variables. The variables with large relative variance tend to dominate the map organization. In order to equalize the contribution of individual variables in the map organization, they are usually normalized to be equivariant. The distance measure used in the SOM training has to be chosen in such a way that applying it to data makes sense. Usually, the Euclidean distance is used. The variable normalization and the distance measure are, of course, data dependent issues and related to the feature extraction phase.

Visualization and interpretation are the key issues for using SOM in data analysis. These include correlation detection, cluster analysis and novelty detection. The scope of this chapter is on the visualization and interpretation phase which are described in the next section. We remind that the data analysis is usually not a flow-through process, but requires iteration, especially between feature extraction and interpretation phases. An integrated software environment is clearly needed. We describe our research software in Sec. 2.4.

2.3 Visualization

The SOM provides a low-dimensional map of the data space. The aim of visualization is both to understand the mapped area and to enable investigation of new data samples with respect to it.

To understand what the SOM really shows, it is important to understand that it actually performs two tasks: vector quantization and vector projection. Vector quantization creates from the original data a smaller, but still representative, data set to be worked with. The set of prototype vectors reflects the properties of the data space. The projection performed by the SOM is nonlinear and restricted to a regular grid (the map grid). The SOM tries to preserve the topology of the data space rather than relative distances.

In contrast, there are several other ways of projecting multidimensional data to lower dimensions. A well-known method is based on Principal Component Analysis (PCA): the eigenvectors with the largest eigenvalues are calculated from the data set, and the data samples are projected on the subspace spanned by these vectors. This is a fast linear operation, but gives misleading results if the ignored directions have significant information.

A different approach is to project the data so that relative distances between samples are as close to the original as possible according to some cost function. Different cost functions lead to different nonlinear algorithms, e.g., Sammon's projection [18] or the Curvilinear Component Analysis (CCA) [4]. Large data sets cause often problems for these, usually iterative, projection methods as the procedure becomes computationally heavy. One possibility is to reduce the computational task by first quantizing the data using some suitable method, e.g., k-means and then applying the projection method. Some recent solutions include [17]. Of course, the SOM can be seen as doing something similar, except that only topology — not distances — is preserved.

2.3.1 *Basic methods for SOM visualization*

The SOM grid provides a basis for various visualizations. Variable values or other features may be shown with respect to the grid.

(a) Unified distance matrix

The unified distance matrix (u-matrix) [7; 22] is a simple and effective tool to show the possible cluster structure on a SOM grid visualization. It shows the distances between neighboring units using a gray scale representation on the map grid. This gives an impression of "mountains" (long distances) which divide the map into "fields" (dense parts, i.e., clusters). See Fig. 2.1(c).

(b) Component planes

The SOM is often "sliced" into component planes in order to see how the values of a certain variable (component) varies on different locations of the map [20]. Each plane represents the value of one variable (component) of the prototype vector in each node of the SOM using, e.g., gray scale representation. One can now see the general behavior of the variable values in different parts of the SOM. See Fig. 2.1(c).

The component planes play an important role in the correlation detection: by comparing these planes even partially correlating variables may be detected by visual inspection — a simple enhancement to this is described in the next section. This kind of comparison could be done using scatter plots as well, but this would require a quadratic amount of displays with respect to the number of variables: each variable against each other variable. When using the component planes the number of displays grows linearly. Furthermore, the vector quantization performed by the SOM removes noise. The component planes can also be easily compared with the cluster representation of the u-matrix.

(c) Hits
When investigating new data with the SOM the question is, which part of the map best corresponds to the data? Traditionally, this has been answered by finding the nearest prototype vector (the best matching unit, BMU) for each investigated data sample and then indicating it from the SOM. See Fig. 2.1(c). For multiple data vectors, one can count the number of times that each unit has been the BMU, and thus, a data histogram is obtained. By comparing different histograms, one can evaluate the similarity of different data sets in terms of the map. Similar histograms imply similar data sets.

(d) Trajectories
If the data have been acquired from a process, one may be interested in visualizing the evolution of the process state in time. The BMU of the current feature vector may be regarded as the operating point on the map which in turn can be regarded as a projection of the multidimensional state space. Trajectory (Fig. 2.1(d)) is a line connecting a sequence of these operating points [10; 21] that shows the change of the process in time. A software tool related to this issue is presented in Sec. 2.4.3.

(e) Combining different projections
To get an idea of the shape of the map in the data space, the prototype vectors of the SOM can be projected to a low dimension using some vector projection method which tries to preserve distances between projected points. A common practice is to use Sammon's projection and to show the topological relations of the map by connecting points that corresponds to neighboring units. The SOM may be considered unreliable if the topological structure is completely twisted or folded. In Fig. 2.1(b) one can see that this has not happened in our artificial example but the map is well ordered in this case.

In order to clarify the connections between visualizations, they may be linked together using color which is a dominant visual hint for grouping objects. This idea has been applied to carrying information from the SOM representation to a geographical map in [1; 3; 8]. We have applied this idea simply to link different presentations of the same data together, e.g., the SOM grid and a scatter plot or Sammon's projection [5; 23]. See Fig. 2.2. Similar linking idea to PCA has been earlier presented by Aristide [3].

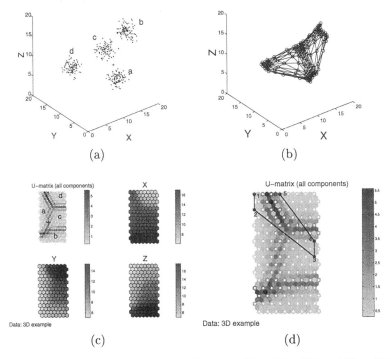

Fig. 2.1 Figure (a) shows a simple three-dimensional (variables X,Y and Z) artificial data set with four clear clusters (a,b,c,d). Figure (b) shows the prototype vectors ("o") of a SOM trained with the data in (a). The topological connections are shown as lines connecting the neighboring prototype vectors. Figure (c) shows the u-matrix and component planes. In the u-matrix dark gray represents long inter-unit distances and light gray short ones. The clusters — that can be seen as light "fields" between the dark "mountains" — have been labeled for convenience. The +-sign shows the BMU for the sample marked by +-sign in (a) (located between clusters a and c). The component planes show how the variables X,Y and Z vary along the map. Figure (d) shows a trajectory of five samples on the u-matrix.

2.3.2 *Correlation hunting*

Correlations between component pairs are revealed as similar patterns in identical positions of the component planes. The correlation detection can be made easier if the component planes are reorganized so that the possibly correlated ones are presented near each other [24]. See Fig. 2.3. Using component planes for correlation hunting in this way is easy, but also rather vague and sometimes even misleading. However, it is easy to select interesting component combinations for further investigation. A more detailed study of interesting combinations can be done using scatter plots which can be linked to the map units by color as has been regularly done in the case studies in Sec. 2.5.*

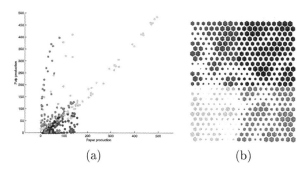

Fig. 2.2 Correlations between vector components can be efficiently visualized using scatter plots. In Fig. (a) each dot corresponds to one map unit. The x- and y-coordinates of the dots have been taken from two components of the prototype vectors. To link the scatter plot to other visualizations, each dot is given a color according to the color coding of the map units shown in Fig. (b). In this grayscale figure only four shades of gray are used. In practice a full color palette is much more informative. In addition to color coding, Fig. (b) also uses size to indicate clusters on the map: small units correspond to cluster borders. It can be seen that for most units, especially those with light gray color coding, the two components are linearly correlated but that there are distinct exceptions.

2.3.3 *Novelty detection*

When investigating new data using SOM, the BMU of each data sample is found and indicated on the map (see Sec. 2.3.1). The problem with this simple approach is that it gives no information of the accuracy of the match. Typically, there are several units with almost as good match as the BMU. Alternatively, the data sample may actually be very far from the map — a novelty in terms of the map.

Instead of simply pointing out the BMU, the response of all map units to the data can be shown. The resulting response surface shows the relative goodness of each map unit in representing the data. The response can be,

---

*For technical reasons we can't use colors in this presentation. In order to sketch the idea, a gray level coding is used instead. A full color version can be found in [27].

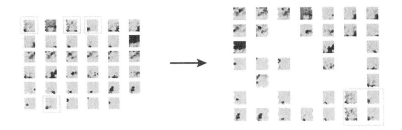

Fig. 2.3 Correlations between components can be hunted from the component planes visualization on the left. The task is easier if the planes are reorganized so that component planes which seem to have high correlation are placed near each other, as shown on the right. For example, this reorganization brings nicely together the four framed components.

e.g., a function of the quantization error as follows:

$$g(\mathbf{x}, \mathbf{m}_i) = \frac{1}{1 + (q_i/a)^2}, \qquad (2)$$

where $q_i = ||\mathbf{x} - \mathbf{m}_i||$ is the quantization error, i.e., distance, between sample $\mathbf{x}$ and map unit i. The scaling factor a is the average distance between each training data sample and its BMU. See Fig. 2.4(a). Perhaps a more interpretative response function results if the SOM is used as a basis for reduced kernel density estimate of the data. Then one can estimate the probability $P(i|\mathbf{x})$ of each map unit representing the data sample, see for example [2; 6].

In both cases above, the response surface is added onto the map afterwards, while the original SOM algorithm has a "crisp" winner-take-all activation function. There are related algorithms that have an intrinsic probabilistic background as the S-Map [11]. However, it seems that a kernel density estimation model added to the SOM gives results that are well comparable with these methods [2].

Another way to show the accuracy of the match is to use, e.g., the size of the sample marker. In Fig. 2.4(b), the fuzzy response function (Eq. 2) has been used to control the size of the sample markers (circles). Now, individual samples can be seen along with their BMUs (position) and accuracy (size).

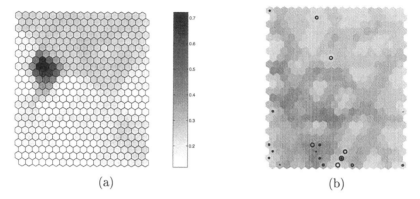

Fig. 2.4 Accuracy of matches. Figure (a) shows the response surface (Eq. 2) for one data sample. Figure (b) shows BMUs and corresponding accuracies of 20 samples. The background texture is averaged u-matrix of the SOM. Each circle represents one sample. The position of the circle indicates the BMU, and its size the accuracy of the match.

2.4 Software

To accomplish the explorative and iterative data analysis scheme, a flexible software environment is needed. It should include domain specific post- and preprocessing capabilities, SOM implementation and different visualizations. The possibility to rapidly customize the code is important. We have tried to achieve this in the SOM Toolbox.

2.4.1 SOM Toolbox

The MathWorks Inc.'s MATLAB [16] has been gaining popularity as the "language of scientific computing", and it employs a high-level programming language with strong support for matrix algebra, graphics and visualization. MATLAB suits for fast prototyping and customizing. The SOM Toolbox[†] [25], hereafter the Toolbox, is an attempt to take advantage of these strengths and provide a customizable and easy-to-use implementation of the SOM as a free function library for the MATLAB environment.

The advantages of the Toolbox are mainly in fast customization and visualization. A major benefit is that as the MATLAB's language is inter-

---

[†]Available in http://www.cis.hut.fi/projects/somtoolbox/

preted, the user may give on-line commands to change various parameters or visualizations. Furthermore, the Toolbox is constructed in a modular manner. Therefore, it is convenient to tailor the code for the specific needs of each user. Other toolboxes — commercial or freeware — may be used together with the Toolbox to provide domain specific processing capabilities. For example, a toolbox related to system simulation might be used in a process control task.

The basic procedures — SOM initialization, training and visualization — have been collected under high level functions which provide heuristic choices for various parameter values. This gives an automated data-to-visualization operation to start with. The Toolbox also implements some variants of the basic SOM. The topology of the SOM can be n-dimensional, and several SOM shapes are supported: rectangular, cylinder and toroid — as well as several neighborhood functions. In order to facilitate the data analysis process, the Toolbox keeps track of labels associated with individual data vectors, vector component names, component normalization information and information on the training procedure.

A standard implementation of the SOM and related tools are available as the SOM_PAK [13]. It is a public domain software package[‡] developed in the Neural Networks Research Centre of the Helsinki University of Technology, written in ANSI C language for UNIX and PC environments. In map training, it is faster than the Toolbox and has a better capability to be applied to large data sets than the Toolbox. However, while the SOM_PAK is the choice for heavy duty, the Toolbox is meant for experimental and/or interactive purposes. If the scalability is a problem, the SOM_PAK can be accessed from the Toolbox. It is possible to first train the map with the SOM_PAK and then use the Toolbox for visualization.

2.4.2 *The SOM visualization as a user interface platform*

The SOM grid is an effective base for building visualizations and user interfaces for accessing multidimensional data. Assume that we need to attach some information (text, symbols, colors) to the projected points. The projection methods that produce a nonuniform visualization may cause problems as the labeling information easily becomes unreadable in the dense parts of the projection.

[‡]Available in http://www.cis.hut.fi/nnrc/som_pak/

In the SOM the amount of the units in a certain region of the space is proportional to the density of the training data in that region, i.e., the map uses more units to represent the dense parts of the data. This increases readability as the map automatically "zooms up" areas that are dense. On the other hand, the topology preserving property gives access to cluster or variable value visualization through u-matrix and component planes which can be easily used as browsers. The nodes can be used as clicking points to access the data underneath. The idea to use the SOM visualization as a user interface has been used earlier, e.g., in the WEBSOM [14] in browsing large document collections.

2.4.3 Interactive tool for time-series exploration

As an example, we shortly describe an interactive time-series tool designed on the SOM Toolbox. The purpose of the tool is to facilitate the inspection of the connections between the multidimensional data space presented by the SOM and the time-series plot. In analysis, the feature data have been extracted and the map is trained using them. The analyst may now evaluate how certain feature variables are distributed and what kind of clusters there are in the map visualization. The analyst sees how different regions of the map are related to a time-series representing the same data from a different point of view. After this, the analyst may reconsider if the feature data really represent the investigated phenomena in a sensible way or if the features should be extracted in some other way. The tool in Fig. 2.5 allows the analyst to

- see the connection between original time-series and the feature space visualized by the SOM.
- run the process using a slider on the time-series. A trajectory — showing the connected BMUs for the current and some past samples of the time-series — is animated on the map.
- define some areas on the map and tag them with specific colors. The same markers are shown on the time-series. Now the analyst may inspect how a region on the map is connected to the time-series. This may be done to the opposite direction, too, in order to see how the time-series is projected to the map.

The Self-Organizing Map as a Tool in Knowledge Engineering 51

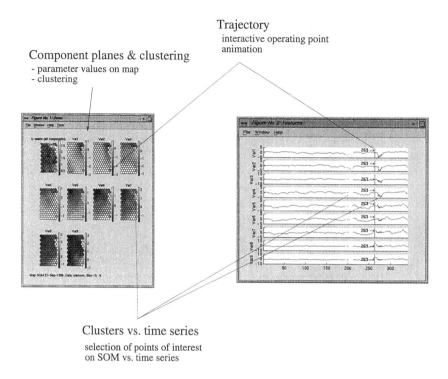

Fig. 2.5 Time-series tool. The analyst may inspect changes in the operation point using a slider. The analyst may mark regions on the map and in the time-series using different colors.

2.5 Case studies

2.5.1 *Analysis of a continuous pulp digester*

In the first case study, behavior of a continuous pulp digester was analyzed. An illustration of the digester and separate impregnation vessel is shown in Fig. 2.6. Wood chips and cooking liquor are fed into the impregnation vessel. After the impregnation, the chips are fed into the digester. At the top of the digester, they are heated to cooking temperature using steam, and the pulping reaction starts. During the cook, the chips slowly move downwards the digester. The cooking ends at extraction screens, where the pulping reaction is stopped by cooling the chips using wash liquor. The wash liquor is fed to the digester bottom and it moves upwards, countercurrent to the chip flow.

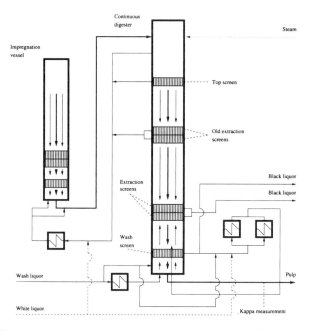

Fig. 2.6 The continuous digester and the impregnation vessel. The cooking and wash liquor flows are marked by thin lines and the chip flow by thick line.

Problems in digester operation indicated by drops of pulp consistency in the digester outlet were the starting point for the analysis. In those situations, end product quality variable (kappa number) values were lower than the target value.

Measurement data were obtained from the automation system of the mill. The analysis was started with several dozens of variables which were gradually reduced down to six most important measurements during data analysis process. The data used in the following experiments consisted of three separate measurement periods during more than one month of normal pulping operation. The periods were segmented by hand in such a way that they mainly consisted of faulty situations of the process. The production speed was required to be constant. During the measurement periods there were no significant errors in the measurements. Process delays between signals were compensated using known digester delays.

In Fig. 2.7, the six signals and production speed of the fiber line are shown. The three segmented parts are shown by solid line and the parts that were left out of the analysis by dotted line. In Fig. 2.8, the compo-

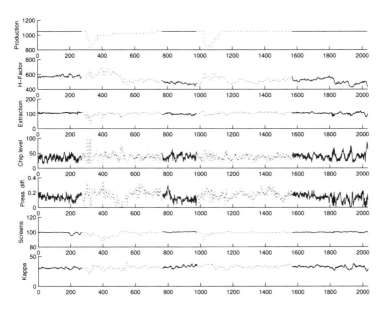

Fig. 2.7   Measurement signals of the continuous digester. The analyzed parts are marked by solid line and the parts that were ignored by dotted line.

nent planes of a 17 by 12 units SOM trained using signals of Fig. 2.7 are presented. Five of them depict behavior of the digester and the last one is the output variable, the kappa number. The problematic process states are mapped to the top left corner of the SOM: the model vectors in that part of the map have too low kappa number value.

Correlations between the kappa number and other variables are shown in Fig. 2.9, where the SOM of Fig. 2.8 has been presented using color coding. The colors were originally chosen in such a way that adjacent map units had almost similar colors; here we are only able to use four gray levels. The five scatter plots are based on *model vector component values* of the SOM. They all have the values of kappa number on the x-axes and the five other

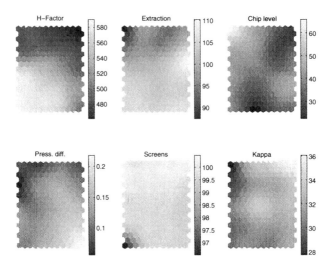

Fig. 2.8 Component planes of the SOM trained using six measurement signals of the digester. Dark color indicates low and light color high variable value, respectively.

variables on the y-axes. In Fig. 2.10, a similar technique for coloring the scatter plots is utilized. In this case, however, the scatter plots are based on *data vectors* — not values of the model vectors of the SOM. The color of each data vector is the one assigned to the the SOM unit that is nearest to the data vector. It should be noted that even though the plots differ from the ones of Fig. 2.9, the SOM has been able to capture the shape of the data cloud quite accurately. The scatter plots indicate that *in the faulty states* denoted by dark grey color (top left corner of the map), there is only weak correlation between kappa number and H-Factor, which is the variable used to control the kappa number. Otherwise, there is a negative correlation as might be expected. On the other hand, the variables *Extraction* and *Chip level* seem to correlate with the kappa number in the faulty process states. Also, the values of *Press. diff.* are low and value of variable *Screens* (which during the analysis was noticed to indicate digester fault sensitivity) is high.

The interpretation of the results is that in a faulty situation, the downward movement of the chip plug in the digester slows down. The plug is so tightly packed at the extraction screens that the wash liquor cannot pass it as it should. There are two consequences: the wash liquor slows down the

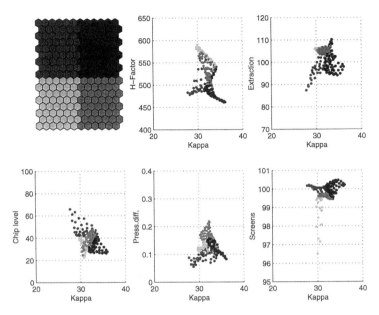

Fig. 2.9 Color map and five scatter plots of model vectors of the SOM. The points have been dyed using the corresponding map unit colors.

downward movement of the plug and the pulping reaction does not stop. Because the cooking continues, the kappa number becomes too small. In addition, the H-factor based digester control fails: in the H-factor computation, cooking time is assumed to be constant, while in reality it becomes longer due to slowing down of the chip plug movement.

2.5.2 Analysis of the quality of the hot rolled strip

In the second case study, a hot rolling system was analyzed. Hot rolling is a process where steel slabs are heated, rolled, cooled and coiled into final products, strips. Figure 2.11 illustrates the composition of the hot strip mill in Raahe (at the time of the data acquisition; currently the mill construction is somewhat different). First, the slab is heated in the slab reheating furnaces (1) into temperature appropriate for the following rolling process. Then, after the formed scale is removed with high-pressure water

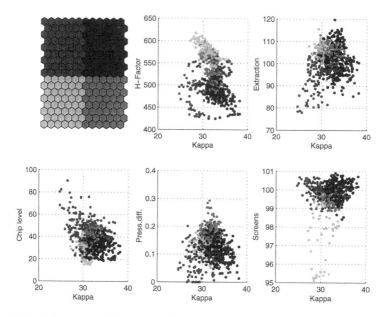

Fig. 2.10 Color map and five scatter plots of data vectors. The points have been dyed using the color of BMU.

shower (2), the slab passes to the roughing mill. The slab is rolled back and forth several times vertically in the edger (3) and horizontally in the reversing rougher (4). The resulting transfer bar travels under the heat retention panels (5) through another descaling and possible shearing of the head (6) into the finishing mill (7), where it is rolled into desired end product. The finishing mill consists of six stands. The transfer bar goes through them with high accelerating speed. After the rolling, the strip is cooled with several water curtains (8) and coiled (9).

The process is controlled hierarchically by several separate automation systems. Basically, each process stage introduced above has its own automation system. Furthermore, a lot of additional computation, control, and information processing is made within and between the systems. This causes difficulties in the data acquisition. Hence, the process data available for this case study consisted only of averages and standard deviations of the measured process variables of one strip.

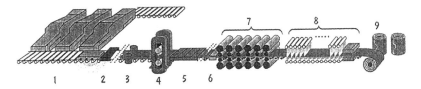

Fig. 2.11 Rautaruukki hot strip mill. The different process stages are marked with numbers. See text for their explanations.

Due to ever increasing competition and customer requirements, the steel producers are under growing pressure to improve the cost efficiency of the production and the quality of their products. This is also the motivation for the analysis, the purpose of which was to study which process parameters and variables affect the quality of the rolled strips. This can be done, e.g., with correlation analysis for process data, which was the approach in this case.

The data was collected from factory data bases in co-operation with the process experts. In the data set it was chosen 47 variables. The average and standard deviation of five process parameters were chosen to represent the quality: width, thickness, profile, flatness and wedge of the rolled strip. The other variables included information about the slab (analyzed chemical content), finishing mill parameters (average bending forces, entry tensions, and axial shifts for each stand), and process state (strip strength, target dimensions, and average and standard deviation of the temperature after the last stand). After preprocessing of data, the amount of the strips included in the study was slightly over 16500.

In the beginning, in order to get to know the general dependencies between the parameters, a very simple global linear correlation analysis was performed. This showed, e.g., that the entry tensions of the stands were controlled based on the tensile strength calculated from the chemical analysis results. Due to redundant information of the variables caused by the controlling principles of the process, the data dimension could be reduced to 36 variables.

The structure of the data set was then studied. This was done by projecting the data on the two largest principal components of the data (Fig. 2.12(a)). As an alternative approach, the prototype vectors of a SOM trained with the data were projected with Sammon's mapping (Fig. 2.12 (b)). The data seem to be somehow clustered as was expected. Furthermore, it can be seen that the different projection algorithms provide more or less similar results and the SOM has approximated the data quite well.

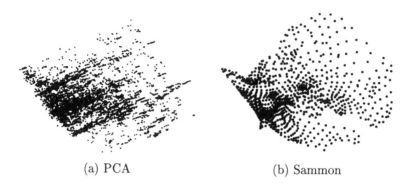

(a) PCA   (b) Sammon

Fig. 2.12 The original data projected with PCA (a) and the prototype vectors of the SOM projected with Sammon's mapping (b).

Due to the quite large amount of variables, finding correlations between them using the typical component plane representation (where the planes are plotted next to each other in the same order as the variables in the data) became extremely difficult. Fortunately, the task could be made easier by reorganizing the component planes using the procedure explained in Sec. 2.3.2 so that the possibly correlating planes were placed near each other. The result is illustrated in Fig. 2.13.

Using this approach, some of the interesting relationships between the variables could be detected. Based on this information and the *a priori* knowledge of the system, the variables to be used in the more detailed analysis of the strip quality could be chosen. In this case, the strip thickness was chosen to be studied further. The variables included in the new data set were quality parameters, thickness average deviation and standard deviation, strip target dimensions, strip strength, bending forces, temperature after the last stand, and strip profile.

Using the scatter plots colored with the continuous coloring of the SOM plane, as explained in Sec. 2.3.2, dependencies between thickness and other parameters in different process states could be found. The approach is illustrated in Fig. 2.14, where all the other variables are plotted against average thickness deviation. Note, that here the color code had to be limited

Fig. 2.13 The reorganized component planes of the SOM.

to four gray levels, which drastically deteriorates the results. However, in the actual study a true continuous color code was used. After some inspection of these plots, the following statements regarding the problems with strip width could be made:

- The thickness deviation of the strip seems to increase as the bending forces decrease, especially when the strips are somewhat thick. Then, also the standard deviations of the thickness, the temperature after the last stand, and the strip profile tend to increase.
- The standard deviation of the strip seems to increase as the thickness of the strip increases, especially with hard steels. As with the deviation of the thickness, the standard deviation seems to increase as the rolling temperature and the bending forces decrease. The standard deviation of the temperature after the last stand and the strip profile tend also to increase. However, this does not hold for quite narrow and thin strips.

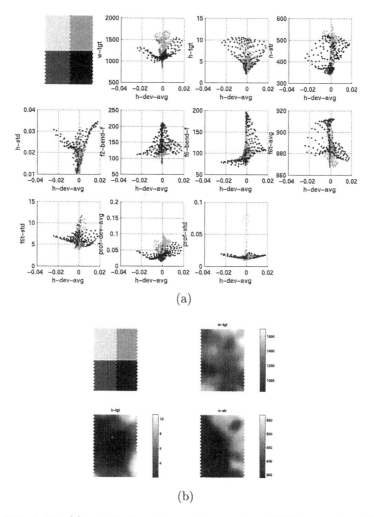

Fig. 2.14 In Fig. (a) variables from the prototype vectors of SOM are scatter plotted using the color coding shown in the upper left picture. For example, the last scatter plot (*prof-std* vs. *h-dev-avg*) shows that on the lightest gray region of the color coded map the thickness deviation (*h-dev-avg*) does not increase/decrease, as on the other regions, when the profile standard deviation (*prof-std*) increases. In Fig. (b), it can be seen that on the lightest gray region of the map are the data samples mostly from quite narrow, thin, and mild strips, as on this region the component planes *w-tgt* (target width), *h-tgt* (target thickness), and *n-str* (strip strength) indicate low values simultaneously.

2.6 Conclusions

The Self-Organizing Map has proven to be a powerful tool in knowledge discovery and data analysis. It combines the tasks, and benefits, of vector quantization and data projection. The various novel visualization methods presented in this chapter offer efficient ways to enhance the visualization of the SOM in data exploration. There are many kinds of tasks in exploratory visualization, but as the proposed principles are simple, they can be easily modified to meet the needs of the task. Future work is still needed to enable the methods to automatically take heed of the properties of the underlying data.

The SOM can be effectively used to find and visualize correlations between process variables in different operational states of the process. The topology preserving property together with the regular presentational form of the SOM visualization gives a compact base where many kinds of visualizations and interfaces may be linked together.

In this chapter, we have used the basic SOM visualizations together with methods that link different kind of visualizations using color. However, there are some aspects in the methods that should be noted:

- One should remember when using color visualizations that there are color-blind people who do not see the color space as the majority of people do.
- The color coding that we have used is of heuristic design, something to start with. Furthermore, a coloring that brings up the cluster structure (see [8; 9]) would certainly be beneficial.
- The linking between the scatter plots and the SOM could be made interactively by highlighting the interesting points. However, the color coding brings an automated overall sight to this procedure.
- The scatter plots connected to the map grid will benefit the analysis only if the dependencies are such that a variable can be considered to be (locally) a function of mainly one other latent variable. If the dependencies are more complex, the scatter plot visualization with the color linking becomes useless.

Despite their evident limitations, the methods presented have facilitated the industrial data analysis, especially in the explorative phase of the work.

It should be emphasized that the data analysis process usually is iterative, i.e., the most important variables can be determined only after various steps of the data mining process. In the beginning, there are usually several dozens of measurements which will then be reduced to the most important ones affecting the behavior of the process. Several tests must be made and interpreted using knowledge of process experts.

2.7 Acknowledgments

The research in this work was carried out in the technology program "Adaptive and Intelligent Systems Applications" financed by the Technology Development Centre of Finland (TEKES) and in the "Application of Neural Network based Models for Optimization of the Rolling Process" (NEUROLL) project financed by the European Union. The cooperation of the following enterprises is gratefully acknowledged: Jaakko Poyry Consulting, Rautaruukki and UPM-Kymmene.

We acknowledge Mr. Juha Parhankangas for carrying out various elaborate programming tasks in our projects.

References

[1] E. J. Ainsworth, "Classification of Ocean Colour Using Self-Organizing Feature Maps," Proceedings of the 5th International Conference on Soft Computing and Information/Intelligent Systems (Eds. T. Yamakawa, G. Matsumoto), Vol. 2, pp. 996–999, World Scientific, 1998.

[2] E. Alhoniemi, J. Himberg, J. Vesanto, "Probabilistic Measures for Responses of Self-Organizing Map Units," Proceedings of International ICSC Congress on Computational Intelligence and Applications (CIMA'99) (Eds. H. Bother, E. Oja. E. Massad, C. Haefke), pp. 286–290, 1999.

[3] V. Aristide, "On the use of two traditional statistical techniques to improve the readability of Kohonen Maps," Proceedings of the NATO ASI on Statistics and Neural Networks, Les Arcs, France, 1993.

[4] P. Demartines, J. Hérault, "Curvilinear Component Analysis: a Self-Organizing Neural Network for Nonlinear Mapping of Data Sets," IEEE Transactions on Neural Networks, Vol. 8, pp. 148–154, 1997.

[5] J. Himberg, "Enhancing SOM-based data visualization by linking different data projections," Proceedings of 1st International symposium on Intelligent Data Engineering and Learning 1998 (IDEAL'98) (Eds. L. Xu, L. W. Chan, I. King, A. Fu), pp. 427–434, Springer, 1998.

[6] L. Holmström, A Hämäläinen, "The Self-Organizing Reduced Kernel Density Estimator," Proceedings of the International Conference on Neural Networks (ICNN'93), San Francisco, pp. 417–421, 1993.

[7] J. Iivarinen, T. Kohonen, J. Kangas, J., S. Kaski, "Visualizing the Clusters on the Self-Organizing Map," Proceedings of the Conference on Artificial Intelligence Research in Finland (Eds. C. Carlsson, T. Järvi, T. Reponen), number 12, pp. 122–126, Finnish Artificial Intelligence Society, 1994.

[8] S. Kaski, J. Venna, T. Kohonen, "Tips for Processing and Color-Coding of Self-Organizing Maps," in Visual Explorations in Finance (Eds. G. Deboeck, T. Kohonen), Ch. 14, pp. 195–202, Springer-Verlag, 1998.

[9] S. Kaski, J. Venna, T. Kohonen, "Coloring that Reveals High-Dimensional Structures in Data," Proceedings of the 6th International Conference on Neural Information Processing (ICONIP'99), Vol. II, pp. 729–734, 1999.

[10] M. Kasslin, J. Kangas, O. Simula, "Process State Monitoring Using Self-Organizing Maps," in Artificial Neural Networks (Eds. I. Aleksander, J. Taylor), Vol. 2, pp. 1531–1534, North-Holland, 1992.

[11] K. Kiviluoto, E. Oja, "S-Map: A network with a simple self-organization algorithm for generative topographic mappings," in Advances in Neural Processing Systems (Eds. M. I. Jordan, M. J. Kearns, S. A. Solla), no. 10, pp. 549–555, MIT Press, 1997.

[12] T. Kohonen, Self-Organizing Maps, Springer Series in Information Sciences 30, Springer, 1995.

[13] T. Kohonen, J. Hynninen, J. Kangas, J. Laaksonen, "SOM_PAK: The Self-Organizing Map Program Package," Technical Report A31, Helsinki University of Technology, Laboratory of Computer and Information Science, 1996.

[14] T. Kohonen, S. Kaski, K. Lagus, T. Honkela, "Very Large Two-Level SOM for the Browsing of Newsgroups, " Proceedings of ICANN'96, pp. 269–274, 1996.

[15] T. Kohonen, E. Oja, O. Simula, A. Visa, J. Kangas, "Engineering Applications of the Self-Organizing Map," Proceedings of the IEEE, 84(10), pp. 1358–1384, 1995.

[16] MathWorks Inc, MATLAB — The Language of Technical Computing: Using MATLAB Version 5, MathWorks Inc., 1997.

[17] N. R. Pal, V. K. Eluri, "Two Efficient Connectionist Schemes for Structure Preserving Dimensionality Reduction," IEEE Transactions on Neural Networks, Vol. 9, no. 6, pp. 1142–1154, 1998.

[18] J. W. Sammon, Jr., "A Nonlinear Mapping for Data Structure Analysis," IEEE Transactions on Computers, C-18(5), pp. 401–409, 1969.

[19] O. Simula, J. Kangas, "Process monitoring and visualization using self-organizing maps," Computer-Aided Chemical Engineering, Vol. 6, Ch. 14, pp. 371–384, Elsevier, 1995.

[20] V. Tryba, S. Metzen, K. Goser, "Designing of Basic Integrated Circuits by Self-Organizing Feature Maps," Proceedings of Neuro-Nimes '89, Int. Workshop on Neural Networks and their applications, pp. 225–235, Nanterre, France, 1989.

[21] V. Tryba, K. Goser, "Self-Organizing Feature Maps for Process Control in Chemistry," in Artificial Neural Networks (Eds. T. Kohonen, K. Mäkisara, O. Simula, J. Kangas), Vol. 1, pp. 847–852, North-Holland, 1991.

[22] A. Ultsch, H. Siemon, "Kohonen's Self Organizing Feature Maps for Exploratory Data Analysis," Proceedings of the International Neural Network Conference (INNC'90), pp. 305–308, Kluwer, 1990.

[23] J. Vesanto, J. Himberg, M. Siponen, O. Simula "Enhancing SOM Based Data Visualization," Proceedings of the 5th International Conference on

Soft Computing and Information/Intelligent Systems (Eds. T. Yamakawa, G. Matsumoto), pp. 64–67, World Scientific, 1998.

[24] J. Vesanto, J. Ahola, "Hunting for Correlations in Data Using the Self-Organizing Map," Proceedings of International ICSC Congress on Computational Intelligence and Applications (CIMA'99) (Eds. H. Bother, E. Oja. E. Massad, C. Haefke), pp. 279-285, 1999.

[25] J. Vesanto, E. Alhoniemi, J. Himberg, K. Kiviluoto, J. Parviainen, "Self-Organizing Map for Data Mining in MATLAB: the SOM Toolbox," Simulation News Europe, 25, p. 54, ARGE Simulation News, 1999.

[27] J. Vesanto, "SOM-based data visualization methods," Intelligent Data Analysis, Vol. 3, No. 2, pp. 111-126, Elsevier, 1999.

Chapter 3
Classification of Oceanic Water Types Using Self-Organizing Feature Maps

Ewa J. Ainsworth
National Space Development Agency of Japan

Abstract

Radiative transfer algorithms in combination with empirical formulae have been the most popular approach to the analysis of ocean primary productivity from remotely sensed images of the Earth. These methods fully rely on the limited amounts of ground truth data available and assumptions regarding how sensor, Earth's surface and atmospheric properties influence the radiation captured in different ranges of the electromagnetic spectrum. As these assumptions are restraining, multi-spectral and fusion techniques based on the application of unsupervised neural networks can contribute to the improvement in ocean colour studies and enable analysis of complex water types. This chapter presents the application of a hierarchy of self-organizing feature maps to clustering and differentiation of oceanic waters. The practical studies are performed on imagery captured all over the Pacific Ocean by the Ocean Colour and Temperature Scanner on board the Japanese satellite ADEOS.

Keywords: neural networks, self-organizing feature maps, multi-dimensional topology, unsupervised learning, feature analysis, classification, hierarchical processing, data fusion, regularity detector, satellite images, multi-spectral analysis, ocean colour, sea surface temperature, case 1 and case 2 waters, chlorophyll

3.1 Introduction

The present state of the ocean is of special interest to those concerned with changes in the Earth climate, environment, and natural resources. Biological productivity of the ocean depends on phytoplankton which use chlorophyll to capture the energy of the sun to produce organic biomass [1]. Phytoplankton support marine food webs and influence global chemical budgets and climate. They utilize carbon dioxide from the atmosphere through photosynthesis affecting the carbon dioxide balance of the planet. Phytoplankton make a contribution to the seasonal warming of ocean surface layers by absorbing and scattering light. They are also responsible for the production of quantities of volatile compounds, such as dimethyl sulphide, which escape to the atmosphere and act as cloud-seeding nuclei.
Chlorophyll rich waters are found in topographically induced upwellings, along continental shelf fronts, and in coastal seas and estuaries. Coastal waters beside phytoplankton normally contain numerous extra residua. The coastal region is of immediate interest to nearly all people since most of human interaction with the ocean takes place in shore waters including fisheries, eutrophication, recreation, and coastal pollution.

3.1.1 *Remote sensing of ocean colour and temperature*

Since the emergence of the first systematic Earth orbital observations in the 1960s, it has become possible to observe environmental changes globally, instantaneously, frequently and in a consistent fashion. Satellites conduct homogeneous and regular measurements of atmospheric and surface parameters in regions with limited access and too broad to allow convincing generalization of *in situ* observations, such as in the oceans, deserts and polar zones. The Earth is remotely scanned with a number of different sensors whose design depends on a desired purpose of their mission. Following the pioneering investigations by Clarke *et al.* [2] on the feasibility of deriving marine chlorophyll concentration from its influence on the spectral composition of light backscattered by the upper oceanic layers, a first especially devoted sensor, Coastal Zone Colour Scanner (CZCS), was launched in 1978. 8 years of the world ocean observation proved capabilities of remote sensing techniques to monitor marine biomass and led to the definition of a new generation of ocean colour sensors supported by the Joint Global Ocean Flux Study.

The Ocean Colour and Temperature Scanner (OCTS) was designed as a successor to CZCS and launched in August 1996 on board of the Japanese satellite ADEOS [3]. OCTS captured electromagnetic energy of the Earth from 12 spectral channels. Channel characteristics are displayed in Table

3.1. Eight channels lie in the visible and near-infrared and four in the thermal infrared range of the electromagnetic spectrum. The signal to noise ratio (SNR) is expressed as the mean square noise divided by the saturation radiance. NEΔT is the noise equivalent differential temperature. The channels were designed to provide a high radiometric sensitivity of readings suitable for the extraction of marine chlorophyll concentration [4]. Each band was scanned with 10 detectors obtaining 10 bit brightness radiances.

Band		wavelength (nm)	SNR
1	violet	402-422	450
2	dark blue	433-453	500
3	blue-green	480-500	500
4	green	510-530	500
5	yellow	555-575	500
6	dark red	660-680	500
7	near-infrared	745-785	500
8	near-infrared	845-885	450
			NEΔT (K)
9	thermal-infrared	3,550-3,880	0.15
10	thermal-infrared	8,250-8,800	0.15
11	thermal-infrared	10,300-11,400	0.15
12	thermal-infrared	11,400-12,700	0.2

Table 3.1 OCTS channel characteristics.

A French sensor POLDER was also present on ADEOS providing data for ocean studies but with much lower spatial resolution of 7km. Since OCTS and POLDER, two other ocean colour sensors have been launched, American SeaWiFS and German MOS. Many new instruments are planned for the future which will perform ocean colour and temperature studies as a part of their mission, such as Japanese GLI, European MERIS and American MODIS.

Practical investigations performed during the current study are applied to archived OCTS imagery. The general concept is universal and can be used with other sensors, such as SeaWiFS and GLI when the sensor becomes available.

3.1.2 *Current applications and algorithms of ocean colour data*

Ocean colour and temperature data have been mostly used to extract sea surface temperature, marine chlorophyll concentrations and atmospheric parameters for the scientific climatological and environmental studies. This information appears as images pixel-by-pixel colour coded with chlorophyll levels and temperature values. They are usually delivered to the scientific community with a delay after time-consuming processing, ordering and shipment, unless a researcher in advance agrees a special capture and delivery programme.

Radiative transfer models have been the most popular approach to processing of ocean colour and temperature data. These methods use selected spectral channels and limited amounts of ground truth information available to model atmospheric and Earth surface phenomena. Usually, land is masked out using superimposed area maps. Clouds are cleared applying empirical threshold algorithms. Remaining ocean radiances undergo a thorough analysis.

For the purpose of remote sensing, water conditions are divided into two categories, case 1 and case 2. Case 1 waters are fully dominated by phytoplankton and their by-products and occur mainly in the open ocean. Case 2 waters contain additional suspended sediments, dissolved organic matter, and terrigenous particles and are largely associated with coastal resumes.

Water-leaving radiances, which are used to extract chlorophyll levels, in most favourable conditions represent only 10% of the total radiance captured by a satellite [5]. The readings are dominated by the atmospheric path radiance originating from photons scattered by air molecules and/or aerosols. Current chlorophyll extraction algorithms perform an atmospheric correction to remove the contribution of the atmosphere in satellite measurements. Under the assumption of separability of radiances, radiative transfer models isolate molecular (Rayleigh), gas, aerosol, and ocean reflectances and model them individually [6]. Radiances originating from air molecular scattering are readily extracted. However, radiances due to aerosol scattering present a difficulty since distributions of their particles cannot be established. Several models of atmospheric aerosols are normally defined. Near-infrared radiances measured over case 1 waters are assumed to be fully dependent on the atmosphere. It is also occasionally postulated that case 1 water leaving radiance is negligibly small in the red visible [6]. These wavelengths are used to extract aerosol properties and extrapolate them towards the visible spectra. Hence, uncorrupted water-leaving radiances are calculated for the subsequent extraction of marine chlorophyll levels.

Chlorophyll concentrations are calculated from normalized water-leaving radiances applying empirical equations fitted to suit a given ground truth data set [7, 8]. Coefficients of the Ocean Chlorophyll Concentration (OCC) equation for OCTS were adjusted to approximate the measurements in the sea around Japan [9]. This causes the algorithms to be less accurate when the conditions are different. The equations utilize only a fraction of information available. The OCTS method uses three spectral channels to calculate chlorophyll levels.

The skill of the radiative transfer models heavily relies on the concept of zero-case-1-water leaving radiance in the near-infrared. They initially presume all waters to be case 1. However, water types within the case 2 category can be of the top interest to the majority of users. Current algorithms are not suitable for case 2 water analysis. In case 2 waters there is a significant water leaving radiance in both the visible and near-infrared [10]. Consequently, the usual aerosol extraction is unfeasible. Regular atmospheric corrections fail because the extrapolation of aerosol path radiance into visible bands results in distorted and even negative reflectances at visible wavelengths.

The 765nm near-infrared channel is largely influenced by the oxygen absorption. Some algorithms, such as OCTS, do not perform the radiative transfer correction for oxygen and have only one near-infrared channel available for aerosol extraction. They overcome the problem by applying an additional assumption that case-1-water leaving radiance is negligible in the red visible range of the spectrum. Thus, they use the red visible, 670nm, and the other near-infrared, 865nm, channels to define aerosols. However, earlier studies and many authors show that case 1 waters can produce a significant reflectance in the red band, especially with high chlorophyll levels [11, 12].

3.1.3 *Motivation for the research*

The current research provides a vision of future utilisation of ocean colour and temperature information. It also addresses the problems encountered by the radiative transfer models when dealing with globally distributed imagery. The purpose is to complement the existing models and contribute to a better differentiation of water types from satellite data. Soft Computing algorithms for feature analysis and classification create most useful tools for this application.

3.1.3.1 *Distributed utilization of data*

Ocean colour and temperature data can bring more benefits and serve a wider range of users. Local coastal resumes are of strong interest to fishermen, environmentalists, policy planners, holiday industry, coastal guards and even life guards concerned with water quality. They would need near real-time information on water types within their local area and upper ocean temporal changes and trends. Such information has not been so far available from remotely sensed observations and would require a novel approach to ocean colour data processing and distribution. Satellite image

receiving stations should be more distributed. The analysis should satisfy the following requirements:
(1) Automatic, near real-time processing and rapid distribution of final products.
(2) Extraction of water types and analysis of ocean state of most practical interest to individual users.
(3) Detailed examination of local marine zones.
(4) Observation of temporal changes in the upper ocean and short-term prediction of change tendencies.
(5) Flexibility in acquiring new or additional information adjusted to user changing needs.

A definition of water types is not objective and depends on water characteristics of most concern to individual users. The classical remote sensing division into case 1 and case 2 waters and chlorophyll levels alone are inappropriate. There is a multitude of water attributes which can be of interest, including phytoplankton, eddies, yellow matter, river plumes, coccolithophorids blooms, red tides, naturally occurring upwellings, pollution due to sewage outfalls, industrial pollution and many others. The data processing should:
(1) objectively discover a multitude of water types,
(2) extract water types of concern to particular users.

The initial extraction of water types can be done independently and stored in a common database for immediate access. User dependent expert system based software can enable a high level manipulation of water type information relying on practical user requirements and local and temporal condition of the investigated region.

3.1.3.2 *Combating the chlorophyll estimation errors*

Due to the assumptions made by the atmospheric correction, standard OCTS OCC products occasionally produce a considerable misinterpretation of chlorophyll levels in areas with an intensified atmospheric attenuation, such as around cloud edges, high phytoplankton concentration, and over case 2 waters. Other algorithms, such as SeaWiFS and POLDER, apply a turbid water test on 555nm channel normalized water leaving radiances after the full correction has been already performed. These approaches label isolated case 2 waters because chlorophyll estimates are unreliable there. The analysis of POLDER products has shown that often not all case 2 waters are discovered and a more consistent method of case 1 and case 2 water separation would be beneficial [12].

3.1.3.3 *Necessity for case 2 water analysis*

Coastal zones are of special importance to the majority of people. However, current algorithms do not provide a means for analysis of case 2 water types. It is most complex to partition radiance at the top of the atmosphere into components due to atmosphere and case 2 waters. Therefore, novel approaches are needed.

3.2 Unsupervised neural networks for ocean colour data processing

Artificial neural networks have been considered as an advantageous tool in solving difficulties of satellite image analysis. They have been applied for a variety of purposes, such as cloud type determination [13] and land cover classification [14]. There have been also attempts to extract chlorophyll concentration from normalized water leaving radiances in the case 1 category using the backpropagation algorithm [15].

In the current study, unsupervised artificial neural networks are used to objectively extract a multitude of water types from ocean colour and temperature imagery. Self-organizing feature maps are selected for their feature analysis and clustering capabilities [16]. They are expected to improve the accuracy of chlorophyll concentration estimates and enable the investigations of case 2 waters.

Neural networks are attractive tools because they do not require detailed *a priori* knowledge about the transfer of radiative energy within the atmosphere, clear ocean and water suspended particles. In earlier studies done by the author, the effectiveness and efficiency of a self-organizing feature map for cloud differentiation from satellite images have been compared with other classification algorithms [17]. The testing set accuracy is usually slightly higher for the neural network than in case of conventional algorithms, such as maximum likelihood and K-nearest neighbour.

3.2.1 *Self-organizing feature maps*

The topology, learning and classification strategies in three-dimensional self-organizing feature maps are explained in Fig. 3.1. A conventional self-organizing feature map topology is two-dimensional, however, any dimension is possible according to the problem being solved. $\mathbf{x}$ is an input feature vector representing pixel multi-channel radiance values, and w_{ij} is a weight between the ith element (channel) of the feature vector and the jth neuron in the self-organizing feature map. The dimension of the feature space is equal to the number of spectral channels used. However, as shown later, different types of information can be fused together, such as spectral and contextual, to provide a refinement of classification decisions.

The neural network data handling is composed of two stages, the training and the classification in actual operational conditions. At the beginning of training neural weights are randomly initialized and neural neighbourhoods are large. During the training all pixels from the training scenes are presented to the neural network for several iterations. With the progress of training neural neighbourhoods and the learning function α shrink to zero. Neural weights first order themselves according to the pattern spread in the multi-spectral radiance domain. The ordering is supported by the neighbourhoods. Neurons located close to one another are associated with similar multi-channel reflectances and, thus, similar pattern classes. When ordered, neural weights learn to approximate multi-spectral radiances representative to all discovered classes. In consequence, pattern classes are defined in terms of their most prevalent spectral response acquired from the investigated channels.

Self-Organizing Feature Maps

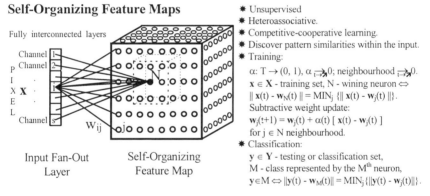

Fig 3.1 Topology, learning and classification strategies in self-organizing feature maps.

As far as the physical processing of data is concerned, self-organizing feature maps perform the least-squares minimum difference separation of radiances defined by the multi-spectral pixel information. They map multi-channel radiance vectors onto their lower-dimensional neural topology. Each neuron or a group of neighbouring neurons represents a different pattern class. Suitably trained self-organizing feature maps learn a large variety of reflectance patterns occurring over an investigated area. Trained neurons need to be labelled with their corresponding geophysical pattern classes.

The classification process in an operational environment involves finding a best matching neuron representing the geophysical pattern class corresponding to the given multi-spectral input.

3.2.2 *Advantages of self-organizing feature maps in satellite data processing*

The main advantages of self-organizing feature maps are the following:
(1) Capability to learn from examples and knowledge generalization so that the knowledge applies in new and different circumstances.
(2) Operation as regularity detectors which by themselves discover statistically salient properties of multi-spectral radiance distributions.
(3) Ability to integrate multi-spectral and multi-source information.
(4) No ground truth data are needed for the training.
(5) Efficiency in the operational classification of remotely sensed data.
(6) Learnt knowledge can be easily adjusted and upgraded.

3.2.2.1 *Training and generalization*

Radiative transfer models rely on ground truth data for the appropriate calibration and validation of their models and empirical algorithms. However, the availability of ground truth data is limited. Open ocean chlorophyll campaigns and coastal water surveys performed from ships, buoys and testing airborne sensors are localised and infrequent. Valid data points constitute a small fraction of all measurements performed due to problems in attaining temporal and spatial alignment of ground tests with satellite passes in cloud free conditions. Self-organizing feature maps do not require ground truth information during the training process. Having been introduced by intense training to the whole valid range of spectral patterns, they learn to adequately represent and associate these patterns within their topology. The patterns are general and representative to the whole of the investigated area, e.g. the Pacific, temporal variations, e.g. seasons, and rare phenomena, e.g. oil spills, eddies.

3.2.2.2 *Regularity detector*

Unlike radiative transfer models, unsupervised neural networks make no assumptions on how spectra are distributed and intertwined together. They are distribution free and support highly complex decision boundaries in the multi-channel spectrum space. Self-organizing feature maps assist data examination related to a statistical analysis but without imposing any statistical distribution. They can objectively find an arbitrary large number of spectrum classes related to a variety of geophysical patterns on the Earth surface and within the Earth's atmosphere.
Self-organizing feature maps preserve topological relations of input samples within their neural architecture because neurons localized close to one another represent similar data classes. Fuzzy class memberships of multi-

channel spectra are visualized in the maps themselves. Fuzzy class assignment depends on an appropriate interpretation and labelling of the network. Consequently, self-organizing feature maps can associate water types which are transitory from one type to another and pixels representing spatial diversity of water resumes.

3.2.2.3 Integration of information from different sources

The understanding of the spectral composition of light backscattered by the upper oceanic layers has enabled the definition of empirical equations for chlorophyll concentration using ratios of channel normalized water leaving radiances. However, these algorithms are solely successful in case 1 waters where the only suspended particles are phytoplankton. In case 2 waters, there can be a variety of suspended sediments, terrigenous particles and dissolved organic matter which individually can be practically indiscernible with the spectral data available. Unlike radiative transfer models, unsupervised neural networks can concurrently use information coming from most of or all available spectral channels. This enhanced knowledge can refine the results and enable differentiation of water types characterised by overlapping radiances in wide sections of the spectrum. Additionally, spectral information can be integrated with contextual information which provides a strong basis, or sometimes the only basis, for the extraction of complex patterns.

3.2.2.4 Ground truth

Ground truth data often are unavailable, insufficient or not-representative. However, unsupervised neural networks do not need ground truth for the training. When the training is complete, oceanographic expertise and/or small amounts of ground truth information are needed to interpret and label the classes.

3.2.2.5 Efficiency

Unsupervised neural networks are very slow in the training process because they need to be introduced to the whole valid range of patterns with no guide which patterns are important and which can be ignored. Once trained, they are very fast in the operational classification. This makes them very efficient tools to fulfill the near real-time objective discovery of a multitude of water types from remotely sensed data.

3.2.2.6 *Upgrades*

Unsupervised neural networks can incorporate information about new patterns and pattern classes to their previously learnt knowledge without initiating the training process from the beginning. Therefore, the water type extraction algorithm can be easily adjusted and upgraded.

3.3 Hierarchy of neural networks for the water type classification

The problem of water type differentiation from ocean colour and temperature data can be separated into four major classification issues:
(1) Isolation of water pixels in images from land and clouds pixels.
(2) Separation of pixels with a relatively high radiance in the near-infrared which is associated with turbid atmosphere and case 2 waters from pixels with relatively low near-infrared readings associated with case 1 waters below a fairly clear atmosphere.
(3) Removal of oceanic regions covered by the turbid atmosphere.
(4) Detailed classification of water types in clear ocean sections within both case 1 and case 2 waters.

The above hierarchy of image processing steps cannot be done in one operation because different data and classification strategies are needed to accomplish each procedure. Thorough feature extraction is required to find the most appropriate set of spectral channels contributing to the differentiation of investigated patterns. Other types of information can also be applied, such as contextual. Neural network design is each time different corresponding to the problem being solved.

3.3.1 *Radiance data studies*

The atmospheric aerosol correction is the most complex and vulnerable to errors and can distort and often jeopardise water type information, *e.g.* in the case 2 category. Thus, the current processing does not perform the full atmospheric correction. It is left up to the feature analysis and clustering abilities of self-organizing feature maps to differentiate both water types in the relatively clear sky conditions and turbid atmosphere over any type of waters. First, brightness radiances obtained by a sensor are radiometrically and geometrically revised, geolocated, and corrected for the molecular (Rayleigh) scattering, "standard aerosols", and systematic variations amongst pixels arising from different satellite viewing and sun zenith angles [18]. The corrected brightness radiances will be from now on called 'radiances'. The pixel-by-pixel classifications are performed on the multi-spectral radiances.

3.3.1.1 Spatial distribution of data

Ten OCTS images portraying coastal sites broadly distributed over the Pacific Ocean were chosen for the practical studies. The scenes are composed of blocks of around 800 by 800 pixels cut out of larger sensor passes constituting a Local Area Coverage. The sites are displayed in Fig. 3.2. Some of these scenes and processes in the upper ocean are described in Jones and Ainsworth [19]. Fig. 3.2 represents monthly average chlorophyll levels of the cloud free Pacific region for April 1997. The colour coded chlorophyll concentration scale is also given.

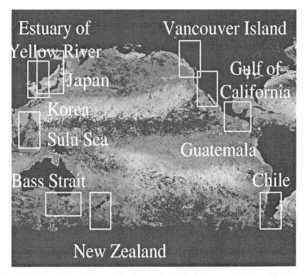

Fig. 3.2 Distribution of the investigated sites over the Pacific Ocean.

3.3.1.2 Spectral choice of data

The application of a larger number of OCTS channels is legitimate. However, the most appropriate channels need still to be chosen. Feature analysis can determine whether different bands provide supplementary information regarding ocean colour and temperature useful to differentiate distinct water types, land and clouds, or whether the information is duplicated and thus redundant. The correlation coefficients amongst all OCTS channels were computed for all investigated scenes. Table 3.2 shows an example of the correlation coefficients amongst 8 visible and near-infrared and 4 thermal-infrared channels for the Sulu Sea scene.

VNIR	1	2	3	4	5	6	7	8
1	1	0.964	0.937	0.932	0.898	0.852	0.628	0.588
2	0.964	1	0.953	0.950	0.922	0.895	0.660	0.620
3	0.937	0.953	1	0.962	0.948	0.928	0.692	0.674
4	0.932	0.950	0.962	1	0.946	0.935	0.733	0.710
5	0.898	0.922	0.948	0.946	1	0.950	0.800	0.798
6	0.852	0.895	0.928	0.935	0.950	1	0.808	0.799
7	0.628	0.660	0.692	0.733	0.800	0.808	1	0.931
8	0.588	0.620	0.674	0.710	0.798	0.799	0.931	1

IR	9	10	11	12
9	1	-0.522	-0.536	-0.558
10	-0.522	1	0.982	0.973
11	-0.536	0.982	1	0.984
12	-0.558	0.973	0.984	1

Table 3.2 Correlation coefficients amongst visible and infrared channels of the OCTS for the Sulu Sea scene captured on 1997/01/02.

The correlation of consecutive visible channels is high. However, nonconsecutive visible channels are less well correlated, significantly below that expected from the amount of noise in a signal. On the other hand, three thermal infrared channels, 10 (8.5μm), 11 (11μm), and 12 (12μm), are strongly interdependent. Values of correlation coefficients amongst channels 10, 11, and 12 for all scenes average to 0.980, with the lowest coefficient being 0.937.

One-dimensional self-organizing feature maps were applied to study the linear ordering of 12 channel spectra. Neural weights were randomly initialized and the networks were trained on six images out of the data set. Fig. 3.3 shows an example of the distribution of multi-spectral radiances within a self-organizing feature map composed of 256 neurons. The network size provides an easy conversion of a winning neuron number to a grey-level intensity which can be displayed for each pixel to form a classified image. For each neuron on the X-axis, the Y-axis shows the 12-channel spectral reflectances which represent that neuron weights. The ordering shows that bands 10, 11, and 12 closely follow one another while graphs of other spectral channels are quite variable. Bands 10, 11 and 12 provide repeated information which, if all applied, would unnecessarily emphasise the temperature of the scenes.

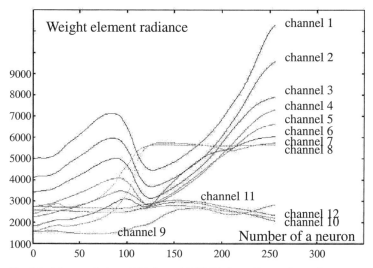

Fig. 3.3 Linear ordering of 12 channel OCTS information performed by a one-dimensional self-organizing feature map.

In accordance with the feature analysis, the final pixel-by-pixel classification makes use of ten spectral channels, all visible and near-infrared and only 9 (3.5µm) and 11 (11µm) from the thermal infrared range. Channel 11 gives the strongest radiation power and contains the water vapour absorption spectrum. Channels 10 and 12 are not applied as they are considered redundant. Occasionally, subsequent stages of the image processing benefit only of the selected channels out of this choice of ten.

3.3.2 Hierarchy of image processing

The current objective for the processing of ocean colour and temperature data is to differentiate a large number of water types based on their spectral and auxiliary characteristics [18]. Because case 1 and case 2 waters have spectrally different characteristics, they require a distinct processing approach. The two water categories are first separated and only then intrinsic water types are observed. The current scheme extracts clear and mixed water types which naturally occur within oceanic regions. However, it does not provide detailed water constituent levels, such as chlorophyll concentration, for which a succeeding study and a different algorithm are needed.

The proposed hierarchy of image processing is displayed in Fig. 3.4. The consecutive stages of the algorithm isolate water pixels in images and separate pixels associated with a relatively low and relatively high radiance in the near-infrared. The two cases are dealt with separately. Relatively low near-infrared radiances are associated with case 1 waters below almost clear atmosphere and a differentiation of ocean colour in the case 1 category is performed. Relatively high near-infrared radiances correspond to the turbid atmosphere over any kind of waters and the case 2 water type below fairly clear skies. The following processing masks out oceanic regions covered by the turbid atmosphere and provides a detailed classification of case 2 water types.

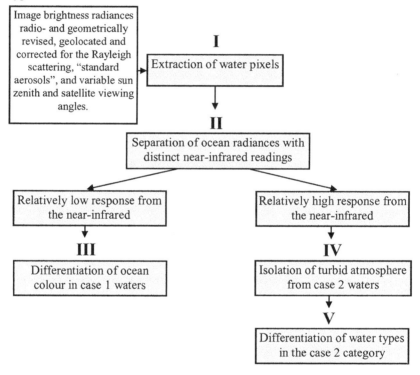

Fig. 3.4 Hierarchy of image processing for water type differentiation.

3.3.3 *Hierarchies of self-organizing feature maps: training, testing and response*

Each stage of the image processing is associated with an individual neural network. Hierarchies of three-dimensional self-organizing feature maps were trained on mixtures of all investigated scenes. Up to six image blocks were applied during training of a single hierarchy of networks. Subsequent scenes were interlaced by lines to provide the best data fusion.

Three-dimensional self-organizing feature maps of the size from 6x6x7 to 9x9x9 neurons were studied. Each network was trained for a large number of iterations, up to 100 on six scenes. The best initial learning rate was experimentally established to be equal to 0.2. Initial neuron neighbourhoods in all the experiments were large and corresponded to half a diameter of the network. Each neuron within self-organizing feature maps was considered to represent a different pattern class.

Testing scenes were acquired from sites not used in the training. To display classified images, neurons in trained networks were mapped onto colours in the RGB colour cube. Consequently, neurons close to one another represented similar pattern classes and had allocated similar colour shades. Testing images were visually compared to standard OCTS OCC products.

The design of the neural networks was studied to answer two major questions regarding the fine tuning of the classifier.

(1) Do self-organizing feature maps focus on spectrum classes which are predominant in the training set or is their allocation of neurons only dependent on mathematical differences amongst established classes, regardless of class occurrences in the training set? Within OCTS scenes some water types or special upper-ocean phenomena can constitute only a small fraction of all pixels. The classification algorithm should still be able to extract the rarer classes.

(2) Can self-organizing feature maps be sensitive to minute changes in the spectra or are they confounded by large changes? Large spectrum differences occurring in a comprehensive data set, e.g. the entire Pacific Ocean, could disable the detection of detailed variations amongst water types. In this case, regional studies rather than global data analyses should be more appropriate.

In order to investigate these issues, charts of neural network weight values were drawn against image histograms. Fig. 3.5 displays the comparison between histograms and graphs representing the number of neurons allocated to corresponding radiances by a self-organizing feature map. A three-dimensional 9x9x9 neuron network constituting the first stage of image processing was trained on a combination of six scenes scattered over the Pacific Ocean.

Fig. 3.5 demonstrates that the neural network can create a detailed representation of the entire spectrum domain. Similar graphs were obtained for all satellite channels. Neurons portray spectra uniformly spread throughout entire domains of each of the channels. Histogram peaks, such as cloud spectra above the 6000 radiance in visible channels, are not represented by a significantly larger number of neurons. It should be noted that the self-organizing feature map is three-dimensional and classes represented by neurons are ordered in a three-dimensional neural space. Distinct patterns defined by ten spectral channels can have similar radiances in a single chosen channel. Consequently, a larger number of neurons allocated to similar single-channel reflectances can be a necessity. For example, Fig. 3.5 shows the 865nm near-infrared channel in which the peak at 6000 value delineates two predominant patterns, clouds and land, compelling more neurons to be assigned to the peak.

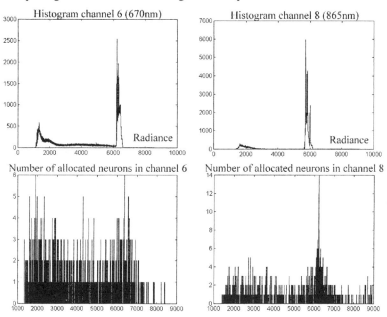

Fig. 3.5 Comparison of histograms and spectrum allocation by a self-organizing feature map, channels 6 (670nm) and 8 (865nm).

Self-organizing feature map response is dependent on mathematical differences amongst classes. If a certain category of radiances is widely spread over a large domain but very different from all other categories distributed over a small domain, the first single category will be best represented. Therefore, feature extraction needs to find and eliminate such problems. When the spectrum domain is uniformly represented, all major classes can be covered. Fortunately, radiance data has a very strict domain defined by the spectral resolution of detectors for each channel. Neurons are duly allocated where histograms are both high and low. The fineness of the spectral domain coverage depends on the number of neurons employed by the network. In this study, from 256 to 729 neurons were used enabling detection of small spectral differences.

3.3.4 Self-organizing feature map topologies and their results

Detailed statistical examinations and feature analyses of multi-spectral radiance distributions and behaviour were performed. They are allowed to effectively define neural topologies and interpret classification results. To ease the neuron labelling, weights in each of self-organizing feature maps are semi-randomly initialized applying the knowledge of pattern distributions.

3.3.4.1 Extraction of water pixels

The first stage of the processing separates water pixels from land and cloud pixels. The classification was preceded by a thorough feature analysis. Histogram studies showed that near-infrared channels provide a good separation of water patterns from patterns of land and clouds. A histogram of the 765nm near-infrared channel is displayed in Fig. 3.6. Pixel radiances representative for waters, clouds and land are superimposed onto the histogram. Waters are associated with low near-infrared readings while land and clouds with high near-infrared values showing as a single histogram peak at 6000 radiance.

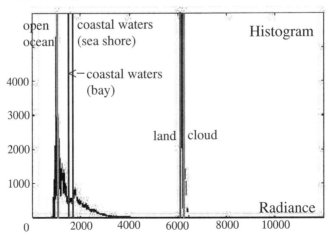

Fig. 3.6 The 765nm near-infrared channel histogram and corresponding locations of sea, cloud, and land patterns for the Japan scene, 1997/04/26.

One-dimensional self-organizing feature maps, such as in Fig. 3.3, can by themselves discover the regularity in data creating a clear separation of water from clouds and land. This is because 765nm and 865nm near-infrared channel radiances over 4000-5000 value represent clouds and land while smaller values denote waters. Thus, the first 100 neurons were automatically designated to water pixels.

The initial knowledge of pattern spectral distribution helped to design the most suitable neural topology for the water pixel separation. All ten spectral channels are used in the classification. Weights in the three-dimensional self-organizing feature map are initialized in a semi-random manner. The intialization strategy and colours of the eight corners of the RGB cube are shown in Fig. 3.7.

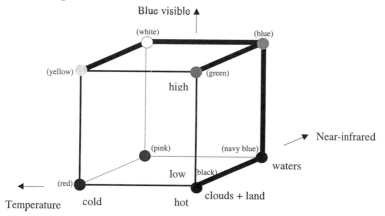

Fig. 3.7 Semi-random initialization of weights in the self-organizing feature map performing separation of water pixels from land and cloud pixels.

Before the training, the weight elements corresponding to the 11μm thermal-infrared channel are generated in a semi-random decreasing order with the neuron co-ordinates increasing along the X-axis. During the training, this encourages the network to allocate cold cloud patterns to neurons positioned on the left-hand side of the neural cube. Weight elements corresponding to the 443nm dark blue channel are initialized in a semi-random increasing order along the Y-axis of the network. The decreasing semi-random initialization of weight elements corresponding to both near-infrared channels along the Z-axis encourages the network to allocate water patterns to neurons on the back of the cube. All other weight elements are fully randomly generated. Consequently, different water types are roughly associated with neurons in the upper middle and on the back of the three-dimensional self-organizing feature map.

An example of water pixel extraction using a 9x9x9 neuron self-organizing feature map is displayed in Fig. 3.8. Waters have characteristically blue to light green and, on other images, pink colours. Clouds are usually yellow and land is dark green, red and navy. Colour and, thus, class differences enable water pixel differentiation.

Fig. 3.8 Water pixel extraction for the Guatemala scene, 1997/03/31.

3.3.4.2 *Separation of ocean radiances with distinct near-infrared readings*

The second three-dimensional self-organizing feature map is designed to reclassify only water pixels. The network uses all visible and both near-infrared channels to extract radiance distributions related to oceanic and atmospheric near-infrared readings. Visible channels are also applied because some case 2 waters are more explicitly differentiable with visible than near-infrared data, *e.g.* coloured dissolved organic matter, pheopigments, detritus and bacteria absorb light most strongly at 412nm. Weights in the self-organizing feature map are semi-randomly initialized to facilitate the separation of ocean reflectances dominated by the atmosphere and case 2 waters from that representing case 1 waters. The weight initialization supervises distribution of the following spectra:
(1) 412nm violet visible channel on the X-axis.
(2) 765nm near-infrared channel on the Y-axis.
(3) 865nm near-infrared channel on the Z-axis.
The weight arrangement encourages the network to assign case 1 waters to neurons associated with low values corresponding to the near-infrared channels and high values at 412nm (because the absorption is inversely proportional to the reflectance). Low near-infrared readings are allocated in the upper part and on the back of the neural cube. This corresponds to blue and light coloured RGB shades.

Fig. 3.9 shows an example of a standard OCC product for the Southern Island of New Zealand and a classification result where clouds and land are masked in black. Standard OCTS OCC products are level 3 output of the conventional processing. They are in the Mercator projection while classified images originate from lower level standard products and are in the satellite natural projection. This creates a slightly different appearance of both images.

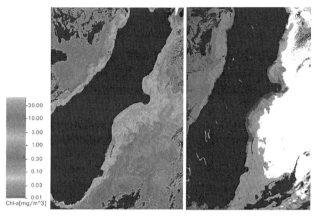

Fig. 3.9 Standard OCTS OCC product and differentiation of water radiances with different near-infrared reading on the New Zealand scene, 1997/01/26.

In the classification result oceanic zones with relatively high near-infrared readings have distinctive green, red and brow dark colours making them effectively discernible. Some of high near-infrared zones correspond to coastal areas shown by the standard product as having elevated chlorophyll levels, such as along the central eastern shore of the island. However, conventional chlorophyll estimations cannot be trusted in case 2 waters. The standard algorithm also misinterprets some near cloud pixels for high chlorophyll concentrations and shows them in red. In this early stage of image processing, the classification approach is able to discover many regularities in water types. Ocean colour on both sides of the island is different. It is most likely due to different water constituents in the Tasman Sea and in the open ocean. Clear sky open ocean is almost white since the near-infrared energy is nearly all absorbed.

3.3.4.3 *Differentiation of ocean colour in case 1 waters*

The purpose of the third level of image processing is to analyse water types within the case 1 category and, possibly, extract waters with different

Classification of Oceanic Water Types ... 87

phytoplankton types and levels. Most of the empirically derived OCC algorithms use ratios of two spectral channels. The SeaWiFS equation applies the ratio 490nm/555nm which yields the highest correlation on a testing data set [8]. The POLDER algorithm uses the ratio 443nm/565nm [7]. The current scheme benefits from the application of all six visible OCTS channels to differentiate ocean colour. It is also assisted by the experience with the choice of spectral channels gained by the conventional studies. The weights in the three-dimensional self-organizing feature map for case 1 water analysis are semi-randomly initialized in the following manner:
(1) 443nm dark blue visible channel on the X-axis.
(2) 490nm blue-green visible channel on the Y-axis.
(3) 565nm yellow visible channel on the Z-axis.

Fig. 3.10 shows the OCTS OCC standard product and the neural result of case 1 water type differentiation for the Gulf of California scene, Mexico. In the standard product, coastal boundaries are very blurry with many pixels masked in black. The analysis of near-shore waters is not feasible using the conventional algorithm. The classification result shows sharp coastal line and clearly separates case 2 waters from the case 1.

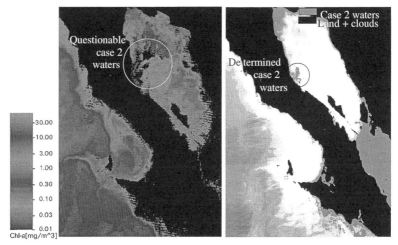

Fig. 3.10 Standard OCTS OCC product and the result of case 1 water type differentiation for the Gulf of California scene, 1997/03/19.

In the head of the Gulf of California there are some water patterns masked out from the standard OCC product. Only a small share of blanked out pixels encircled in the second image is determined as case 2 water by the neural classification. The spectral analysis showed that the masked out pixels girdled in the first image are characterized by considerably high response from the red visible channel. It is thus conceivable that the standard algorithm cannot contest high chlorophyll levels because the OCTS atmospheric model is based on the inaccurate assumption of zero water-leaving radiance in the red visible spectrum. The high level of phytoplankton at the head of the Gulf of California is a persistent phenomenon discussed by Santamaria-del-Angel *et al.* [20]. Coastal waters at the north shore of the Gulf are classified by the neural network as case 2 but given high chlorophyll levels by the conventional approach. There is also a distinct water contamination in the bottom part of the Gulf which is eliminated by both methods. The contamination is perhaps a pollution coming from the Sonora river.

3.3.4.4 *Isolation of turbid atmosphere from case 2 waters*

Radiances associated with case 2 waters below relatively clear skies and high atmospheric attenuation over any kind of waters are closely intertwined together. They cannot be adequately differentiated with the spectral data available. Analysis of pattern distributions in channel histograms showed that visible spectra of the turbid atmosphere and case 2 waters are not differentiable. However, the 670nm red visible channel in combination with both near-infrared and one thermal-infrared 11μm channels can support the separation.

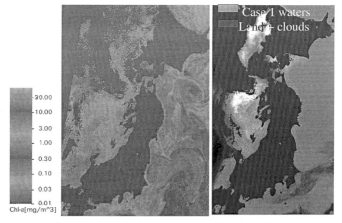

Fig. 3.11 Standard OCTS OCC product and the result of turbid atmosphere and case 2 water separation for the Japan scene, 1997/04/26.

The four channel spectral information is fused with additional expert system like knowledge on pixel proximity to land and clouds. As land and clouds are extracted during the first stage of image processing, the percentage of land and cloud pixels within a given radius can be readily calculated for each water pixel. The closer to land the higher is the probability of a pixel to represent case 2 waters and the closer to clouds the higher is the likelihood for the pixel to be contaminated by the turbid atmosphere.

The weights in the three-dimensional self-organizing feature map are semi-randomly initialized in the following manner:

(1) 11µm thermal infrared channel and proximity of clouds on the X-axis.
(2) Proximity of land on the Y-axis.
(3) Both 765nm and 865nm near-infrared channels on the Z-axis.

The classified image in Fig. 3.11 contains turbid atmosphere patterns shown in distinguishable red, orange, yellow and dark colours. Case 2 waters are mostly characterised by discernible light blue shades.

3.3.4.5 *Differentiation of water types in the case 2 category*

The last stage of the image processing extracts a multitude of water types in the case 2 water category. All visible and near-infrared channels are used. The weights are initialized in a semi-random fashion to associate the following:

(1) 412nm violet visible channel on the X-axis.
(2) 765nm near-infrared channel on the Y-axis.
(3) 865nm near-infrared channel on the Z-axis.

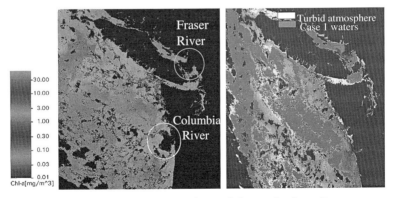

Fig. 3.12 Standard OCTS OCC product and the result of case 2 water type differentiation for the Vancouver Island scene, 1997/05/01.

Fig. 3.12 displays the standard OCTS OCC product and the result of the case 2 water type differentiation for the Vancouver Island scene, Canada. The area contains estuaries of two rivers, Fraser and Columbia. River plumes are masked out from the standard OCTS OCC product due to their high contents of terrigenous particles, sediments, dissolved organic matter and pollution. However, the neural classifier is able to analyse the case 2 river outlets. It can be even recognized that both rivers carry waters with similar characteristics.

3.3.5 *Class labelling*

Neural networks are well suited for the current application. They have the capability to reason under uncertainties and the water type separation is a very imprecisely defined decision problem. An accurate and objective definition of clouds, land, case 1 waters, case 2 waters and turbid atmosphere in terms of spectral radiance on the top of the atmosphere (with the defined corrections) is infeasible due to complexity of patterns, unstable atmospheric residua and noise. In this study, reflectance classes are roughly interpreted and a detailed neuron-by-neuron labelling of self-organizing feature maps is based on observations and experience with standard OCC products. A large number of extracted spectrum classes and their ordering support the grouping. Future research can hopefully use improved oceanographic expertise and ground truth data to revise the class identification.

3.4 Accomplishments of the hierarchical image processing

The proposed hierarchical image processing separates radiances related to case 1 waters, case 2 waters and ocean reflectances highly influenced by the atmosphere. It also creates a detailed differentiation of water types in the case 1 and case 2 instance. The system has undergone thorough studies and a large number of simulations. The results of the following steps of image processing are displayed in Fig. 3.13 for an example of Yellow River scene.
Yellow River is the second largest river in China running over 4,845km. It carries enormous amounts of yellow soil and sand which on average amount to 34kg/m^3 and maximally reach 580kg/m^3. It makes Yellow River the world's biggest as far as the outflow is concerned. The river flows into the Gulf of Chihli depositing soil at its estuary. It is recognized that the entire Gulf of Chihli and waters around the Shantung Peninsula are engrossed with the circulated river outflow. Fig. 3.13 in the left-hand side bottom corner

includes the standard product of OCTS OCC for the scene. The conventional OCC algorithm blanked out the whole of the Gulf of Chihli. This is probably due to negative water leaving radiances in the visible spectrum produced by the atmospheric correction over case 2 waters with a high concentration of yellow soil. The OCTS standard routine detected high phytoplankton levels in the water band surrounding the Shantung Peninsula. Around the Peninsula, there are case 2 waters discharging from the Gulf of Chihli where conventional chlorophyll estimates cannot be trusted. The stage V differentiation of case 2 water types proves that the Yellow River estuary contains varying degrees of yellow soil contents, from the heavy concentration shown in black to the low concentration in light blue on the boundary of case 1 waters.

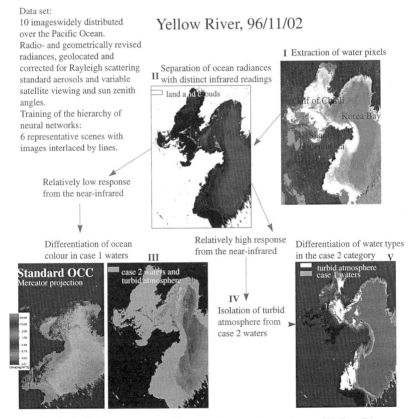

Fig. 3.13 Subsequent stages of water type extraction, estuary of Yellow River.

OCTS standard products mask out some of case 2 waters and misinterpret the others for high chlorophyll concentration. High chlorophyll levels, *e.g.* the Gulf of California scene, and water pixels influenced by elevated atmospheric attenuation, *e.g.* the New Zealand scene, are also occasionally misunderstood. Conversely, the neural network scheme is able to uniformly identify all genuine case 2 waters. The classification approach extracts and analyses case 2 waters in a consistent and objective manner. It can also discover a large number of water type classes which can be suitably labeled and generalized to suit requirements of the users of the future ocean colour information systems.

3.5 Conclusions

The assumptions taken by the standard radiative transfer models occasionally provide dubious results in chlorophyll estimation. The conventional algorithms are also not suitable for water type extraction in the case 2 category. This chapter has introduced a concept of water type analysis based on a hierarchical classification using unsupervised neural networks.
Self-organizing feature maps have turned out extremely beneficial for the feature analysis and classification of multi-spectral remotely sensed data. The scheme can objectively discover a multitude of water types. It does not require ground truth information to learn a comprehensive range of upper ocean patterns and its knowledge can be successively upgraded. The neural processing is very effective and efficient. The scheme has shown its skill in identifying case 1 and case 2 water types on a comprehensive set of OCTS scenes widely distributed over the Pacific Ocean. The algorithm can complement the existing models and contribute to the development of better products of chlorophyll estimation throughout the globe. The technique forms the basis for automatic assessment and monitoring of oceanic water types for future information systems aimed at a wide community of users.

Acknowledgements

This work is supported by the Science and Technology Agency, Japan International Science and Technology Exchange Center. The author would like to thank Professor Ian S.F. Jones for his unestimated support and inspiration and the team from the Earth Observation Research Center in Tokyo.

References

[1] S.W. Jeffrey, R.F.C. Mantoura, S.W. Wright., *Phytoplankton Pigments in Oceanography*, UNESCO Publishing, Paris (1997).
[2] G.L. Clarke, G.C. Ewing, C.J. Lorenzen, "Spectra of Backscattered Light from the Sea Obtained from Aircraft as a Measure of Chlorophyll Concentration", *Science*, **167** (1970).
[3] H. Kawamura, and the EORC team, "OCTS Mission Overview", *Journal of Oceanography*, **54** (1998).
[4] S. Shimada, H. Oaku, Y. Mitomi, H. Murakami, A. Mukaida, Y. Nakamura, J. Ishizaka, H. Kawamura, T. Tanaka, M. Kishino, H. Fukushima, "Calibration and Validation of the Ocean Color Version-3 Product from ADEOS OCTS", *Journal of Oceanography*, **54** (1998).
[5] D. Antoine, A. Morel, "Atmospheric Correction Over the Ocean (Case 1 Waters)", *ESA, MERIS ESL* (1997).
[6] H. Fukushima, A. Higurashi, Y. Mitomi, T. Nakajima, T. Noguchi, T. Tanaka, M. Toratani, "Correction of Atmospheric Effect on ADEOS/OCTS Ocean Color Data: Algorithm Description and Evaluation of Its Performance", *Journal of Oceanography*, **54** (1998).
[7] P.-Y. Deschamps, F.-M. Bréon, M. Leroy, A. Podaire, A. Bricaud, J.-C. Buriez, G. Sèze, "The POLDER Mission: Instrument Characteristics and Scientific Objectives", *IEEE Transaction on Geoscience and Remote Sensing*, **32**, no. 3 (1994).
[8] E.R. Firestone, S.B. Hooker, "SeaWiFS Prelaunch Technical Report Series Final Cumulative Index", *NASA Technical Memorandum* 1998-104566, **43** (1998).
[9] M. Kishino, T. Ishimaru, K. Furuya, T. Oishi, K. Kawasaki, "In-Water Algorithm for ADEOS/OCTS", *Journal of Oceanography*, **54** (1998).
[10] J. Aiken, G. Moore, "Algorithm Theoretical Basis Document 2.6, Case 2 (S) Bright Pixel Atmospheric Correction", *ESA, MERIS ESL* (1997).

[11] A. Morel, "Bio-Optics of Case 1 Waters and Ocean Color Remote Sensing", *Proceedings of the 4th Pacific Ocean Remote Sensing Conference*, Qingdao, China (1998).
[12] E.J. Ainsworth, "Neural Network Ocean Colour Extraction in Comparison with Standard POLDER and OCTS Chlorophyll Concentration Products", *ALPS'99, CNES Conference: Aerosols, Radiation budget -Land surfaces -Ocean colour, Meribel, France* (1999).
[13] K. Valkealahti, J. Iivarinen, A. Visa, O. Simula, "An Operational Cloud Classifier Based on a Self-Organized Feature Map", *Internal Report* A19, Helsinki University of Technology (1993).
[14] I. Kanellopoulos, A. Varfis, G.G. Wilkinson, J. Mégier, "Land Cover Discrimination in SPOT Imagery by Artificial Neural Network - A Twenty Class Experiment", *International Journal of Remote Sensing*, 13, no. 5, pp. 917-924 (1992).
[15] L. Gross, S. Thiria, R. Frouin, B.G. Mitchell, B.G. (May 1999) "Artificial Neural Networks for Modeling the Transfer Function between Marine Reflectance and Phytoplankton Pigment Concentration", *IEEE Transaction on Geoscience and Remote Sensing*, 37, no. 3 (1999).
[16] T. Kohonen, "Self-Organization and Associative Memory", Springer-Verlag (1989).
[17] E.J. Kwiatkowska (Ainsworth), "Neural Network System for Cloud Classification from Satellite Images", *PhD thesis*, University of Bradford, Great Britain (1997).
[18] E.J. Ainsworth, I.S.F. Jones, "Radiance Spectra Classification from the Ocean Colour and Temperature Scanner on ADEOS", *IEEE Transaction on Geoscience and Remote Sensing*, 37, no. 3 (1999).
[19] I.S.F. Jones, E.J. Ainsworth, "Phytoplankton Distributions at Sites in the Pacific Ocean", *EORC Bulletin*, Technical Report No. 1, Tokyo, pp. 26-37 (1998).
[20] E. Santamaria-del-Angel, S. Alvarez-Borrego, F.E. Muller-Karger, "The 1982-1984 El Niño in the Gulf of California as Seen in CZCS Imagery", *Journal of Geophysical Research*, 99, pp. 7423-7432 (1994).

# Chapter 4
Feature Selection by Artificial Neural Network for Pattern Classification

Basabi Chakraborty

Iwate Prefectural University, Japan

Abstract

Feature selection is very important for the success of any automated pattern recognition system. Removal of redundant features improves the efficiency of a classifier as well as cut down the cost of feature extraction. Recently artificial neural networks (ANN) are becoming popular for solving pattern classification problems. But the choice of proper architecture and model from various alternatives is still an open problem for research. In this work a new architecture, a modified version of multilayer feed forward neural network, proposed earlier for pattern classification has been used as a tool for feature selection. A proper algorithm for feature subset selection has been proposed in which the features are evaluated according to their contribution to classification rate of the net for the unknown samples. Simulation of the proposed algorithm has been done with two types of data sets and the results seem to be promising.

Keywords : pattern classification, feature selection, feature evaluation, feature ranking, optimal feature subset, artificial neural network, neural classifier, multilayer perceptron, connection weight, backpropagation training, saliency measure, output error function, network accuracy, fractal neural network, statistically fractal, fractal dimension, similarity dimension, fractal connection structure, sparse network, average connectivity

4.1 Introduction

Feature selection is an important prerequisite of any automated classification system. The main objective of feature selection, prior to classification, is to retain the optimum salient characteristics necessary for the recognition process and at the same time to discard unwanted information to reduce the complexity of the classifier. The most crucial thing is to assess the quality of a feature that is whether it is redundant or relevant in the decision process. The research on pattern classification has a strong statistical background and many well accepted techniques for feature selection have been designed so far [1] [2]. Most of the techniques define some measure to evaluate the quality of any particular feature or a feature subset from the whole feature set and rank them accordingly. Some near optimal search process is then used to find out the optimal feature subset.

However, the complexity of computation for statistical techniques increases with the number of features involved. In many problems statistical measures seem to be inappropriate as for nonparametric measures the evaluation of the criterion function for a feature subset is computationally difficult and for parametric measures where the distribution is known, the computation is easier, but in case of small sample size the estimation error on parameters of gaussian distribution conceal the true discriminatory power of the feature evaluation criterion. Moreover real life problems are often characterized by vagueness rather than randomness which are difficult to be modelled by statistical tools.

Recently the application of artificial neural network (ANN) to the problem of pattern classification has gained wide acceptance as the design of these networks mimic the behaviour of human brain, the best of all such cognitive tasks. Among various proposed architectures of ANN feed forward multilayer perceptron models are the most popular ANN models for pattern classification problems. ANN models are known to be capable of extracting useful information from the raw data and represent them via layers of neurons and weights associated with the connections between different layers of neurons. Thus by analyzing the working of these models they can be used as an efficient tool for feature selection problem.

Ruck et al. [3] used a multilayer perceptron for feature selection where they proposed a saliency metric which represents the sensitivity of the network's output to its input to rank the input feature's usefulness. The saliency measure used in their work has been found to be effective in determining the significance of input features irrespective of the training rule used. They further validated the measure by comparing with the traditional method of ranking input features according to the probability of error criterion. Another simpler form of the saliency metric is used by Tarr [4] for determining the relative significance of the input features. Belue et al. [5]

used feedforward three-layer neural model and different forms of relative saliency measures for discrimination of relavant features from irrelavant ones. Those measures of saliency of an input feature involve the derivative of the output error function and the connection weights. To have a reliable average of the saliency measures the networks have to be trained repeatedly. This requirement makes these methods time consuming, specially with backpropagation training rule which is rather slow.

Pal et al. [6] proposed a connectionist model, a multilayer perceptron architecture with some major differences, for selection of a subset of good features for pattern recognition problems. Rudy et al. [7] developed a method to identify the salient features in which the network is trained to minimize an augmented error function. With the use of this error function, after training the network retains large connection weights only for those inputs that are needed to represent the characteristics of the pattern to be classified, there by distinguishing relevant inputs from the irrelevant ones. They proposed an efficient algorithm for discarding irrelevant features based on the network accuracy of the trained net on the training data set as the criterion.

In the present work a similar algorithm for ranking the effectiveness of an input feature based on the recognition rate of the trained network on the test set as the criterion and a sparsely connected neural network as the tool has been proposed. A modified version of multilayer perceptron, proposed in our earlier work [8] for pattern classification and was found to be effective than the fully connected perceptron model, has been used here for feature selection. The architecture and the implementation of the network is described in the next section. The following section describes the proposed algorithm for feature selection. Simulation has been done with different data sets and the results are reported in the next section. The final section contains the discussion and conclusion.

4.2 Fractal Neural Network Model

The proposed model is a modification of multilayered feed forward architecture with input, output and one or more hidden layers in which the connection structure between the upper layer neurons other than the output layer and the immediate lower layer neurons is statistically fractal. The neurons are arranged in a layered hierarchy where each layer is an array

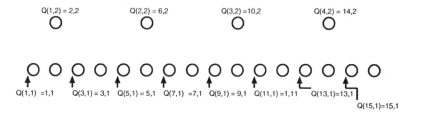

Fig. 4.1 Spatial Positions of the Upper and Lower layer Neurons

of neurons in one or two dimension depending on the type of inputs to be processed.

Each neuron in the array can be defined by a spatial position coordinate, Q_{ik} representing ith neuron (considering one dimensional layers) in the kth layer. The upper layer neurons other than the input layer are positioned relative to the position of the immediately previous layer depending on the number of neurons available in both the layers. Thus Q_{ik} is calculated as

$$Q_{ik} = [\lceil n_{k-1}(2i-1)/2n_k \rceil, k] \text{ for } i = 1, 2, \ldots, n_k \qquad (1)$$

where n_{k-1} and n_k represent the number of neurons in $(k-1)$th and kth layers respectively. The input layer neurons have Q_{ik} value defined as $Q_{ik} = [i, 1]$.

Fig. 4.1 explains the positioning of neurons according to Eq. (1) in case of 16 and 4 neurons in the lower and upper layer respectively.

4.2.1 Fractal Connection Structure

Fig. 4.2 depicts the architecture of the proposed network with one dimensional layers. The probability of an upper layer neuron other than the output layer neuron to receive connection from the lower layer neurons follow an inverse power law generating a self similar scale invariant connection pattern between the neurons in corresponding layers resembling fractal like structure. However, the output layer is fully connected to the immediate lower hidden layer. Unlike fully connected network this network is sparsely connected and the sparseness depends on the similarity dimension of the fractal connection set. The probability that ith neuron in the kth layer receives connection from the jth neuron of the previous layer, defined by

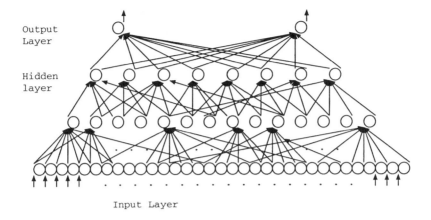

Fig. 4.2 The architecture of the proposed fractal net

CP_{ijk} follows the law

$$CP_{ijk} = Ar_{ij}^{D-d} \tag{2}$$
$$i = 1, 2 \ldots n_k$$
$$j = 1, 2 \ldots n_{k-1}$$
$$0 \leq D \leq d$$

where r_{ijk} is the Euclidean distance between the spatial locations of the ith neuron in the kth layer and the jth neuron of the previous layer defined as

$$r_{ijk} = ||Q_{ik} - Q_{j(k-1)}||, \; r_{ijk} \geq 1 \tag{3}$$

d denotes dimension of the array of neurons in k th layer. A represents a constant, D represents the fractal dimension (similarity dimension [9]) of the synaptic connection distribution which controls the sparseness in the average connectivity of the network.

The fractal connection structure in the proposed model allows low probability of long range connection links and high probability of short range connection links, generating a partially localized statistically fractal connection structure.

4.2.2 Implementation & Operation of the Proposed Network

To implement such a sparse neural network for each i, j, k a uniform random number ρ in the interval [0,1] has been generated and the connectivity C_{ijk} of the link from ith neuron in the kth layer to the jth neuron of the previous layer is assigned as

$$\begin{aligned} C_{ijk} &= 1 \text{ if } CP_{ijk} \geq \rho \\ &= 0 \text{ Otherwise} \end{aligned} \qquad (4)$$

Average connectivity (AC) in percentage for a given network is defined as the ratio of the number of connections present (NC_p) and the total number of connections possible in case of full connections (NC_f) expressed in percentage. Mathematically speaking,

$$AC = \frac{NC_p}{NC_f} \times 100. \qquad (5)$$

NC_p is proportional to (N^D) where N is the total number of neurons in the network. NC_f is proportional to the square of N. Thus for a given fractal dimension, the average connectivity is inversely proportional to the size of the network (the number of the neurons in the network). For a given fractal dimension, the larger network has a lower average connectivity. For a given size of the network, increase in fractal dimension increases the average connectivity.

We apply a sample pattern to the input layer processing elements and compute the activation to the ith processing element in the kth layer other than the input layer as

$$I_{ik} = \sum_j W_{ijk} C_{ijk} O_{j(k-1)}. \qquad (6)$$

Here W_{ijk} represents the connection strength of the link to ith processing element in the kth layer from jth processing element of the previous layer. O_j denotes the output of jth processing element of the $(k-1)$th layer. The output of the ith processing element in the kth layer is given by

$$O_{ik} = G[I_{ik} - \theta] \tag{7}$$

where G[] being the usual sigmoid function defined by

$$G[x] = 1/(1 + \exp^{-x}) \tag{8}$$

and θ denotes the bias value.

4.3 Feature Selection Algorithm

A simple algorithm for removing irrelevant features with the help of fractal neural network has been devised. The network is trained by back propagation training algorithm for optimum efficiency determined by the highest classification rate for the problem at hand by suitable set up of the different parameters using all the features. The necessary details of the initial set up of the fractal network has been explained in the simulation section. The features are then removed one by one, selection for their removal is done by examining the change in efficiency in terms of the classification rate. Depending on the problem and the required classification accuracy, the final set of features (optimal feature subset) is determined. The actual steps of the algorithm are as follows.

(1) Let $(F = F_1, F_2, \ldots, F_N)$ be the set of N features and C be the number of classes in a sample data set for a particular pattern classification problem. For feature subset selection by fractal neural model the whole data set is randomly divided into three parts named as training set, validation set and test set.

(2) A fractal neural network discussed in the earlier section with the input layer of N neurons and the output layer of C neurons is to be set up. The number of hidden layers and the number of neurons in each hidden layer are to be chosen heuristically by trial and error depending on the problem. The fractal dimension of the synaptic connection distribution is also chosen by trial and error by gradually varying the value in order have the most efficient network structure with the least average connectivity. The connection structure has to be set up according to Eq. (2) and Eq. (4) with proper selection

of d (we considered $d = 1$ that is one dimensional input layers only in our experiment) and A.

(3) The network is to be trained with the training sample for a preassigned minimum allowable output error (attainable for the given problem with the given network structure) and is to be examined after each iteration for validation using the validation set. After training the network is to be tested with the test set of samples for the classification rate.

(4) Several networks are to be trained for the selection of the best network configuration which has the optimum number of hidden layers, the optimum number of neurons in each hidden layer and the optimum value of the fractal dimension for which the classification rate for the test samples is the highest. This optimum network configuration is to be retained for later steps.

(5) The fractal network configuration selected in the previous step has to be retrained with the same training and validation samples with the set of input features one less from the full set. (e.g remove F_k th input from the set of input features $(F = F_1, F_2, \ldots, F_N)$ by making F_k th input and all the connection weights from this input zero). The classification rate with the one less input has to be calculated with the same test samples.

(6) All the inputs are to be removed one by one from the whole set and the whole procedure in the previous step has to be repeated. In each case only one feature is withdrawn. For example when F_j is removed, all other F_k, $k \neq j$ are retained. In each case the classification rate is to be calculated over the test samples.

(7) The inputs are to be ranked according to the classification rate of the network without that particular input. The highest classification rate obtained, corresponds to the most irrelevant input.

(8) Now after removal of the most irrelevant input selected in the previous step, the whole procedure is to be repeated from step 5 to step 7 for removal of the next irrelevant feature.

(9) The process is to be stopped when any one of the following stopping criteria is met.

   (a) The total number of features attains a pre-assigned limit.
   (b) The classification or recognition rate falls below a preassigned limit.

4.4 Simulation and Results

The efficiency of the proposed algorithm for feature selection has been tested by simulation with two different data sets. One of them is Anderson's IRIS data set [10], commonly used to test pattern recognition problems and the other one is SONAR data set used earlier for underwater target recognition [11].

4.4.1 *Simulation with IRIS data*

This data set contains three classes that is three varieties of IRIS flowers, namely Iris Setosa, Iris Versicolor & Iris Virginica each with 50 sample vectors. Each sample has four feature vectors (Sepal length F_1, Sepal width F_2, Petal length F_3 & Petal width F_4). As the number of features are small, the feature set has been extended to include combinations of the four features for our experiment. It will also give an idea about the relevance of the combined features. The extended feature set is $(F_1, F_2, F_3, F_4, |F_1 - F_2|, |F_1 - F_3|, |F_1 - F_4|, |F_2 - F_3|, |F_2 - F_4|, |F_3 - F_4|, F_1/F_2, F_1/F_3, F_1/F_4, F_2/F_3, F_2/F_4, F_3/F_4)$. Actual feature name and the corresponding number is given in Table 4.1. The whole sample set has been divided to training and test set with 75 samples in each group (25 samples per class). The training set is further divided into 60 and 15 samples for the training and the validation set.

The fractal network with 16 neurons in the input layer, 3 neurons in the output layer and one hidden layer has been set up. The number of neurons in the hidden layer is varied to take values $(4, 6, 8)$ and different networks are set up. The values of the fractal dimension ranging from 0.85 to 0.98 have been used for setting up networks of various sparseness for our experiment. The connection structure of the network has been set up according to Eq. (2) and Eq. (4), considering A and d to be 1. Each network has been trained and validated by the training and validation set respectively with backpropagation algorithm. The initial weight values are selected randomly from 0.1 to -0.1. The network with one hidden layer of 6 neurons and fractal dimension 0.9 has been chosen for the *optimum net* for feature selection (step 4 of the algorithm).

Now the feature removal has been carried out according to the proposed algorithm (step 5 to step 9). In each case the average classification rate is used after training the network several times for different initial weight

Table 4.1 Generated features for IRIS data

Feature name	Feature number
F_1	1
F_2	2
F_3	3
F_4	4
$F_1 - F_2$	5
$F_1 - F_3$	6
$F_1 - F_4$	7
$F_2 - F_3$	8
$F_2 - F_4$	9
$F_3 - F_4$	10
F_1/F_2	11
F_1/F_3	12
F_1/F_4	13
F_2/F_3	14
F_2/F_4	15
F_3/F_4	16

configuration. The result has been tabulated in Table 4.2. The feature number represents the feature according to Table 4.1. Average recognition rate represents the average over different networks (with different initial weight setup) and over different classes. The order of the features in the column *features removed* indicates the order in which they are removed. From the table it is seen that the recognition rate initially increases with the removal of the redundant features and finally decreases with the removal of 2 more features after removing 12 features. Thus for this problem the feature set containing feature 3, 4, 8 and 9 are considered to be the most important features for efficient classification. Depending on other requirements (e,g cost of feature extraction, complexity of classifier design) the stopping criterion should be set such that the ultimate feature set contains 2 or 4 features.

Table 4.2 Removal of features from IRIS data set

Features removed	Average recognition rate
all features	97.21%
7	97.43%
7, 2, 11	97.76%
7, 2, 11, 1, 5, 16	98.01%
7,2,11,1,5,16,10,13,14	98.19%
7,2,11,1,5,16,10,13,14, 12,16,15,	98.21%
7,2,11,1,5,16,10,13,14, 12,16,15,8,9	97.54%

4.4.2 Simulation with SONAR data

This data set, collected from underwater target classification problem using sonar signals, consists of two types of sonar returns one from a metal cylinder and the other from a cylindrically shaped rock, both of them positioned on a sandy ocean floor. The impinging pulse was a wideband linear FM chirp and the returns were obtained from each target at various aspect angles. A set of 208 returns (111 cylinder and 97 rock returns) were selected on the basis of the strength of the specular return (4.0 -15.0 dB signal-to-noise ratio), making certain that a variety of aspect angles were represented. Each sample signal was preprocessed to produce power spectral envelope and 60 sample points were obtained for each envelope. These samples were normalized to take on values between 0.0 and 1.0 for using as the input to the network. The details of the preprocessing can be found in [12].

The samples are divided into training and testing set with 104 samples each. The training set is further divided into training and validation set with 70 and 34 samples respectively. The fractal network with 60 neurons

Table 4.3 Feature selection for SONAR data set

Number of features retained	Average recognition score
60	92.53%
45	92.79%
20	93.14%
5	93.27%
2	90.82%

in the input layer and 2 neurons in the output layer and a single hidden layer has been used for simulation. The connection structure has been set up according to Eq. (2) and Eq. (4) with the values of A and d taken as 1. The number of neurons in the hidden layer is varied between 4 to 24 for experiment. The value of the fractal dimension has also been varied to find out the optimum sparseness (average connectivity) of the fractal network in this particular problem. The network has been trained with backpropagation algorithm over training samples. Initial weights were selected from random numbers between 0.3 and −0.3. In each case networks with different initial setup have been used for training and their average performance has been taken into account.

The network with one hidden layer of 6 neurons and connection structures for fractal dimension 0.8 has been selected as the optimum network for further processing. The feature removal has been done according to step 5 to step 9. The result have been shown in Table 4.3. Here as the number of features is large, the actual features that are removed from the set are not given in the table. From the table it is seen that the selected 5 feature set is the best one and here the removal process has to be stopped.

4.5 Discussion and Conclusion

Feature evaluation and selection are very important for the success of an automated pattern recognition system. Most of the collected real data sets contain redundant or irrelevant informations. The removal of redundant informations helps minimizing the cost of future data collection related to the same problem. The cost and complexity of the classifier design increases with the number of input features. Restricting the number features to a minimum by retaining only good features also decreases the time required for classifying a new pattern.

In this work an algorithm for feature selection using a fractally connected network, a modified version of multilayer perceptron, has been proposed and tested by simulation over two types of data sets. The sparse structure of the network makes the training quicker than the conventional fully connected network. For finding out the optimum size and structure of the network we need to run the network a number of times by trial and error, but the network's low average connectivity makes the process much easier and quicker than fully connected network. Moreover controlling the parameter *fractal dimension*, we can systematically control the connectivity of the network to match the redundancy of the sample data set. The effect of low connectivity and hence reduction in training time should be better understood for high dimensional input data.

Fractal architecture, being structured, is easier for efficient hardware implementation [13] and also supports biological reality [14]. The choice of the classification rate as the criterion for feature ranking instead of network accuracy seems to be more practical in real world problems as the efficiency of an automated pattern classification system should be judged by its correct decision power.

Simulations of the proposed network with the two data sets using the simple algorithm have shown promising results. The results are in accordance with the earlier findings with the same data set. However, the proposed algorithm has to be implemented with more different and large real world data sets for proper judgement of its effectiveness for feature subset selection by an artificial neural network.

References

[1] R. Duda and P. Hart, *Pattern Classification and Scene Analysis*, Wiley New York(1973).

[2] P. A. Devijver and J. Kittler, *Pattern Recognition: A Statistical Approach*, Prentice–Hall International(1982).

[3] D. W. Ruck, S. K. Rogers and M. Kabrisky, "Feature Selection Using a Multilayer Perceptron", *Neural Network Computation*, Vol.20, pp.40–48(1990).

[4] G. Tarr, "Multi-layered feedforward neural networks for image segmentation",*Ph. D dissertation prospectus*, School of Engineering, Air Force Institute of Technology, Wright-Patterson AFB OH(1991).

[5] L. M. Belue and K. W. Bauer, "Determining input features for multilayer perceptrons", *Neurocomputing*, Vol.7, No.2, pp.111–121(1995).

[6] N. R. Pal and K. Chintalapudi, " A connectionist system for feature selection", *Neural, Parallel and Scientific Computation*, Vol. 5, No. 3, pp. 359–381(1997).

[7] R. Setiono and H. Liu, "Neural-Network Feature Selector", *IEEE Transactions on NN*, Vol.8, No.3, pp.654–662(1997).

[8] B. Chakraborty, Y. Sawada and G. Chakraborty, 'Layered Fractal Neural Net: Computational Performance as a Classifier', *Knowledge-Based Systems*, Vol. 10, No. 3, pp. 177–182(1997).

[9] B. B. mandelbrot, *The fractal geometry of Nature*, Freeman, San Francisco,CA(1982).

[10] J. C. Bezdek, *Pattern Recognition with Fuzzy Objective Functions*, Plenum Press, NY(1981).

[11] P. R. Gorman & T. J. Sejnowski, "Analysis of Hidden Units in a Layered Network Trained to Classify Sonar Targets", *Neural Networks*, Vol. 1, pp. 75–89(1988).

[12] P. R. Gorman and T. J. Sejnowski, "Learned Classification of Sonar Targets using a Massively-parallel Network.", *IEEE Trans. ASSP*, Vol.36, No. 7, pp. 1135–1140(1988).

[13] J. N. H. Heemskerk, "Overview of Neural Hardware", in *Neurocomputers for Brain Style Processing*, Ph D Thesis, Leiden University, Netherlands(1995).

[14] B. L. M. Happel and J. M. J. Murre, "Design and evolution of modular neural network architectures", *Neural Networks*, Vol. **7**, No.6 , Pp. 985–1004(1994).

Chapter 5
MLP Based Character Recognition using Fuzzy Features and a Genetic Algorithm for Feature Selection

Shamik Sural[1], P.K.Das[2]

[1]*NIIT Limited, 6B Pretoria Street, Calcutta 700 071, India.*
[2]*Dept. of Computer Science & Engineering,*
Jadavpur University, Calcutta 700 032, India.

Abstract

We present a soft computing approach to character recognition from printed documents. For feature extraction, we define a number of fuzzy sets on the Hough transform of character pattern pixels and synthesize additional fuzzy sets by t-norms. The height of each t-norm constitutes a feature element and a set of 'n' such feature elements form an n-dimensional feature vector for the character. A 3n-dimensional vector is then generated from the n-dimensional feature vector by defining three linguistic fuzzy sets, namely, weak, moderate and strong. These 3n-dimensional vectors form a Multilayer Perceptron (MLP) input for training by back propagation. The MLP outputs represent fuzzy sets denoting the belongingness of an input pattern to a number of fuzzy pattern classes. The feature set is chosen by optimizing a Feature Quality Index (FQI) using genetic algorithm. A two-state Markov chain is used to model degraded document images for simulation tests. The system can recognize characters with an accuracy of 98%.

Keywords : Pattern Recognition, Optical Character Recognition, Classification, Hough Transform, Multilayer Perceptron, Back Propagation, Feature Extraction, Fuzzy Sets, Linguistic Sets, α-cut, t-norm, Feature Vector, Feature Selection, Feature Quality Index, Genetic Algorithm, Noise Model, Misclassification, Classifier Failure, Markov Chain.

5.1 Introduction

Optical Character Recognition (OCR) is a classification problem in which an unknown character is classified into a standard character pattern class. A number of methods have been suggested for the recognition of characters from optically scanned documents [17,38]. The two fundamental approaches to character recognition are feature based classification and template matching. In the template matching approach, recognition is based on the correlation of a test character with a set of stored templates. In the feature classification method, features are extracted from standard character images to generate feature vectors. A decision tree is formed based on the presence or absence of some of the elements in these feature vectors. When an unknown character pattern is encountered, the tree is traversed from node to node till a unique decision is reached. Template matching techniques are usually more sensitive to font and size variations of the characters than the feature classification methods. However, selection and extraction of useful features is not always straightforward.

Multilayer Perceptron (MLP) and other neural networks are also often used for character recognition after they are trained with a set of standard patterns by supervised learning [18,23]. The advantage of using neural networks is that a high computation rate can be achieved through their massive parallelism. However, if a neural network is trained with the character patterns directly, recognition performance is strongly affected by the presence of noise and image segmentation errors. Segmentation is a pre-processing step in which text blocks are identified from a scanned document image [36]. An alternative approach is to extract features from standard character patterns and train a neural network with these features. In this process, usually a threshold is introduced to determine the presence of a particular feature in an image. As a result of image degradation due to noise, one or more features might be missed resulting in incorrect classification by the neural network. It may be mentioned that human beings are more efficient than computers in handling several complex recognition problems including character recognition from document images. Human reasoning is somewhat fuzzy in nature, which enables us to combine even visually degraded features in the brain using the millions of neurons working in parallel. Fuzzy sets have the ability to model vagueness and ambiguity in data which is often encountered in character recognition as well as in other pattern recognition problems. Thus, to enable an OCR system to recognize characters even from degraded text images, it is felt necessary to incorporate fuzzy concepts in the operation of a neural network. Our approach combines the robustness of feature extraction with the speed of execution of neural networks in a framework of fuzzy systems. In section 5.2, we explain the operation of a multilayer perceptron and in section 5.3 we give an introduction to the properties of fuzzy sets.

Hough transform is a method for the extraction of lines and curves from images [11,24]. It has also been used for the detection of skew in a scanned document [21]. We give an introduction to Hough transform in the next section. Fuzzy and probabilistic concepts have been introduced by some researchers to generalize the basic Hough transform technique [8,30]. Han et al [19] have proposed a fuzzy Hough transform technique in which an image point is treated as a fuzzy point. In our approach, a number of fuzzy set membership values are calculated from the standard Hough transform accumulators. These fuzzy sets are combined to generate individual feature elements for each character. A set of such feature elements together form a feature vector, and the feature vectors from all the standard character patterns are used to train an MLP by supervised learning. In section 5.3 we explain the process of fuzzy feature extraction using Hough transform. The expected MLP outputs denote the grade of membership of an input pattern in the fuzzy sets representing similarities to the different character pattern classes. The highest value MLP output is normally selected as the detected character during recognition. Due to degradation of the image by noise, more than one output fuzzy set may have a high membership value. A dictionary search for ascertaining the correct choice is then made with these possible characters only. The search is thus confined to a small subset, which reduces the search time. The operation of the MLP with fuzzy input and output is explained in section 5.4.

Any pattern recognition system typically consists of selection and extraction of useful features from a pattern and use of a classifier to distinguish it from a set of similar looking patterns. A pattern can have a large number of measurable attributes, all of which may not be necessary for uniquely identifying it from other patterns in the particular domain of classification problem using a chosen classifier. It is, therefore, imperative that from a p-domain feature space consisting of all possible features, a projection be taken on a q-dimensional subspace of useful features where q <= p. This process of selecting q features from a set of p possible features for each pattern is called feature selection. The feature selection process, thus, reduces the space-time complexity of the classification process by removing the redundant or unimportant features. It should be noted that the optimum feature set chosen by a feature selection process depends on the classifier and the class structures in the feature space. A number of feature selection techniques have been proposed in the literature [10,13]. Use of fuzzy set theoretic measures for feature selection has been proposed by Pal [41]. Ruck et al [45], Belue and Bauer [6] and Pal and Chintalapudi [40] have proposed neural network based techniques for the evaluation of features. De et al [9] have recently proposed an MLP-based approach for feature ranking and selection. We have improved this method using a genetic algorithm to reduce the search time effectively in this method. We explain the feature selection process in section 5.5.

Traditionally, OCR algorithms are tested with a large number of documents for evaluating their performance. Often, a clean document is modified by shifting one or more pixel positions to generate the test characters [33]. Most of the character recognition systems of today are found to be suitable for a specific type and quality of image. The methods and algorithms used in the development of these OCRs are often biased by the researcher's choice of the training and the test data sets. As a result, such systems perform excellently for the data sets chosen by the researcher. In many cases, however, the recognition accuracy falls sharply when a slightly degraded image is chosen. It has, therefore, been felt necessary to model the defects quantitatively and experiment with extensive simulation to determine the nature of image defects that result in higher failure rate. Baird [1,2] first described a document defect model which includes a number of document image parameters, namely, size, resolution, horizontal and vertical scaling factors, translational offsets, jitter, defocussing, sensitivity and binarization threshold. Methods of calibrating image defect models were later discussed by him [3]. Review of the state of the art of calibration methods and further discussions on document image defect models, specially the defects due to the physics of apparatus for printing and imaging, was also made by Baird [4]. Ho and Baird [22] have presented a more recent report on similar defect models. An alternative approach to modeling is the morphological document degradation model proposed by Kanungo et al [28]. Their model simulates both the statistically independent pixel inversion that occurs in images and the blurring caused by point spread function of the scanner optical system. Subsequent to the development of document image degradation / defect models, different methods for validating such models have also been developed [34,39]. Kanungo et al [27] have proposed a statistical methodology for the validation of document image models and estimation of parameters.

We use a two-state Markov chain to model noisy document images for a formal mathematical treatment of the recognition accuracy of the fuzzy OCR system and selection of the system parameter values. This model has earlier been used for modeling communication channels with memory [12,15]. We have used the statistical methodology proposed by Kanungo et al [27] for validation of the noise model. We describe the model along with the simulation results in section 5.6. Finally, we present the implementation results and draw conclusions from our work in the last section.

5.2 Hough Transform and Multilayer Perceptron

5.2.1 *Hough Transform*

For line detection, Hough transform uses a parameterization to map an arbitrary straight line in the image plane to a point in the parameter space. A straight line can be parametrically represented by its distance from the origin denoted by ρ and the angle θ of its normal as shown below :

$$x\cos\theta + y\sin\theta = \rho \qquad (1)$$

If $\{(x_1,y_1), (x_2,y_2), ..., (x_n,y_n)\}$ is a set of n points in the image plane, the line detection problem is to find the different straight lines passing through these image points. Hough transform maps the points (x_i,y_i) into sinusoidal curves in the ρ-θ plane defined by :

$$\rho = x_i\cos\theta + y_i\sin\theta \qquad (2)$$

The curves in the transformed plane corresponding to all collinear points in the image have a common point of intersection. The parameters of the point of intersection, say (ρ_0,θ_0), represent the line passing through the image points. Hough transform thus maps the problem of detecting collinear points in the image plane into one of finding concurrent curves in the transformed plane. To determine the concurrent curves, the ρ-θ plane is quantized into quadruled grids forming a two-dimensional accumulator array. For each black pixel point (x_i,y_i) in the image, ρ values are computed for all the quantized values of θ using eq. (2). Accumulator cell counts are incremented by one for each ρ-θ combination so obtained. When all the black pixels are transformed and the accumulator array is updated, a given cell in the two-dimensional accumulator holds the total number of curves that pass through the ρ-θ values represented by it. If the count of a cell (ρ_i,θ_j) is 'm' then exactly m image points lie on a straight line with normal parameters (ρ_i,θ_j). A thresholding is done on each ρ-θ accumulator cell count and if the count is greater than the threshold, a corresponding line is detected in the input pattern. Otherwise, the cell is ignored.

The Hough transform technique may be extended to detect curves apart from straight lines [5]. An appropriate transform similar to eq. (1) is chosen to map points lying on the curve to a surface in the transformed plane. Detection of points lying on a circle is achieved by using the following equation:

$$(x-a)^2 + (y-b)^2 = c^2 \qquad (3)$$

An arbitrary point (x_i,y_i) in the image is thus transformed into a surface in the a-b-c parameter space defined by :

$$c = \sqrt{(x_i - a)^2 + (y_i - b)^2} \qquad (4)$$

If the surfaces corresponding to a number of image points meet at a point (a_0,b_0,c_0), then all the image points lie on a circle defined by these three parameter values. The curve detection technique using Hough transform can be implemented with a quantized three dimensional (a,b,c) accumulator array similar to line detection. Parametric representation of circles can also be used for the detection of curves from an image [52]. We use Hough transform for feature extraction from character patterns as explained in section 5.3.

5.2.2 *Multilayer Perceptron*

A multilayer perceptron is a network of simple processors, which are connected in a manner similar to the biological neurons [20,35]. The processors, often

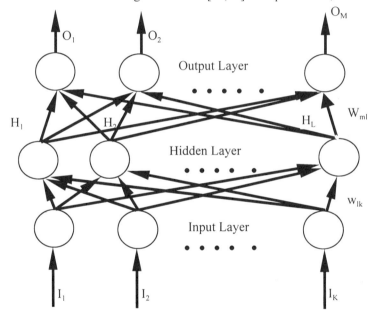

Fig. 5.1. Schematic of an MLP with one hidden layer.

called neurons, usually have sigmoid transfer functions and are arranged in a number of layers. The lowermost layer is the input to the MLP and the topmost layer is the MLP output. There can be any number of hidden layers between the input and the output. In multilayer perceptron architecture, there is no interconnection among neurons within a layer while neurons of adjacent layers are fully connected through weighted links. Information flow is only in the forward direction, i.e., from input to hidden layers and from hidden layers to output. A two-layered MLP, that is a network with one hidden layer, is shown in Fig. 5.1. For each neuron, the total input is the sum of the weighted outputs from the previous layer.

The transfer function normally used for a neuron is $f(x) = 1/(1+e^{-x})$ where x is the total weighted input to the neuron. In Fig. 5.1, k^{th} component of the input vector is I_k (k = 1, 2, .. K), K being the total number of inputs. The hidden layer outputs are labeled as H_l (l = 1, 2, .. L), where L is the number of hidden units and the outputs are O_m (m = 1, 2, .. M), M being the total number of outputs. w_{lk} is the weight from input k to the hidden unit l and W_{ml} is the weight from hidden unit l to the output unit m.

Thus,

$$H_l = f(\sum_k I_k w_{lk}) \text{ and} \tag{5}$$

$$O_m = f(\sum_l H_l W_{ml}) \tag{6}$$

An MLP can be trained by many supervised algorithms, of which back propagation is the most popular [46]. The back propagation (BP) algorithm minimizes the square error at the MLP output in a gradient descent process. For any pattern p, if T_m (m = 1, 2, .. M) is the desired output, then the back propagation algorithm minimizes the total error E for all patterns in the training set where

$$E \cong 1/2 \sum_{p=1}^{P} \sum_m (O_m - T_m)^2, \tag{7}$$

P being the total number of patterns.

The error is minimized by changing the appropriate weights in the back propagation process. For hidden layer to output connection,

$$\Delta W_{ml} = -\eta \frac{\partial E}{\partial W_{ml}} \tag{8}$$

$$\frac{\partial E}{\partial W_{ml}} = (O_m - T_m) f'(\sum_l H_l W_{ml}) H_l \tag{9}$$

$$= \delta_m H_l \tag{10}$$

For input to hidden layer connection, Δw_{lk} can be obtained by applying the chain rule :

$$\Delta w_{lk} = -\eta \frac{\partial E}{\partial w_{lk}} \quad \text{where } \eta \text{ is the learning rate.} \quad (11)$$

$$\frac{\partial E}{\partial w_{lk}} = (\sum_m \delta_m W_{ml}) f'(\sum_k I_k w_{lk}) I_k \quad (12)$$

$$= \delta_l I_k \quad (13)$$

The P input patterns are normally applied sequentially. One training epoch consists of a forward pass followed by updating of weights in the backward pass of one pattern and repetition of the whole process for all the P patterns. This process is continued till the total error falls below a specified limit. The MLP can then be used to classify unknown patterns presented at the input. This method of training a neural network with sample patterns is called supervised learning. The problem of character recognition where the expected patterns are known, is a typical application of supervised learning of multilayer perceptron acting as a classifier [47].

5.2.3 *Character Recognition with MLP*

To train an MLP with character patterns in the English alphabet, each character can be represented by a rectangular grid of size, say X by Y. The number of units 'K' in the input layer is then XY and the number of output neurons 'M' is the same as the number of letters in the alphabet. When a particular character from the alphabet is presented at the MLP input for training, the expected output of the corresponding neuron is set to '1' and the rest to '0'. After an MLP is trained with all the letters in the alphabet, it is able to recognize an unknown character presented at the input from a segmented document image. The performance of the MLP trained with the character patterns is directly affected by segmentation errors during the recognition phase. Due to incorrect segmentation, the same image pattern may appear to be different to the MLP because of its position within the rectangular grid. Attempts have been made to solve this problem by training the MLP with each pattern as well as with extra patterns generated by dithering [18,33]. This approach, however, increases the number of training patterns resulting in higher computation time and complexity.

Instead of training an MLP with the character patterns directly, it may also be trained with a number of feature vectors. The feature vectors are formed by extracting relevant features from each pattern by a feature extraction technique. Hough transform is one of the methods for extracting such features from a character image. Other methods are also available for feature extraction [51] from document images. The MLP-based classification method using feature vectors is less susceptible to segmentation errors than an MLP trained with the character patterns directly. However, if a pattern is distorted by noise so that the features are degraded, the MLP may fail to identify it due to incorrect feature extraction. As mentioned earlier in this section, a thresholding is done on the accumulator cell counts in the Hough transform technique for the extraction of line and circle from an image pattern. Due to the presence of noise, if the accumulator cell count goes even slightly below the threshold, a feature may be completely missed out. To overcome the drawbacks of Hough transform for feature extraction and character recognition with crisp MLP, we use a *fuzzy* Hough transform technique followed by recognition with a *fuzzy* MLP so that a higher character recognition efficiency is achieved.

5.3 Fuzzy Feature Extraction using Hough Transform

In this section, we give an introduction to fuzzy sets and how fuzzy features can be extracted from Hough transform by defining a number of fuzzy sets.

5.3.1 *Fuzzy Sets and their Properties*

For a universal set U of objects, a crisp subset A is defined by specifying the objects in U that are members of the set A. The membership of the objects of U in the set A may also be defined in terms of a characteristic function :

$u_A : U \rightarrow \{0,1\}$, so that

$$\forall x \in U, u_A(x) = \begin{cases} 1 \text{ if } x \in A \\ 0 \text{ if } x \notin A \end{cases}$$

In the pattern recognition paradigm, if there are N pattern classes $C_1, C_2, ..., C_N$, then a classifier can classify an unknown pattern 'r' into only one of these classes. We, therefore, write :

$$u_{C_i}(r) = \begin{cases} 1 \text{ if } r \in C_i \\ 0 \text{ if } r \notin C_i \end{cases}$$

Fuzzy sets are obtained by generalizing the concept of characteristic function to that of a membership function. A fuzzy set membership function is a mapping $\mu : U \rightarrow [0,1]$, so that if a fuzzy set A is defined on the universal set U, $\mu_A(x) \in [0,1]$, $\forall x \in U$. The fuzzy set A is thus characterized by the pair $\langle x, \mu_A(x) \rangle$ for all x. The α-cut, $^\alpha A$ of a fuzzy set A is the crisp set $^\alpha A = \{x \mid x \in U, \mu_A(x) \geq \alpha\}$. The 1-cut, $^1 A$ is called the core of A. The support of a fuzzy set A in a universal set U is the crisp set that contains all the elements of U with non-zero membership grades in A. The Height h(A) of a fuzzy set A is the largest membership grade in that set. Thus $h(A) = \underset{x \in U}{\text{Sup}} A(x)$ where Sup denotes Supremum. A fuzzy set A is called Normal if $h(A)=1$.

Zimmermann [53] and Klir and Yuan [31] have given more detailed discussions on the theory and properties of fuzzy sets while Kandel [26] and Bezdek and Pal [7] have described a number of applications of fuzzy sets to pattern recognition problems. Using fuzzy set-theoretic concepts, a pattern point 'r' belonging to the universe U, may be assigned different grades of membership in different fuzzy pattern classes C_i. The fuzzy pattern classes are defined in terms of their membership functions as $C_i = \{(\mu_{C_i}(r), r)\}$ where $\mu_{C_i}(r) \in [0,1]$, $\forall r \in U$.

The advantage of fuzzy sets as applied to pattern recognition problems in general and character recognition in particular is that, an ambiguous object need not be assigned to one class only. Fuzzy techniques specify to what degree the object belongs to a number of classes, a reasoning similar to the human thought process in pattern recognition.

5.3.2 *Hough Transform and Fuzzy Feature Extraction*

An important observation on Hough transform for line detection is that it provides three important characteristics of a straight line in an image pattern. These are the values of ρ, θ and count of a ρ-θ accumulator cell. ρ and θ specify the position and orientation of a straight line, while count specifies the length of the line in terms of the number of black pixels lying on it. Keeping this in mind, we define a number of fuzzy sets whose membership functions are listed in table 5.1 for θ values in the first quadrant. Similar membership functions are defined for θ values in the other quadrants for these sets.

All the black pixels in a character pattern are first mapped to the ρ-θ plane using the transform of eq. (2) and the ρ-θ accumulator is updated. The membership values for the fuzzy sets of table 5.1 are then determined for each ρ-θ accumulator cell. For other pattern recognition problems, similar fuzzy sets can be defined on the Hough transform accumulator.

Table 5.1. Fuzzy set membership functions defined on Hough transform accumulator cells for line detection from a pattern of height X and width Y.

Fuzzy Set	Membership Function		Notation
Long line	$count/[(X^2+Y^2)^{1/2}]$		LL
Short line	2LL	if $count \leq [(X^2+Y^2)^{1/2}]/2$	SL
	2(1-LL)	if $count > [(X^2+Y^2)^{1/2}]/2$	
Nearly horizontal line	$\theta/90.0$		HL
Nearly vertical line	1-HL		VL
Slant line	2HL	if $\theta \leq 45.0$	TL
	2(1-HL)	if $\theta > 45.0$	
Line near top border	ρ/X	if HL > VL	NT
	0	otherwise	
Line near bottom border	1-NT	if HL > VL	NB
	0	otherwise	
Line near vertical centre	2NT	if (HL > VL and $\rho \leq X/2$)	NVC
	2(1-NT)	if (HL > VL and $\rho > X/2$)	
	0	otherwise	
Line near right border	ρ/Y	if VL > HL	NR
	0	otherwise	
Line near left border	1-NR	if VL > HL	NL
	0	otherwise	
Line near horizontal centre	2NR	if (VL > HL and $\rho \leq Y/2$)	NHC
	2(1-NR)	if (VL > HL and $\rho > Y/2$)	
	0	otherwise	

Since thresholding is not used in this method, it retains all the information contained in the original image in terms of length, position and orientation of the different lines. By fuzzy Hough transform, we map the characteristics of the lines in an image pattern into properties of these fuzzy sets. LL and SL of table 5.1 extract length information of the different lines in a character pattern. HL, VL and TL represent their skew while NT, NB, NVC, NR, NL and NHC give the spatial distribution of these lines. Each of the fuzzy sets satisfies the following properties:
1. $\mu_A(x) \in [0,1]$ where A denotes any of the fuzzy sets in table 5.1.
2. $h(A) = 1$ and hence each fuzzy set is normal.
3. The 1-cuts i.e., the core of the fuzzy sets TL, NT, NB, NVC, NR, NL, NHC represent crisp features. The core of the fuzzy sets HL and VL denote the

strictly horizontal and strictly vertical lines, respectively, while the core of LL is a diagonal line.
4. Support of the fuzzy sets LL and SL represent straight lines with all possible lengths in the pattern.

Table 5.2. Fuzzy set membership functions defined on Hough transform accumulator cells for circle detection from a pattern of height X and width Y.

Fuzzy Set	Membership Function		Notation
Large circle	c/(X/2)		LC
Small circle	2LC	if $c \leq (X/4)$	SC
	2(1-LC)	if $c > (X/4)$	
Centre near right border	a/Y		CRB
Centre near left border	1-CRB		CLB
Centre near horizontal mid-point	2CRB	if $a < (Y/2)$	CHM
	2(1-CRB)	otherwise	
Centre near top border	b/X		CTB
Centre near bottom border	1-CTB		CBB
Centre near vertical mid-point	2CTB	if $b < (X/2)$	CVM
	2(1-CTB)	otherwise	
Centre near mid-point	(2CHM)CVM		CMP
Dense circle	count/$2\pi c$		DC
Sparse circle	2DC	if count $\leq \pi c$	PC
	2(1-DC)	Otherwise	

We define similar fuzzy sets on the (a,b,c) accumulator cells for circle extraction using the transform $c = \sqrt{(x-a)^2 + (y-b)^2}$ as shown in table 5.2. Based on the fuzzy sets defined in table 5.1, we synthesize an additional number of fuzzy sets to represent each line in the image as a combination of its length, position and orientation. These fuzzy sets represent the dominant line features present in the different character patterns. The basic fuzzy sets of table 5.2 for circle extraction are also combined in terms of their position, size and sparseness to represent the circular features in a character pattern. The synthesized set definitions for line and circle extraction are given in table 5.3. Membership values for the synthesized fuzzy sets of table 5.3 are determined for each ρ-θ accumulator cell using t-norm.

Table 5.3. Synthesized fuzzy set definitions using t-norms.

Synthesized Fuzzy Set	Definition (i ≡ t-norm)	Notation
Long slant line	i(TL,LL)	LSL
Short slant line	i(TL,SL)	SSL
Nearly horizontal short line near vertical centre	i(HL,i(SL,NVC))	HSVC
Nearly horizontal short line near top border	i(HL,i(SL,NT))	HLT
Nearly vertical long line near left border	i(VL,i(LL,NL))	VLL
Nearly vertical long line near right border	i(VL,i(LL,NR))	VLR
Nearly horizontal long line near top border	i(HL,i(LL,NT))	HLT
Nearly horizontal long line near bottom border	i(HL,i(LL,NB))	HLB
Nearly vertical long line near horizontal centre	i(VL,i(LL,NHC))	VLHC
Nearly vertical short line near horizontal centre	i(VL,i(SL,NHC))	VSHC
Large dense circle with centre near mid-point	i(LC,i(DC,CMP))	LDM
Large sparse circle with centre near mid-point	i(LC,i(PC,CMP))	LPM
Large sparse circle with centre near bottom border on horizontal mid-point	i(LC,i(PC,i(CBB,CHM)))	LPBM
Small sparse circle with centre near left border on vertical mid-point	i(SC,i(PC,i(CLB,CVM)))	SPLM
Small dense circle with centre near top border on horizontal mid-point	i(SC,i(DC,i(CTB,CHM)))	SDTM
Small sparse circle with centre near top left border	i(SC,i(PC,i(CTB,CLB)))	SPTL
Small sparse circle with centre near top right border	i(SC,i(PC,i(CTB,CRB)))	SPTR
Small sparse circle with centre near bottom border on horizontal mid-point	i(SC,i(PC,i(CBB,CHM)))	SPBM
Small sparse circle with centre near mid-point	i(SC,i(PC,CMP))	SPM
Small dense circle with centre near mid-point	i(SC,i(DC,CMP))	SDM

A fuzzy intersection or t-norm i is a binary operation on the unit interval that satisfies the following properties for any p,q,r $\in$ [0,1] where p,q,r denote membership values in arbitrary fuzzy sets :
1. $i(p,1) = p$
2. $q \leq r \Rightarrow i(p,q) \leq i(p,r)$
3. $i(p,q) = i(q,p)$
4. $i(p,i(q,r)) = i(i(p,q),r)$

A number of t-norms are available as fuzzy intersection [31] of which we use the standard intersection : $i(p,q) = \min(p,q)$. For other pattern recognition problems, suitable fuzzy sets may be similarly synthesized from the corresponding basic sets of fuzzy Hough transform. A non-null support of a synthesized fuzzy set implies the presence of the corresponding feature in a pattern. We, therefore, choose the height of each synthesized fuzzy set to define a feature element and the set of 'n' such feature elements constitute an n-dimensional feature vector for the character. Thus, if $\overline{F}_1, \overline{F}_2, ..., \overline{F}_P$ denote P feature vectors derived from the P input characters using fuzzy Hough transform, the feature elements of each pattern are defined as $F_{i1} = h(LSL) = \underset{(\rho\text{-}\theta)}{\text{Sup LSL}}$,

$F_{i2} = h(SSL) = \underset{(\rho\text{-}\theta)}{\text{Sup SSL}}$, etc. The values of the feature elements constituting the feature vectors from 10 character patterns 'A' – 'J' are shown in Fig. 5.2. We have presented preliminary results on this method of feature extraction in [48-50]. The feature vectors extracted from all the character patterns are used to train a multilayer perceptron as described in the next section.

5.4 Multilayer Perceptron with Fuzzy Input and Output

A number of fuzzy perceptrons and other fuzzy neural networks have been described in the literature. Keller and Hunt [29] have introduced fuzzy set theory into the perceptron algorithm to ease convergence problems when data sets are linearly separable. Pal and Mitra [43] also have introduced fuzzy concepts in MLP input and output. Pedrycz [44] has discussed about neurocomputations in relational systems. Gader et al [14] have proposed a fuzzy neural system for handwritten character recognition. We use a multilayer perceptron with fuzzy feature vectors as inputs and fuzzy pattern class memberships as outputs, which is structurally similar to the crisp perceptron shown in Fig. 5.1. In this section, we explain the MLP input and output as well as character recognition with the MLP using fuzzy set theoretic concepts.

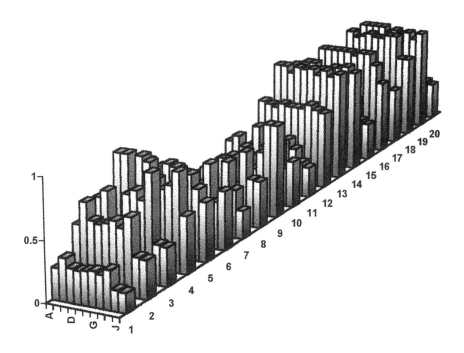

Fig. 5.2 Values of the feature elements for the character patterns 'A' – 'J'.

5.4.1 *Fuzzy MLP Input*

The elements of the n-dimensional feature vectors generated from the fuzzy Hough transform as discussed in the last section represent the heights of synthesized fuzzy sets and hence are real numbers. When such a feature vector is extracted from a degraded pattern for recognition, the strength of the features in the vector may vary due to the presence of noise. To combat the effect of noise, we generate membership values in three linguistic fuzzy sets, namely, *weak, moderate* and *strong* from the individual feature elements. The linguistic set membership functions are derived from the Butterworth filter transfer functions [37] as shown below.

$$\mu_{weak}(x) = [1+(x/a)^{2m}]^{-1/2}$$
$$\mu_{moderate}(x) = ([1+(x/a_1)^{2m}][1+(a_2/x)^{2m}])^{-1/2}$$
$$\mu_{strong}(x) = [1+(a/x)^{2m}]^{-1/2} \qquad (14)$$

Here $x = a$ (a_1, a_2 for $\mu_{moderate}$) is the cut-off point for all values of 'm' where m controls the slope of the functions. The n-dimensional feature vectors extracted from Hough transform are thus mapped into 3n-dimensional vectors which form the MLP input both during training and recognition. The advantage of using linguistic features is that, for small variations in the extracted feature values, the linguistic set memberships remain unchanged. The system can then recognize even degraded character patterns.

5.4.2 *Fuzzy MLP Output*

In a conventional MLP, an input pattern belongs only to a particular output pattern class. We, however, use fuzzy pattern classes as outputs and the MLP is trained to learn the degree by which an input character belongs to each of these pattern classes. The pattern classes are defined as "similar to character 'A' ", "similar to character 'B' ", etc and represented by C_1, C_2, ..., etc. When the MLP is trained with sample patterns, the expected outputs corresponding to each input pattern is computed based on a distance measure between the input vector and the feature vector of the character represented by the particular output unit. The membership function denoting belongingness to the different character pattern classes for an input pattern is determined using the following method.

Consider a P-class problem domain with P nodes in the output layer of the MLP with fuzzy membership values. Each pattern, before converting to linguistic sets, is represented by the feature vector $\overline{F_i}$, $i = 1, 2, ..., P$. The Euclidean distance between $\overline{F_i}$ and other feature vectors is :

$$d_{ik} = [\sum_j (F_{ij} - F_{kj})^2]^{1/2} \quad k = 1, 2, ..., P \qquad (15)$$

We use eq. (15) to calculate the distances of all the P patterns from the ith input pattern where the summation is done over all the feature elements subscripted by j. The membership of the ith character pattern to the kth fuzzy pattern class C_k, and hence the value of the kth expected output of the MLP for input vector $\overline{F_i}$ is determined as follows :

$$O^i_{k(exp)} = \mu_k(\overline{F_i}) = 1/[1+(d_{ik}/f_{den})^{fpow}] \qquad (16)$$

Here 'f_{den}' and 'f_{pow}' control the membership grades by which the pattern $\overline{F_i}$ belongs to the different output fuzzy sets. This method of using fuzzy pattern classes at the MLP output has been suggested by Pal and Mitra [43] as well as by Pal and Dutta Majumder [42] The following properties are satisfied by the fuzzy class membership functions of eq. (16).

1. $\mu_k(\overline{F_i}) \in [0,1]$
2. $\mu_k(\overline{F_i}) = \mu_i(\overline{F_k})$
3. $\mu_k(\overline{F_k}) = 1$
4. $d_{ik} \geq d_{il} \Rightarrow \mu_k(\overline{F_i}) \leq \mu_l(\overline{F_i})$
5. For $f_{den} \rightarrow 0$ and $f_{pow} \rightarrow \infty$, the fuzzy MLP output reduces to conventional MLP output with $O^i_{k(exp)} = 1$ for i = k and 0, otherwise.

Fig. 5.3 shows the plot of the expected outputs of the nodes representing fuzzy sets "similar to character 'A' ", ..., "similar to character 'J' " for the input patterns 'A',...,'J'. Distance measures other than Euclidean distance may also be considered in a similar manner. The MLP is trained with the input fuzzy feature vectors and fuzzy expected outputs by the standard back propagation algorithm. The error between the actual output and the expected output is minimized through updation of weights, initially set with random values.

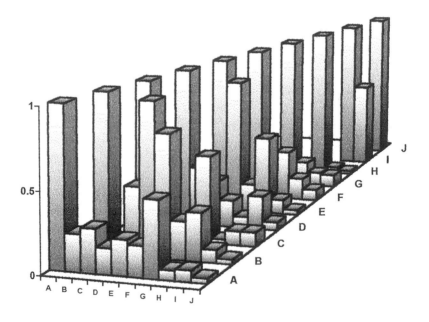

Fig. 5.3. Expected values of 10 MLP output nodes for the corresponding input patterns.

5.4.3 Fuzzy Character Recognition

The recognition decision of the MLP is based on the α-cuts of the output fuzzy sets for $\alpha = th\_opt$, where th_opt is a threshold value. The α-cuts are determined by the parameters f_{den} and f_{pow} of eq. (16). For $f_{den} > d_{ik}$, the number of elements in the α-cuts increases with higher values of f_{pow}. For a fixed value of the parameters f_{den} and f_{pow}, if th_opt is low, α-cuts of the output fuzzy sets may contain more than one element while a high value of th_opt results in null α-cuts for some of the outputs. If each of the α-cuts contain more than one element, then during recognition, only one of the MLP outputs goes above the threshold. The highest value output is then considered as the detected character. If, however, the membership value is above the threshold for more than one output, it indicates a possibility of *misclassification*. All these outputs are then considered for a dictionary search to ascertain the character. In the dictionary search step, a lexicon is consulted to correctly determine the character using word level knowledge. The advantage of using fuzzy set membership functions at the MLP output is that the search space is shortened and only the outputs with high membership values are considered for the search. Since the MLP outputs denote their similarities to the correct pattern class, this decision making process is justified. In the third possibility, when all the outputs of the MLP are less than the threshold th_opt for an input pattern, it indicates a *classifier failure*. The dictionary search is made with a wildcard at the unknown character position, i.e., the search space includes all the pattern classes. If more than one choice of possible characters form a valid word in the dictionary, the characters are considered to be unresolved and are marked for identification by user intervention. The values of th_opt, f_{den} and f_{pow} are chosen by simulation so that each α-cut contains more than one element and the combined error due to *misclassification* and *classifier failure* is minimized. In section 6 we discuss the simulation results for *misclassification* and *classifier failure* of the character recognition system.

5.5 Feature Selection using Genetic Algorithm

As discussed in sections 5.3 and 5.4, we choose a number of fuzzy features for the classification of characters using a multilayer perceptron. However, there is no *a priori* knowledge about the effectiveness as well as adequacy of this set of features. It is therefore, imperative that some feature selection method should be adopted to decide which features are redundant and which ones are necessary for complete classification of all possible characters. De *et al* [9] have suggested the use of a Feature Quality Index (FQI) for the ranking and selection of features using multilayer perceptron. This feature ranking process is based on the concept that the influence of a feature on an MLP output is related to the importance of the feature in discriminating among classes. The impact of the qth feature on the MLP output out of a total of 'p' features is measured by setting the feature value to zero for each input pattern x_i, i = 1,2,...,n. FQI is defined as the deviation of the MLP output with q^{th} feature value set to zero from the output with all features present. Thus,

$$FQI_q = \frac{1}{n}\sum_{i=1}^{n}\|\mathbf{O}_i - \mathbf{O}_i^{(q)}\|^2 \qquad (17)$$

Here $\mathbf{O}_i$ and $\mathbf{O}_i^{(q)}$ are the output vectors with all the p features present and with the qth feature set to zero, respectively. The features are ranked according to their importance as $q_1, q_2, ..., q_p$ if $FQI_{q1} > FQI_{q2} > ... > FQI_{qp}$. In order to select the best p′ features from the set of p features, $^pC_{p\prime}$ possible subsets are tested, one at a time. The quality index $FQI_k^{(p\prime)}$ of the kth subset S_k is measured as :

$$FQI_k^{(p\prime)} = \frac{1}{n}\sum_{i=1}^{n}\|\mathbf{O}_i - \mathbf{O}_i^k\|^2 \qquad (18)$$

Here $\mathbf{O}_i^k$ is the MLP output vector with x_i^k as the input. x_i^k is derived from x_i as follows :

$$x_{ij}^k = \begin{cases} 0 & \text{if } j \in S_k \\ x_{ij} & \text{otherwise} \end{cases} \qquad (19)$$

A subset S_j is selected as the optimal set of features if $FQI_j^{(p\prime)} \geq FQI_k^{(p\prime)} \ \forall k; k \neq j$.

An important observation on this method of feature selection is that the value of p′ should be pre-determined and that $^pC_{p\prime}$ number of possible choices are to be verified to arrive at the best feature set. It is evident that no *a priori* knowledge is usually available to select the value of p′ and an exhaustive search is to be made for all values of p′; p′ = 1,2,..., p. The number of possible trials then becomes (2^p - 1) which is prohibitively large for high values of p.

To overcome the drawbacks of the above method, we select the best feature set by the use of genetic algorithm [16]. We define a mask vector **M** where $M_i \in \{0,1\}$; i=1,2,...,p and each feature element q_i, i = 1,2,...,p is multiplied by the corresponding mask vector element before reaching the MLP input. The MLP inputs may then be written as :

$$I_i = q_i M_i \,;\, i = 1, 2, \ldots, p. \tag{20}$$

$$= \begin{cases} 0 & \text{if } M_i = 0 \\ q_i & \text{otherwise} \end{cases} \tag{21}$$

Thus, a particular feature q_i reaches the MLP if the corresponding mask element is one. To find the sensitivity of a particular feature q_j, we have to set the mask bit M_j to zero. In light of the above discussions, when we select the kth subset S_k of the feature set $\{q_1, q_2, \ldots, q_p\}$, all the corresponding mask bits are set to zero and the rest are set to one. When the feature set multiplied by these mask bits reaches the MLP we get the effect of setting the features of the subset S_k to zero and calculate the value of FQI_k. It should be kept in mind that the kth subset thus chosen may contain any number of feature elements and not a pre-specified p' number of elements. A schematic representation of the feature selection process using genetic algorithm is shown in Fig. 5.4.

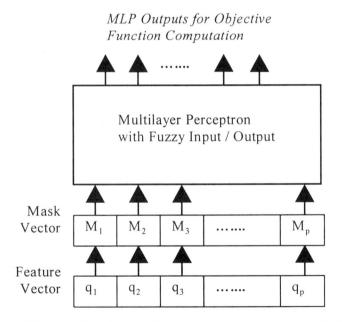

Fig. 5.4. Schematic of the feature selection process using genetic algorithm.

Starting with an initial population of strings representing the mask vectors, we use a genetic algorithm with *reproduction*, *crossover* and *mutation* operators to determine the best value of the objective function. The objective function is the

FQI value of the feature set S_k selected with the mask bits set to zero for the selected features and is given by :

$$FQI_k = \frac{1}{n}\sum_{i=1}^{n} \left\| \mathbf{O}_i - \mathbf{O}_i^k \right\|^2 \qquad (22)$$

In this process, we solve both the problems of pre-determining the value of p' and searching through the ${}^pC_{p'}$ possible combinations for each value of p'. In the genetic algorithm implementation, we start with 20 features generated from the fuzzy Hough transform as listed in table 5.3 so that the number of elements in the mask vector is also 20. After running the genetic algorithm for a sufficiently large number of generations, the mask string with the best objective function value is determined. The feature elements corresponding to the mask bits zero are chosen as the selected set of features. The algorithm has been first tested on two benchmark data sets, namely, Iris data and Crude Oil data [25] and the results match with those obtained in most of the experiments done by other researchers [29]. The parameters for the genetic algorithm are as follows :

Chromosome Length : 20
Population Size   : 20
Mutation Probability : 0.002
Crossover Probability : 0.67

The selected set of features is $(q_2 q_3 q_5 q_6 q_7 q_9 q_{10} q_{11} q_{12} q_{13} q_{15} q_{16} q_{17} q_{19} q_{20})$. The number of features is reduced from 20 to 15 which is a reduction of 25%. The time and resource requirements during classification are, thereby, greatly reduced. The MLP is next trained with only this set of features for classification.

5.6 Noise Model and Simulation Results

5.6.1 *Document Image Degradation Model*

We model a degraded document image as a two-state Markov chain in which one state produces errors in the image with a probability 'r' while the other state corrupts the image pixels with a probability 'b'. Here $r \ll b$ and the state with lower error probability is called the Random state (R) while the other is referred to as the Burst state (B). The transition probabilities are 'q' and 'Q' where q is the conditional probability that the image remains in the Random state for the next pixel position, given that it is in the Random state for the current pixel. With probability (1-q), it makes a transition to the Burst state. Q is also defined similarly for the Burst state. The transition probability matrix for the Markov chain is:

$$P = \begin{bmatrix} q & 1-q \\ 1-Q & Q \end{bmatrix} \qquad (23)$$

Here p_{ij}, $i,j = 1,2$ is the transition probability from state i to state j in one step. The steady state probabilities of the document image being in the Random state and in the Burst state are $P_R = (1-Q)/(2-Q-q)$ and $P_B = (1-q)/(2-Q-q)$, respectively. The average pixel error probability P_e on the document is $P_e = bP_B + rP_R$.

In communication channel models, a Burst is defined as a sequence in which contiguous transmitted bits have a higher probability of error. However in a document image, which is inherently two-dimensional in nature, we define a Burst start as an event when pixels lying on the neighborhood of the current pixel are affected with higher error probability. The burst first propagates to the 8 neighboring pixels of the current pixel, then to the next 16 neighbors, followed by the next 24 neighbors and so on. Thus, propagation of Burst is spatial in a noisy document unlike communication channels where it is temporal in nature. The parameters of the noise model are, therefore, $\theta = (q, Q, r, b)^T$. Here the parameters q and r control the random noise in the document. Q, on the other hand, controls the duration and propagation of a noise Burst while b determines the probability of a pixel getting affected during the Burst. It should be noted that a Burst does not necessarily mean that all the pixels are reversed in this state. Rather, it signifies that pixels falling in a Burst sequence have a higher probability of getting reversed. From the primary parameters of the noise model, two other parameters can be derived which are suitable for the actual process of simulation. The error density ratio, which is the ratio of the Burst state error probability and the Random state error probability, is defined as $\Delta = b/r$. For different document images with the same pixel error probability P_e, Δ is an indicator of the severity of the bursts in the image. The average burst length, λ is defined as the average number of pixels for which the image remains in the burst state. Here, $\lambda = Q/(1-Q)$. We have used the statistical validation method proposed by Kanungo et al [27] for the validation of the noise model.

5.6.2 *Simulation Results*

The distance between each pair of input patterns presented to the MLP is determined by the linguistic set parameters 'm', 'a', 'a_1' and 'a_2' of eq. (14). If a flat membership function is considered by choosing a high value of m, patterns with nearly equal heights in the synthesized fuzzy sets of table 5.3 tend to have almost identical linguistic set membership values. As a result, more than one MLP output becomes high for the same input pattern. On the other hand, if a small value of m is chosen, the same input pattern generates significantly different linguistic feature vectors, even when the noise level is low. Most of the MLP outputs then show low membership values. The requirement of an OCR system to correctly differentiate between similar looking patterns (thus reducing *misclassification*), and to correctly recognize a pattern in the presence of noise (thus reducing *classifier failure*), are mutually contradictory in nature. We, therefore, choose the values of m and f_{pow} from the simulation results so that the total error of the fuzzy OCR system is minimized. Since, this set of simulations is done to test the sensitivity of the classifier to the input and output parameters, we have not used dictionary search to aid the recognition process in this case. The variation of the two types of error with the parameter m of eq. (14) are shown in Fig. 5.5(a)-(b). The results are shown for different values of the output parameter f_{pow}. From the figures, it is seen that *misclassification* error increases with m while recognition error due to *classifier failure* goes down drastically with increasing values of m.

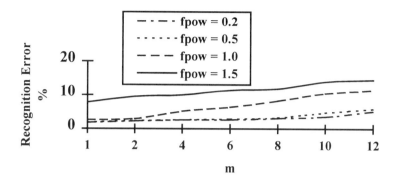

(a)

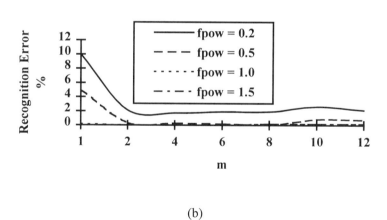

(b)

Fig. 5..5 (a) Variation of error due to *misclassification* for different values of linguistic set parameter m. (b) Variation of error due to *classifier failure* for different values of linguistic set parameter m.

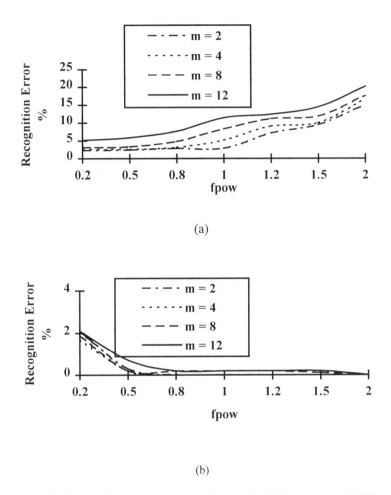

Fig. 5.6 (a) Variation of error due to *misclassification* for different values of MLP output parameter f_{pow}. (b) Variation of error due to *classifier failure* for different values of MLP output parameter f_{pow}.

The expected values of the MLP output for each fuzzy input vector represent the similarity to the respective fuzzy pattern class. The parameters f_{den} and f_{pow} of eq. (16) control this measure of similarity for the output pattern classes. The factor f_{den} is used to restrict the distance measure d_{ik} to a value less than unity and f_{pow} controls the closeness to the fuzzy pattern classes. If the value of the parameter

f_{pow} is decreased, the membership values $\mu_k(\overline{F_i})$ of eq. (16) decrease except for i = k. This effectively increases the distance between the correct output and the other outputs for a given input pattern. When an unknown pattern is encountered during testing, the chance of *misclassification* is reduced while that of *classifier failure* increases in the presence of noise. Thus, decreasing the value of f_{pow} enhances the 'contrast' in the output pattern classes. Fig. 5.6(a)-(b) show the variation of the two types of recognition error with the parameter f_{pow} for different values of the linguistic set parameter m.

The ability to correctly identify a character through dictionary search depends on the noise distribution in the document image. If, within a word, one or only a few characters are affected and the rest are recognized correctly, dictionary search can uniquely identify the unrecognized characters. Recognized characters in their positions within the word and unrecognized possibilities in their positions are considered for this search. As an example, let the word *house* is to be recognized where 'h', 'o', 'u' and 'e' are uniquely detected by thresholding and the possible choices for the fourth position are 'u', 'r' and 's' (i.e., outputs corresponding to these character classes have membership values more than the threshold *th_opt*). Then, a dictionary search can identify the character as 's'. However, if the noise distribution is such that a number of short bursts occur in more than one character position within a word, the possible choices may be numerous, increasing the search time. It may not also be possible to uniquely determine the character from word level knowledge only. Continuing with the above example, if low noise bursts affect the letters 'h' and 'u', it is possible that the choices for the first position are 'h' and 'm' while that for the third position are 'u' and 'r'. In this case, more than one character is affected in the word, where each character is distorted to a lesser degree so that the possible choices are two for each position. The possible combinations are thus 'house', 'horse', 'mouse' and 'morse', the first three of which are valid words in the dictionary. Hence, the characters remain unresolved and are identified by user intervention.

Fig. 5.7(a) shows the variation of unresolved error after dictionary search for different values of λ, the average burst length. We fix the total probability of error $P_e = 0.005$, keeping b = 0.5 and r = 0.0005. λ is varied from 10 to 200. From the figure, it is seen that for small values of λ, the recognition error percentage is higher and it goes down with increase in the value of λ. When λ is small, there are a large number of noise bursts, each with short length. As a result, the number of recognized characters is less resulting in ambiguous choice from the dictionary search. As λ increases, the number of bursts goes down and the affected characters are resolved by dictionary search, reducing the recognition error.

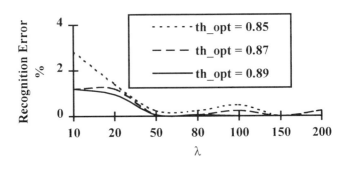

(a)

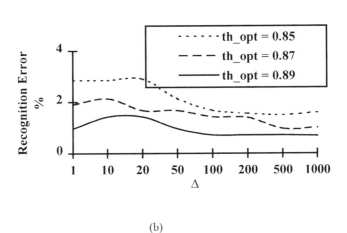

(b)

Fig. 5.7 (a) Variation of unresolved error with λ for different values of *th_opt*. (b) Variation of unresolved error with Δ for different values of *th_opt*.

The noise distribution in the document image has also been varied for different values of Δ, the ratio of burst state error probability and the random state error probability. The recognition results are shown in Fig. 5.7(b). Here also, the total probability of error $P_e = 0.005$. We maintain q = 0.999 and Q = 0.99. Δ is varied from 1 to 1000. From the figure it is seen that for small values of Δ, unresolved error is higher. The error percentage then decreases and remains almost constant for higher values of Δ. For small values of Δ, error occurs with almost equal probability in both the random state and the burst state, increasing the number of unresolved errors. For higher values of Δ, error due to random noise is corrected by the fuzzy MLP itself while the errors caused by dense bursts are resolved in the dictionary search step.

From Fig. 5.7(a)-(b), it is also seen that the unresolved error percentage is lower for higher values of output threshold *th_opt*. For low *th_opt* values, the number of possible choices is high for each character position and, hence, the dictionary search often cannot uniquely determine the characters. However, for very high *th_opt* values, many of the MLP outputs fall below the threshold and hence dictionary search is to be made with wildcards, increasing the search time.

5.7 Implementation Results and Discussions

The fuzzy OCR system is used to recognize characters from printed documents. Document scanning and binarization is done by a 300-dpi HP scanner. The input and output parameters of the MLP are selected based on the simulation test results. The linguistic set parameter m and the MLP output parameter f_{pow} are typically chosen as 4 and 0.87, respectively. The ratio (d_{ik}/f_{den}) is kept less than unity by choosing f_{den} as the maximum value of d_{ik}. The character recognition efficiency of the system is more than 98% for single font documents written in Times New Roman font. When trained with the fonts Times New Roman, Courier and Arial, the recognition efficiency of the system is in the range of 96-98% for multi-font documents.

The advantage of soft computing is harnessed in a number of ways in the character recognition system discussed here. First, the proposed fuzzy Hough transform method does not reject any feature since thresholding is not done on the Hough transform accumulators cells. All the pattern features are, therefore, retained for decision making at a higher level. Secondly, the choice of multilayer perceptron as a classifier enables the system to perform classification faster than a conventional nearest neighbor classifier. The use of fuzzy sets at the MLP output allows the system to segregate characters, which are suitable candidates for final selection from word level knowledge. Here also, we do not use the *winner-take-all* logic of crisp perceptrons. Finally, the genetic algorithm for feature selection makes the process fast and elegant.

The linguistic set definitions and the MLP with fuzzy input/output can be used with other fuzzy feature extraction techniques also. Fuzzy features like *thick* lines, *thin* lines, *nearly parallel* lines, lines *slightly above* or *slightly below* fixed lines, similar to those proposed by Krishnapuram et al [32] may also be extracted from document as well as non-document images using this technique. The genetic algorithm based feature analysis can be applied to a wide variety of pattern recognition problems including the example problems cited by De et al [9]. The present work can be extended to include fuzzy rule based systems to combine features extracted by fuzzy Hough transform instead of using a fuzzy MLP.

References

[1] H.S. Baird, "Document image defect models," *Proc. IAPR Workshop on Syntactic and Structural Pattern Recognition.* Murray Hill, NJ, pp. 38-46, 1990.

[2] H.S. Baird, "Document image defect models," in *Structured Document Image Analysis* (Eds. H.S.Baird, H.Bunke and K.Yamamoto), Springer Verlag, New York, 1992.

[3] H.S. Baird, "Calibration of document image defect models," *Proc. Fourth Annual Symposium on Document Analysis and Information Retrieval.* Las Vegas, Nevada, pp. 1-16, 1993.

[4] H.S. Baird, "Document image defect models and their uses". *Proc. Second International Conf. on Document Analysis and Recognition,* Japan, pp. 62-67, 1993.

[5] D.H. Ballard, "Generalizing the Hough transform to detect arbitrary shapes," *Pattern Recognition* **13**, pp. 111-122, 1981.

[6] L.M. Belue and K.W. Bauer Jr., "Determining input features for multilayer perceptrons," *Neurocomputing* **7**, pp. 111-121, 1995.

[7] J.C. Bezdek and S.K. Pal (Eds.), *Fuzzy models for pattern recognition - Methods that search for structure in data,* IEEE Press, NY, 1992.

[8] S.M. Bhandarkar, "A fuzzy probabilistic model for the generalized Hough transform," *IEEE Trans. on Systems Man and Cybernetics* **24**, pp. 745-759, 1994.

[9] R.K. De, N.R. Pal and S.K. Pal, "Feature analysis : Neural network and fuzzy set theoretic approaches," *Pattern Recognition* **30**, pp. 1579-1590, 1997.

[10] P.A. Devijver and J. Kittler, *Pattern recognition – A statistical approach,* Prentice Hall, London, 1982.

[11] R.O. Duda and P.E. Hart, "Use of the Hough transform to detect lines and curves in pictures," *Commun. ACM* **15**, pp. 11-15, 1972.

[12] E.O. Elliott, "Estimation of error rates for codes on burst channels," *Bell Systems Technical Journal* **42**, pp. 1977-1997, 1963.

[13] K. Fukunaga, *Introduction to statistical pattern recognition,* Academic Press, New York, 1972.

[14] P.D. Gader, M. Mohamed and J.-H. Chiang, "Comparison of crisp and fuzzy character neural networks in handwritten word recognition," *IEEE Trans. on Fuzzy Systems* **3**, pp. 79-86, 1997.

[15] E.N. Gilbert, "Capacity of a burst-noise channel," *Bell Systems Technical Journal* **39**, pp. 1253-1265, 1960.

[16] D.E. Goldberg, *Genetic Algorithms in Search, Optimization and Machine Learning*, Addison-Wesley, Reading, Mass., 1989.

[17] V.K. Govindan and A.P. Shivaprasad, "Character recognition - A review," *Pattern Recognition* **23**, pp. 671-683, 1990.

[18] I.A. Hadar I.A, T.A. Diep and H. Garland, "High accuracy OCR using neural network with centroid dithering," *IEEE Trans. on Pattern Analysis and Machine Intelligence* **17**, pp. 218-224, 1995.

[19] J.H. Han, L.T. Koczy and T. Poston, "Fuzzy Hough transform," *Pattern Recognition Letters* **15**, pp. 649-658, 1994.

[20] J. Hertz, A. Krogh and R.G. Palmer, *Introduction to the theory of neural computation*, Addison-Wesley, CA, USA, 1991.

[21] S.C. Hinds, J.L. Fisher and D.P. D'Amato, "A document skew detection method using run length encoding and the Hough transform," *Proc. 10th International Conf. on Pattern Recognition*, pp. 464-468, 1990.

[22] T.K. Ho and H.S. Baird, "Large scale simulation studies in image pattern recognition," *IEEE Trans. on Pattern Analysis and Machine Intelligence* **19**, pp. 1067-1079, 1997.

[23] B. Hussain and M.R. Kabuka, "A novel feature recognition neural network and its application to character recognition," *IEEE Trans. on Pattern Analysis and Machine Intelligence* **16**, pp. 98-106, 1994.

[24] J. Illingworth and J. Kittler, "A survey of the Hough transform," *Computer Vision, Graphics and Image Processing* **44**, pp. 87-116, 1988.

[25] R.A. Johnson and D.W. Wichern, *Applied multivariate statistical analysis*, 3rd edition, Prentice Hall, Englewood Cliffs., NJ, USA, 1992.

[26] A. Kandel, *Fuzzy techniques in pattern recognition*, John Wiley & Sons, USA, 1982.

[27] T. Kanungo, H.S. Baird and R.M. Haralick, "Validation and estimation of document degradation models," *Proc. Fourth Annual Symposium on Document Analysis and Information Retrieval*, Las Vegas, Nevada, pp. 217-225, 1995.

[28] T. Kanungo, R.M. Haralick and I. Phillips, "Global and local document degradation models," *Proc. Second International Conf. on Document Analysis and recognition*, Tsukuba, Japan, pp. 730-734, 1993.

[29] J.M. Keller and D.J. Hunt, "Incorporating fuzzy membership functions into the perceptron algorithm," *IEEE Trans. on Pattern Analysis and Machine Intelligence* **7**, pp. 693-699, 1985.

[30] N. Kiryati, Y. Eldar and A.M. Bruckstein, "A probabilistic Hough transform," *Pattern Recognition* **24**, pp. 303-316, 1991.

[31] G.J. Klir and B. Yuan, *Fuzzy sets and fuzzy logic - Theory and applications*, Prentice Hall Inc., Englewood Cliffs, NJ, USA, 1995.

[32] R. Krishnapuram, J.M. Keller and Y. Ma, "Quantitative analysis of properties and spatial relations of fuzzy image regions," *IEEE Trans. on Fuzzy Systems* **1**, pp. 222-233, 1993.

[33] H.K. Kwan and Y. Cai, "A fuzzy neural network and its application to pattern recognition," *IEEE Trans. on Fuzzy Systems* **2**, pp. 185-202, 1994.

[34] Y. Li, D. Lopresti and A. Tomkins, "Validation of document defect models for optical character recognition," *Proc. Third Annual Symposium on Document Analysis and Information Retrieval*, Las Vegas, Nevada, pp. 137-150, 1994.

[35] R.P. Lippmann, "An introduction to computing with neural nets," *IEEE ASSP magazine* April, pp. 4-22, 1987.

[36] Y. Liu, "Machine printed character segmentation - An overview," *Pattern Recognition* **28**, pp. 67-80, 1995.

[37] J. Millman and C.C. Halkias, *Integrated Electronics : Analog and Digital Circuits and Systems*, McGrawhill, Singapore, 1972.

[38] S. Mori, C.Y. Suen and K. Yamamoto, "Historical review of OCR research and development," *Proc. IEEE*, pp. 1029-1058, 1992.

[39] G. Nagy, "Validation of OCR data sets," *Proc. Third Annual Symposium on Document Analysis and Information Retrieval*, Las Vegas, Nevada, pp. 127-135, 1994.

[40] N.R. Pal and K.K. Chintalapudi, "A connectionist system for feature extraction," *Neural, Parallel and Scientific Computation* **5**, pp. 359-382, 1997.

[41] S.K. Pal, "Fuzzy set theoretic measures for automatic feature evaluation: II," *Information Sciences* **64**, pp. 165-179, 1992.

[42] S.K. Pal and D.K. Dutta Majumder, *Fuzzy mathematical approach to pattern recognition*, John Wiley and Sons, New York, 1986.

[43] S.K. Pal and S. Mitra, "Multilayer perceptron, fuzzy sets and classification," *IEEE Trans. on Neural Networks* **3**, pp. 683-697, 1992.

[44] W. Pedrycz, "Neurocomputations in relational systems," *IEEE Trans. on Pattern Analysis and Machine Intelligence* **13**, pp. 289-297, 1991.

[45] D.W. Ruck, S.K. Rogers and M. Kabrisky, "Feature selection using a multilayer perceptron," *Journal of Neural Network Computing*, pp. 40-48, fall 1990.

[46] D.E. Rumelhart, G.E. Hinton and R.J. Williams, "Learning internal representation by error propagation," in *Parallel Distributed Processing : Explorations in the microstructure of cognition, Vol. 1 : Foundations* (Eds. D.E. Rumelhart and J.L. McClelland), MIT Press, 1986.

[47] S. Sural and P.K. Das, "A document image analysis system on parallel processors," *Proc. Fourth International Conf. on High Performance Computing*, pp. 527-532, 1997.

[48] S. Sural and P.K. Das, "Fuzzy Hough transform, linguistic sets and soft decision MLP for character recognition," *Proc. Fifth International Conf. on Soft Computing and Information / Intelligent Systems*, Iizuka, Japan, pp. 975-978, 1998.

[49] S. Sural and P.K. Das, "A soft computing approach to character recognition," *Proc. International Conf. on Information Technology*, Bhubaneswar, India, pp. 39-44, 1998.

[50] S. Sural and P.K. Das, "Fuzzy Hough transform and an MLP with fuzzy input/output for character recognition," *Fuzzy Sets and Systems* **105**, pp. 489-497, 1999.

[51] O.D. Trier, A.K. Jain and T. Taxt, "Feature extraction methods for character recognition – A survey," *Pattern Recognition* **29**, pp. 641-662, 1996.

[52] S.Y. Yuen and C.H. Ma, "An investigation of the nature of parameterization for the Hough transform," *Pattern Recognition* **30**, pp. 1009-1040, 1997.

[53] H.-J. Zimmermann, *Fuzzy set theory and its applications, Second edition*, Kluwer Academic publishers, Norwell, Massachusetts, 1991.

Chapter 6
A New Clustering with Estimation of Cluster Number Based on Genetic Algorithms

Katsuki Imai, Naotake Kamiura, and Yutaka Hata
Himeji Institute of Technology

Abstract

Clustering is primarily used to uncover the true underlying structure of a given data set. Most algorithms for clustering often depend on initial guesses of the cluster centers and assumptions made as to the number of subgroups presents in the data. In this paper, we propose a method for fuzzy clustering without initial guesses on cluster number in the data set. Our method assumes that clusters will have the normal distribution. Our method can automatically estimate the cluster number and form the clusters according to the number. In it, Genetic Algorithms (GAs) with two chromosomic coding techniques are evaluated. Graph structured coding can derive high fitness value. Linear structured can save the number of generation.

Keywords : Fuzzy clustering, hard clustering, FCM, k-means, supervised, unsupervised, GA, sGA, evolutionary computing, linear structured coding, graph structured coding, normal distribution, standard deviation, normal density curve, cluster number estimation, cluster validity, Neyman-Scott's method, center of cluster, prototype of cluster, probabilistic degree, belongingness, objective function.

6.1 Introduction

Recently, database users must treat large amounts of stored data that generally forms complex distribution. Because clustering methods split up a group of object into some subgroups and the objects inside a subgroup show a certain degree of similarity, these are primarily used to discover the true underlying structure of a given data [1]-[3]. The clustering problem is solved on the basis of a measure function, such that the distance between objects within subgroups is smaller than the distance between objects belonging to different ones.

Hard clustering assigns each data point to one and only one of the clusters with a degree of membership equal to 1 under the assumption that each cluster has a well-define boundary. Fuzzy clustering permits each data with a fuzzy value to belong to plural cluster and hence it is effective for the data in the subgroups whose boundaries might be fuzzy [4]. Fuzzy C-Means (FCM for short) is the well-known fuzzy clustering methods, and often used for numerous problems in the life science in recent years [5]-[8]. FCM method is based on fuzzy extension of the least-square error criterion, and often converges a local minimum. Though the number of clusters must be given previously to FCM, it is very difficult if we have only a little knowledge about database. Most of previously clustering methods never divide databases without the information on the number of the cluster. An unsupervised clustering, which can automatically estimate the important factor, are also proposed, but these methods require some complex parameters, magic numbers or procedures [9]-[12].

In this paper, we propose an unsupervised clustering method. In order to estimate the cluster number automatically, we assume that every cluster has the normal distribution. The normal density curve, which gives probability of belonging to each cluster, is characterized by given standard deviation. The probability expressed by normal density curve is regarded as the membership degree belonging to the cluster. Each distribution of cluster always overlaps with the other ones. Because this overlap disables us from clearly recognizing each cluster, we define the objective function that decreases the overlap and the distance between objects and each cluster centers.

As search algorithm, we introduce Genetic Algorithms (GAs for short) hard to fall into local minimum to our clustering. For every datum, the probabilistic like degree is calculated by the normal density curve formed according to the given standard deviation. An objective function in GAs evaluates the degree. Then our method can achieve a clustering according to the standard deviation. From the viewpoint of necessary generations in GAs, we evaluate two coding techniques. One is the graph structured coding called structured GA (sGA for short). We encode a candidate solution of our clustering method in two-level structure chromosome. The higher level of chromosome shows existence of each cluster by 0 or 1, and the lower one shows the centers of clusters by real number. This coding technique can obtain precise values of centers. The other technique is linear structured coding with classical chromosomes. It approximates a cluster center to given data point and encodes index numbers assigned to data points. It is useful in reducing the number of generations. The two methods depend on the standard deviation given in advance. We therefore define a measure based on the probability for comparison with different results on various standard deviations. The experimental results on data generated by Neyman-Scott's method show that our clustering method can estimate the precise number of clusters.

This paper is organized as follows. Section 2 introduces FCM method. Section 3 describes the fuzzy clustering method based on the normal distribution. Section 4 explains search algorithms based on sGA and classical GA. Section 5 describes the validity measure for our clustering method. Section 6 shows the experimental results on artificially generated data. Section 7 contains our conclusions.

6.2 Preliminaries

Let $X = \{x_1, x_2, \cdots, x_n\}$ be a set of all data. Each element of X has an N-dimensional vector specified by values of variables $x_1, x_2, \cdots,$ and x_N. Let c be the number of clusters. The objective function Q of FCM is defined as the sum of squared errors. Namely,

$$Q = \sum_{i=1}^{c} \sum_{k=1}^{n} u_{ik}^{m} \|x_k - v_i\|^2 \qquad (1)$$

where v_i is the center of the i-th cluster and $\|x_k - v_i\|$ is a distance function between x_k and v_i. u_{ik} is the degree of membership of the k-th data x_k in the i-th fuzzy cluster and $U = [u_{ik}]$ is called partition matrix. u_{ik} satisfies the following condition.

$$\begin{cases} u_{ik} \in [0,1] \\ 0 < \sum_{k=1}^{n} u_{ik} < n \text{ for any } i \\ \sum_{i=1}^{c} u_{ik} = 1 \text{ for any } k \end{cases} \qquad (2)$$

As m in Q equals 1, u_{ik} takes 0 or 1 for optimum solution. In this case, FCM method converges in theory to the traditional k-means solution. Already known fuzzy clustering method including FCM usually set m to the value over

1 to set u_{ik} to a fuzzy value [4]. The local minimal solution of Equation (1) in FCM is calculated as follows.

$$u_{ik} = \left[\sum_{j=1}^{c} \left(\frac{\|x_k - v_i\|^2}{\|x_k - v_j\|^2} \right)^{\frac{1}{m}} \right]^{-1} \quad (3)$$

$$v_i = \frac{\sum_{k=1}^{n} u_{ik}^{m} x_k}{\sum_{k=1}^{n} u_{ik}^{m}} \quad (4)$$

A procedure of FCM method consists of a two-stage alternative optimization.

STEP 1) Give m in Q, the number of clusters c and set random initial values for partition matrix U and the cluster center v_i.

STEP 2) Minimize Q with respect to U by Equation (3) and let the optimal solution be U.

STEP 3) Minimize Q with respect to v_i by Equation (4) and let the optimal solution be v_i.

STEP 4) Check the stopping criterion. If it is not satisfied, go to STEP 2.

In conventional clustering method, as the number of clusters increase, u_{ik} approaches 0 or 1, and the minimal value of Q approaches 0. If the number of clusters equals the number of data, Q becomes 0 and u_{ik} takes 0 or 1 for optimum solution. Then, we never estimate the number of clusters from Q. Besides we do not obtain global minimum solutions because FCM method is considered on only the local minimum solutions [10][13].

6.3 Fuzzy clustering based on the normal distribution

6.3.1 Overview

FCM method requires the knowledge about the number of clusters because u_{ik} approaches 0 or 1. The reason why solutions fall into local minimum is because conventional methods modify the initial guess of the centers v_i and that of u_{ik} to search minimal solutions alternatively. To keep u_{ik} from taking these values, we assume that each cluster has the normal distribution. Besides we use GAs as search algorithms without initial guess of the centers to obtain the global minimal solution.

Figure 6.1 shows our flow diagram. In advance, we set a standard deviation of every cluster: σ_0, that determines the distribution of cluster. Then GAs search the number of clusters and the center of each cluster. According to them, we calculate the fitness functions of GAs, and we obtain the clustering result.

6.3.2 *Our clustering method*

In the normal distribution, probability distribution of random variable is described by the normal density curve with the center of distribution and the standard deviation. The normal density curve $f(\chi)$ is calculated as follows.

$$f(\chi) = \frac{1}{\sqrt{2\pi}\sigma} \exp\left[-\frac{(\chi-\mu)^2}{2\sigma^2}\right] \quad (5)$$

where χ is the random variable, μ is the center of distribution, and σ is the standard deviation. Figure 6.2 shows the normal density curve.

Let $H_i \in [0,1]$ be the membership function for the i-th cluster. From the assumption of normal distribution, the normal density curve gives the

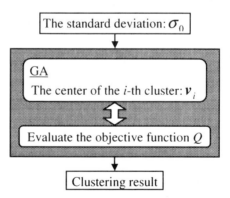

Fig. 6.1 Flow diagram

belongingnesses of the i-th cluster H_i as probability of selecting each cluster. The degree u_{ik} is calculated by setting the sum of H_is to 1 for x_k. Because the distribution of each cluster at least overlaps with the adjacent ones, the sum of H_is is always bigger than each of H_is, and the degree u_{ik} never takes 0 and 1.

In the following discussion, we denote x_k $(1 \le k \le n)$ by $(x_1^k, x_2^k, \cdots, x_N^k)$ and denote v_i $(1 \le i \le c)$ by $(v_1^i, v_2^i, \cdots, v_N^i)$. We derive a normal distribution h_i for given standard distribution σ_0 and calculate the membership function of the i-th cluster H_i from h_i. Suppose that all variables in data are independent. According to Equation (5), we show the following formula $h_i(x_k)$ that expresses the degree of N-dimensional normal distribution of x_k to the i-th cluster.

$$h_i(x_k) = \prod_{t=1}^{N} \frac{1}{\sqrt{2\pi}\sigma_0} \exp\left[-\frac{(x_t^k - v_t^i)^2}{2\sigma_0^2}\right]$$

h_i takes the maximum value on the center of the i-th cluster. This value $h_{i\max}$ is

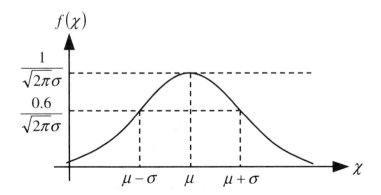

Fig. 6.2 Normal density curve

$$h_{i\max}(v_i) = \left(\frac{1}{\sqrt{2\pi}\sigma_0}\right)^N$$

We calculate the fuzzy membership function $H_i(x_k)$ from h_i as follows.

$$H_i(x_k) = \frac{h_i(x_k)}{h_{i\max}(v_i)} = \prod_{t=1}^{N} \exp\left[-\frac{(x_t^k - v_t^i)^2}{2\sigma_0^2}\right] \quad (6)$$

This value signifies the probability of x_k belonging to the i-th cluster when the probability of v_i belonging to the i-th cluster is 1. Because we consider only the i-th cluster for this belongingness, the value of the i-th membership function on x_k is calculated by comparison of $H_i(x_k)$ with the other belongingnesses. Namely, the membership value of x_k in the i-th cluster: u_{ik} is defined as follows.

$$u_{ik} = \frac{H_i(x_k)}{\sum_{i=1}^{c}\{H_i(x_k)\}} \quad (7)$$

u_{ik} satisfies Equation (2).

[Example 1]
The $H_i(x_k)$ of the clusters on Figure 6.3 are shown in Figure 6.4(a). The

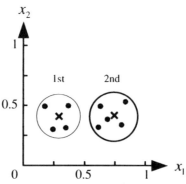

Fig. 6.3 An example of clustered data.

data marked with x_k belongs to the 1st cluster and 2nd cluster with the degrees 0.9 and 0.2, respectively. In our method, since the membership value u_{ik} is set to Equation (7), u_{1k} and u_{2k} are calculated as follows.

$$u_{1k} = \frac{0.9}{0.9+0.2} = 0.82$$

$$u_{2k} = \frac{0.2}{0.9+0.2} = 0.18$$

Figure 6.4(b) shows the membership value u_{ik}. Then, the overlap of clusters is shown by gray area.

[End of Example]

As the number of clusters increases, the overlap with the adjacent ones increases and hence the variance of u_{ik} s becomes smaller. Therefore this increasing overlap prevent us from recognizing each cluster clearly. As the

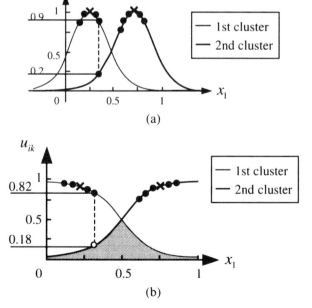

Fig. 6.4   Membership functions.
(a) Membership function of the cluster: H_i.   (b) Membership value on each data: u_{ik}.

number of clusters decreases, $u_{ik}\|x_k - v_i\|^2$ increases. This signifies that data within an identical cluster are not similar. So the objective function must decrease depending on the overlap and $u_{ik}\|x_k - v_i\|^2$. We define the objective function Q as follows.

$$Q = \sum_{i=1}^{c}\sum_{k=1}^{n} u_{ik}^{\frac{1}{2}} \|x_k - v_i\|^2 \qquad (8)$$

In Equation (8), u_{ik} takes neither 0 nor 1 and is constrained to be fuzzy value by Equations (6) and (7).

When we set the standard deviation to the value smaller than σ_0, the normal density curve becomes thin and overlap of clusters becomes smaller than σ_0. Therefore the result obtained by this method depends on the standard deviation σ_0. That is to say, if we set σ_0 to a small value in advance, the number of clusters is estimated to be large, and if we set σ_0 to large one, the number is estimated to be small.

[**Example 2**]
Figure 6.5 shows the case that the data of Figure 6.4 are separated into three clusters. Figures 6.6(a) and 6.6(b) show the membership function H_i and the membership value u_{ik}, respectively. In Figure 6.6(b), the overlap of the clusters is shown by gray area. Comparing Figure 6.6(b) with Figure 6.4(b), clearly, overlap increases.
[**End of example**]

A New Clustering with Estimation of Cluster ... 151

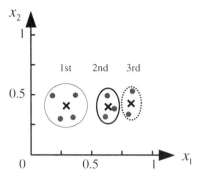

Fig. 6.5 An example of 3 cluster.

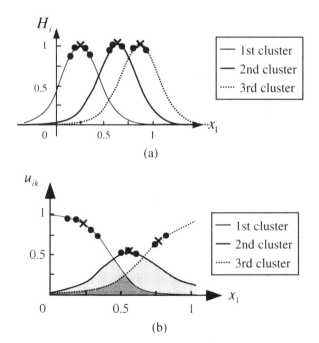

Fig. 6.6 Membership functions on Figure 6.5.
(a) Membership function of the cluster: H_i. (b) Membership value on each data: u_{ik}.

6.4 Genetic algorithms

6.4.1 *Overview of genetic algorithms*

Genetic Algorithms (GAs for short) proposed by Holland [14] are a class of optimization procedures modeled after genetics and evolution. Because they never require differentiability or continuity of search space, they have been used to efficiently search for attractive solutions to large, complex problems [15]. The search proceeds in survival-of-the-fitness fashion by gradually manipulating a population of potential problem solutions until the most superior ones dominate the population.

In GAs, a candidate solution is encoded in a data structure called a chromosome, whose fitness can be evaluated by the fitness function to be optimized. A population of such candidate solutions is first randomly chosen at first. Then, this population is successively changed by mating the two well-fitted individuals in population. The mating strategy, namely the genetic operators act to search for optimum solution. GAs run in five steps:

STEP 1) Randomly initialize a population of chromosomes.
STEP 2) Calculate the fitness of each individual in the population.
STEP 3) Select individuals to become parents of the next generation according to the fitness of individuals.
STEP 4) Create a new generation from the parent pool by chromosome crossover between parent pairs and its mutation.
STEP 5) If the stopping criterion is not satisfied, return to STEP 2.

In this paper, we use GAs to globally search the number of clusters and the center of each cluster with two encoding techniques. One technique is called structured Genetic Algorithm (sGA for short) that utilizes chromosomes with a largely hierarchical directed graph genetic structure [15][16]. The other is classical linear coding technique that enables us to reduce the number of necessary generations.

6.4.2 *Graph structured coding*

The chromosome of graph structured coding has a directed two-level hierarchical graph structure of genes. Figure 6.7(b) shows the chromosome representing cluster centers in Figure 6.7(a). The higher level expressed by a set of binary strings searches the existence of each cluster. If the i-th cluster can not be found, we assign 0 to the *i*-th gene, otherwise we assign 1. The sum of all higher genes' values, therefore, equals the number of clusters c. The lower level expressed by a set of real numbers searches cluster center. The *i*-th higher gene is linked to N lower genes with the values of variables in the *i*-th center. The length of the higher level, L, is shorter than or equal to the number of clusters. The maximum length of L is equal to the number of data, n. The total length of the lower level is $L \times N$.

Crossover and mutation are applied to either the higher level or the lower level. We employ the two-point crossover available to sGA as our crossover operator. Our crossover operator swaps substrings together with genes in the lower level between two randomly selected points. On the other hand, crossover on the lower level never influences the higher level. Figure 6.8(a) (or 6.8(b)) shows crossover on the higher (or lower). Our mutation operator on the higher level changes the value 1 into 0 or 0 into 1, whereas it adds the random value to the gene in the lower level.

The fitness function of GA evaluates a fitness of chromosome. A chromosome is more suitable as its fitness function becomes higher. According to Equation (8), our fitness function is defined as follows.

$$fitness = \frac{1}{Q} \qquad (9)$$

This coding method enables us to obtain precise vectors of the cluster centers. GA with this coding, however, requires a lot of generations to obtain a solution because of extensive continuous searching space.

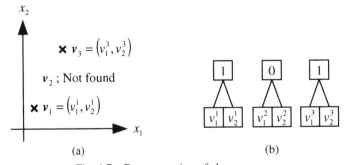

Fig. 6.7 Representation of chromosome.
(a) An example of the cluster centers.   (b) 2-level structure of chromosome.

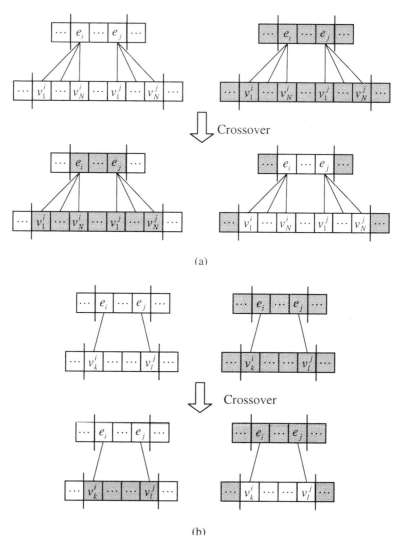

Fig. 6.8 Crossover.
(a) Crossover on the higher level. (b) Crossover on the lower level.

6.4.3 Linear structure coding

We can reduce the number of generations by approximating the center of each cluster to the nearest datum. Then we encode a candidate solution as linear structured classical chromosome. We call the nearest datum to the center of i-th cluster the i-th prototype. The chromosome consists of a list of prototypes, namely the i-th prototype is stored in the i-th gene. Each gene takes one of the integers $1, 2, \ldots, n$ which index a data points. If the i-th cluster can not be found or the i-th prototype agrees with the previous prototype, we assign -1 to the i-th gene. The length of the chromosome is permitted maximal number of clusters. The maximal length equals the number of data: n. Figure 6.9(b) shows the chromosome that represents the approximated cluster centers in Figure 6.9(a).

Our crossover used in this coding method is the two-point one in which substrings between two randomly selected points are swapped. Our mutation changes the value of each of randomly selected genes for one of integers $1, 2, \ldots, n$.

Let p_i be the i-th prototype. Then, according to Equation (9), the fitness function is defined as follows.

$$fitness = \left(\sum_{i=1}^{c} \sum_{k=1}^{n} u_{ik}^{\frac{1}{2}} \left\| x_k - p_i \right\|^2 \right)^{-1}$$

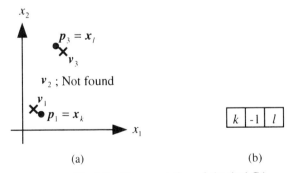

(a) (b)

Fig. 6.9 Representation of classical GA.
(a) An example of the prototypes. (b) Linear structure of chromosome.

6.5 Validity measure for clustering result

Our method depends on the standard deviation σ_0 given in advance. Generally the problem in clustering with respect to comparison between two solutions is called the cluster validity one, and some criteria are proposed [4] and [10]. These criteria are based on whether the resulting clusters are clearly separated and a lot of data points are concentrated in the vicinity of the cluster centers. Since our method the decreases the overlap of clusters, our results obtained always satisfy the above criteria. So we must discuss more suitable criterion for our method. We employ the following measure based on the probability for comparison with different result on various σ_0 s.

$H_i(x_k)$ is equal to the probability of selecting the i-th cluster for the given k-th data point x_k under the assumptions that each cluster has the normal distribution and the above probability for the i-th center v_i equals 1. We denote i for which u_{ik} takes the maximum value by i_{max}. Then the k-th data point x_k should belong to the i_{max}-th cluster.

We define the measure M_{sd} equal to the following average of probability as an indicator to evaluate the clustering result.

$$M_{sd} = \frac{\sum_{k=0}^{n} H_{i_{max}}(x_k)}{n} \quad \text{subject to } (n \gg c > 1)$$

Our clustering results are more suitable as M_{sd} becomes higher.

6.6 Experimental result

This section shows our clustering results for a numerical example. The example is the two-dimensional distribution generated by following Neyman-Scott's method [17].

STEP 1) Set the number of clusters: c, the mean number of data belonging to each cluster: r, and the standard deviation of each cluster: s.

STEP 2) Assign 2-dimensional uniform random vector to each center of cluster.

STEP 3) Determine the number of data belonging to each cluster by

Poisson random number for r.

STEP 4) Generate the data belonging to every cluster by two-dimensional Gaussian random number for every cluster center and standard deviation: s.

Figure 6.10 shows the example of 4 clusters with 69 data synthesized artificially by the above. We applied our method to the example. We set the population size to 60, probability of crossover to 30% and that of mutation to 10%. The results are reported averaged over 5 independent runs.

Figures 6.11(a) and 6.11(b) show our clustering results obtained by sGA and classical GA under the assumption of $\sigma_0 = 0.2$, respectively. Each one of the two techniques are estimated to be 5. Figures 6.12(a) and 6.12(b) show our clustering results obtained by sGA and classical GA under the assumption of $\sigma_0 = 0.21$, respectively. The numbers of clusters are estimated to 3 and 4 by sGA and classical GA, respectively. Table 6.1 shows the number of clusters obtained by sGA and classical GA under different σ_0 s. Figure 6.13(a) shows the cluster validity M_{sd} calculated from the solution by sGA. In the case of $\sigma_0 = 0.205$, the number of clusters c equals 4 and M_{sd} takes the maximum value 0.75. Figure 6.13(b) shows the cluster validity M_{sd} calculated from the solution by classical GA. In the case of $\sigma_0 = 0.217$, the number of clusters c equals 4 and M_{sd} takes the maximum value 0.72. Figure 6.14 shows our clustering result by sGA under the assumption of $\sigma_0 = 0.205$. The clustering result obtained by classical

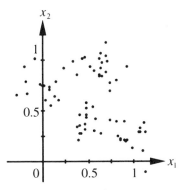

Fig. 6.10 The artificial generated 69 data.

GA under the assumption of $\sigma_0 = 0.217$ is the same as Figure 6.12(b). The artificial clusters are divided clearly in them. Table 6.2 shows comparison results between sGA and classical GA on the number of generations and fitness value with various σ_0 s. Classical GA requires fewer generations than sGA. The maximum fitness value obtained by sGA is higher than that by classical GA.

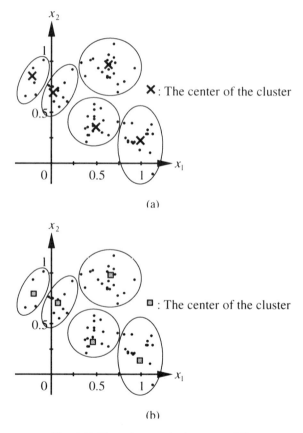

Fig. 6.11 Clustering results for $\sigma_0 = 0.2$.
(a) Clustering result obtained by sGA. (b) Clustering result obtained by classical GA.

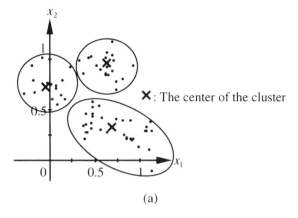

(a)

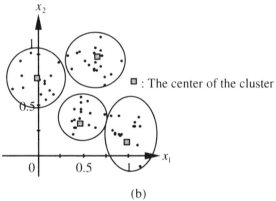

(b)

Fig. 6.12 Clustering results for $\sigma_0 = 0.21$.
(a) Clustering result obtained by sGA. (b) Clustering result obtained by classical GA.

Table 6.1 The number of cluster on 69 data.

The number	The standard deviation	
of cluster	sGA	classical GA
1	$0.285 < \sigma_0$	$0.285 < \sigma_0$
2	$0.240 < \sigma_0 \leq 0.285$	$0.235 < \sigma_0 \leq 0.285$
3	$0.205 < \sigma_0 \leq 0.240$	$0.217 < \sigma_0 \leq 0.235$
4	$0.120 < \sigma_0 \leq 0.205$	$0.125 < \sigma_0 \leq 0.217$
5	$0 < \sigma_0 \leq 0.120$	$0 < \sigma_0 \leq 0.125$

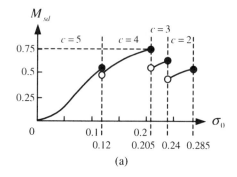

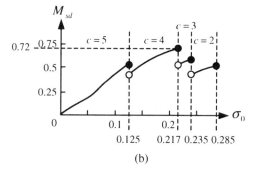

Fig. 6.13 The value of M_{sd}.
(a) sGA. (b) classical GA.

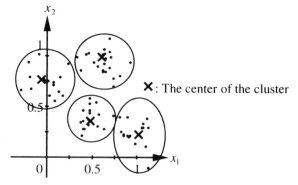

Fig. 6.14 Clustering results by sGA for $\sigma_0 = 0.205$.

Table 6.2. Comparison results between sGA and classical GA

	Generations	Fitness
sGA	6700	0.125557
GA	406	0.12208

6.7 Conclusions

In this paper, we proposed an unsupervised clustering method which forms the clusters according to a given standard deviation. We assume that every cluster has the normal distribution. The standard deviation gives the probability of selecting a cluster to each data, and a membership degree to the data in the cluster is calculated by the probability. The objective function of our clustering method conducts a solution according to both the overlap among clusters and the distance between data and the cluster center. GA based search can prevent the solution from falling into local minimum. We introduced the following two coding techniques: one called sGA with graph structured chromosome and the other called classical GA with linear structured chromosome. To compare several solutions under the assumption of the different standard deviation, we defined the validity measure for clustering result such that the standard deviation gives high probability to a cluster that the data should belong to. The experimental results of application to artificially generated data showed that our clustering method could correctly estimate the number of cluster.

Following subjects remain as future work: determining an optimum standard deviation in GAs and reducing the number of generation required for GAs.

References

[1] M. Holsheimerh and A. Siebes, "Data mining: the search for knowledge in databases," Report CS-R9406, The Netherlands, 1994.
[2] P. Adriaans and D. Zantinge, *Data mining*, Addison Wesley Longman Limited, London, 1996.
[3] U. Fayyad, G. P. Shapiro, P. Smyth and R. Uthurusamy, *Advances in knowledge discovery and data mining*, AAAI/MIT Press, Boston, MA, 1996.
[4] J. C. Bezdek and S. K. Pal, *Fuzzy models for pattern recognition*, IEEE Press, 1992.

[5] S. Miyamoto and M. Mukaidono, "Fuzzy c-means as a regularization and maximum entropy approach," in *Proc. of Seventh IFSA World Congress, Prague*, pp. 86-92, 1997.

[6] L. J. Mazlack, "Aspect of approximate reasoning applied to unsupervised data mining," in *Proc. of IEEE Biennial Conference of the North American Fuzzy Information Processing Society - NAFIPS*, pp.268-272, 1996.

[7] W. Pedrycz, "Data mining and fuzzy modeling," in *Proc. of IEEE Biennial Conference of the North American Fuzzy Information Processing Society - NAFIPS*, pp.263-267, 1996.

[8] S. Miyamoto, K. Umayahara and M. Mukaidono, "Fuzzy classification functions in the methods of fuzzy c-means and regularization by entropy," *Journal of Japan Society for Fuzzy Theory and Systems*, Vol.10, No. 3, pp. 548-557, 1998, (in Japanese).

[9] P. Cheeseman and J. Stutz, "Bayesian classification (Auto Class): Theory and results," in *Advances in knowledge discovery and data mining*, ed. U. M. Fayyad, AAAI/MIT Press, pp.153-180, 1996.

[10] R. P. Li and M. Mukaidono, "A maximum entropy approach to fuzzy clustering," in *Proc. of the 4th IEEE Intern. Conf. on Fuzzy Systems (FUZZ IEEE/ IFES'95)*, Yokohama, Japan, March 20-24, pp.2227-2232, 1995.

[11] S. Inui, K. Kamei and K. Inoue, "An advanced fuzzy c-means algorithm with cluster number estimation," *T. IEE Japan*, Vol. 114-C, No.11, pp. 1166-1171, 1994, (in Japanese).

[12] Y. Endo and S. Yamaguchi, "Tournament fuzzy clustering algorithm with automatic cluster number estimation," *Trans. IEICE of Japan*, Vol. J79-A, No. 7, pp.1276-1288, 1996.

[13] T. Ohta, M. Nemoto, H. Ichihashi and T. Miyoshi, "Hard clustering by fuzzy c-means," *Journal of Japan Society for Fuzzy Theory and Systems*, Vol. 10, No. 3, pp. 532-540, 1998, (in Japanese).

[14] J. Holland, *Adaptation in natural and artificial systems*, The University of Michigan, 1975, and MIT Press, 1992.

[15] R. J. Bauer, Jr., *Genetic algorithms and investment strategies*, John Wiley & Sons Inc., N. York, 1994.

[16] D. Dasgupta and D. R. McGregor, "Designing application-specific neural networks using the structured genetic algorithm," in *Proc. of COGANN-92 International Workshop on Combinations of Genetic Algorithms and Neural Networks*, Baltimore, Maryland, June 6, pp.87-96, 1992.

[17] T. Kato and K. Ozawa, "Non-hierarchical clustering by a genetic algorithm," *Journal of Information Processing Society of Japan*, Vol.37, No.11, pp.1950-1959, 1996, (in Japanese).

Chapter 7

Associative Classification Method

Akihiro Kanagawa, Hiromitsu Takahashi

Okayama Prefectural University

Abstract

This chapter deals with classification problems, such as diagnosis, in which classes are defined by categorical forms. Recently, soft computing techniques including learning algorithm in neural networks and fuzzy expert system are applied to the classification problems. Kanagawa *et al.* present an associative classification method using the cellular neural networks. This chapter proposes a new classification method using the associatron as an associative memory machine. We alter the associatron so as to have three stable leveled outputs, following in the steps of a method given by Kanagawa *et al.* Examples of diagnosis of liver disease and the problem of iris classification are demonstrated.

Keywords : Associatron, Associative Memory, Classification, Neural Networks, Bit Map Pattern

7.1 Introduction

Let q_i^* be an actual value of an item q_i $(i = 1, \ldots, n)$. For given n number of data $\{q_1^*, q_2^*, \ldots, q_n^*\}$, the problem of classifying these data into m number of classes $\{C_1, C_2, \ldots, C_m\}$ is known as a classification problem. It has long been studied as an important subject of mathematical statistics, above all in multivariate analysis, and methods based on the Maharanobis generalized distance or methods that construct a discriminant function have been discussed. However, these methods not only require the assumption that the attribute data follow a multivariate normal distribution, there is also the strong restriction that the variance-covariance matrix must have equality throughout the class. Methods based on the discriminant function are free from this variance-covariance equality restriction; however, in this case, calculation of the discriminant function grows extremely complex. In contrast to this approach, research has been conducted to make classifications by utilizing the learning functions of neural networks or a rule base that employs fuzzy systems. Keller and Hunt[1] have discussed methods of solving classification problems using the perceptron. In addition, Ripley[2] has conducted a survey on a classification method using multilayer neural networks. Shigenaga et al.[3] have taken the acquisition method of fuzzy if-then rules for classification using a rough set and applied it to diagnosis of liver disease, demonstrating its effectiveness. These trends are known as soft computing, and the present mainstream in regard to the classification problem lies in acquiring fuzzy if-then rules through learning in hierarchical neural networks according to training data [4].

On the other hand, Kanagawa et al.[5][6] have demonstrated the possibility of an approach to classification problems using associative memory performance in mutually interconnected neural networks. They avoided the memory-poor Hopfield network and used for the associative medium a cellular neural network (CNN)that can denote changes in conditions via differential equations. However, this method requires a complicated matrix operation known as singular value decomposition. In addition, isolated cells often arise in the use of CNN. In this chapter a method to make the associative classification system given by Kanagawa et al., using the associatron [7],which they had proposed as a dedicated device of associative memory, into a more high-level, more complete classification system is introduced. We apply it to the problem of iris classification and liver disease to demonstrate its effectiveness.

7.2 Associatron and Associative memory

7.2.1 *The Principle of the Associatron*

The associatron is a model for a neural network proposed by Nakano[7][8]; its special features lie in the way that it provides a model for the cerebral neural network. It expresses an item of memory in a pattern of the excitement of nerve cells across a neural network. It embeds Hebb's law by using a method to strengthen the synapse connection that interprets as follows: " the synapse connection between simultaneously excited cells grows stronger." First, let us look at the mutually interconnected neural network. Each neuron has 3 values: $-1, 0, 1$. Let us assume that when there is an input from outside, the value is -1 or 1, and that when there is no input from outside, the value is 0. The pattern is expressed according to the state that the neurons take in the overall neural network.

The synapse connections between cells that are excited simultaneously in the same way grow stronger, so that if we suppose that there are multiple neurons in a -1 state in the input pattern, then the connections between these neurons will be strengthened. In the same way, the connections between the 1 neurons will also be strengthened. Conversely, connections between neurons in the -1 state and neurons in the 1 state will be weakened. Now, let us assume that the pattern of all neurons in the -1 state, or alternatively the pattern of all neurons in the 1 state is embedded, and that this pattern has been partly input. A previously embedded pattern is known as an embedded pattern, and the input pattern is called the recalled pattern. For example, in Fig. 7.1, the embedded pattern is shown on the left, and the input pattern is shown on the right (in Fig.7.1, a black pixel corresponds to 1, a neutral gray pixel corresponds to 0, and a white pixel corresponds to -1).

The associatron expresses the relationship among the various neuron connections at the synapse. In associative classification, the embedded pattern usually contains plural items. Every time a new pattern is embedded, the connections between the neurons with the same value are strengthened, and the connections between neurons with different values are weakened. If the same pattern is repeatedly embedded, then that pattern is strongly memorized. In this way, even if many patterns are embedded, only the connection relationships change, and there is no need for new areas of memory.

When a single pattern is recalled from among many embedded patterns,

Fig. 7.1 Embedded pattern and recalled pattern

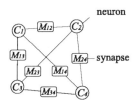

Fig. 7.2 Structure of an Associatron

recall takes place as if there were only one embedded pattern. However, when there are plural embedded patterns, some neurons are stimulated to become −1, and some neurons are stimulated to become 1. In this type of situation, decisions are made by majority decision of the neural network as a whole. It is decided by the neural network thus, so that even if there is some noise, or a slightly deviant pattern is input, a correct decision can be achieved. However, the fact cannot be avoided that the more embedded patterns there are, the harder it is to achieve a correct result.

7.2.2 Mechanism of Associative memory

In this section, embedment and recall based on the associatron are described.

Let us consider a neural network model such as that represented in Fig.7.2. It shows the state of the neuron C_i as x_i and the strength of the synapse between C_i and C_j as M_{ij}. The relationship $M_{ij} = M_{ji}$ holds. The embedded pattern is expressed in a column vector as in Eq.(7.1) below. The value of x_i is taken as −1, 0 or 1, and n denotes the number of neurons in the associatron.

$$x = (x_1, x_2, ..., x_n)^T. \tag{7.1}$$

If there are m items in the embedded pattern, then

$$x^k = (x_1^k, x_2^k ..., x_n^k)^T : k = 1, 2..., m, \tag{7.2}$$

and to express the kth pattern, the entire embedded pattern is treated as a matrix, as follows:

$$X = \begin{bmatrix} x_1^1, & x_2^1, & \cdots & , x_n^1 \\ x_1^2, & x_2^2, & \cdots & , x_n^2 \\ \vdots & \vdots & \vdots & \vdots \\ x_1^k, & x_2^k, & \cdots & , x_n^k \\ \vdots & \vdots & \vdots & \vdots \\ x_1^m, & x_2^m, & \cdots & , x_n^m \end{bmatrix}^T \tag{7.3}$$

By finding the inner product of this matrix X and its transposed matrix X^T, the following memory matrix M with n rows and n columns obtained.

$$M = XX^T. \tag{7.4}$$

If we take the input pattern as Y [Eq.(7.6)] and the recall result as Z [Eq.(7.7)], we can use the quantizing function

$$\phi(x) = \begin{cases} -1 & : x < 0 \\ 0 & : x = 0 \\ 1 & : x > 0 \end{cases} \tag{7.5}$$

to derive Eq.(7.8). Note that, in regard to matrix $A = (a_{ij})$, we assume $\phi(A) = (\phi(a_{ij}))$.

$$Y = (y_1, y_2, ..., y_n)^T \tag{7.6}$$

$$Z = (z_1, z_2, ..., z_n)^T \tag{7.7}$$

$$Z = \phi\{\phi(M)Y\}. \tag{7.8}$$

It can be seen from Eqs.(7.1)-(7.4) and (7.8) that embedment and recall are given according to an exceedingly simple calculation process.

7.3 Classification procedure based on associative memory

7.3.1 *Associative classification via CNN*

Now we introduce associative classification using cellular neural networks (CNN) as given in Kanagawa et al.[5]. The CNN is composed of cell neurons systematically arrayed in a lattice. The cell entity is a nonlinear analog circuit, and each cell is influenced by its neighbor cells. The state of cell x_{ij}, from column i, row j may be described by the following differential equations:

$$\dot{x}_{ij} = -x_{ij} + Ty_{ij} + I \quad (7.9)$$

$$y_{ij} = \text{sat}(x_{ij}), \quad (7.10)$$

where, T is for the template matrix, and the cell connection is being described. I is the threshold vector. Function $\text{sat}(x)$ is the output function, and it corresponds to the quantizing function of the associatron. Kanagawa et al. demonstrates how a multi-valued CNN may be constructed by making this output function into a piecewise linear multi-step function. A 3-valued output function [Eq.(7.11)] is shown in Fig.7.3.

$$\text{sat}(x) = \begin{cases} -1 & : \quad x < -1.5 \\ x + 0.5 & : \quad -1.5 \leq x \leq -0.5 \\ 0 & : \quad -0.5 \leq x \leq 0.5 \\ x - 0.5 & : \quad 0.5 \leq x \leq 1.5 \\ 1 & : \quad 1.5 < x \end{cases} \quad (7.11)$$

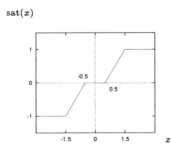

Fig. 7.3 Output function of the CNN

Categories for blood tests or the like are often expressed in phases of 3 value levels, such as " low, normal, high" or " normal, excessive, highly excessive." For example, $\gamma-\text{GTP} = 0 - 50[\text{IU}/l]$ is in the normal range, but the $50 - 100[\text{IU}/l]$ level is mildly excessive, while a level higher than $100[\text{IU}/l]$ is seriously excessive and will result in a diagnosis of illness. On the other hand, the normal range for ChE (cholinesterase) lies in the $200 - 400[\text{IU}]$ range; levels below this raise suspicions of hepatitis, while higher ranges prompt suspicions of a fatty liver. That is why 3-stage levels for the various items are considered. Using the 4×4 CNN shown in Fig.7.4, typical patterns as shown in Fig.7.5 for a healthy person, chronic hepatitis, liver cirrhosis and hepatoma are derived.

They take these as embedded patterns and derived a threshold matrix as the template matrix using the singular value decomposition method given by Liu and Michel[9]. They also give a scaling function to map various diagnostic items taken from medical technical papers, etc. into the 3 levels, $-1, 0$, and 1. Based on this, certain patient data served as the initial 4×4 CNN pattern made by using the scaling function.

UA	BUN	LDH	Plt
ALb	γGTP	GOT	LAP
TBill	$\frac{\text{GOT}}{\text{GPT}}$	GPT	AFP
DBill	ChE	ALP	AFP

Fig. 7.4 4×4 CNN for diagnosis of liver disease

It is highly probable that the pattern obtained through the dynamics of the differential equation of the CNN that takes the results of these data as its initial value will be one of the 4 embedded patterns in Fig.7.5. The illness named by the associated pattern thus obtained is the diagnosis result. In this associative diagnosis by CNN, the complex matrix operation known as singular value decomposition is required. Moreover, the cell states are altered by the differential equations, so that simulation by digital computer

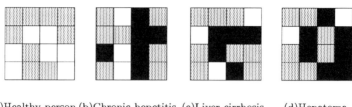

(a)Healthy person (b)Chronic hepetitis (c)Liver cirrhosis (d)Hepatoma

Fig. 7.5   Patterns of four liver diseases

takes some time. In automatic diagnosis, in which huge volumes of data must be processed rapidly, this might be said to be a somewhat fatal weakness. In addition, as long as the CNN is being used, one must be prepared for the danger that isolated cells may arise, as pointed out by Kawabata *et al.*[10]. In the case of associative memory designed by the Liu and Michel, isolated cells are cells that are electrically neutral and are isolated in the cell linkage. When isolated cells arise, classification becomes impossible due to abnormal convergence.

7.3.2   Alteration of the Associatron

In this study, we make inquiries into a classification system that uses the associatron in place of the CNN. The reasons for using the associatron for associative memory are as follows:

(1) Developed as a dedicated associative memory device, it is a medium that sufficiently takes Hebb's law, etc., into account.

(2) Not only is the procedure for embedment and recall simple, recall results can be obtained rapidly.

(3) It is a neural network whose original pattern comes from neurons which already have three values.

The above reasons can be brought up, but one point of caution should be the quantizing function given in Eq.(7.5). In this system, $\phi(x) = 0$ when $x = 0$ is used formally for a kind of softened result that will not strengthen the connections more than is needed by the neurons according to Hebb's law, and to bring the input vector order into agreement. In actuality, in the recall results of the original associatron, neurons almost never become $x = 0$. Accordingly, to obtain a stable three-level recall result, we give the quantizing function (Fig. 7.6) as in Eq.(7.12) below:

$$\phi(x) = \begin{cases} -1 & : x < x_{-1} \\ \frac{x - x_{-0}}{x_{-0} - x_{-1}} & : x_{-1} \leq x \leq x_{-0} \\ 0 & : x_{-0} < x < x_{+0} \\ \frac{x - x_{-0}}{x_{-0} - x_{-1}} & : x_{+0} \leq x \leq x_{+1} \\ 1 & : x > x_{+1} \end{cases} \qquad (7.12)$$

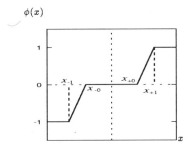

Fig. 7.6 Quantizing function

This form may be said to be the quantizing function given by Nakano[8] extended with a piecewise linear function. In this chapter, we refer to this associatron that positively contains three values as the altered associatron.

7.3.3 Classification rule based on Hamming distance

In association via the associatron, whenever the quantizing function in Eq.(7.12) is given, there is a possibility that the neuron state takes a value other than $-1, 0, 1$; it is possible to obtain a recall result that differs slightly from the embedded pattern. Therefore, in order to clarify into which category classification is to be made, we define the " distance" between the two patterns. The Hamming distance $d_H(x, y)$ between the two nth dimension vectors, $x = (x_1, x_2..., x_n)$ and $y = (y_1, y_2..., y_n)$, is defined in Eq.(7.13):

$$d_H(x, y) \equiv \sum_{i=1}^{n} \delta(x_i, y_i), \qquad (7.13)$$

where

$$\delta(x_i, y_i) = \begin{cases} 0 & : \quad x_i = y_i \\ 1 & : \quad x_i \neq y_i. \end{cases} \quad (7.14)$$

This time we have given the Hamming distance in Eq.(7.15) to express the distance between patterns that take multiple values.

$$d_H^k = \sum_{i=1}^{n} |x_i^k - z_i| (k = 1, 2, ..., m) \quad (7.15)$$

where x^k represents the kth recalled pattern among the m kinds of embedded patterns, and z represents the recall result. In this case, even if we have a piecewise linear continuous function as in Eq.(7.12) for the quantizing function, Eq.(7.15) can still give a measurement for the distance. It compares all the recall results, obtained by multiplying the recalled pattern by the memory matrix, with all the embedded patterns and treats that with the shortest Hamming distance as the recall result. If a value equals to the Hamming distance emerges, it assumes that a recall result has not been obtained.

7.3.4 Design of the classification system

We will use the altered associatron to demonstrate the order in which associative classification occurs. In this section, it is assumed that training data for each category $\{C_1, C_2, ..., C_m\}$ have been given.

i) We create a bitmap pattern to express each category based on the items $\{q_1, q_2, ..., q_n\}$. The size of the pattern is decided so that the pixels will be positioned quadrate as nearly as possible. For example, if the number of items $n = 8$, we will adopt an $n = 9 : 3 \times 3$ bitmap pattern by increasing the number of items from among $\{q_1, q_2, ..., q_n\}$ by the one item that we consider to be the most important. Then we allot each pixel in the pattern to an item. By classifying the level of each item into one of three levels, " small-medium-large," based on the representative value (average value, etc.) of the training data for each category, we allot the elements, -1, 0, 1, respectively, to the above bitmap pattern. When the pattern expressing each category has been allotted in this way, we embed it into the altered associatron. Concretely, we create the memory matrix given in Eq.(7.4).

ii) The m patterns created in i) are typical patterns for each category, and classification occurs if the given characteristic values $q_1^*, q_2^* ..., q_n^*$ recall one of these m patterns. At this time, in order to transform the characteristic value vector $(q_1^*, q_2^*, ..., q_n^*)$ onto the input pattern elements in Eq(7.6), proper scaling is required. Therefore, if the scaling functions are assumed to be $\{f_1, f_2, ..., f_n\}$, it is desirable that these be functions that map the three-level representative values set in i) into -1, 0 and 1 respectively. Thus, now, Eq.(7.16) can be considered as an example giving a function, that is, $f(a) = -1, f(b) = 0, f(c) = 1$, which maps this into -1, 0, 1, in regard to an item for which we assume that representative values are given in three levels, from smallest to largest, a, b, c.

$$f(q) = \begin{cases} 2\left(\dfrac{q-a}{c-a}\right)^p - 1 & : \quad q \geq a \\ -1 & : \quad q < a, \end{cases} \qquad (7.16)$$

where

$$p = \frac{-\log 2}{\log \dfrac{b-a}{c-a}} \qquad (7.17)$$

When $q < a$ in Eq.(7.16), the fact that $f(q) = -1$ is a mathematical restriction of the real exponent function, and even if $f(q) < -1$ is reached using a different function, it will not be supported.

iii) With the above as preparation, it still remains to set the quantizing function $\phi(x)$ in order to apply Eq.(7.8) as $(y_1, y_2, ..., y_n) = \{f_1(q_1^*), f_2(q_2^*), ..., f_n(q_n^*)\}$, and to conduct associative memory, when characteristic values $q_1^*, q_2^*, ..., q_n^*$ is given. There is no other way to do this but to set $x_{-1}, x_{-0}, x_{+0}, x_{+1}$ in Eq.(7.12). In the case of training data, we know the right answer to the classification problem, so we can define the Hamming distance d_H^{k*} of the actually recalled pattern with the pattern that should have been recalled in connection with the characteristic value vector belonging to the category C_k. Taking the sum of all the data belonging to category C_k and further taking the sum total of that through all categories of m number, the following classification performance function can be obtained:

$$S = \sum_{k=1}^{m} \sum d_H^{k*}. \qquad (7.18)$$

When proper classification has taken place through complete recall of all the data for all categories, then $S = 0$. S becomes larger as improper classification increases. Consequently, by requiring $x_{-1}, x_{-0}, x_{+0}, x_{+1}$ which minimizes S, we set the quantizing function accordingly. There is a restriction on these parameters:

$$x_{-1} < x_{-0} < 0 < x_{+0} < x_{+1}$$

In order to reduce the search range, we may set

$$x_{+0} > 0.5,\ x_{+1} \leq 2.0,$$

or,

$$x_{+0} = -x_{-0},\ x_{+1} = -x_{-1}.$$

iv) We calculate the Hamming distance defined in Eq.(7.15) for the pattern for which the altered associatron has carried out association against the data to be classified and the initial pattern that performed the scaling function obtained in ii), and for each of $\{C_1, C_2, ..., C_m\}$, and assume the smallest class as the classification category.

7.4 Example of associative classification using the Associatron

7.4.1 *Application to the problem of iris classification*

We apply this method to Fisher's well-known iris classification problem[11]. The problem is to classify three kinds of irises $\{C_1, C_2, C_3\} = \{setosa, veriscolor, virginica\}$ from four values, petal width and length, sepal width and length. Following the general rule, we create a classification standard using the first 75 data items and then classify and verify the second 75 data items. We apply the order described in 3.4, as follows:

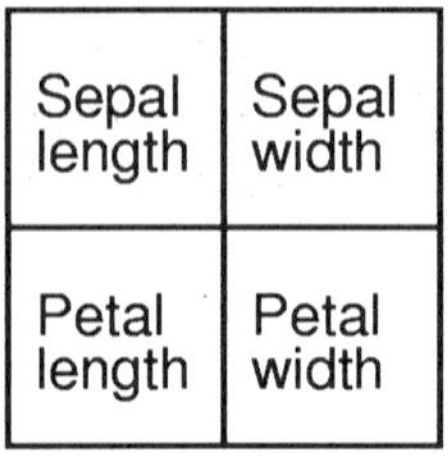

Sepal length	Sepal width
Petal length	Petal width

Fig. 7.7 Associatron for classification of irises

i) It is best to consider a 2 × 2 bitmap pattern to cover the four items, sepal length and width, petal length and width. We consider the neuron allocation shown in Fig. 7.7 as q_1:sepal length, q_2:sepal width, q_3:petal length, q_4:petal width. Next we calculate the average of the individual items in the training data. The result is shown in Table 1. From this, *setosa*, for example, comes out to be q_1:small (-1), q_2:large $(+1)$, q_3:small (-1), q_4:small $(+1)$; the resulting pattern, shown in Fig.7.8 (a), becomes the pattern that expresses *setosa*. Patterns for the other irises are derived in the same fashion. These four patterns are embedded in the altered associatron.

ii) We set the scaling function $\{f_1, f_2, f_3, f_4\}$ based on the values in Table 1. Employing Eq.(7.16), we obtain the value for q_1:

$$f_1(q_1) = \begin{cases} 2\left(\frac{q_1-5.028}{1.548}\right)^{1.53} - 1 & : \quad q_1 \geq 5.028 \\ -1 & : \quad q_1 < 5.028 \end{cases}$$

iii) In order to determine the quantizing function, we conducted the search at 0.1 intervals with the following limiting conditions:

$$x_{+0} = -x_{-0}, x_{+1} = -x_{-1} \tag{7.19}$$

$$x_{+0} < x_{+1} \tag{7.20}$$

$$0.5 \leq x_{+1} \leq 2.0 \tag{7.21}$$

By carrying out associative classification on the pattern transformed by the scaling function in ii), we obtained $x_{+0} = 1.9, x_{+1} = 2.0$ as the x_{+0}, x_{+1} group minimizing Eq.(7.18). Using the above classification system, we verified the second half of the data. The results obtained were no result 0, misclassified 1. In this respect, research results on this official problem using various fuzzy rules and neural nets are detailed in Simpson[12]. In addition, in regard to this problem, Abe and Lan[13] very recently obtained misclassified 2, which was the record at that time.

7.4.2 Application to the diagnosis of liver disease

For reference' sake, in this section, with the intention of direct comparison to associative classification heretofore, we compare its diagnostic ability to methods using CNN. based as much as possible on the methods given by

Kanagawa et al.. Therefore, we used the same allocation and the same sense of each neuron as in the associatron system to which we are making comparison, and we used the embedded pattern in Fig. 7.5 as is. We used the same scaling function as that of Kanagawa et al., and the quantizing function $\phi(x)$ given in Eq.(7.11).

We also used the some verification data as in Kanagawa et al.. Table 2 shows the diagnosis results. The diagnosis sensitivity for hepatoma is far better; we can concretely verify the superiority of the proposed method. We also make comparison to that used fuzzy rules employing the rough set of. The diagnostic sensitivities in [3] are as follows:

Method 1	Method 2
(a) Healthy person ...100%	(a) Healthy person ...100%
(b) Chronic hepatitis ...80%	(b) Chronic hepatitis ...61.5%
(c) Liver cirrhosis ...70%	(c) Liver cirrhosis ...64.7%
(d) Hepatoma ...50%	(d) Hepatoma ...58.8%

Verification methods differ from those in Kanagawa et al.[5], so that direct comparison with the fuzzy rule method is improper, but we can infer the superiority of the proposed method.

7.5 Conclusion

In this chapter, we have proposed a method possessing effective classification properties, employing an extended version of the associatron associative memory device used in the CNN (cellular neural network) of Kanagawa et al. : a classification method by association that has demonstrated its practicality. The particular features of this classification method can be summarized as follows:

(1) Not only are the embedment and recall procedures extremely simple, without the need for complicated matrix calculations as in the CNN, but it also possesses powerful associative [recall] performance. Moreover, recall time is remarkably short in comparison to the CNN.

(2) There is no worry that isolated cells will arise, as in the CNN. By taking into consideration Hebb's law, we were able to obtain more powerful associative [recall] performance. As examples, we applied the proposed method to the iris classification problem and to the liver disease diagnosis problem.

On the iris classification problem, it demonstrated the fact that it can

Table 7.1 Parameters of scaling functions

	sepal length	sepal width	petal length	petal width
setosa	5.028 (a)	3.480 (c)	1.460 (a)	0.248 (a)
versicolor	6.012 (b)	2.776 (a)	4.312 (b)	1.344 (b)
virginica	6.576 (c)	2.928 (b)	5.640 (c)	2.044 (c)
p	1.529812	0.452181	1.813141	1.403431

Table 7.2 Inference results and comparison of the other method

Class	No. of data	No. of rights by proposed method	No. of rights by CNN
healthy person	10	10	10
chronic hepetitis	10	6	6
liver cirrhosis	10	6	4
hepatoma	10	10	5

employ a tremendously superior classification performance of misclassified 1 out of 75 verification data items. In the liver disease example, in comparison to the CNN system, and under exactly the same conditions, it showed a high percentage of rights. Although comparison conditions differed, comparison at the same time with a fuzzy expert system obtained equal or superior results. However, at the present time, there are three values for levels of expression for a single characteristic. As fuzzy systems employ 3-5 levels of fuzzy variables, it can be inferred that the proposed system will have difficulty in dealing with an increase in the number of classes. In this chapter, we introduce an associative classification by associatron.

However, it does not necessarily follow that the use of associatron is best. Recently, Zhang et al.[14] give an efficient CNN associatron memory by making use of optimized saturation function, and demonstrate its effectiveness by diagnosing of liver diseases. Design of optimal classification system is an important subject for the future study.

7.6 Acknowledgment

We are pleased to thank Miss Mitsue Senoo(Matsushita AVC Multimedia Software Co., Ltd.) for her helpful contributions. This research has been supported by the Grand-in-Aid for Sientific Research(C), No. 11680450.

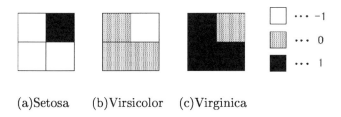

(a)Setosa (b)Virsicolor (c)Virginica

Fig. 7.8 Patterns of three irises

Bibliography

[1] Keller, J. and Hunt, D. (1985) " Incorporating fuzzy membership functions into the perceptron algorithm", *IEEE Trans. Patt. Anal. Mach. Intell.*, **7**, 693.
[2] Ripley,B.D. (1994) " Neural networks and related methods for classification", *J. Royal Statist. Soc. B*, **56**, 409.
[3] Shigenaga, T., Ishibuchi, H. and Tanaka, H. (1993) " Fuzzy inference of expert system based on rough sets and its application to classification problems", *J. of Japan Society for Fuzzy Theory and Systems*, **5**, 358.
[4] Ishibuchi, H., Fujioka, R. and Tanaka, H. (1993) " Neural networks that learn from fuzzy if-then rules", *IEEE Trans. on Fuzzy Systems*, **1**, 85.
[5] Kanagawa, A., Kawabata, H. and Takahashi, H. (1996) " Cellular neural networks with multiple-valued output and its application", *IEICE Trans. on Fundamentals*, **E79-A**, 1658.
[6] Kanagawa, A. Kawabata, H. and Takahashi, H.(1998) " Classification method by using the associative memories in cellular neural networks", Data Science,Classification, and Related Methods, 334, Springer-Verlag Tokyo.
[7] Nakano,K.(1972) " Associatron-a model of associative memory", *IEEE Trans. on Systems Man and Cybernetics*, **2**, 380.
[8] Nakano, K. (1994) Basics of Neuro Computer, Corona, 140.
[9] Liu, D. and Michel, A. (1993) " Cellular neural networks for associative memories", *IEEE Trans. on Circuits Syst. -II*, **40**, 119.
[10] Kawabata, H., Zhang, Z., Kanagawa, A., Takahashi, H. and Kuwaki, H. (1997) " Associative memories in cellular neural networks using a singular value decomposition", *Electronics and Communications in Japan*, Part 3, **80**, 59.
[11] Fisher, R.A.(1936) " The use of multiple measurements in taxonomic problems",*Annals of ugenics*, **7**, Part II, 179.
[12] Simpson R (1992) " Fuzzy min − max neural networks part I classlfication", *IEEE Trans. on Neural Networks*, **3**,776.

[13] Abe S. and Lan. M. (1995) " A method for fuzzy extractlon directly from numerical data and its application to pattern classification" , *IEEE Trans. on Fuzzy Systems*, **3**, 18.

[14] Zhang, Z., Liu, Z. Q. and Kawabata, H.(1999) "Tri-output cellular neural network and its application to diagnosing liver diseases", *Proc. of IEEE SMC*, III, 372

Chapter 8
Recognition of Shapes and Shape Changes in 3D-objects by GRBF Network: A Structural Learning Algorithm to Explore Small-sized Networks

Masahiro Okamoto, Miwako Hirakawa, Noriaki Kinoshita,
Takanori Katsuki, Tetsuya Miyazaki, Masami Ishibashi

Kyushu Institute of Technology

Abstract

Poggio and Edelman have shown that for each object there exists a smooth mapping from an arbitrary view to its standard view and that the mapping can be learnt from a sparse data set. They have demonstrated that such a mapping function can be well approximated by Gaussian GRBF(Genaralized Radial Basis Function) network. In this paper, we have applied this network to the recognition of three kinds of hand shape changes, such as grasp, stroke and flap. Also during learning stage, we have introduced a structural learning algorithm to GRBF network in order to explore the small-sized and essential network structure for the recognition. Finally, we have designed a system to capture motion of the hand with this GRBF by using data glove.

keywords: neural network, 3D-object recognition, flexible objects, Gaussian GRBF, structural learning, data glove, hand-shape change, standard 2D-view, rigid object, regularization theory, radial basis function, artificial intelligence, robot eye, memory-based view, canonical view, snap-shot, interpolation, ill-posed problem, clustering, receptive field, hand's motion capture

8.1 Introduction

Automatic acquisition of 3D models from images is usually a very difficult problem. One way to overcome the need of 3D model is to exploit methods for representing objects by a collection of 2D views (2D projection('snap shots')) rotating 3D object. Poggio and Edelman [1], Edelman and Poggio [2], Poggio [3], Poggio and Girosi [4], and Maruyama et al. [5] have proposed such a view-based object-recognition method named GRBF(Generalized Radial Basis Function) network which relys on multiple 2D views instead of 3D models. This network resembles to the conventional artificial neural network, however, each unit in a hidden layer is represented by radial basis function such as Gaussian. In this paper, we have applied GRBF network to the recognition of shape changes of flexible object; three kinds of hand shape changes such as grasp, stroke and flap. We [6] have also designed structural learning algorithm to explore the small-sized and essential GRBF network structure. We show their performance by computer simulations and by using data glove.

8.2 GRBF network for rigid objects

A Gaussian GRBF network is shown in Figure 8.1, which consists of three layers (input layer + one hidden layer + output layer). Since 3D object is supposed to be a collection of 2D coordinates (perspective view) of the feature points on the image, each 'snap-shot' 2D view is represented as a 2n vector $X_1, Y_1, X_2, Y_2, ..., X_n, Y_n$ of the coordinates on the image plane of n labelled and visible feature points on the object. We assume here that all features are visible. Each basis unit in hidden layer can be represented by Eq.(1), where T_x and T_y are centers of Gaussian functions for X-axis and Y-axis, respectively, m is the number of basis units in hidden layer. The W is supposed to be binding coefficient (weight) between units in input layer and those in hidden layer. The resulting value $G_k(k = 1, 2, .., m)$ can be regarded as the 'activity' of the unit. The output of GRBF network is the linear superposition of the activities of all the basis unit (G_k) in hidden layer as shown in Eq.(2). Since GRBF network is designed to explore the mapping that transforms each 'snap-shot' 2D view to its standard 2D view of the object, the objective function of the network can be written in Eq.(3), where $(X_{st,i}, Y_{st,i})(i = 1, 2, ..., n)$ is standard coordinate of the ith

$$G_k = exp\left(\sum_{i=1}^{n} -(X_i - T_{x_k})^2 W_{k(2i-1)}^2\right)$$
$$\times exp\left(\sum_{i=1}^{n} -(Y_i - T_{y_k})^2 W_{k(2i)}^2\right) \quad (k=1,2,...,m) \quad (1)$$

$$f_j = \sum_{k=1}^{m} C_{k,j} G_k \quad (j=1,2,...,2n) \quad (2)$$

$$E = \sum_{q=1}^{N} \sum_{i=1}^{n} \left((X_{st,i} - f_{2i-1})^2 + (Y_{st,i} - f_{2i})^2\right) \quad (3)$$

$$f_{2n+p+1} = \sum_{k=1}^{m} C_{k,2n+p+1} G_k \quad (p=0,1,..,obj-1) \quad (4)$$

$$H = \sum_{q=1}^{N} \left(\sum_{i=1}^{n} \left((X_{st,i} - f_{2i-1})^2 + (Y_{st,i} - f_{2i})^2\right)\right.$$
$$\left. + A \sum_{p=0}^{obj-1} (F_{st,p} - f_{2n+p+1})^2\right) \quad (5)$$

object, N is the number of learning data set (examples). In order to learn several kinds of 3D objects in one Gaussian GRBF network, teacher flags for recognition of object, $F_{st,i}(i=0,1,...,obj-1)$, were prepared, where obj represents the number of 3D objects to be learnt. For example, suppose three kinds of objects should be learnt, when 2D projection view of the 1st. object is given to the system $(F_{st,0}, F_{st,1}, F_{st,2})$ is set to be $(1,0,0)$. For the case of that 2D projection views of the 2nd. and 3rd. objects are given, $(F_{st,0}, F_{st,1}, F_{st,2})$ will be $(0,1,0)$ and $(0,0,1)$, respectively. In the same manner as in Eq.(2), flag output $(f_{2n+p+1}, (p=0,1,..,obj-1))$ will be calculated according to Eq.(4). In this study, we consider the mean squared error between flag output and teacher flag to define the objective function (H) as in Eq.(5), where A is an arbitrary coefficient.

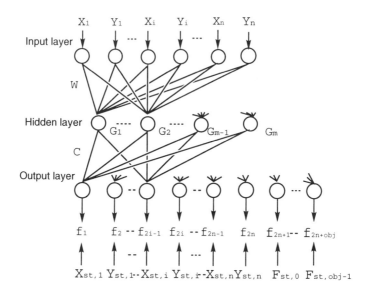

Fig. 8.1 GRBF network structure

8.3 GRBF network for flexible objects

If the shape of a flexible object changes smoothly, the mapping from an arbitrary view of the object to standard view is expected to be synthesized by smooth interpolation of shape-specific mappings. We demonstrate that the mapping which gives the standard view of a flexible object can be synthesized by learing in GRBF network shown in Figure 8.2, where situation 0 and 1 represent arbitrary feature status before shape-changing and the feature status after shape-changing, respectively. The other symbols and definition are the same as in Figure 8.1. In this study, we have applied this Gaussian GRBF network to the recognition of three kinds of hand shape changes, such as grasp, stroke and flap. Figure 8.3 shows wire frame models for hand shape change where situation A represents basic status of hand before shape changing, B, C and D are the status after shape-changing ,where broken lines in B, C and D show basic status A. Grasp can be regarded as $A \to B$ where angle drawn by arrow, α, is 90 degree. Stroke can be regarded as $A \to C$ where angle drawn by arrow, β, is 45 degree. Flap can be shown as the moving $A \to D$ where angle drawn by arrow, γ, is 60 degree. Thus, in learning process, 2D view of status A is given to situation

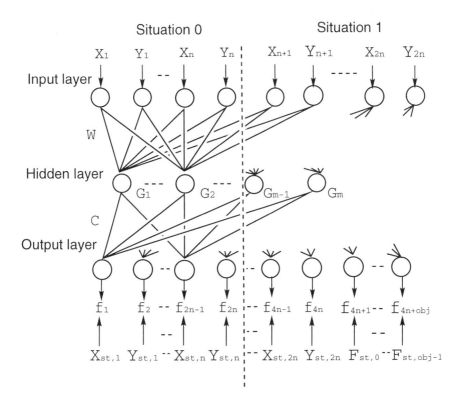

Fig. 8.2 GRBF network structure for the recognition of shape change

0 at input layer and that of B, C or D is given to situation 1 at input layer. The value of teacher flags for recognition, $(F_{st,0}, F_{st,1}, F_{st,2})$, is $(1,0,0)$ for grasp, $(0,1,0)$ for stroke, and $(0,0,1)$ for flap, respectively.

8.4 Structural learning of GRBF network

To use this network, first we have to decide on the number of basis units (m) in the hidden layer. Like most other feedforward network, usually we do not have any guidelines far this and hence learning with trial and error becomes inevitable. The flexibility of GRBF network structure in accordance with the difficulty in recognition of shapes or shape changes should be required. We shall show here a structural learning algorithm which is focused on

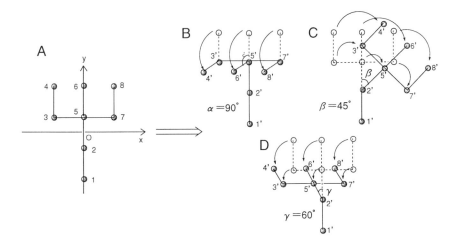

Fig. 8.3 Wire frame models for hand shape change

Table 8.1 Evaluation of normalized error for the recognition of rigid objects

object	ave. of Error* aginst object A-st	ave. of Error* against object B-st	ave. of Error* agianst object C-st
A	0.0151	1.27	1.39
B	1.25	0.0193	1.18
C	1.32	1.14	0.0200

object	flag output $(f_{2n+1}, f_{2n+2}, f_{2n+3})$**	teacher flag $(F_{st,0}, F_{st,1}, F_{st,2})$
A	(0.994, 0.00279, 0.00289)	(1, 0, 0)
B	(-0.00351, 1.00, 0.0237)	(0, 1, 0)
C	(-0.00513, 0.00237, 1.00)	(0, 0, 1)

* the value of Eq.(6), ** average value of 100 2D views

automatic adjustment of the number of basis units in hidden layer. The structural learning method aims at exploring the small-sized and essential network structure enough to recognize 3D shapes or shape changes. In this section, the recognition of three kinds of rigid objects having 8 apexes shown in Figure 8.4 was examined using Gaussian GRBF network shown in Figure 8.1. The algorithm for structural learning is described next:

(1) Set up the number of basis units (m) in hidden layer arbitrary.
(2) Start training (learning) using training data.
(3) If the network can succeed in learning (objective function (H shown in Eq.(5) is converged to a certain threshold value within fixed iterations), proceed to the module for decreasing m (go to step (4)). Otherwise proceed to the module for increasing m (go to step (6)).

(decreasing module)

(4) Initially set the value of k to 1. After cutting off one basis unit in hidden layer (G_k) and all relative connection lines binding to G_k, calculate the value of objective function H_k written in Eq. (5). Repeat this procedure (4) with changing k with increment 1 until $k = m$. Go to step (5).
(5) If k is equal to m, search the minimum value among H_i ($i = 1, 2, .., m$), consider a new network cutting off the ith basis unit (G_i) which provides the minimum value of H. Set m to m-1 and back to (2).

(increasing module)

(6) If training was successful previously, back to the previous trained network structure and proceed to (8) (the module for cutting unnecessary connection lines); the current m-value is determined to be the final number of basis units in hidden layer. Otherwise proceed to (7).
(7) Increase the value of m with α% (m: integer value) and go back to (2).

(cutting unnecessary connection lines)

(8) After determining final number of basis units in hidden layer (m-value), cut the unnecessary connection lines between input layer and hidden layer, and between hidden layer and output layer; cut the connection lines of which weighting coefficient (W and C in GRBF network) has less than a certain absolute threshold value (=cutting-off value).

Efficiency of our algorithm of structural learning was examined with initial value of m (the number of basis units in hidden layer) as 20. The performance of the GRBF network was evaluated by the following normalized error:

$$Error = \frac{\sqrt{\sum_{i=1}^{n} \left((X_{st,i} - f_{2i-1})^2 + (Y_{st,i} - f_{2i})^2\right)}}{\sqrt{\sum_{i=1}^{n} \left((X_{st,i} - g_{xst})^2 + (Y_{st,i} - g_{yst})^2\right)}} \quad (6)$$

where g_{xst} and g_{yst} represent x-coordinate and y-coordinate of the center of gravity in standard 2D view, respectively. The program could automatically decide the final number of m at 11. For fixed m-value at 11, the performance of the Gaussian GRBF network for recognition of rigid objects A, B, and C was calculated by using the normalized error function written in Eq.(6). The results are shown in Table 8.1. With 100 unknown arbitrary 2D views of object A to the GRBF network, the average values of normalized error function against A, B and C were found to be 0.0151, 1.27, 1.39, respectively. Observe that the value against A (object A-st) takes the minimun among them. The average value of flag output ($f_{2n+1}, f_{2n+2}, f_{2n+3}$) is (0.994,0.00279,0.00289), which is very close to the value of the teacher flag for object A(($F_{st,0}, F_{st,1}, F_{st,2}$)=(1, 0, 0)). Setting the absolute threshold value for cutting off of W and C at 1.0e-7 and 9.5, respectively, 62% of con nection lines between input and hidden layers, and 15% of those between hidden and output layers were deleted by our algorithm. Applying 100 unknown arbitrary 2D views of objects A, B, C, one by one to the final trained GRBF network, the correct recognition rate was examined by evaluating the values of flag output. The results are shown in Table 8.2. In the table, for instance, among 100 unknown data, the final trained GRBF network could correctly classify 95 unknown arbitrary 2D views of object A into the object A. Thus the correct recognition rate is 95%. For the remaining 5 unknown data, the network could classify into neither A, B nor C, because the output flag was close to neither (1,0,0), (0,1,0) nor (0,0,1). We should emphasize here the network has not made misclassification. In the same manner, for the cases of objects B and C, the trained GRBF network also showed high capability of recognition over 94%.

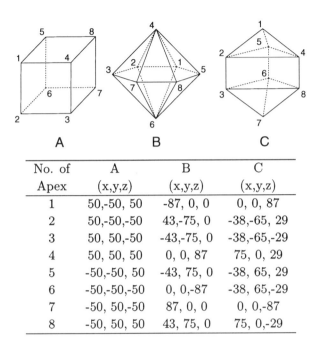

Fig. 8.4 Model of rigid objects having 8 apexes. The lower parts represent coordinate (x,y,z) of each apex.

No. of Apex	A (x,y,z)	B (x,y,z)	C (x,y,z)
1	50,-50, 50	-87, 0, 0	0, 0, 87
2	50,-50,-50	43,-75, 0	-38,-65, 29
3	50, 50,-50	-43,-75, 0	-38,-65,-29
4	50, 50, 50	0, 0, 87	75, 0, 29
5	-50,-50, 50	-43, 75, 0	-38, 65, 29
6	-50,-50,-50	0, 0,-87	-38, 65,-29
7	-50, 50,-50	87, 0, 0	0, 0,-87
8	-50, 50, 50	43, 75, 0	75, 0,-29

Table 8.2 Correct recognition rate for rigid objects

| unknown-object | recognition | | | correct recognition rate |
	object A	object B	object C	
A	95	0	0	95 %
B	0	94	0	94 %
C	0	0	98	98 %

Table 8.3 Evaluation of normalized error for the recognition of hand shape change

shape -change	ave. of Error* against grasp-st	ave. of Error* against stroke-st	ave. of Error* against flap-st
grasp	0.0355	0.563	0.240
stroke	0.600	0.0210	0.608
flap	0.231	0.553	0.0291

shape -change	flag output $(f_{4n+1}, f_{4n+2}, f_{4n+3})^{**}$	teacher flag $(F_{st,0}, F_{st,1}, F_{st,2})$
grasp	(0.982, -0.0178, 0.0454)	(1, 0, 0)
stroke	(0.00420, 0.977, 0.0330)	(0, 1, 0)
flap	(0.0175, -0.0291, 1.02)	(0, 0, 1)

* the value of Eq.(6)(change n to $2n$), ** average value of 100 2D views

Table 8.4 Correct recognition rate for hand shape change

unknown- shape change	recognition			correct recognition rate
	grasp	stroke	flap	
grasp	97	0	0	97 %
stroke	0	97	0	97 %
flap	0	0	98	98 %

8.5 Recognition of hand shape change

As for the hand shape change shown in Figure 8.3, we prepared 20 2D views for each shape change (total 20 × 3=60 sets) as training examples. The values of parameter set, Tx, Tx, W and C were optimized to minimize the value of objective function in Eq.(5) (change n to $2n$). After learning, 100 unknown 2D views (data not being used in learning process) are provided to the Gaussian GRBF network (*Figure* 8.2). Setting the initial guess of the number of basis unit (m) in hidden layer at 20, our program could automatically decide the final number of m at 8. With $m=8$, the performance of the Gaussian GRBF network for recognition of three kinds of flexible objects was calculated by using the normalized error function written in Eq.(6)(change n to $2n$). The results are shown in Table 8.3. Table 8.3 shows the performance of Gaussian GRBF network for recognition of hand shape change. Providing 100 unknown 2D views of grasp to the trained GRBF network, the average normalized errors defined by Eq.(6) against

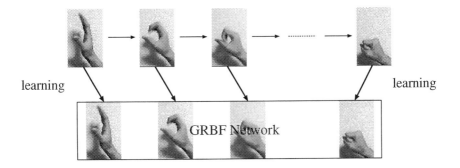

Fig. 8.5 Concept of GRBF network for hand's motion capture

standard 2D views of grasp (grasp-st), stroke (stroke-st) and flap (flap-st) are found to be 0.0355, 0.563, 0.240, respectively. The average value of flag output $(f_{4n+1}, f_{4n+2}, f_{4n+3})$ is (0.982, -0.0178, 0.0454), which is very close to the value of teacher flag for grasp ((1, 0, 0)). In the same manner, the average normalized error against standard 2D view of stroke takes the minimum value (0.0210) when unknown 2D views of stroke are provided. These results show that the Gaussian GRBF network defined by Figure 8.2 can recognize three kinds of hand shape change: grasp, stroke and flap. Setting the absolute threshold value for cutting off W and C at 1.0e-5 and 10.0, respectively, 32% of connection lines between input and hidden layers, and 29% of those between hidden and output layers were deleted by our algorithm. With this reduced net, we used 100 unknown arbitrary 2D views among grasp, stroke and flap, one by one and the correct recognition rate was examined by evaluating the values of flag output. The results are shown in Table 8.4. In the same manner as in Table 8.2, the trained GRBF network showed high capability of recognition for all three kinds of shape changes over 97% and has not made misclassification.

8.6 Hand's motion capture system

In the section 8.3, we described GRBF network for flexible objects as shown in Figure 8.2. Supposing arbitrary feature status before shape changing (situation 0) and the feature status after shape changing (situation 1), 2D coordinates of situations 0 and 1 were given to the input layer in the learning

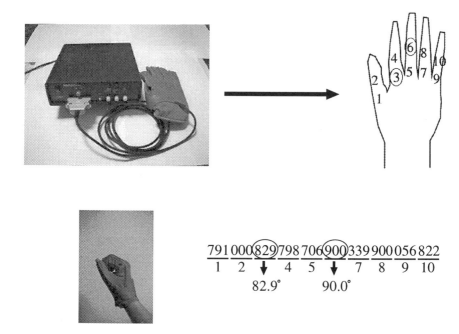

Fig. 8.6 Data globe and joint's position of hand

process. It is obvious that the system in Figure 8.2 cannot be applied to the recognition of more complex hand's motion bacause of lack of input data. Input data are the collection of only two situations (situations 0 and 1). Figure 8.5 shows the sequential motion of grasp. Since sequential motion consists of a lot of frames, we can pick up typical several canonical frames of the motion and those frames can be applied to the GRBF network for learning. In this study, we used data glove (Figure 8.6, Super Glove (Nissho Electronics, Inc., Japan)) to collect the angle information of hand's joints. (see Figure 8.6). After the calibration, this data glove can simultaneously calculate the angle (between 0° and 90°) at 10 joints of one hand at an arbitrary frame and can send those angle data to a computer through RS-232C. These data are fed to the GRBF system shown in Figure 8.1, where n=5 and $X_1, Y_1, X_2, Y_2, ..., X_5, Y_5$ represent angle information of 10 joints, respectively. As an example Y_1 and Y_5 show the angle data at the joints 2 and 10 in Figure 8.6, respectively. At a certain frame of hand

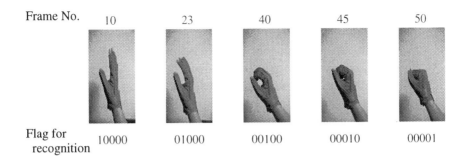

Fig. 8.7 Teacher frames and flags for recognition

motion shown in Figure 8.6, the angle data at joints 3 and 6 are 82.9° and 90.0°, respectively. Suppose one motion, such as grasp, consists of sequential 50 frames and 5 such frames (in this study, frame number, 10, 23, 40, 45 and 50 (see Figure 8.7)) are picked up among them for learning. We set up 5 kinds of flag for recognition (teacher flag) as shown in Figure 8.7. The flag number 10000 is assigned to the frame number 10, 01000 is to the frame number 23, 00100 is to the frame 40, 00010 is to the frame 45, 00001 is to the frame 50. Preparing 6 sets of angle data of 10 joints at frame 1 to 50 and picking up the data at the frame number 10, 23, 40, 45 and 50 from them, 5 sets of angle data were applied to learning of GRBF network and the remaining 1 set of angle data was used for standard angle of this motion (teacher angle). The learning procedures are the same as in section 8.2 (GRBF network for rigid objects). After the learning, 100 sets of unknown angle data, frame by frame (from frame 1 to 50), were applied to the final trained GRBF network, the correct recognition score was examined by evaluating the order of the values of flag outputs. If the order of the resulting flag output is 10000 → 01000 → 00100 → 00010 → 00001, this motion can be regarded as the template hand motion ('grasp' in this case). The trained GRBF network could acheive a recognition over 84%.

8.7 Conclusions

1) Structural learning algorithm to explore the small-sized GRBF network structure was designed.

2) The designed GRBF network was applied to the recognition of rigid and flexible 3D-objects.
3) The minimum number of basis units in hidden layer enough to recognize, was automatically decided.
4) After deletion of unnecessary connection links between hidden and output layers, the final small-sized GRBF network showed high recognition capability over 94%.
5) Using the glove data to generate angle data of hand's joints, we could design a system to capture hand's motion.

Acknowledgement

This study was supported by Grant-in-Aid for Scientific Research C from the Ministry of Education, Science, Sports and Culture, Japan $No.10680387$.

References

[1] Poggio T. and Edelman S., (1990), "A network that learns to recognize 3D objects", *Nature*, **343**, pp.263-266.

[2] Edelman S. and Poggio T., (1990), "Bringing the grandmother back into the picture: a memorybased view of object recognition", *MIT AI Lab. Memo*, No.1181.

[3] Poggio T., (1990), "A theory of how the brain might work", *MIT AI Lab. Memo*, No.1253.

[4] Poggio T. and Girosi, F., (1990), "Regularization algorithms for learning that are equivalent to multilayer networks", *Science*, **247**, pp.978-982.

[5] Maruyama, M., Teraoka, T., Abe, S., (1994), "Recognition of 3D flexible objects by GRBF", *Biological Cybernetics*, **70**, pp.377-385.

[6] Kinoshita, K., Katsuki, T., Miyazaki, T., Hirakawa, M., Okamoto, M., (1998), "Recognition of shape and shape-changes in 3D objects by GRBF network", *Proc. of 3rd. Int. Symp. on Artificial Life and Robotics (AROB III'98)*, **1**, pp.228-233.

Chapter 9
Non-linear Discriminant Analysis Using Feed-forward Neural Networks

Takashi Koshimizu[1], and Masaaki Tsujitani[2]
[1] *Bayer Yakuhin, Ltd.*
[2] *Osaka Electro-Communication University*

Abstract

Neural computing has emerged as a practical and powerful tool for "nonlinear" multivariate statistical analysis. In this paper, nonlinear discriminant analysis using a neural network is considered and applied to a medical diagnosis problem. The probabilistic interpretation of the network output is discussed in classification problems. The principle of the likelihood in network models is employed based on a probabilistic approach regarding the connection weights of the network as unknown parameters, and the maximum likelihood estimators of outputs are also introduced. Additionally, statistical techniques are formulated in terms of the principle of the likelihood of network models. The statistical tools for the inference illustrated here include *i*) deviance to evaluate the goodness-of-fit of a network model, *ii*) selection of the best fit model among several competing network models, and *iii*) likelihood-ratio chi-square statistics for pruning of neural network parameters and selection of a "best" subset of predictor variables.

Keywords : feed-forward neural network, nonlinear discriminat analysis, Kullback-Leibler measure, AIC, cross-entropy, likelihood ratio statistic, deviance, medical classification, pruning, information compression

9.1 Introduction

Feed-forward neural networks, also known as multi-layer perceptrons, are now widely applied to many classification problems such as pattern recognition [3, 19], speech recognition, diagnostic image analysis, molecular modeling [7], clinical diagnosis [21], prediction of action for new cancer drugs [25] and survival data analysis [8].

As a learning procedure for feed-forward neural networks, the back-propagation algorithm was introduced [20]. In the case of classification problems, several modifications to the back-propagation method such as the maximum likelihood approach and alternative cost functions have been suggested in previous work [4, 12, 15, 23]. In principle, these algorithms have been developed for obtaining the maximum likelihood estimators of network outputs. Richard and Lippmann [17] showed the relationship between network outputs and Bayesian *a posteriori* probabilities and that Bayesian probabilities are estimated when desired network outputs use the 1-of-M target coding scheme and the sum-of-squares error or cross-entropy cost function is used.

In recent years, alternatively, neural computing techniques have received increasing attention from statisticians. White [26] showed some limiting properties of the back-propagation technique. Gish [9] took a probabilistic view of neural networks to derive the maximum likelihood estimators for binary classification data. Ripley [18] presented the basic ideas of the neural network and provided some comparisons with standard statistical techniques, and Cheng and Titterington [6] reviewed neural networks from a statistical point of view. As a result, neural computing has emerged as a practical and powerful tool for "nonlinear" multivariate statistical analysis. Many papers have discussed problems which arise in dimensionality reduction or in information compression, comparing neural networks with the conventional statistical methods such as discriminant analysis, principal component analysis and so on. For optimizing the architecture of a neural network, one approach is to remove connections gradually by use of second derivatives or penalty functions, which is known as *pruning algorithm* [5, 11, 13, 14, 22].

The objective of this paper is to derive a nonlinear discriminant analysis using a feed-forward neural network, which is closely related to statistical pattern recognition, and apply it to classification problems in medical fields. We first discuss the probabilistic interpretation of a network output in a two-class problem. The principle of the likelihood in network models is introduced based on a probabilistic approach regarding connection weights of the network as unknown parameters, and the maximum likelihood estimators (MLE) of outputs are also introduced. We clarify the relationship between the sum-of-squares error function and the Kullback-Leibler measure. The statistical inference is also formulated in terms of the likelihood of networks. The statistical tools for the inference presented here include *i*) *deviance* to evaluate the goodness-of-fit of a network model, *ii*) selection of the best fit model among several competing network models using Akaike's [1] Information

Criterion (AIC), and *iii*) the likelihood-ratio chi-square statistics to test a null hypothesis for neural network parameters and for selection of a "best" subset of predictor variables.

9.2 Neural Discriminant Analysis

9.2.1 Model Building for Two Classes

An example of a feed-forward neural network with a single hidden layer for two-class problem is shown in Fig. 9.1. There are I input variables $x_1, \cdots, x_I$; one hidden layer with H neurons and one neuron in the output layer. The connection weight vector between the i-th unit in the input layer ($i = 1, \cdots, I$) and the j-th unit in the hidden layer ($j = 1, \cdots, H$), is $\alpha_j = (\alpha_{0j}, \alpha_{1j}, \cdots, \alpha_{Ij})^T$, where α_{0j} is a bias. Similarly, the weight vector connected to the output unit is $\beta = (\beta_0, \beta_1, \cdots, \beta_H)^T$, where β_0 is a bias.

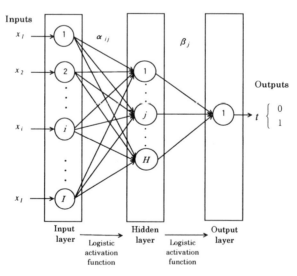

Fig. 9.1   Feed-forward neural network for a two-class problem

The input to the j-th hidden unit is a linear projection of the input vector $x^{<d>} = \left(1, x_1^{<d>}, \cdots, x_I^{<d>}\right)$ for the d-th case, i.e.,

$$u_j = \sum_{i=0}^{I} \alpha_{ij} x_i .$$

The output of the hidden unit is

$$y_j = f(u_j) = f\left(\sum_{i=0}^{I} \alpha_{ij} x_i\right)$$

where $f(\cdot)$ is a nonlinear activation function. The most commonly used activation function is the logistic sigmoid function

$$f(u_j) = \frac{1}{1 + \exp(-u_j)} .$$

The input to output unit is

$$v = \sum_{j=0}^{H} \beta_j y_j$$

and the output is

$$o = g(v) = g\left(\sum_{j=0}^{H} \beta_j y_j\right)$$

where $g(\cdot)$ is an alternative nonlinear activation function. When the logistic sigmoid function is used for $f(\cdot)$ and $g(\cdot)$, the functional representation of the output from the neural network for a given input vector x is

$$o(x; \alpha, \beta) = g\left(\sum_{j=0}^{H} \beta_j \cdot f\left(\sum_{i=0}^{I} \alpha_{ij} x_i\right)\right) = \frac{1}{1 + \exp\left(-\sum_{j=0}^{H} \beta_j \frac{1}{1 + \exp\left(-\sum_{i=0}^{I} \alpha_{ij} x_i\right)}\right)} \quad (1)$$

where α, β denote the vectors of unknown parameters. The number of parameters included in the function (1) is $p=H(I+1)+H+1$.

In a two-class problem, the task is to assign an input vector x to one of class C_k ($k=1,2$). Using Bayes' theorem, the posterior probability of membership of class C_1 can be written as

$$P(C_1 \mid x) = \frac{P(x \mid C_1)P(C_1)}{P(x \mid C_1)P(C_1) + P(x \mid C_2)P(C_2)} \qquad (2)$$

where $P(x \mid C_k)$ is the likelihood or conditional probability of the input vector if the class is C_k, and $P(C_k)$ is the prior probability of C_k. Neural network outputs closely estimate Bayesian posterior probabilities when the desired outputs are a 1-of-K target coding scheme and an appropriate cost function such as the sum-of-squares cost function or cross-entropy cost function is used [17]. The sum-of-squares error function has been frequently used. With this error function, the network parameters are estimated by minimizing

$$E = \frac{1}{2} \sum_{d=1}^{D} \left\{ o^{<d>} - t^{<d>} \right\}^2 \qquad (3)$$

where this desired output $t^{<d>}$ is called a target value in the neural network context. In case of the sum-of-squares error function, we assume that the distribution of the target data can be defined by a smooth deterministic function, added with normally distributed noise,

$$t = z(x) + \varepsilon, \quad \varepsilon \sim N(0, \sigma^2), \qquad (4)$$

and seek to model $z(x)$, with outputs $E(t^{<d>} \mid x) \equiv o^{<d>}(x; \alpha, \beta)$, which maximize the likelihood function. The principle of this maximum likelihood method is based on the assumption of normally distributed target data. For classification problems, however, the targets are binary variables, and the normally distributed noise model does not provide a good description of their distribution. A more appropriate choice of error function is needed [3]. When a input vector, $x^{<d>} = \left(x_1^{<d>}, x_2^{<d>}, \cdots, x_I^{<d>}\right)$, $d = 1, \cdots, D$, is given in two-class problem, an output of a classifier, $o^{<d>} = o^{<d>}(x; \alpha, \beta)$, is viewed as an estimators of the conditional probability that target value for $x^{<d>}$ is 1,

$$P\{t^{<d>} = 1 | x^{<d>}\} \cong o^{<d>}.$$

The conditional probability that target value is 0 is given by

$$P\{t^{<d>} = 0 | x^{<d>}\} \cong 1 - o^{<d>}.$$

With this interpretation of network outputs, we can present a particular case of the binomial distribution, called the Bernoulli distribution

$$f(t^{<d>}) = \{o^{<d>}\}^{t^{<d>}} \{1 - o^{<d>}\}^{1-t^{<d>}}. \tag{5}$$

The variance of this distribution can be given by

$$Var[t^{<d>}] = o^{<d>}(1 - o^{<d>}). \tag{6}$$

Assuming that data are drawn independently from the distribution, the likelihood of observing the training data set $t = \left(t^{<1>}, t^{<2>}, \cdots, t^{<D>}\right)^T$ and $x = \left(x^{<1>}, x^{<2>}, \cdots, x^{<D>}\right)^T$ is given by

$$L(\alpha, \beta; x, t) = \prod_{d=1}^{D} \{o^{<d>}\}^{t^{<d>}} \{1 - o^{<d>}\}^{1-t^{<d>}}. \tag{7}$$

The logarithm of the likelihood is written in the form

$$\ln L(\alpha, \beta; x, t) = \sum_{d=1}^{D} \{t^{<d>} \ln o^{<d>} + (1 - t^{<d>}) \ln(1 - o^{<d>})\}. \tag{8}$$

Consequently, the estimated outputs, $\hat{o}^{<d>}$, (i.e., the connection weights, $\hat{\alpha}_{ij}, \hat{\beta}_j$) are the maximum likelihood estimators of these parameters provided we compute α and β maximizing (8). The negative logarithm of the likelihood is cross-entropy error function [10, 12, 23].

$$F(\alpha, \beta) = -\sum_{d=1}^{D} \left\{ t^{<d>} \ln o^{<d>} + \left(1 - t^{<d>}\right) \ln\left(1 - o^{<d>}\right) \right\}. \tag{9}$$

The Kullback-Leibler measure

$$I(t;o) = \sum_{d=1}^{D} \left\{ t^{<d>} \ln\left(\frac{t^{<d>}}{o^{<d>}}\right) + \left(1 - t^{<d>}\right) \ln\left(\frac{1 - t^{<d>}}{1 - o^{<d>}}\right) \right\} \tag{10}$$

may be expanded explicitly as

$$\begin{aligned}
\sum_{d=1}^{D} &\left\{ t^{<d>} \ln\left(\frac{t^{<d>}}{o^{<d>}}\right) + \left(1 - t^{<d>}\right) \ln\left(\frac{1 - t^{<d>}}{1 - o^{<d>}}\right) \right\} \\
&= \underbrace{-\sum_{d=1}^{D} \left\{ t^{<d>} \ln\left(\frac{1}{t^{<d>}}\right) + \left(1 - t^{<d>}\right) \ln\left(\frac{1}{1 - t^{<d>}}\right) \right\}}_{\equiv -\ln L(\max)} \\
&\quad + \underbrace{\left[-\sum_{d=1}^{D} \left\{ t^{<d>} \ln o^{<d>} + \left(1 - t^{<d>}\right) \ln\left(1 - o^{<d>}\right) \right\} \right]}_{F(\alpha,\beta) \equiv -\ln L(\alpha, \beta; x, t)}
\end{aligned} \tag{11}$$

Since the first term of the right side in (11), which depends on only $t^{<d>}$, is constant, the smaller second term, i.e. the cross-entropy, yields the smaller Kullback-Leibler measure. Maximizing the logarithm of the likelihood function corresponds to minimizing the cross-entropy error function and minimizing the Kullback-Leibler measure [15]. The outputs are good estimators of the conditional expectation of target values.

The Kullback-Leibler measure also has a relationship with the sum-of-squares error function as in Theorem 1.

Theorem 1. The Kullback-Leibler measure is approximately equivalent to the sum-of-squares error function with the weighting factor of the reciprocal of the variance of Bernoulli distribution according to

$$\sum_{d=1}^{D}\left\{t^{<d>}\ln\left(\frac{t^{<d>}}{o^{<d>}}\right)+\left(1-t^{<d>}\right)\ln\left(\frac{1-t^{<d>}}{1-o^{<d>}}\right)\right\} \quad (12)$$

$$\cong \frac{1}{2}\sum_{d=1}^{D}\left\{\frac{1}{o^{<d>}\left(1-o^{<d>}\right)}\left(t^{<d>}-o^{<d>}\right)^{2}\right\}$$

Proof. Using the formula,

$$s\ln\left(\frac{s}{t}\right) \cong (s-t) + \frac{1}{2}\frac{(s-t)^{2}}{t} + \cdots,$$

we have that

$$\sum_{d=1}^{D}\left\{t^{<d>}\ln\left(\frac{t^{<d>}}{o^{<d>}}\right)+\left(1-t^{<d>}\right)\ln\left(\frac{1-t^{<d>}}{1-o^{<d>}}\right)\right\}$$

$$= \sum_{d=1}^{D}\left[\left(t^{<d>}-o^{<d>}\right)+\frac{1}{2}\frac{\left(t^{<d>}-o^{<d>}\right)^{2}}{o^{<d>}}+\left(1-t^{<d>}-1+o^{<d>}\right)+\frac{1}{2}\frac{\left(1-t^{<d>}-1+o^{<d>}\right)^{2}}{1-o^{<d>}}\right]$$

$$\cong \frac{1}{2}\sum_{d=1}^{D}\left\{\frac{\left(t^{<d>}-o^{<d>}\right)^{2}}{o^{<d>}\left(1-o^{<d>}\right)}\right\} = \frac{1}{2}\sum_{d=1}^{D}\left\{\frac{1}{o^{<d>}\left(1-o^{<d>}\right)}\left(t^{<d>}-o^{<d>}\right)^{2}\right\} \quad \text{(Q.E.D.)}$$

9.2.2 Model Building for Multiple Independent Attributes

In the classification problems, which we have discussed in the previous section, the aim of the classification is to assign new vectors to one of two mutually exclusive classes. However, in some applications we may wish to use a network to determine the probabilities of presence or absence of a number of attributes, which need not be mutually exclusive. In this case the network has multiple outputs and the value of output $o_k^{<d>}$ represents the probability that the k-th attribute is present. A neural network model with a single hidden layer for multiple independent attributes is illustrated in Fig. 9.2.

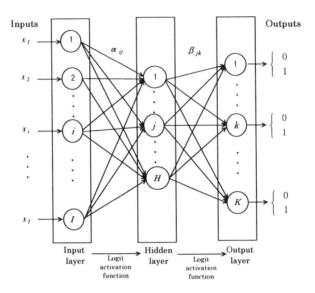

Fig. 9.2 Feed-forward neural network for a multiple independent attributes

In this case, the weight vector connected from the hidden unit to the k-th output unit is $\beta_k = (\beta_{0k}, \beta_{1k}, \cdots, \beta_{Hk})^T$, where β_{0k} is a bias. The input from hidden unit to the k-th output unit is

$$v_k = \sum_{j=0}^{H} \beta_{jk} y_j$$

and the output is formulated as

$$o_k = g(v_k) = g\left(\sum_{j=0}^{H} \beta_{jk} y_j\right)$$

where $g(\cdot)$ is an nonlinear activation function, the logistic sigmoid function, commonly used in the previous section. The number of parameters included in the feed-forward neural network model here is $p=H(I+K)+H+K$. If we treat the K attributes as independent, we can use the product Bernoulli distribution

$$f(t^{<d>}) = \prod_{k=1}^{K} \{o_k^{<d>}\}^{t_k^{<d>}} \{1-o_k^{<d>}\}^{1-t_k^{<d>}}. \tag{13}$$

The variance of this distribution can be given by

$$Var[t_k^{<d>}] = o_k^{<d>}(1-o_k^{<d>}).$$

The likelihood function of the training data for the k-th output unit is thus given by

$$L(\alpha,\beta;x,t) = \prod_{d=1}^{D}\prod_{k=1}^{K} \{o_k^{<d>}\}^{t_k^{<d>}} \{1-o_k^{<d>}\}^{1-t_k^{<d>}}. \tag{14}$$

The logarithm of the likelihood is written in the form

$$\ln L(\alpha,\beta;x,t) = \sum_{d=1}^{D}\sum_{k=1}^{K} \{t_k^{<d>}\ln o_k^{<d>} + (1-t_k^{<d>})\ln(1-o_k^{<d>})\}, \tag{15}$$

and the cross-entropy error function for multiple independent attributes is expressed as

$$F(\alpha,\beta) = -\sum_{d=1}^{D}\sum_{k=1}^{K} \{t_k^{<d>}\ln o_k^{<d>} + (1-t_k^{<d>})\ln(1-o_k^{<d>})\}. \tag{16}$$

Theorem 1 can be extended as

$$\sum_{d=1}^{D}\sum_{k=1}^{K} \left\{ t_k^{<d>}\ln\left(\frac{t_k^{<d>}}{o_k^{<d>}}\right) + (1-t_k^{<d>})\ln\left(\frac{1-t_k^{<d>}}{1-o_k^{<d>}}\right) \right\}$$
$$\cong \frac{1}{2}\sum_{d=1}^{D}\sum_{k=1}^{K} \left\{ \frac{1}{o_k^{<d>}(1-o_k^{<d>})}(t_k^{<d>}-o_k^{<d>})^2 \right\} \tag{17}$$

We now derive the back-propagation algorithm for a feed-forward network with multiple independent outputs. We can apply the chain rule for partial derivatives to give

$$\frac{\partial F^{<d>}(\alpha,\beta)}{\partial \beta_{jk}} = \frac{\partial F^{<d>}(\alpha,\beta)}{\partial o_k^{<d>}} \frac{\partial o_k^{<d>}}{\partial \beta_{jk}} \tag{18}$$
$$= \frac{o_k^{<d>}-t_k^{<d>}}{o_k^{<d>}(1-o_k^{<d>})} o_k^{<d>}(1-o_k^{<d>})y_j = (o_k^{<d>}-t_k^{<d>})y_j.$$

9.2.3 Model Building for Multiple Classes

We now return to conventional classification problems which involve mutually exclusive classes when the number of classes is greater than two. A neural network model for multiple classes is shown in Fig. 9.3. Consider the output o_k for each class and target data, which has a 1-of-K target coding scheme. In a multple classification problem, the task is to assign an input vector x to one of class C_k (k=1,...,K). Using Bayes theorem, the posterior probability of membership of class C_k can be written in the form

$$P(C_k \mid x) = \frac{P(x \mid C_k) P(C_k)}{\sum_{k=1}^{K} P(x \mid C_k) P(C_k)}$$

where $P(x \mid C_k)$ is the likelihood or the conditional probability of the input vector if the class is C_k. Neural network outputs closely estimate Bayesian posterior probabilities when the desired outputs are 1-of-K target coding scheme [17].

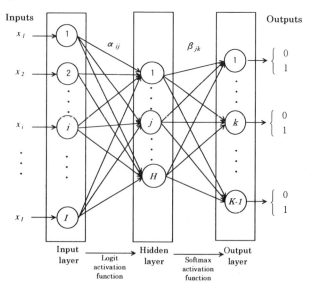

Fig. 9.3   Feed-forward neural network for a multiple classes

The value of the conditional distribution for the pattern can be written as

$$f(t^{<d>}) = \prod_{k=1}^{K} \{o_k^{<d>}\}^{t_k^{<d>}}. \qquad (19)$$

The cross-entropy function is in the form

$$F(\alpha,\beta) = -\sum_{d=1}^{D}\sum_{k=1}^{K}\{t_k^{<d>}\ln o_k^{<d>}\} \qquad (20)$$

and the Kullback-Leibler measure is given as

$$I(t;o) = \sum_{d=1}^{D}\sum_{k=1}^{K}\left\{t_k^{<d>}\ln\left(\frac{t_k^{<d>}}{o_k^{<d>}}\right)\right\}. \qquad (21)$$

The number of parameters included in the feed-forward neural network model here is $p=H(I+K-1)+H+K-1$. We next consider the functional representation of neural network models for the multiple classes. Since the logistic sigmoid function is used for the input to the j-th hidden unit

$$u_j = \sum_{i=0}^{I}\alpha_{ij}x_i, \qquad (22)$$

the output of the hidden unit is expressed as

$$y_j = \frac{1}{1+\exp(-u_j)}. \qquad (23)$$

The input to the k-th output unit is

$$v_k = \sum_{j=0}^{H}\beta_{jk}y_j. \qquad (24)$$

The activation function of network outputs for the multiple classes can be achieved by using the *softmax* activation (normalized exponetial) function. The softmax activation function can be regarded as a generalization of the logistic function, since it can be written in the form,

$$o_k = \frac{\exp(v_k^{<d>})}{\sum_{k=1}^{K}\exp(v_k^{<d>})} = \frac{1}{1+\exp(-V_k)} \qquad (25)$$

where V_k is given by

$$V_k = v_k - \ln\left\{\sum_{k'\neq k}^{K}\exp(v_{k'})\right\}.$$

In evaluating the derivatives of the softmax activation function, we obtain

$$\frac{\partial F^{<d>}(\alpha, \beta)}{\partial \beta_{jk}} = \left(o_k^{<d>} - t_k^{<d>}\right) y_j,$$

which is the same result for multiple independent classes with the use of the logistic activation function [3, 4].

9.2.4 Statistical Inference

Introducing the maximum likelihood principle into the neural network models, the deviance allows us to test the goodness-of-fit of the neural network models;

$$Dev = 2\left[\ln L(max) - \ln L(\alpha, \beta; x, t)\right] \sim \chi^2_{D-p} \quad (26)$$

where $\ln L(max)$ denotes the maximum log likelihood in a saturated model, which has as many parameters as observations and provides a perfect fit to the data, and $\ln L(\alpha, \beta; x, t)$ denotes that in the applied neural network model, respectively. The deviance has the same form as the G^2 likelihood-ratio statistic for the goodness-of-fit of the model. The degrees of freedom, $D-p$, equal the difference between the number of independent observations and the number of parameters (connection weights and biases) in the neural network model. The greater the deviance, the poor the model fits. The deviance is seen to be equivalent to twice the Kullback-Leibler measure,

$$Dev = 2 \times I(t;o).$$

The likelihood-ratio test is a general method of testing a null hypothesis against an alternative hypothesis. For two neural network models M_1 and M_2, suppose that M_1, which has the parameters $\alpha_{j_1} = (\alpha_{0j}, \alpha_{1j}, \cdots, \alpha_{Ij_1})^T$ and $\beta_1 = (\beta_0, \beta_1, \cdots, \beta_{J_1})^T$, is a special case of M_2, which has the parameters $\alpha_{j_2} = (\alpha_{0j}, \alpha_{1j}, \cdots, \alpha_{Ij_2})^T$ and $\beta_2 = (\beta_0, \beta_1, \cdots, \beta_{J_2})^T$. The deviances for M_1

and M_2 are $G^2(M_1) = -2(L_1 - L_s)$ and $G^2(M_2) = -2(L_2 - L_s)$ where L_i and L_s denote the maximum likelihood under model M_i and the maximum likelihood in the saturated model, respectively. Giving that M_2 holds, we can denote the likelihood-ratio statistic for testing whether certain parameters in M_2, but not in M_1, equal zero by $G^2(M_1|M_2)$. The statistic for comparing these two models equals

$$G^2(M_1|M_2) = -2(L_1 - L_2) = -2(L_1 - L_s) - \{-2(L_2 - L_s)\} \\ = G^2(M_1) - G^2(M_2). \tag{27}$$

One can therefore compare two neural network models by comparing their deviances. $G^2(M_1|M_2)$ is a large-sample chi-squared statistic. The degrees of freedom equal the number of additional non-redundant parameters that are in M_2 but not in M_1.

In conventional statistics, various criteria have been developed for assessing the generalization performance. Akaike's information criterion (AIC) helps us to decide which of several competing network architectures is "best" for a given problem:

$$AIC = -2\ln L(\alpha, \beta; x, t) + 2p, \tag{28}$$

where p is the number of parameters in the neural network model and the AIC approach selects the model with minimum value of (28).

The likelihood-ratio test method and the AIC approach presented in this section can be applied to a variety of tasks in the maximum likelihood-based neural network models, such as selection of the best subset of predictor variables, pruning of connection weights, and pruning of input or hidden units.

9.3 Application

9.3.1 Application for Two-class Classification

We used a data set on the physical characteristics of urine with and without crystals [2] illustrated in Tab. 9.1. The data set consists of 79 urine specimens, which are analyzed to determine if certain physical characteristics of the urine might be related to the formation of calcium oxalate crystals. The six physical characteristics of urine are (1) specific gravity x_1, (2) pH, the negative logarithm of the hydrogen ion x_2, (3) osmolarity (mOsm) x_3, (4) conductivity (milliMho) x_4, (5) urea concentration in millimoles per liter x_5, and (6) calcium concentration in millimoles per liter x_6. Feed-forward neural network models with a single hidden layer are applied to the data set of 77 observations by omitting two observations with missing data.

Tab. 9.1 Data presentation of the physical characteristics of urine with and without crystals

Patient No.	Specific gravity x_1	pH x_2	Osmolarity (mOsm) x_3	Conductivity (milliMho) x_4	Urea concentration x_5	Calcium concentration x_6	Crystals
1	1.017	5.74	577	20.0	296	4.49	no crystal
2	1.008	7.20	321	14.9	101	2.36	no crystal
:	:	:	:	:	:	:	:
44	1.020	5.68	876	35.8	308	4.49	no crystal
45	1.021	5.94	774	27.9	325	6.96	crystal
:	:	:	:	:	:	:	:
77	1.015	6.03	416	12.8	178	9.39	crystal

We firstly fitted a neural network model to the data by minimizing the sum-of-squares error function (3). The distribution of the residuals is clearly non-normal as shown in Fig. 9.4. It indicates that the assumption of the normally distributed noises is no longer appropriate in a classification problem.

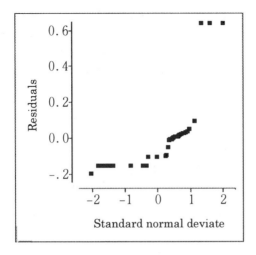

Fig. 9.4 Normal probability plot of residuals in the neural network model with the sum-of-squares error function

(1) *Determination of the Number of Hidden Units*

The neural network model as shown in Fig. 9.5 was applied to the data using the maximum likelihood to yield the estimators of the unknown parameters α and β. Some results for models with various hidden units are given in Tab. 9.2. Since the addition of hidden units introduces a rapid increase in the number of parameters in the neural network model, over-fitting of the data may occur. We may use AIC to select a model with the most appropriate number of hidden units, which is statistically called "parsimonious model".

Inspecting of Tab. 9.2 reveals that the neural network models with two to six hidden units fit the data very well. Comparing AIC values for each neural network model, the model with two hidden units yields AIC of 102.87, the minimum value among five neural network models. This indicates that the neural network with two hidden units is the most appropriate. Although the neural network model with more than four-hidden units yielded only one misclassification, the increase in AIC values for these models indicated that over-parameterization may be induced. For the purpose of comparison, we also applied the linear discriminant function, the quadratic discriminant function, the logistic discriminant function and the tree-based classification method [24]. The numbers of misclassifications were 13, 13 12 and 11, respectively. There was a decrease in the number of misclassifications by neural network models, comparing them to those of other conventional statistical techniques.

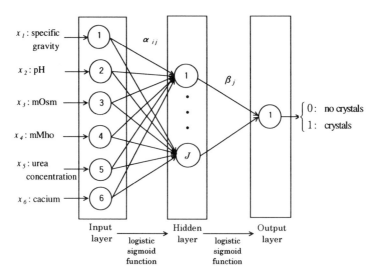

Fig. 9.5   Neural network model for the data set of physical characteristics of urine with and without crystals

Tab. 9.2   Summary results obtained using the neural network models

	The number of the hidden units				
	2	3	4	5	6
Log-likelihood	-34.43	-33.79	-29.41	-28.42	-25.98
Number of parameters	17	25	33	41	49
AIC	102.87	117.57	124.82	138.84	149.96
Deviance	18.80	17.51	8.76	6.78	1.90
Number of missclassifications	7	7	3	1	1

(2) *Selection of Best Subset of Predictor Variables*

Suppose that we test $H_0: \alpha' = 0$, where α' denotes a subset of model parameters (weights connected from a predictor variable to hidden units) in order to evaluate the magnitude of the contribution of each predictor variable to the neural network model. Tab. 9.3 indicates the results using the likelihood-ratio statistic for a neural network with two-hidden units.

The likelihood-ratio statistic of 11.66 for x_6, corresponding to a p-value of 0.003, provides strong evidence that the weight parameters connected from the input unit of x_6 are not zero. Alternatively, the likelihood-ratio statistic of 2.42 for x_4, corresponding to p-value of 0.298, reveals that the null hypothesis of the weight parameters connected from the input unit of x_4 being zero is not rejected.

Tab. 9.3 Likelihood-ratio tests for each predictor variable

Predictor variable	Likelihood-ratio statistic	d.f.	p-value
x_1 :specific gravity	3.60	2	0.166
x_2 :pH	6.45	2	0.040
x_3 :osmolarity	6.27	2	0.044
x_4 :conductivity	2.42	2	0.298
x_5 :urea concentration	4.31	2	0.116
x_6 :calcium concentration	11.66	2	0.003

We now intend to select a "best" subset of six predictor variables, focusing on the statistically significant changes of the likelihood-ratio statistic when applying a simpler model.

Since there are a number of subsets of six predictor variables, a backward eliminating procedure based on the likelihood-ratio test approach is employed as follows;

Step 1: At the k-th stage of the algorithm, remove an i-th ($1 \leq i \leq I - k + 1$) predictor variable among $I - k + 1$ predictor variables and train the neural network with the remainder subset of I-k variables.

Step 2: Compute each $\Delta\text{Dev}_{(i)}$ for the neural network model when removing the i-th variable, comparing with Dev for the neural network model with I-k+I variables.

Step 3: If $\min\{\Delta\text{Dev}_{(1)}, \cdots, \Delta\text{Dev}_{(l-k)}\} < \chi_2^2(\alpha)$ at each successive stage, eliminate the corresponding predictor variable and return to *Step 1* at the $(k+1)$th stage.

Tab. 9.4 summarizes the results obtained using the neural network models with subsets of predictor variables in the above procedure. AIC values for each model are also presented. In this case it is considered to be statistically significant at α level of 0.15.

Fig. 9.6 shows the process of selecting the subsets of predictor variables at each stage in the backward eliminating procedure. We finally selected the subset $\{x_1, x_3, x_6\}$, which was considered to be "best". The smallest AIC value of 93.99 was also obtained for the model with the subset $\{x_1, x_3, x_6\}$. Seven misclassifications still remained in the neural network, while a rapid increase to fourteen misclassifications was found in the linear discriminant function with the predictor variables $\{x_1, x_3, x_6\}$.

Tab. 9.4 The log-likelihood and AIC for neural network models with subsets of six predictor variables

Subsets of predictor variables	Log-likelihood	Number of parameters	Deviance	ΔDev		AIC
x_1,x_2,x_3,x_4,x_5,x_6	-34.43	17	18.80			102.87
x_1,x_2,x_3,x_4,x_5	-40.26	15	30.46	11.66		110.52
x_1,x_2,x_3,x_4,x_6	-36.59	15	23.11	4.31		103.17
x_1,x_2,x_3,x_5,x_6	-35.65	15	21.23	2.42	$<\chi^2_2(0.15)$	101.29
x_1,x_2,x_4,x_5,x_6	-37.57	15	25.07	6.27		105.13
x_1,x_3,x_4,x_5,x_6	-37.66	15	25.25	6.45		105.32
x_2,x_3,x_4,x_5,x_6	-36.23	15	22.40	3.60		102.46
x_1,x_2,x_3,x_5	-37.20	13	24.34	3.11		100.40
x_1,x_2,x_3,x_6	-37.87	13	25.67	4.45		101.74
x_1,x_2,x_5,x_6	-37.09	13	24.11	2.88		100.17
x_1,x_3,x_5,x_6	-35.74	13	21.42	0.19	$<\chi^2_2(0.15)$	97.48
x_2,x_3,x_5,x_6	-39.32	13	28.58	7.36		104.65
x_1,x_3,x_5	-41.84	11	33.63	12.20		105.69
x_1,x_3,x_6	-35.99	11	21.92	0.50	$<\chi^2_2(0.15)$	93.99
x_1,x_5,x_6	-38.05	11	26.04	4.62		98.11
x_3,x_5,x_6	-39.54	11	29.03	7.61		101.09
x_1,x_3	-45.13	9	40.19	18.26		108.25
x_1,x_6	-40.09	9	30.11	8.18	$>\chi^2_2(0.15)$	98.17
x_3,x_6	-42.85	9	35.63	13.71		103.69

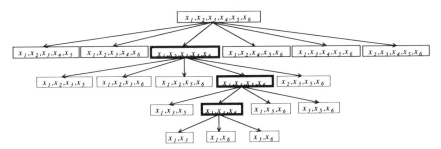

Fig 9.6 Summary of the process of the backward eliminating procedure

9.3.2 Application for Multiple-class Classification

We have applied a feed-forward neural network with a single hidden layer to the data set on the diabetes classification [2] shown in Tab. 9.5. The data set consists of 145 non-obese individuals, who were divided into three groups (overt diabetes, chemical diabetes and normal) on the basis of conventional clinical criteria. Overt diabetes group was defined as having fasting hyper glycaemia (plasma glucose levels in excess of 110mg/dl). The remaining subjects were subdivided into two groups. Chemical diabetes group is those with plasma glucose levels greater than 185mg/dl and 140mg/dl at one and two hours after the glucose load, and others were defined as normal group. The three variables used for the analysis are area under the curve of plasma glucose for the three-hour oral glucose tolerance test (OGTT) x_1, area under the curve of the plasma insulin area the three-hour OGTT x_2 and the steady-state plasma glucose (SSPG) x_3. These variables are the measures of glucose intolerance, insulin response to oral glucose and insulin resistance, respectively. Reaven and Miller [16] originally analyzed using these three variables in order to examine the relationship between chemical diabetes and overt diabetes.

Tab. 9.5   Data presentation of the diabetes classification

Subject No.	Glucose area x_1	Insulin area x_2	SSPG x_3	Classification
1	356	124	55	Normal
2	289	117	76	Normal
⋮	⋮	⋮	⋮	⋮
85	465	237	111	Chemical diabetes
⋮	⋮	⋮	⋮	⋮
113	1468	28	455	Overt diabetes
⋮	⋮	⋮	⋮	⋮
145	1568	15	243	Overt diabetes

The neural network model as shown in Fig. 9.7 is fitted to the data set using the maximum likelihood method to yield the estimate of the unknown parameters α and β. In the neural network model, the outputs for overt diabetes group, chemical diabetes group and normal group represent $(t_1,t_2)=(1,0)$, $(t_1,t_2)=(0,1)$ and $(t_1,t_2)=(0,0)$, respectively.

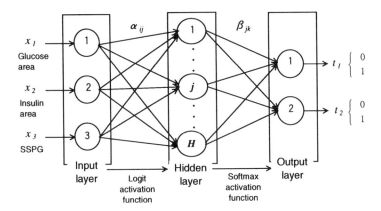

Fig. 9.7 Feed-forward neural network model for the diabetes classification data

(1) *Determination of the Number of Hidden Units*

The results when applying the neural network model with hidden units from one to eight are given in Tab. 9.6. The deviances suggest that a neural network model with two or more hidden units works fairly well. AIC by the proposed method is derived from the maximum log-likelihood of multinomial distribution and AIC with sum-of-squares is computed from the sum-of-squares error function under the assumption of the normally distributed error. Focusing the magnitude of the AIC values by the proposed method, the minimum value of AIC is obtained at the model with two hidden units and AIC values increase monotonically as the number of hidden units increases. Based on these results, the optimal number of hidden units is considered to be two. Concerning another AIC, which is computed from the sum-of-squares, we don't have any insights into the determination of the hidden units. The behavior of two types of AIC calculated after fitting the model with from one to eight hidden units is illustrated in Fig. 9.8.

Tab. 9.6   Summary results obtained using the neural network model for the diabetes classification data

	The number of hidden units							
	1	2	3	4	5	6	7	8
A I C (Proposed method)	191.23	152.06	163.86	171.61	182.99	192.78	204.70	214.66
A I C (Sum-of-squares)	-133.61	-529.32	-747.72	-709.10	-868.03	-713.24	-824.05	-875.15
Deviance	60.85	9.68	9.48	5.24	4.62	2.41	2.32	0.29
(d.f.)	(137)	(131)	(125)	(119)	(113)	(107)	(101)	(95)
Number of missclassifications	11	2	2	2	0	0	0	0

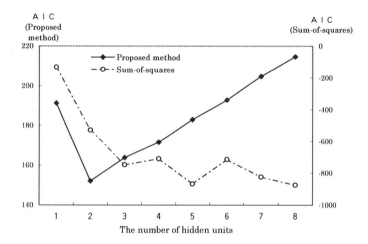

Fig. 9.8   Behavior of AIC by the proposed method and AIC based on the sum-of-squares.

(2) *Pruning of connection weights*

The complexity of a network model does not always achieve the best performance on new data not used for training. It can be optimized by removing redundant connections through "*pruning*". Network pruning allows us to 1) extract some rules from a network with small number of connections, and 2) achieve a higher accuracy on new patterns [22].

Consider the effect of a connection weight to be pruned. The likelihood-ratio test approach for testing null hypothesis, $H_0 : \alpha_{ij} = 0$ uses the test statistic

$$2\left[\ln L(\hat{\alpha},\hat{\beta};x,t)-\ln L(\hat{\alpha}',\hat{\beta};x,t)\right] \sim \chi_1^2$$

where $\ln L(\hat{\alpha},\hat{\beta};x,t)$ is the log likelihood with parameters $\theta=\{\alpha,\beta\}$, $\ln L(\hat{\alpha}',\hat{\beta};x,t)$ is the log likelihood with parameters θ' from which α_{ij} is excluded. Our pruning algorithm based on the likelihood-ratio test approach is presented as follows;

1) Specify a network model with ˘, and train this network until predetermined accuracy rate.
2) Remove each connection weight and train this network with parameters θ' until predetermined accuracy rate.
3) If $\min\left|2\left[\ln L(\hat{\theta};x,t)-\ln L(\hat{\theta}';x,t)\right]\right| < \chi_1^2(\alpha)$,

   remove the corresponding connection weight and return to 1). If no weight satisfies, retain the network with ˘.

The results of the weights pruning in the model with two hidden units based on the proposed algorithm are illustrated in Tab. 9.7. In this case, $\alpha=0.15$ is considered to be appropriate. We finally obtained the pruned network model as shown in Fig. 9.9.

Tab. 9.7 The results of pruning connection weights

Connection weight to be pruned		Likelihood-ratio chi-square statistic			
		Step1	Step2	Step3	Step4
α_{ij}	1→1	9.756	47.324	46.808	45.144
	1→2	9.756	9.968	46.808	48.734
	2→1	0.302	-	-	-
	2→2	0.524	0.524	-	-
	3→1	2.068	1.780	1.802	6.398
	3→2	2.068	2.313	1.802	-
β_{jk}	1→1	3.344	3.262	3.330	8.040
	1→2	3.556	3.714	3.694	8.216
	2→1	3.344	3.630	3.330	3.192
	2→2	3.556	3.758	3.694	3.568

$\chi_1^2(0.15)=2.07$

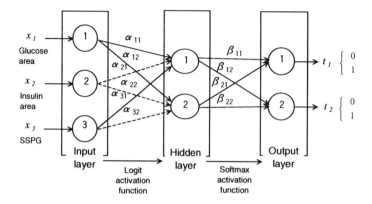

Fig. 9.9 Pruned neural network model with two hidden units

(3) *Information compression*
A method to interpret some relationship of multivariate data may be a visualization of the data. It allows us to reduce the dimension of the information and do the graphical presentation of the data. Using formula (22), we shall define the compression score as the linear combination of predictor variables expressed as

$$\hat{u}_j = \sum_{i=0}^{I} \hat{\alpha}_{ij} x_i .$$

It may be a similar technique to the canonical scores in the multi-dimensional canonical analysis. Two dimensional plots of the compression scores, $\hat{u}_1$ and $\hat{u}_2$, is given in Fig. 9.10, when applying the neural network with two hidden units. For reference, two dimensional plots of the canonical scores in the linear canonical analysis is also shown in Fig. 9.11. Inspecting the distributions of the compression scores, it is considered that the non-linear neural network model classifies the data among the three groups fairly well. On the other hand, the distributions of the canonical scores in the linear canonical analysis are not fully classified among the three groups.

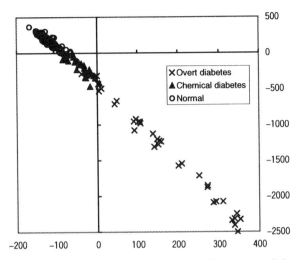

Fig. 9.10 Two dimensional plots of the compression scores of the neural network with two hidden units

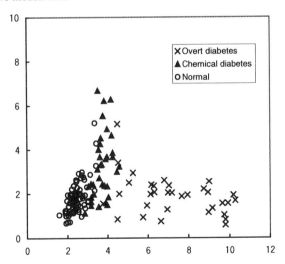

Fig. 9.11 Two dimensional plots of the canonical scores in the linear canonical discriminant analysis

9.4 Conclusion

We introduced the probabilistic interpretation of a network output and constructed the maximum likelihood principle of the network models based on the probabilistic approach in classification problems. We also discussed the learning algorithm by maximizing the log likelihood function, that is, minimizing the cross-entropy error function and minimizing the Kullback-Leibler measure We then derived the theorem of the relationship of two types of error function, i.e., the sum-of-squares error function and the Kullback-Leibler measure. Statistical inference based on the likelihood approach on the network models was formulated by using the deviance, the likelihood-ratio test statistic. We suggested the use of AIC based on the likelihood of the discrete distribution, an alternative to AIC with the sum-of-squares, for determination of the appropriate number of hidden units. In medical classification problems, we developed the pruning algorithm of the connection weights using the likelihood-ratio statistic in order to test the significance of the connection weights. We also showed the procedure with the likelihood-ratio statistic for selecting the best subset of predictor variables. From the point of dimensionality reduction, we presented the relationship between the discriminant analysis and the feed-forward neural networks used for classification. Similar technique for the canonical scores in the multi-dimensional canonical discriminant analysis, we derived the compression scores as the linear combination of predictor variables. It allows us to reduce the dimensions of the information due to graphical presentation of the data.

References

[1] Akaike, H., "Information Theory and An Extension of the Maximum Likelihood Principle", in *Proceedings of the 2nd International Symposium on Information Theory*, eds. B.N. Petrov and F. Caski, Akademiai Kiado, Budapest, pp.267-281, 1973.

[2] Andrews, D.F., Herzberg, A.M., "Data -A Collection of Problems from Many Fields for the Student and Research Worker-", Springer-Verlag, 1985.

[3] Bishop, C.M., "Neural Networks for Pattern Recognition", Clarendon Press, 1995.

[4] Bridle, J.S., "Probabilistic Interpretation of Feed-forward Classification Network Outputs, with Relationships to Statistical Pattern Recognition", in Soulié, F.F. and Hérault, J., (eds) *Neurocomputing: Algorithms, Architectures and Applications*, pp.227-236, 1990.

[5] Buntine, W.L., Weigend, A.S., "Computing Second Derivatives in Feed-forward Networks: A review", *IEEE Transaction on Neural Networks*, **5**, pp.480-488, 1994.

[6] Cheng, B., Titterington, D.M., "Neural Networks: A Review from Statistical Perspective", *Statistical Science*, **9**, (1), pp.2-54, 1994.

[7] Devillers, J., "Neural Networks in QSAR and Drug Design", Academic Press, 1996.

[8] Faraggi, D., Simon, R., "A Neural Network for Survival Data", *Statistics in Medicine*, **14**, pp.73-82, 1995.

[9] Gish, H., "Maximum Likelihood Training of Neural Networks", in Hand, D.J., (eds) *Artificial Intelligence Frontiers in Statistics*, 241-255, Chapman and Hall, 1993.

[10] Hampshire, J.B., Pelmutter, B.A., "Equivalence Proofs for Multi-layer Perceptron Classifiers and the Bayesian Discriminant Function", *Proceedings of the 1990 Connectionist Models Summer School*, pp.159-172, 1990.

[11] Hassibi, B., Stork, D.G., "Second Order Derivatives for Network Pruning: Optimal Brain Surgeon", in *Advanced in Neural Information Processing Systems*, 5, Morgan Kaufmann, San Mateo CA, pp.164-171, 1993.

[12] Hinton, G.E., "Connectionist Learning Procedure", *Artificial Intelligence*, **40**, pp.185-234, 1989.

[13] Kapur, J.N., Kesavan, H.K., "Entropy Optimization Principles with Applications", Academic Press, 1992.

[14] Le Cun, Y., Denker, J.S., Solla, S.A., "Optimal Brain Damage", in *Advanced in Neural Information Processing Systems*, 2, Morgan Kaufmann, San Mateo CA,

pp.598-605, 1990.
[15] Ooyen, A.V., Nienhuis, B., "Improving the Convergence of Back-propagation Algorithm", *Neural Networks,* **5**, pp.465-471, 1992.
[16] Reaven, G.M., Miller, R.G, "An Attempt to Define the Nature of Chemical Diabetes Using A Multidimensional Analysis", *Diabetologia,* **16**, pp.17-24, 1979.
[17] Richard, M.D., Lippmann, R.P., "Neural Network Classifiers Estimate Bayesian A Posteriori Probabilities", *Neural Computation,* **3**, pp.461-483, 1991.
[18] Ripley, B.D., "Neural Networks and Related Methods for Classification", *Journal of the Royal Statistical Society,* B **56**, (3), pp.409-456, 1994.
[19] Ripley, B.D., "Pattern Recognition and Neural Networks", Cambridge University Press, 1996.
[20] Rumelhart, D.E., Hinton, G.E., Williams, R.J., "Learning Internal Representations by Error Propagation", in *Parallel Distributed Processing,* **1**, pp.318-362, 1986.
[21] Setiono, R., "Extracting Rules from Pruned Neural Networks for Breast Cancer Diagnosis", *Artificial Intelligence in Medicine,* **8**, pp.37-51, 1996.
[22] Setiono, R., "A Penalty-function Approach for Pruning Feed-forward Neural Networks", *Neural Computation,* **9**, pp.185-204, 1997.
[23] Solla, S.A., Levin, E., Fleisher, M., "Accelerated Learning in Layered Neural Networks", *Complex Systems,* **2**, pp.625-640, 1988.
[24] Venables, W.N., Ripley, B.D., "Modern Applied Statistics with S-PLUS", Springer-Verlag, 1997.
[25] Weinstein, J.N., Kohn, K.W., Grever, M.R., Viswanadhan, V.N., Rubinstein, L.V., Monks, A.P., Scudiero, D.A., Welch, L., Koutsoukos, A.D., Chiausa, A.J., Paull, K.D., "Neural Computing in Cancer Drug Development: Predicting Mechanism of Action", *Science,* 258, pp.447-451, 1992.
[26] White, H., "Learning in Artificial Neural Networks: A Statistical Perspective", *Neural Computation,* **1**, pp.425-464, 1989.

Chapter 10
Minimizing the Measurement Cost in the Classification of New Samples by Neural-Network-Based Classifiers

Hisao Ishibuchi and Manabu Nii

Osaka Prefecture University

Abstract

In this chapter, we show that the measurement of all attribute values is not always necessary when new patterns are classified by trained neural networks. We assume that a neural network with n input units has already been trained for an n-dimensional pattern classification problem. Our goal is to reduce the average (or expected) number of attributes that are to be measured for classifying new patterns by the trained neural network. Our task is different from the feature selection because the number of measured attributes for classifying each new pattern is not the same. That is, some patterns can be classified by a few attributes while other patterns require the measurement of all the n attributes. Our interval-arithmetic-based approach, in which each unmeasured attribute is represented by an interval that includes its possible values, tries to reduce the number of attributes to be measured with no deterioration of the classification performance.

Keywords : pattern classification, neural networks, back-propagation algorithm, input selection, measurement cost, measurement order, incomplete information, interval arithmetic, inclusion monotonicity, excess width, subdivision method

10.1 Introduction

In classification methods based on decision trees [1, 2], all attributes are not always measured for classifying new patterns. Some patterns are classified by a few attributes while others require the measurement of many attributes. On the contrary, usually all input values are to be measured for classifying new patterns by trained neural networks [3]. While pruning and feature selection techniques [4–7] have the ability to reduce the number of input units of neural networks in the learning phase, the measurement of all input values of pruned neural networks is necessary for classifying new patterns. That is, the number of attributes to be measured in the classification phase is the same as the number of input units of trained (or pruned) neural networks. Let us consider a pattern classification problem in Fig.10.1 where the classification boundary by a trained neural network is shown together with training patterns from three classes. In this pattern classification problem, we need both attribute values (i.e., x_1 and x_2) for the classification task. If we remove x_2, the classification between Class 2 and Class 3 becomes impossible. Thus we have to use a neural network with two input units. The classification boundary depicted in Fig.10.1 was obtained after the learning of a three-layer feedforward neural network with two input units, five hidden units, and three output units.

While two input units are necessary for the classification task in Fig.10.1, we can reduce the number of measurements in the classification phase by measuring the two attribute values in the order of $x_1 \to x_2$. If x_1 of a new pattern is smaller than 0.5, we can see from Fig.10.1 that the new pattern is classified as Class 1 without measuring x_2. On the other hand, we have to measure x_2 if x_1 is not smaller than 0.5. In this manner, we can reduce the average (or expected) number of measurements in the classification phase for new patterns by the trained neural network. This simple example suggests that we have to specify two procedures for decreasing the number of measurements. One procedure is related to the determination of the order of attributes to be measured. In Fig.10.1, we can not decrease the number of measurements if the attribute value x_2 is measured first. The other procedure is related to the classification of new patterns based on partial information. In Fig.10.1, we can see that a new pattern is classified as Class 1 without measuring x_2 if x_1 is smaller than 0.5. Usually, the classification of new patterns based on partial information is not so easy especially in the case of high-dimensional problems.

In our former work [8], we proposed an interval-arithmetic-based approach for determining the order of attributes to be measured. Interval-arithmetic-based neural networks were also used for the learning from interval data [9] and the modelling of interval systems [10]. The aim of this chapter is to clearly demonstrate that our approach can significantly decrease the average number of measurements in the classification phase by computer simulations on real-world pattern classification problems. In this chapter, we first formulate a minimization problem of the measurement

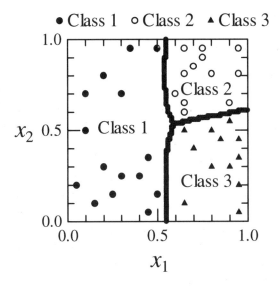

Fig. 10.1 Classification boundary and training patterns.

cost for new patterns where the cost for each measurement is added to the formulation in our former work [8]. Next we propose a procedure for determining the measurement order of attributes to minimize the measurement cost. In our approach, each unmeasured attribute is represented by an interval that includes its possible values. In this manner, all the possible values of each unmeasured attribute can be taken into account when a new pattern is classified. A new pattern with unmeasured attributes is denoted by an interval vector, which is presented to the trained neural network. The classification of the new pattern is based on the corresponding interval output vector from the trained neural network, which is calculated by interval arithmetic [11–14]. Our approach tries to reduce the number of attributes to be measured with no deterioration of the classification performance on new patterns. Then we illustrate how a subdivision method [12] in interval arithmetic can be utilized in our approach. Finally we show simulation results on some real-world pattern classification problems for demonstrating the ability of our approach to decrease the number of attributes to be measured. Our computer simulations also examine the effectiveness of the subdivision method.

10.2 Problem Formulation

10.2.1 Assumptions

In this chapter, we assume that a multi-layer feedforward neural network with n input units has already been trained by a set of training patterns. While we explain our approach using a three-layer feedforward neural network, it is easy to extend our approach to the case of neural networks with four or more layers. Limitation of our approach is that the activation function in the trained neural network should be monotonic. It is not impossible to extend our approach to the case of non-monotonic activation functions as in radial basis function networks. Such extension, however, involves complicated calculations when interval input vectors are presented to neural networks. Thus we restrict the application of our approach within feedforward neural networks with monotonic activation functions.

We also assume that we have a set of new patterns $\mathbf{x}_p$, $p = 1, 2, \ldots, m_{\text{new}}$ to be classified by the trained neural network where $\mathbf{x}_p$ is an n-dimensional vector $\mathbf{x}_p = (x_{p1}, \ldots, x_{pn})$ and m_{new} is the total number of the given new patterns. It should be noted that no element of $\mathbf{x}_p = (x_{p1}, \ldots, x_{pn})$ has been measured at first. Our goal is to minimize the total measurement cost by decreasing the number of attributes to be measured for classifying each new pattern. Let us denote the set of the n attributes by $\{a_1, a_2, \ldots, a_n\}$, and the measurement cost of a_i by c_i. In this notation, x_{pi} is the attribute value of the i-th attribute a_i of the p-th new pattern $\mathbf{x}_p$.

When the measurement cost of every attribute is negligible, our effort to decrease the number of measured attributes does not make sense. The significance of such effort totally depends on the measurement cost. We believe that there are many application areas where the measurement cost is high.

10.2.2 Objective Function

Let $\pi = (\pi_1, \pi_2, \ldots, \pi_n)$ be the measurement order of the given n attributes where $\pi_i \in \{a_1, a_2, \ldots, a_n\}$, $i = 1, 2, \ldots, n$. That is, π is a permutation of the n attributes. In the classification phase, attribute values of each new pattern are measured in the order of π. When the first attribute π_1 is measured, we examine whether the new pattern is classifiable by the trained neural network based on only the attribute value of π_1. A mechanism for checking the classifiability is explained in the next section. If the new pattern is classifiable, the other attributes of this pattern are not measured. On the other hand, if the new pattern is not classifiable based on the attribute value of π_1, the next attribute π_2 is measured. Then we examine whether the new pattern is classifiable by the trained neural network based on the attribute values of π_1 and π_2. This procedure is iterated for each new pattern until it becomes classifiable by the trained neural network.

Let $\phi(\pi, p)$ be the number of measured attributes of the p-th new pattern $\mathbf{x}_p = (x_{p1}, \ldots, x_{pn})$ when the measurement is performed in the order of π. That is, the first $\phi(\pi, p)$ attributes $\{\pi_1, \pi_2, \ldots, \pi_{\phi(\pi,p)}\}$ are measured and the other attributes $\{\pi_{\phi(\pi,p)+1}, \ldots, \pi_n\}$ are not measured for classifying $\mathbf{x}_p$. Thus the measurement cost for classifying $\mathbf{x}_p$ is written as follows:

$$C(\pi, p) = \sum_{i=1}^{\phi(\pi,p)} c_{\pi_i}, \tag{1}$$

where c_{π_i} is the measurement cost of the attribute π_i. The total measurement cost for classifying the given set of new patterns is

$$C(\pi) = \sum_{p=1}^{m_{\text{new}}} C(\pi, p) = \sum_{p=1}^{m_{\text{new}}} \sum_{i=1}^{\phi(\pi,p)} c_{\pi_i}, \tag{2}$$

where m_{new} is the number of the given new patterns. Our task is to determine the order π of the n attributes for minimizing the total measurement cost $C(\pi)$.

When the measurement cost c_i for each attribute is the same (e.g., $c_i = 1$ for $i = 1, 2, \ldots, n$), the total measurement cost $C(\pi)$ can be written as

$$C(\pi) = \sum_{p=1}^{m_{\text{new}}} C(\pi, p) = \sum_{p=1}^{m_{\text{new}}} \phi(\pi, p). \tag{3}$$

In this case, $C(\pi)$ is the total number of measured attribute values for classifying the m_{new} new patterns.

10.3 Classification of New Patterns

10.3.1 Interval Representation

The attribute values of each new pattern are denoted by an n-dimensional vector $\mathbf{x}_p = (x_{p1}, \ldots, x_{pn})$. It should be noted that no attribute values x_{pi}'s have been measured at first. The attribute values are measured in the order of $\pi = (\pi_1, \pi_2, \ldots, \pi_n)$. So some attribute values are measured, and others are not measured when $\mathbf{x}_p$ is classified in the classification phase. This means that the n-dimensional vector $\mathbf{x}_p = (x_{p1}, \ldots, x_{pn})$ is not complete. We denote this incomplete vector by an interval vector $\mathbf{X}_p = (X_{p1}, \ldots, X_{pn})$. When the attribute value x_{pi} is measured, the interval X_{pi} has no width:

$$X_{pi} = [x_{pi}, x_{pi}] \quad \text{if } x_{pi} \text{ is measured.} \tag{4}$$

On the other hand, when the attribute value x_{pi} is not measured, X_{pi} is specified so as to include all the possible values of x_{pi}. In computer simulations of this chapter, all the attribute values were normalized in the unit interval [0,1]. Thus we used the unit interval for unmeasured attributes:

$$X_{pi} = [0, 1] \quad \text{if } x_{pi} \text{ is not measured.} \tag{5}$$

10.3.2 Neural Network for Interval Input Vectors

When we try to classify the p-th new pattern based on incomplete information, we present the interval input vector $\mathbf{X}_p = (X_{p1}, \ldots, X_{pn})$ to the trained neural network. The input-output relation of each unit can be written for the interval input vector as follows [8]:

$$\text{Input units}: \quad O_{pi} = X_{pi}, \quad i = 1, 2, \ldots, n. \tag{6}$$

$$\text{Hidden units}: \quad Net_{pj} = \sum_{i=1}^{n} O_{pi} \cdot w_{ji} + \theta_j, \quad j = 1, 2, \ldots, n_H. \tag{7}$$

$$O_{pj} = f(Net_{pj}), \quad j = 1, 2, \ldots, n_H. \tag{8}$$

$$\text{Output units}: \quad Net_{pk} = \sum_{j=1}^{n_H} O_{pj} \cdot w_{kj} + \theta_k, \quad k = 1, 2, \ldots, c. \tag{9}$$

$$O_{pk} = f(Net_{pk}), \quad k = 1, 2, \ldots, c. \tag{10}$$

This input-output relation is the same as the standard three-layer feedforward neural network except that the inputs X_{pi}, Net_{pj}, Net_{pk} and the outputs O_{pi}, O_{pj}, O_{pk} are intervals. As shown in (6)-(10), we denote real numbers and intervals by lowercase letters (e.g., i, j, k, w_{ji}, θ_j) and uppercase letters (e.g., X_{pi}, O_{pi}), respectively.

An interval is usually represented by its lower limit and upper limit as $A = [a^L, a^U]$ where the superscripts "L" and "U" indicate the lower limit and upper limit, respectively. The interval $A = [a^L, a^U]$ is formally defined as

$$A = [a^L, a^U] = \{x \mid a^L \leq x \leq a^U, x \in \Re\}. \tag{11}$$

The calculation of the input-output relation of each unit in (6)-(10) is performed by interval arithmetic [11–14]. In (6)-(10), we use the following operations on intervals:

$$A + B = [a^L, a^U] + [b^L, b^U] = [a^L + b^L, a^U + b^U], \tag{12}$$

$$a \cdot B = a \cdot [b^L, b^U] = \begin{cases} [a \cdot b^L, a \cdot b^U], & \text{if } a \geq 0, \\ [a \cdot b^U, a \cdot b^L], & \text{if } a < 0, \end{cases} \tag{13}$$

$$f(A) = f([a^L, a^U]) = [f(a^L), f(a^U)], \tag{14}$$

where (14) is valid only when the activation function $f(\cdot)$ is a monotonically increasing function. When $f(\cdot)$ is not monotonic, we can not simply calculate its input-output relation for interval inputs. In this chapter, we use the following sigmoidal activation function $f(\cdot)$ as in many studies on standard feedforward neural networks:

$$f(x) = \frac{1}{1 + \exp(-x)}. \tag{15}$$

We illustrate the nonlinear mapping of an interval by the sigmoidal activation function $f(\cdot)$ in Fig.10.2.

10.3.3 Classification Procedure

We assume that the classification of each new pattern is done by a single winner output. When all the n attribute values are measured, the complete n-dimensional input vector $\mathbf{x}_p = (x_{p1}, \ldots, x_{pn})$ is presented to the trained

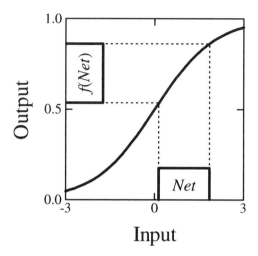

Fig. 10.2 Illustration of the mapping of intervals by the sigmoidal activation function.

neural network. Then the corresponding output vector $\mathbf{o}_p = (o_{p1}, \ldots, o_{pc})$ is calculated. In this case, the new pattern $\mathbf{x}_p$ is classified as Class h that satisfies the following relation (i.e., the h-th output is the winner):

$$o_{pk} < o_{ph} \quad \text{for } k = 1, 2, \ldots, c \; (k \neq h). \tag{16}$$

The classification boundary in Fig.10.1 was drawn based on the classification rule with (16).

Our problem is to determine whether Class h in (16) can be identified based on the partial information included in the interval input vector $\mathbf{X}$. If Class h in (16) can be identified, the measurement of the other attributes is not necessary. On the contrary, if Class h in (16) can not be identified, the next attribute is measured according to the measurement order π.

From the inclusion monotonicity of interval arithmetic [11–14], we can see that the relation in (16) always holds if the following relation holds for the interval output vector $\mathbf{O}_p = (O_{p1}, \ldots, O_{pc})$ corresponding to the interval input vector $\mathbf{X}_p$:

$$o_{pk}^U < o_{ph}^L \quad \text{for } k = 1, 2, \ldots, c \; (k \neq h), \tag{17}$$

where $O_{pk} = [o_{pk}^L, o_{pk}^U]$ and $O_{ph} = [o_{ph}^L, o_{ph}^U]$.

In Fig.10.3, we show some examples of interval output vectors. In Fig.10.3 (a), the new pattern can be classified as Class 3 because the interval output from the third output unit satisfies the inequality relation in (17). On the other hand, the new pattern is not classifiable in Fig.10.3 (b) where there are two possible classes for the new pattern: Class 1 and Class 2.

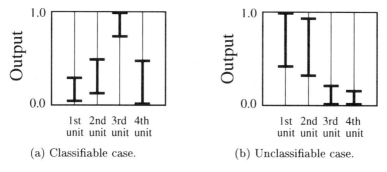

Fig. 10.3   Example of interval output vectors.

Let us briefly explain the inequality relation in (17). Because the interval input vector $\mathbf{X}_p$ includes all the possible values of $\mathbf{x}_p$ (i.e., $x_{pi} \in X_{pi}$, $i = 1, 2, \ldots, n$), the corresponding interval output vector $\mathbf{O}_p$ includes all the possible values of $\mathbf{o}_p$ (i.e., $o_{pk} \in O_{pk}$, $k = 1, 2, \ldots, c$). Thus the following relation holds when the inequality in (17) is satisfied:

$$o_{pk} \leq o_{pk}^U < o_{ph}^L \leq o_{ph} \quad \text{for } k = 1, 2, \ldots, c \; (k \neq h). \tag{18}$$

This means that (16) always holds when (17) is satisfied by the interval output vector $\mathbf{O}_p$. That is, when (17) holds, we know that any input vectors included in the interval input vector $\mathbf{X}_p$ are always classified as Class h.

From the above discussions, we have the following procedure for classifying the new pattern $\mathbf{x}_p$ based on incomplete information.

[Classification procedure]
Step 1 : Measure the value of the first attribute π_1 of the new pattern $\mathbf{x}_p$.
Step 2 : Denote the incomplete information about the new pattern $\mathbf{x}_p$ by the interval input vector $\mathbf{X}_p$.
Step 3 : Present $\mathbf{X}_p$ to the trained neural network, and calculate the interval output vector $\mathbf{O}_p$.

Step 4 : If (17) is satisfied by $\mathbf{O}_p$, classify the new pattern $\mathbf{x}_p$ as Class h. If there is no class which satisfies (17), measure the value of the next attribute according to the measurement order π, and return to Step 2.

By this classification procedure, we can reduce the number of attributes to be measured for classifying each new pattern. It should be noted that the classification result by this procedure is exactly the same as the result based on the measurement of all the n attributes (i.e., the classification result based on (16)). This means that our approach involves no deterioration of the classification performance while it can reduce the measurement cost.

10.3.4 Illustration

In the two-dimensional pattern classification problem in Fig.10.1, there are two possible measurement orders of the two attributes: $\pi_A = (a_1, a_2)$ and $\pi_B = (a_2, a_1)$. Let us consider a new pattern $\mathbf{x}_p = (x_{p1}, x_{p2}) = (0.3, 0.8)$. When the attribute a_1 is first measured, we have the incomplete information $(0.3, ?)$ about this new pattern. This incomplete information is denoted by the interval input vector $\mathbf{X}_p = ([0.3, 0.3], [0, 1])$. The interval input vector is presented to the trained neural network, and we calculate the corresponding interval output vector $\mathbf{O}_p = ([0.996, 1.0], [0.0, 0.0008], [0.0, 0.002])$. Because this interval output vector satisfies (17) for $h = 1$, the new pattern is classified as Class 1 by measuring only x_{p1}. In fact, the output vector corresponding to the complete input vector $\mathbf{x}_p = (0.3, 0.8)$ is $\mathbf{o}_p = (0.999, 0.001, 0.0)$. That is, the classification result (i.e., Class 1) based on the incomplete information $(0.3, ?)$ is the same as the result based on the complete information $(0.3, 0.8)$.

On the other hand, if we first measure the attribute value x_{p2} according to the order π_B, we have the incomplete information $(?, 0.8)$. This information is denoted by the interval input vector $\mathbf{X}_p = ([0, 1], [0.8, 0.8])$, which is presented to the trained neural network. Then we calculate the corresponding interval output vector as $\mathbf{O}_p = ([0.001, 0.999], [0.0, 1.0], [0.0, 0.001])$. Because there is no class that satisfies (17), we have to measure the next attribute (i.e., a_1) according to the order π_B.

10.4 Determination of Measurement Order

Our goal is to minimize the total measurement cost $C(\pi)$ in (2) for classifying the new patterns. It is, however, impossible to know the number of required measurements for classifying each new pattern $\mathbf{x}_p$ before measuring all the attribute values of $\mathbf{x}_p$. Thus we can not directly minimize the total measurement cost for the new patterns. In this chapter, we use the total measurement cost for the training patterns for determining the measurement order.

When the number of attributes (i.e., the number of input units: n) is not large, we can examine all the permutations of the n attributes. For example, it is not difficult to examine all the 24 permutations of four attributes in four-dimensional pattern classification problems. On the other hand, if the number of attributes is large, we can not examine all the $n!$ permutations (i.e., all the possible orders of the n attributes). In this case, we have to use a heuristic procedure. In preliminary computer simulations, we examined two procedures. One procedure is a forward step-wise procedure that determines the measurement order from the first attribute (i.e., from π_1). The other procedure is a backward step-wise procedure that determines the measurement order from the last attribute (i.e., from π_n). In this chapter, we only explain the backward procedure because its simulation results were better than those by the forward procedure.

In the backward procedure, we start with the set of the n attributes $A = \{a_1, \ldots, a_n\}$. First we determine the last attribute π_n by examining the n subsets $A_1, \ldots, A_n$ of A where $A_i = A - \{a_i\} = \{a_1, \ldots, a_{i-1}, a_{i+1}, \ldots, a_n\}$. Let r_i be the number of rejected training patterns in the classification based on the measurement of the attributes in A_i. This means that the measurement of the attribute a_i is necessary for those r_i training patterns. The other patterns do not require the measurement of a_i. Thus the following measurement cost can be reduced by omitting the measurement of a_i:

$$C_i = c_i \cdot (m_{\text{training}} - r_i), \qquad (19)$$

where c_i is the measurement cost of a_i and m_{training} is the total number of the given training patterns. The last attribute π_n is specified as the attribute a_i with the maximum reduced cost C_i. Next, the attribute π_{n-1} is determined in the same manner after updating the attribute set A as $A := A - \{\pi_n\}$. In this manner, the other attributes are ordered in turn.

Let us explain the backward procedure using the two-dimensional pattern classification problem in Fig.10.1. Since two attributes are involved in each pattern, the attribute set A is specified as $A = \{a_1, a_2\}$. Our task is to determine the measurement order $\pi = (\pi_1, \pi_2)$. The backward procedure first determines the last attribute π_2 by examining two subsets A_1 and A_2 where $A_1 = A - \{a_1\} = \{a_2\}$ and $A_2 = A - \{a_2\} = \{a_1\}$. When the subset A_1 is examined, each training pattern $\mathbf{x}_p = (x_{p1}, x_{p2})$ is handled as an incomplete pattern $\mathbf{x}_p = (?, x_{p2})$ with an unmeasured attribute, which is represented by an interval vector $\mathbf{X}_p = ([0, 1], [x_{p2}, x_{p2}])$. Such an interval vector is presented to the trained neural network, and its classifiability is examined. When the first attribute value x_{p1} of each training pattern is replaced with the interval $[0, 1]$, no patterns are classifiable by the trained neural network (i.e., $m_{\text{training}} - r_2 = 0$) in Fig.10.1. This means that no measurement cost can be reduced in (19).

On the other hand, when the subset A_2 is examined, the training pattern $\mathbf{x}_p = (x_{p1}, x_{p2})$ is handled as an incomplete training pattern $\mathbf{x}_p = (x_{p1}, ?)$ and denoted by $\mathbf{X}_p = ([x_{p1}, x_{p1}], [0, 1])$. In this case, 15 training patterns are classifiable (i.e., $m_{\text{training}} - r_2 = 15$). Thus the last attribute π_2 is determined as $\pi_2 = a_2$. Then the attribute set A is updated as $A := A - \{\pi_2\} = \{a_1\}$. Since the attribute set A includes only a single attribute a_1, the measurement order $\pi = (\pi_1, \pi_2)$ is determined as $\pi = (a_1, a_2)$. That is, the first attribute a_1 is measured first, then the second attribute a_2 is measured in the classification phase.

10.5 Computer Simulations

10.5.1 Simulation Conditions

In computer simulations, we used iris data with four attributes, appendicitis data with seven attributes, cancer data with nine attributes, wine data with 13 attributes, and Australian credit approval data with 14 attributes. The iris data set with 150 patterns may be the most frequently used classification problem in the literature, which is available from UC Irvine database (via anonymous ftp from *ftp.ics.uci.edu* in directory */pub/machine-learning-databases*). The appendicitis data with 106 patterns and the cancer data with 286 patterns were used in Weiss and Kulikowski [15] for evaluating various classification methods such as statistical methods, neural networks, and machine learning techniques. The wine data with 178 patterns and the credit data with 690 patterns are also available from UC Irvine database.

All the attribute values of these data sets were normalized as real numbers in the unit interval [0, 1]. The learning of neural networks was performed by the standard back-propagation algorithm under different conditions for each data set. Parameter specifications for each data set are summarized in Table 10.1 where the number of input units is the same as the number of attributes, and the number of output units is the same as the number of classes. The number of hidden units was appropriately specified by preliminary computer simulations. The learning rate and the momentum constant in the back-propagation algorithm, and the number of learning iterations (i.e., the number of epochs) were also specified by preliminary computer simulations.

Table 10.1 Simulation conditions.

Data Sets	Network Architectures			Learning Parameters		
	Input	Hidden	Output	Learning	Momentum	Epochs
Iris	4	2	3	0.25	0.9	2000
Appendicitis	7	5	2	0.25	0.9	2000
Cancer	9	5	2	0.25	0.9	2000
Wine	13	2	3	0.25	0.9	2000
Credit	14	10	2	0.10	0.9	1000

When we examined the performance of our approach on training patterns, all the given patterns in each data set were used for training a neural network and determining a measurement order. The backward procedure was used for the determination of the measurement order. Then the same training patterns were used in the classification phase as test patterns (i.e., they are handled as new patterns), which were classified by the trained neural network. This computer simulation was iterated five times for each data set for calculating the average number of attributes to be measured in the classification phase.

On the other hand, when we examined the performance of our approach on new patterns, we used the 10-fold cross-validation technique [15] where each data set was divided into ten subsets. Nine subsets were used as training patterns for training a neural network and determining a measurement order. The other subset was used as new patterns (i.e., test patterns), which were classified by the trained neural network. In the 10-fold cross-validation, this evaluation procedure was iterated ten times so that each subset was used as test patterns just once. We iterated the 10-fold cross-validation procedure two times by differently dividing each data set into ten subsets. This means that we evaluated 20 trained neural networks for each data set.

In our computer simulations, we used the same measurement cost for all attributes. Thus our goal was to minimize the total number of attributes to be measured in the classification phase.

10.5.2 Simulation Results on Training Patterns

In Table 10.2, we summarize simulation results on training patterns. From this table, we can see that the measurement of all attributes was not necessary in the classification phase. Of course, we used all attributes in the learning phase. We can also see from Table 10.2 that the effectiveness of our approach is problem-dependent.

The effect of our approach also depends on the complexity of neural networks. In the same manner as in Table 10.2 except for the number of hidden units, we performed computer simulations for the iris data set. We used various specifications for the number of hidden units. Simulation results are summarized in Table 10.3. From this table, we can see that the number of attributes to be measured in the classification phase was small when the number of hidden units was small. When the number of hidden units was large, our approach could not significantly decrease the number of measured attributes. This deterioration of the effectiveness of our approach is due to excess widths involved in interval output vectors from trained neural networks. Large excess widths are included in interval output vectors from trained neural networks with many hidden units. This issue will be discussed in the next section.

10.5.3 Simulation Results on Test Patterns

In Table 10.4, we summarized simulation results on test patterns. Computer simulations were performed under the simulation conditions shown in Table 10.1. From the comparison between Table 10.2 and Table 10.4, we can see that our approach worked well on test patterns as well as training patterns. That is, it could decrease the number of attributes to be measured for classifying new patterns.

Table 10.2 Simulation results on training patterns.

Data Sets	Number of Attributes	Number of Measurements
Iris	4	2.83
Appendicitis	7	4.44
Cancer	9	7.66
Wine	13	8.24
Credit	14	12.28

Table 10.3 Simulation results for the iris data set.

Number of hidden units	2	4	6	8	10	20
Number of measurements	2.83	3.24	3.28	3.32	3.41	3.48

Table 10.4 Simulation results on test patterns.

Data Sets	Number of Attributes	Number of Measurements
Iris	4	2.91
Appendicitis	7	4.60
Cancer	9	7.33
Wine	13	8.42
Credit	14	12.44

10.6 Subdivision Methods

10.6.1 *Excess Width Involved in Interval Arithmetic*

Our approach employs interval arithmetic for calculating interval output vectors from trained neural networks. Since the determination of the measurement order and the classification of incomplete patterns totally depend on the interval output vectors, accuracy of interval arithmetic in the trained neural networks has a large effect on the effectiveness of our approach. It is well-known in the literature that interval arithmetic involves excess widths [11–14]. A typical example is $X - X \neq 0$ where $X = [x^L, x^U]$ is an interval (i.e., $x^L \neq x^U$). For example, $[1, 2] - [1, 2] = [-1, 1]$. In this section, we try to improve the performance of our approach by reducing the excess widths included in interval output vectors from trained neural networks.

Let us illustrate excess widths involved in interval arithmetic by another example. We assume that we have a nonlinear function $g(x) = 1 - x + x^2$ and an interval input $X = [0, 2]$. Our task is to calculate the corresponding interval output. By replacing the real number input x with the interval input X, we have the following interval function:

$$G(X) = 1 - X + X^2. \tag{20}$$

In interval arithmetic [11–14], $G(X)$ is called the natural interval extension of $g(x)$. For $X = [0, 2]$, $G(X)$ is calculated by interval arithmetic as

$$\begin{aligned} G([0,\ 2]) &= 1 - [0,\ 2] + [0,\ 2]^2 \\ &= [1,\ 1] + [-2,\ 0] + [0,\ 4] \\ &= [-1,\ 5]. \end{aligned} \tag{21}$$

On the other hand, the exact interval output (i.e., the united extension of $g(x)$) is defined as

$$g(X) = \{g(x) \mid x \in X\}. \tag{22}$$

For $X = [0, 2]$, $g(X)$ is calculated as

$$\begin{aligned} g([0,\ 2]) &= \{1 - x + x^2 \mid x \in [0,\ 2]\} \\ &= [0.75,\ 3] \subset [-1,\ 5] = G([0,\ 2]). \end{aligned} \tag{23}$$

The difference between $g([0, 2])$ and $G([0, 2])$ is the excess width included in $G([0, 2])$. The inclusion relation $g(X) \subset G(X)$ in (23) always holds for any interval input X between the united extension (i.e., exact interval output) and the natural interval extension (i.e., interval arithmetic). Such an inclusion relation also holds for interval outputs in the case of multi-input functions (i.e., when the inputs are interval vectors).

The calculation of the exact interval output $g(X)$ requires some optimization technique for finding the maximum and minimum values of $g(x)$ in X. This is usually a very difficult task especially when $g(x)$ is a highly nonlinear and multi-input function. Neural networks are typical examples of such a complicated function.

Let $\mathbf{g}(\mathbf{x}) = (g_1(\mathbf{x}), \ldots, g_c(\mathbf{x}))$ be the output vector from the neural network in (6)-(10) for the real input vector $\mathbf{x} = (x_1, x_2, \ldots, x_n)$. That is,

$g_k(\mathbf{x})$ is the output value from the k-th output unit when $\mathbf{x}$ is presented to the neural network ($k = 1, 2, \ldots, c$). From the input-output relation of each unit in (6)-(10), $g_k(\mathbf{x})$ can be written as a non-linear function of $\mathbf{x} = (x_1, \ldots, x_n)$:

$$g_k(\mathbf{x}) = \cfrac{1}{1 + \exp\left\{-\sum_{j=1}^{n_H} w_{kj} \cdot \cfrac{1}{1 + \exp(-\sum_{i=1}^{n} w_{ji} \cdot x_i - \theta_j)} - \theta_k\right\}}. \quad (24)$$

The exact interval output $g_k(\mathbf{X})$ is defined as follows for the interval input vector $\mathbf{X} = (X_1, \ldots, X_n)$:

$$g_k(\mathbf{X}) = \{g_k(\mathbf{x}) \mid x_i \in X_i,\ i = 1, 2, \ldots, n\}. \quad (25)$$

From (24), we can imagine the difficulty in calculating the maximum and minimum value of $g_k(\mathbf{X})$ in $\mathbf{X} = (X_1, \ldots, X_n)$.

On the contrary, the interval-arithmetic-based calculation of the interval output vector is very simple as shown in (6)-(10). It only requires simple operations on intervals in (12)-(14). The main drawback of interval arithmetic is that excess widths are included in calculated interval outputs. In the remaining of this chapter, we explain how excess widths can be decreased by subdividing interval input vectors. The decrease in excess widths leads to the decrease in the number of attributes to be measured for classifying new patterns.

10.6.2 Simple Subdivision

A simple technique for decreasing the excess width included in $G(X)$ is to subdivide the interval input X into multiple subintervals of the same width [12]:

$$X = Y_1 \cup Y_2 \cup \ldots \cup Y_m. \quad (26)$$

A sharper estimation of the exact interval output $g(X)$ is obtained as the union of the interval outputs corresponding to the subintervals $Y_1, Y_2, \ldots, Y_m$:

$$G^{(m)}(X) = G(Y_1) \cup G(Y_2) \cup \ldots \cup G(Y_m), \quad (27)$$

where the calculation of $G(Y_j)$ is performed by interval arithmetic.

The estimated interval output $G^{(m)}(X)$ is always included in the natural interval extension $G(X)$ calculated by interval arithmetic: $G^{(m)}(X) \subset G(X)$. This can be explained by the inclusion monotonicity of interval arithmetic [11–14] as follows. From (26), the inclusion relation $Y_j \subset X$, $j = 1, 2, \ldots, m$ holds between interval inputs. From the inclusion monotonicity, we have the inclusion relation $G(Y_j) \subset G(X)$, $j = 1, 2, \ldots, m$ for interval outputs. Thus we have the inclusion relation $G^{(m)}(X) \subset G(X)$ from (27).

On the other hand, the estimated interval output $G^{(m)}(X)$ always includes the exact interval output $g(X)$: $g(X) \subset G^{(m)}(X)$. This can be explained as follows. For the subinterval Y_j, we have $g(Y_j) \subset G(Y_j)$ because interval arithmetic is used for calculating $G(Y_j)$. Thus we have the inclusion relation:

$$g(Y_1) \cup g(Y_2) \cup \ldots \cup g(Y_m) \subset G(Y_1) \cup G(Y_2) \cup \ldots \cup G(Y_m). \quad (28)$$

This inclusion relation is equivalent to $g(X) \subset G^{(m)}(X)$ from (26) and (27).

In the case of a multi-input function $g(\mathbf{x}) = g(x_1, x_2, \ldots, x_n)$, the natural interval extension $G(\mathbf{X})$ of $g(\mathbf{x})$ is obtained by simply replacing the real input vector $\mathbf{x}$ with the interval input vector $\mathbf{X} = (X_1, \ldots, X_n)$. The simple subdivision method divides each element X_i of the interval vector $\mathbf{X} = (X_1, \ldots, X_n)$ into m subintervals of the same width as

$$X_i = Y_{i1} \cup Y_{i2} \cup \ldots \cup Y_{im}, \ i = 1, 2, \ldots, n. \quad (29)$$

Since each element X_i of the n-dimensional interval vector $\mathbf{X} = (X_1, \ldots, X_n)$ is subdivided into the m subintervals, $\mathbf{X} = (X_1, \ldots, X_n)$ is subdivided into m^n interval vectors. A sharper estimation of $g(\mathbf{X})$ is calculated as the union of the interval outputs corresponding to those m^n interval vectors. The subdivision of an interval vector is illustrated in Fig.10.4 in the case of $n = 2$ and $m = 5$.

The number of subintervals (i.e., m) should be specified from the viewpoint of the available computation time. In the case of Fig.10.4, 25 cells (i.e., small interval vectors) are presented to the trained neural networks, and the interval output vector corresponding to each input cell is calculated for obtaining the interval output vector corresponding to the interval input vector $\mathbf{X}$.

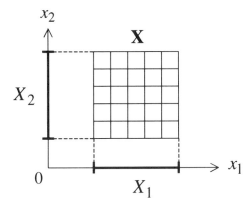

Fig. 10.4 Subdivision of a two-dimensional interval vector.

10.6.3 Hierarchical Subdivision

While the simple (or plain) subdivision method in the previous subsection works well on low-dimensional interval input vectors, its application to high-dimensional vectors is very difficult due to the exponential increase in the number of cells (i.e., interval vectors). A hierarchical subdivision method called "cyclic bisection [12]" was proposed in interval arithmetic for handling high-dimensional interval vectors. In the hierarchical subdivision method, the lower limit and the upper limit of $g(\mathbf{X})$ are independently estimated. That is, two different subdivision structures are constructed for obtaining a sharper estimation of $g(\mathbf{X})$.

Let us illustrate how the lower limit of $g(\mathbf{X})$ is estimated by the hierarchical subdivision method. First, the first element X_1 of the interval vector $\mathbf{X} = (X_1, \ldots, X_n)$ is subdivided into two intervals with the same width:

$$X_1 = Y_1^A \cup Y_1^B. \tag{30}$$

That is, $\mathbf{X} = (X_1, \ldots, X_n)$ is subdivided into the following two interval input vectors:

$$\mathbf{Z}_{(1)}^A = (Y_1^A, X_2, \ldots, X_n), \tag{31}$$

$$\mathbf{Z}_{(1)}^B = (Y_1^B, X_2, \ldots, X_n). \tag{32}$$

Next the interval output for each interval input vector is calculated by interval arithmetic. Among the two interval outputs, one with the smaller lower limit is found. The interval input vector corresponding to that interval output is chosen. Its second element X_2 is subdivided into two subintervals with the same width:

$$X_2 = Y_2^A \cup Y_2^B. \tag{33}$$

For example, when $\mathbf{Z}_{(1)}^A$ is chosen, it is further subdivided as

$$\mathbf{Z}_{(2)}^A = (Y_1^A, Y_2^A, X_3, \ldots, X_n), \tag{34}$$

$$\mathbf{Z}_{(2)}^B = (Y_1^A, Y_2^B, X_3, \ldots, X_n). \tag{35}$$

Then one of the three interval input vectors that have not been subdivided yet is selected for further subdivision. This selection is also based on the minimum lower limit of the interval outputs. In the same manner as in the above subdivision, its third element X_3 is subdivided into two intervals with the same width. Such subdivision is iterated until a pre-specified stopping condition is satisfied. When the last element of an interval input vector is subdivided, the first element is subdivided in the next subdivision procedure. The hierarchical subdivision is illustrated in Fig.10.5 for the case of a two-dimensional interval input vector. The subdivision in Fig.10.5 is also represented in a tree structure in Fig.10.6. A stopping condition should be specified from the viewpoint of the available computation time. The number of cells (i.e., the number of leaf nodes in the tree representation) is used as the stopping condition in computer simulations in the next subsection. When the number of cells reaches a pre-specified one, the iteration of the hierarchical subdivision method is terminated.

When the upper limit of $g(\mathbf{X})$ is to be estimated, a hierarchical subdivision structure is constructed in the same manner except that the choice of an interval input vector to be subdivided is based on the maximum upper limit of interval outputs. In the application of the hierarchical subdivision method to a neural network with c output units, the lower limit and the upper limit of the interval output from each output unit are independently estimated. That is, the hierarchical subdivision method is employed $2 \times c$ times for estimating the c-dimensional interval output vector from the neural network.

In the hierarchical subdivision method called "cyclic bisection [12]", the element to be subdivided is cyclically chosen with no consideration about its effect on the decrease in the excess width. The efficiency of the hierarchical

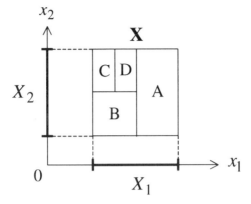

Fig. 10.5 Hierarchical subdivision of a two-dimensional interval vector.

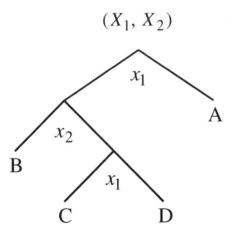

Fig. 10.6 Tree representation of the hierarchical subdivision.

subdivision method can be improved by carefully selecting an element to be subdivided at each subdivision step. We modify the selection procedure of the subdivided element in the following manner. When an interval input vector is chosen, one of its n elements should be subdivided. In our modified method, the subdivision of each of the n elements is examined. That is,

$g(\mathbf{X})$ is estimated from each of those n alternatives. When the lower limit is concerned, one element whose subdivision leads to the maximum lower limit (i.e., minimum excess width) is chosen and subdivided. On the other hand, one element whose subdivision leads to the minimum upper limit (i.e., minimum excess width) is chosen and subdivided when the upper limit is concerned.

10.6.4 Simulation Results

In the same manner as in Section 10.5.2, we examined the effectiveness of our approach with the modified hierarchical subdivision method. In our computer simulations, the hierarchical subdivision was terminated when original interval input vectors were subdivided into 50 interval vectors. We examined the effect of the hierarchical subdivision on the number of measured attributes by comparing the following three situations:

Case 1 : With no subdivision method. This is exactly the same as the situation in Section 10.5.2.

Case 2 : The use of the hierarchical subdivision only in the classification phase of incomplete patterns.

Case 3 : The use of the hierarchical subdivision in the determination phase of the measurement order and the classification phase of incomplete patterns.

Computer simulations were performed in the same manner as in Table 10.2. Simulation results are summarized in Table 10.5. From this table, we can see that the number of attributes to be measured in Case 2 and Case 3 with the hierarchical subdivision method is smaller than in the case

Table 10.5 Simulation results on training patterns.

Data Sets	Number of Attributes	Number of Measurements		
		Case 1	Case 2	Case 3
Iris	4	2.83	2.32	2.32
Appendicitis	7	4.44	4.42	4.37
Cancer	9	7.66	7.46	7.28
Wine	13	8.24	8.24	8.19
Credit	14	12.28	12.17	11.39

of interval arithmetic with no subdivision method (i.e., Case 1). This is because sharper output vectors were calculated by the hierarchical subdivision method than interval arithmetic. In our approach, the check of the classifiability of each incomplete pattern is based on the corresponding interval output vector. Thus a sharper interval output vector is more likely to be classifiable. This leads to the decrease in the number of measured attributes in Case 2 and Case 3.

10.7 Conclusions

In this chapter, we demonstrated that the number of attributes to be measured for classifying new patterns by trained neural networks could be decreased by denoting each unmeasured attribute by an interval. This means that the measurement of all input values is not always necessary in the classification phase by trained neural networks. We also suggested the use of a subdivision method for decreasing the number of measured attributes further. While the feature selection and the pruning have been often studied in the field of neural networks as a part of learning procedures, there are few studies that discuss the measurement cost in the classification phase for classifying new patterns. Our approach is useful in application areas where the measurement cost of each attribute is not negligible.

References

[1] L. Breiman, J. H. Friedmaan, R. A. Olshen, and C. J. Stone, Classification and Regression Tree, Wadsworth and Brooks, Pacific Grove, California, 1984.

[2] J. R. Quinlan, C4.5: Programs for Machine Learning, Morgan Kaufmann Publishers, San Mateo, California, 1993.

[3] D. E. Rumelhart, J. L. McClelland, and the PDP Research Group, Parallel Distributed Processing, MIT Press, Cambridge, 1986.

[4] Y. Le Cun, J. S. Denker, and S. A. Solla, "Optimal brain damage," Advances in Neural Information Processing Systems II, Morgan Kaufmann Publishers, San Mateo, California, pp.598–605, 1990.

[5] M. Ishikawa, "Structural learning with forgetting," Neural Networks, vol. **9**, no. **3**, pp.509–521, 1996.

[6] C. Schittenkopf, G. Deco, and W. Brauer, "Two strategies to avoid overfitting in feedforward networks," Neural Networks, vol. **10**, no. **3**, pp.505–516, 1997.

[7] R. Setiono and H. Liu, "Neural-network feature selector," IEEE Trans. on Neural Networks, vol. **8**, no. **3**, pp.654–662, 1997.

[8] H. Ishibuchi and A. Miyazaki, "Determination of inspection order for classifying new samples by neural networks," Proc. of ICNN'94, pp.2907–2910, 1994.

[9] H. Ishibuchi and H. Tanaka, "An extension of the BP-algorithm to interval input vectors," Proc. of IJCNN'91, pp.1588–1593, 1991.

[10] H. Ishibuchi, H. Tanaka, and H. Okada, "An architecture of neural networks with interval weights and its application to fuzzy regression analysis," Fuzzy Sets and Systems, vol. **57**, no. **1**, pp.27–39, 1993.

[11] R. E. Moore, Interval Analysis, Prentice-Hall, Englewood Cliffs, NJ, 1966.

[12] R. E. Moore, Methods and Applications of Interval Analysis, SIAM, Philadelphia, 1979.

[13] G. Alefeld and J. Herzberger, Introduction to Interval Computations, Academic Press, New York, 1983.

[14] K. Okumura, "Recent topic on circuit analysis - Application of interval arithmetic," System/ Control/ Information, vol. **40**, no. **9**, pp.393–400, 1996. (in Japanese)

[15] S. M. Weiss and C. A. Kulikowski, Computer Systems That Learn, Morgan Kaufmann Publishers, San Mateo, California, 1991.

Chapter 11
Extraction of Fuzzy Rules from Numerical Data for Classifiers

Nikhil R. Pal[1] and Anujit Sarkar[2]
[1] *Indian Statistical Institute*
[2] *Macmet Interactive Technologies Pvt. Ltd.*

Abstract

We propose a method for fuzzy rule generation directly from numerical data for designing classifiers. First a fuzzy partition is imposed on the domain of each feature, which results in a set of fuzzy values for each feature. Then a descriptor-pattern table is constructed using the training data and the fuzzy feature values. Rules are now discovered from the descriptor-pattern table. The rule generation process finds the distinct descriptors to discover simple rules and if required generates further rules using conjunction of common descriptors or conjunction of common descriptors and negation of distinct descriptors. A rule minimization process is then initiated to retain a small set of rules adequate to learn the training data. We suggest three possible schemes for generation of the initial fuzzy partitioning of the feature space and a genetic algorithm based tuning scheme is used to refine the rule base. Finally, the proposed scheme is tested on some real data. Unlike, most of the classifiers, the proposed method can detect ambiguous data and declare them to be unclassified - this is a distinct advantage.

Keywords : Rule Extraction, Classifiers, Rule Based Systems, Distinct Descriptor, Common Descriptor, Fuzzy Portioning.

11.1 Introduction

Pattern recognition may involve two types of data. The first category is called the *object* data while the second one is called *relational* data. In object data a pattern or an object (say, a human being, tank, animal etc.) is characterized by a set of measurements like height, weight etc. On the other hand, in relational representation a set of n objects is represented by an

$n * n$ proximity (similarity /dissimilarity) relation. The proximity relation may be computed from the object representation or could be obtained by experts or by some other means. In this chapter, we concentrate only on object data.

There are three major tasks of pattern recognition: *Feature analysis*, *Clustering* and *Classification*. Feature analysis is an essential and important step towards designing effective clustering and classification algorithms. Clustering looks for substructures present in a data set, i.e., it partitions the data set into homogeneous groups. For example, in case of a remotely sensed image, the goal of clustering may be to group the pixels based on gray values and properties of neighboring pixels in such a manner that pixels corresponding to each type of surface (land, vegetation, water etc.) form a separate cluster. Note that, for clustering we do not know the actual type of region a pixel corresponds to, but we expect our clustering algorithm to identify such groups. We emphasize that clustering only finds "homogeneous" groups but cannot say which group corresponds to what. A classifier, on the other hand, partitions the feature space so that any unlabeled data point can be assigned the appropriate class label. A classifier is designed using some training data for which the actual class labels are known. For example, to design an analysis system for remotely sensed images we may be given one or more images with known class label for every pixel; in other words, for every pixel we know whether it corresponds to water, land or vegetation etc. Based on these (training) images we can devise a scheme so that when new images come, we can assign possible class label to every pixel considering "similarity" of the pixels in the new image with the pixels in the training images. The principal function of a classifier is to yield decisions concerning the class membership of unknown patterns.

Features can be of three types : numerical, categorical or non-numerical and fuzzy or ambiguous. Numerical values of features have a proximity relation between them. Categorical values are non-numeric. Each feature can take a number of values, called attribute values and an object is characterized by values of these attributes. Finally, the fuzzy feature values (like HIGH, LOW) are ambiguous, and it is not well defined, so one cannot expect a precise value for such a feature. Several models have been developed to resolve the uncertainties in decision making like prototype based model, neural network based system, decision theoretic system, rule based system etc.[9; 10; 11]. We consider here a rule based approach.

The ID3 [1] algorithm is a procedure for synthesizing an efficient discrimination tree for classifying patterns that have non-numeric values. The Pao-Hu method (PHM) [2] also has the same goal of "discovering" a set of necessary and sufficient conditions that describe different classes of objects. PHM directly finds rules to discriminate patterns from different classes. Two serious limitations of both ID3 and PHM approaches are : they use categorical data only and thus cannot deal with partial information. Pal et al. [6] proposed a generalization of ID3, named RID3, which can handle real data. Several other authors have also proposed fuzzy generalization of ID3 [3; 4]. There are other approaches to fuzzy rule extraction for classifiers too [9; 12]. Here we propose a fuzzy rule based classifier which is motivated by the PHM. This can deal with real valued numerical data as well as fuzzy test input.

11.2 Pao-Hu Method (PHM)

Pao-Hu method [2] provides a mechanism for extracting rules for classification. Here a pattern is regarded as a conjunction of descriptors, where a descriptor comprises at least a feature name and one of the possible feature values. Consider a set of n patterns each of which has p features. Without loss of generality we assume that each feature has J possible values. Thus, there are Jp descriptors. The first task of this rule induction method consists of partitioning these descriptors into common descriptors and first level distinct descriptors. To achieve this a table of association is prepared between the patterns and each of these descriptors. This can be done taking each pattern and making p entries, one for each of the p - feature values associated with the pattern, in an array of possible Jp sites. This process is repeated for all n patterns. At the end, the descriptors would be divided into common descriptors and the first level distinct descriptors, each with an associated pattern set.

To infer rules the algorithm proceeds as follows:
Step 1. Number the patterns and rewrite them in terms of descriptors. Retain the class labels of the patterns.
Step 2. The association table is now formed. If only patterns from a particular class is associated with a descriptor, call that descriptor a *distinct* descriptor (DD). These are the first-level distinct descriptors, in contrast to the second-level distinct descriptors obtained subsequently. All other

descriptors which are not DDs are called common descriptors (CDs). The first-level DDs are then used to form rules. A rule is considered complete if all patterns of a particular class is covered by the rule. Otherwise, it is a partial rule.

Step 3. The rule induction process is continued to extract additional rules, if required, to cover the remaining patterns. There are three possible ways to form the second level distinct descriptors:

(a)conjunction of a CD and the negation of a first level DD.
(b)conjunction of the negations of two first level DDs.
(c)conjunction of two CDs.

Step 4. In the event that the first-level and second level distinct descriptors do not suffice to classify all patterns, we form the third level distinct descriptors using combinations of first level and second level distinct descriptors, and so on, to get higher level descriptors as required.

The advantages of the Pao-Hu method are that only simple set operations and list processing are involved. A drawback of this method is that it can deal with only categorical data, not real valued data.

Next we discuss the proposed method which can be viewed as a fuzzy generalization of the Pao-Hu method.

11.3 Proposed Method

We are given a p-dimensional data set $X = \{\mathbf{x}_1, \mathbf{x}_2, \cdots, \mathbf{x}_N\}$, where $\mathbf{x}_i \in R^p$ with c classes $C = \{c_1, c_2, \cdots, c_c\}$. For simplicity, without loss of generality, we represent the class labels as $C = \{1, 2, \cdots, c\}$. The jth component of any data point $\mathbf{x}_i$, represents the value of the jth feature and is denoted by x_{ij}. The problem is to construct a set of rules so that not only we are able to classify the training data but also unknown incoming data points.

We denote the domain of the jth feature by D_j. Let us define n_j fuzzy sets, $A_{j,1}, A_{j,2}, \cdots, A_{j,n_j}$, on the domain of the jth feature. The fuzzy set $A_{j,k}$ is characterized by a membership function $\mu_{j,k}$. For the ith data point $\mathbf{x}_i$, the membership of the jth feature value (x_{ij}) to the kth fuzzy set defined on the domain D_j of the jth feature is denoted by $A_{j,k}(x_{ij}) = \mu_{j,k}(x_{ij})$.

Consider $\mathbf{x}_i \in R^p$. Let $\mu_{j,l}^i = max_{k=1,2,\cdots,n_j}\{\mu_{j,k}(x_{ij})\}$. Then x_{ij} has the highest membership to the lth fuzzy set defined on D_j. Note that, the jth component may also have non-zero memberships to some other fuzzy sets defined on D_j but $A_{(j,l)}$ is the best representation for the given x_{ij}.

We can now describe $\mathbf{x}_i$ and its associated class as follows : If x_{i1} is A_{1,l_1} AND x_{i2} is A_{2,l_2} AND $\cdots$ AND x_{ip} is A_{p,l_p}, then the class is k.

Here k is the class label for the data point $\mathbf{x}_i$ and l_j is the index of the fuzzy set defined on D_j for which x_{ij} has the maximum membership value. The preceding facts (description of the data points), in short, can be written as : If $\mu_{1,l_1}^i \wedge \mu_{2,l_2}^i \wedge \ldots \wedge \mu_{p,l_p}^i$ then the class is k.

In this way, for every data point we can write a description. But this will result in n such statements which are to be aggregated. To do the aggregation, we generate a table exhibiting the association between different descriptors (fuzzy sets defined on different D_j s) and the pattern classes; we call this table *descriptor-pattern* table or DP table, in short.

11.3.1 Computation of DP Table

The DP table has $(1+c)$ columns - the first one is for *descriptors*; i.e., for the fuzzy feature values while the rest, columns 2 through $(1+c)$ are for the c *pattern* classes. The table will have $n = \sum_{j=1}^{p} n_j$ rows, each row corresponds to a distinct fuzzy set defined on one of the p features; in other words, every row corresponds to a unique fuzzy set. For example, the first n_1 rows may correspond to $A_{1,l}, l = 1, \cdots, n_1$. So the table comprises $n * (1+c)$ cells. Entries in the cells corresponding to the first column will be a list of descriptors. Each cell entry corresponding to other columns will hold two lists : a list containing the identity of the patterns (may be the pattern number) falling in the corresponding class and another list containing membership value of the associated patterns.

To make notations simple, we use $(A_{j,l}, k)$ to represent the cell corresponding to the row $A_{j,l}$ and column k. If the description of the ith pattern is : $\mu_{1,l_1}^i \wedge \mu_{2,l_2}^i \wedge \cdots \wedge \mu_{p,l_p}^i$ and the class is k, then in the membership list M_{j,l_j}^k corresponding to the cell (A_{j,l_j}, k) (i.e., the membership list in the column corresponding to the class k for the row A_{j,l_j}) we include the value μ_{j,l_j}^i. Also we include the pattern number i in the pattern identity list L_{j,l_j}^k corresponding to the cell (A_{j,l_j}, k). And this is done for all $j = 1, \cdots, p$.

Now we examine each row of DP table.

Step 1. If we find a row in which all of the c pattern lists for the c columns are empty, then the associated fuzzy set in column 1 is redundant and can be ignored.

Step 2. If we find a row in which only one of the c columns for pattern identity contains a non-empty list, then the associated fuzzy set in column

1 is a distinct descriptor. Since patterns from only one class are associated with this fuzzy descriptor, we call it a DD.

Let A_{j,l_j} be one such row and only the column for class k has a nonempty list L_{j,l_j}^k. Let $\hat{\mu}_{l_j} = min_{\mu \in M_{j,l_j}^k} \{\mu\}$ i.e., $\hat{\mu}_{l_j}$ is the minimum of all the membership values contained in M_{j,l_j}^k. Then we can summarize the information in row A_{j,l_j} as: If "x_{ij} is A_{j,l_j}" is satisfied at least to the extent $\hat{\mu}_{l_j}$, then it is from class k. Thus, we get a rule : If $A_{j,l_j}(x_{ij}) \geq \hat{\mu}_{l_j}$ then the class is k.

Fuzzy feature values such as A_{j,l_j} will be called the first level distinct descriptors. All other descriptors are called common descriptors. Note that, this rule alone may not be enough to describe the class k completely; if it can, it is called a *complete* rule else a *partial* rule. In this way all rules using the first level DDs are found out.

Now all rows corresponding to the distinct descriptors are moved to a new DP table. From now on, we will refer to this new table as the *distinct descriptor table*. The old table, with the distinct descriptors removed will henceforth be called the *common descriptor table*.

Step 3. After all rules with the first level DDs are found, we create a new DP table for discovering the second level DDs.

To form the second level descriptors, we use the conjunction of a common descriptor from the CD table and the "negation" of a first level distinct descriptor from the DD table. Here "negation" does not mean a fuzzy complement. In the crisp case "negation" of a feature may mean absence of the feature. So $\neg A_{j,l}$ means absence of the fuzzy feature $A_{j,l}$; in other words, the jth feature of the data point is *not* adequately represented by the fuzzy concept $A_{j,l}$. Thus "negation" may be interpreted as: $\mu_{j,l}$ is not greater than $\hat{\mu}_{l_j}$.

Let us now explain how the second level DP table can be constructed. Suppose $A_{j,l}$ is a first level DD and $A_{m,s}$ be a common descriptor. Then $A_{m,s} \wedge \neg A_{j,l} (m \neq j)$ forms a second level descriptor. Let $L_{m,s}^g$ and $L_{j,l}^g$ be the lists of pattern identifiers associated respectively with $A_{m,s}$ and $A_{j,l}$ for class g, $g = 1, \cdots, c$. Also let $L_{m,s-j,l}^g = L_{m,s}^g - L_{j,l}^g$ = the list of patterns which are in $L_{m,s}^g$ but not in $L_{j,l}^g$. Hence, in the row for $A_{m,s} \wedge \neg A_{j,l}$ we create the list $L_{m,s-j,l}^g$ in the column for class $g, g = 1, \cdots, c$.

Once this is done, then like *step 1* we look for redundant descriptors. As in *step 2*, we now look for a row in which only one column has non-empty list of pattern identifiers and get the second level distinct descriptors. Let a second level DD be $A_{m,s} \wedge \neg A_{j,l}$ and the only non-empty column be the one corresponding to class k. We now find $\hat{\mu}_{s_m} = min_{\mu \in M_{m,s_m}^k} \{\mu\}$ and $\hat{\mu}_{l_j} = min_{\mu \in M_{j,l_j}^k} \{\mu\}$. We can now write a rule of the form : If $A_{m,s}(x_{im}) > \hat{\mu}_{s_m}$ AND $A_{j,l}(x_{ij}) NOT \geq \hat{\mu}_{l_j}$ then class is k. Equivalently, if $A_{m,s}(x_{im}) > \hat{\mu}_{s_m}$ AND $A_{j,l}(x_{ij}) < \hat{\mu}_{l_j}$ then the class is k.

We can also consider negation of more than one first level DDs to construct second level descriptors. In this way if we are able to find a set of rules that can classify unambiguously all patterns in the training data, then we are done. Otherwise, proceeding in the same manner we find the third level descriptors and the associated rules and so on.

But steps 1 through 3 may not be enough to find all rules required to classify the training data. In such a case, we need to consider conjunction of the common descriptors as described next in *step 4*.

Step 4. Let $A_{m,s}$ and $A_{j,l}$ be two CDs. Let $L_{m,s}^g$ and $L_{j,l}^g$ be the list of pattern identifiers associated respectively with $A_{m,s}$ and $A_{j,l}$ for class g, $g = 1, \cdots, c$. Also denote $L_{m,s \cap j,l}^g = L_{m,s}^g \cap L_{j,l}^g$ - the list of patterns which are common to both $L_{m,s}^g$ and $L_{j,l}^g$. Now suppose only one (say $g = k$) of the c lists thus obtained is non-empty. In other words, $L_{m,s \cap j,l}^g = NULL \; \forall g \neq k$ and $L_{m,s \cap j,l}^k \neq NULL$. Then $A_{m,s} \wedge A_{j,l}$ is a distinct descriptor and it can be used to describe a partial or complete rule of the form : If $A_{m,s}(x_{im}) > \hat{\mu}_{s_m}$ AND $A_{j,l}(x_{ij}) > \hat{\mu}_{l_j}$ then the class is k.

11.4 Choice of Membership Functions

So far we talked about quantization of the feature space by fuzzy sets but did not say anything about their choices/definitions. Such membership functions (MFs) may be triangular, Gaussian etc. We discuss next about three such choices that we have used.

11.4.1 *MFs using Equispaced Symmetric Triangles*

Here we consider equispaced, normal and symmetric triangular membership functions. For each feature, we create as many symmetric triangles as the number of fuzzy sets we want, such that they cover the entire domain of that feature. The domain (as obtained from the training patterns) is extended on either side (minimum and maximum) by 5%. Any two adjacent triangles overlap such that the peak of one triangle is connected to the midpoint of the base of adjacent triangles, i.e., a 50% overlap is there between adjacent membership functions. If F^i_{min} and F^i_{max} are the minimum and maximum values for the i-th feature, then 5% adjustment is made at both ends such that the new extrema are $f^i_{min} = F^i_{min} - (F^i_{max} - F^i_{min})*0.05$ and $f^i_{max} = F^i_{max} + (F^i_{max} - F^i_{min})*0.05$. The 5% adjustment is made on both sides so that future data points, which are not far away from the training data can be dealt with by the classifier. If there are k fuzzy sets defined on the ith feature then the base width of each triangular membership functions will be $2 * (f^i_{max} - f^i_{min})/(k+1)$.

It is convenient to write such membership functions using the formula $\mu_A(x) = 1 - 2 \mid x - a \mid /b, x \in [a - b/2, a + b/2]$ and $\mu_A(x) = o$, otherwise. Here a is the peak, i.e., the point at which MF=1 and b is the width of the MF. Since choice of the MFs has significant impact on the performance of the algorithm, we propose two other schemes.

11.4.2 MFs With FCM Ignoring the Class Information

It may not always be appropriate to use symmetric triangles which are evenly spread over the domain of the feature. Since the patterns belong to different classes, it may be reasonable to assume that patterns belonging to a class tend form a cluster in the feature space. Even if this be the case, each such cluster may be too big to cover by one fuzzy set. Thus it may be required to split the data corresponding to one class to more than one cluster. Here first we try to find the natural clusters ignoring the class information and later in the next scheme we also use the class information. We use the fuzzy c-means (FCM) [8] algorithm to get the natural cluster centroids of the patterns under considerations. For the sake of completeness the FCM algorithm is described next.

The Fuzzy c-Means Algorithm

The FCM algorithm can be used to construct a fuzzy c-partition of a given data set. FCM formulates the clustering problem as an weighted least square optimization problem. Let the *centroid* vectors for the c clusters be $V = \{\mathbf{v_1}, \mathbf{v_2}, \cdots, \mathbf{v_c}\}$, $\mathbf{v_i} \in R^p$ and u_{ik} be the membership of $\mathbf{x_k}$ ($\mathbf{x_k} \in X$) to the ith cluster. Then the FCM algorithm finds $U = [u_{ik}]_{c \times N}$

and V by solving

$$minimize \ J_m(U, V : X) = \sum_{k=1}^{N} \sum_{i=1}^{c} (u_{ik})^m (d_{ik})^2 \quad (1)$$

subject to

i) $0 \leq u_{ik} \leq 1, \ \forall i, k,$
ii) $\sum_i u_{ik} = 1, \ \forall k,$ and
iii) $0 < \sum_k u_{ik} < N, \ \forall i.$

Here $m > 1$ is a fuzzifier which controls the fuzziness in the resultant partition matrix U, and $d_{ik} = \| \mathbf{x}_k - \mathbf{v}_i \|$ is the Euclidean distance between $\mathbf{x_k}$ and $\mathbf{v}_i$. However, $\| \cdot \|$ can be any other inner product induced norm also.

The necessary conditions for optimality of J_m, can be derived using Langrangian method as :

$$\mathbf{v}_i = \sum_{k=1}^{N} (u_{ik})^m \mathbf{x}_k / \sum_{k=1}^{N} (u_{ik})^m, 1 \leq i \leq c \quad (2)$$

and

$$u_{ik} = (\sum_{j=1}^{c} (d_{ik}/d_{jk})^{2/(m-1)})^{-1}, 1 \leq k \leq N, 1 \leq i \leq c. \quad (3)$$

The FCM algorithm iterates between (2) and (3) or between (3) and (2) depending on whether initialization is on U or V. In our implementation we initialized on U randomly. The iteration continues until either $\| U_t - U_{t-1} \| < \epsilon$ or $\| V_t - V_{t-1} \| < \epsilon$ or both are satisfied. Here U_t and V_t represent the membership and the centroid matrices at the tth iteration and ϵ is a small positive value. We calculated the natural centroids $V = \{\mathbf{v_1}, \mathbf{v_2}, \cdots, \mathbf{v_c}\}$, with $m = 2.5$ and $\epsilon = 0.0001$.

These centroids are then used to create MFs and they serve as the peaks of the triangles. If we have p features and decided to create c fuzzy sets for each feature then we obtain c cluster centroids $\{\mathbf{v_1}, \mathbf{v_2}, \cdots, \mathbf{v_c}\}$, $\mathbf{v}_j = (v_{j1}, v_{j2}, \cdots, v_{jp})^T$ from FCM . If f_i^{min} and f_i^{max} are the minimum and maximum values for the i-th feature after 5% allowance on both the sides, then the membership functions of the fuzzy sets will be represented by $(f_i^{min}, v_{1i}, v_{2i})$, (v_{1i}, v_{2i}, v_{3i}) and so on, with a membership value of unity at v_{ji} for the jth fuzzy set. We use (a, b, c) to represent a triangular membership function with base (a, c) and peak at b. Note that these MFs are neither equispaced nor of equal base. We shall see shortly that this provides an improvement over the results that can be achieved using equispaced symmetric triangles.

11.4.3 MFs Using Class Information

In the previous scheme, we ignored the class information that are available. Finding the natural centroids of all patterns taken together may sometimes have a negative effect. The reason being that the centroids of clusters corresponding to a class may be drawn away from their desirable positions because of the impact of patterns that belong to other classes. So another, possibly more attractive, approach may be to obtain fuzzy sets from clusters of patterns belonging to a particular class. Thus, here we cluster the data corresponding to each class separately.

To elaborate it, let $X = X_1 \cap X_2 \cup \cdots \cup X_c$ (where c is the number of classes) and $X_i \cap X_j = \phi$, $i \neq j$ i.e., X_i contains all data points for class i. We now cluster each of X_i into, say, 2 clusters by FCM. So each of X_i will generate 2 centroids, i.e., 2 fuzzy sets for each feature as done in Section 11.4.2. So a total of $2*c$ fuzzy sets will be generated for each feature.

11.5 Illustration of DP Table and Rule Generation

Let us take an example to illustrate how we can construct descriptor pattern table. This will pave the way for extraction of rules for the classifier.

Consider a collection of 18 patterns over 3 classes which are described by 3 features F_1, F_2, F_3 as shown in Table 11.1. We have arbitrarily assigned class label 1 to patterns 0-5, class label 2 to patterns 6-11 and class label 3 to patterns 12-17.

Let us now define 3 fuzzy sets for each feature on the respective domains of the 3 features. The domains of F_1, F_2, F_3 are 0-13, 4-16 and 0-16 respectively. We denote the fuzzy sets by $A_{i,j}$, i=0,1,2 and j=0,1,2 such that $A_{i,j}$ is the jth fuzzy set on the ith feature. Let us assume that membership functions are equispaced symmetric triangles.

Thus, for each feature, we create 3 equispaced symmetric triangles such that they cover the entire domain of that feature. The range of the domain is increased on either side (minimum and maximum) by 5%. As mentioned

Table 11.1 The 18 - point data set

Pattern Id	F_1	F_2	F_3	Class
0	0	4	8	1
1	4	5	8	1
2	1	6	12	1
3	2	8	15	1
4	3	7	13	1
5	4	7	16	1
6	4	8	4	2
7	5	9	1	2
8	6	10	0	2
9	7	16	2	2
1	8	14	3	2
1	7	13	2	2
12	8	4	0	3
13	9	5	1	3
14	10	6	2	3
15	11	7	3	3
16	12	8	4	3
17	13	4	5	3

earlier any two adjacent triangles overlap such that the peak of one triangle is connected to the midpoint of the base of adjacent triangles. Thus, we arrive at the 9 fuzzy sets shown in Table 11.2.

To construct the initial DP table consider a pattern x_i. For is j-th feature x_{ij} find out the fuzzy set $A_{j,k}$ in which it has the highest membership, μ^*. Include x_i and μ^* in the cell corresponding to $A_{j,k}$ and the class to which the pattern belongs. This is done for all feature values for all patterns. The final DP table obtained is shown in Table 11.3. In Table 11.3, the column for each class is split into two subcolumns, the first one corresponds to pattern list and the second one is for the membership list.

Following *step 1* we find that there is no row in which all cells are empty. So none of the rows can be ignored. Next, following step 2, we find that for each of the rows with descriptors $A_{0,2}, A_{1,1}, A_{1,2}, A_{2,1}, A_{2,2}$ only one cell (column) contains entries; we call them distinct descriptors as they are able to classify patterns on their own. Rest of the rows are termed

Table 11.2 Fuzzy sets for the 18 - point data set

Fuzzy Features	Peak	Base (b)	Left end (a)	Right end (c)
$A_{0,0}$	2.925	7.15	-0.65	6.5
$A_{0,1}$	6.5	7.15	2.925	10.075
$A_{0,2}$	10.075	7.15	6.5	13.65
$A_{1,0}$	6.7	6.6	3.4	10
$A_{1,1}$	10	6.6	6.7	13.3
$A_{1,2}$	13.3	6.6	10	16 6
$A_{2,0}$	3.6	8.8	-0.8	8
$A_{2,1}$	8	8.8	3.6	12.4
$A_{2,2}$	12.4	8.8	8	16.8

as common descriptors. The next task is to partition the descriptors into first-level distinct descriptors and common descriptors to get two refined tables shown in Table 11.4 and Table 11.5. In these two tables, instead of showing the list of membership values, we only include the minimum membership value.

In the first level distinct descriptor pattern table there are 5 rows or descriptors. So 5 rules can be formed from these distinct descriptors :
Rule 1: $[A_{0,2} \geq 0.181818] \Longrightarrow 3$. This rule *identifies* $\{13, 14, 15, 16, 17\}$
Rule 2: $[A_{1,1} \geq 0.696969] \Longrightarrow 2$. This rule *identifies* $\{7, 8\}$
Rule 3: $[A_{1,2} \geq 0.181818] \Longrightarrow 2$. This rule *identifies* $\{9, 10, 11\}$
Rule 4: $[A_{2,1} = 1] \Longrightarrow 1$. This rule *identifies* $\{0, 1\}$
Rule 5: $[A_{2,2} \geq 0.181818] \Longrightarrow 1$. This rule *identifies* $\{2, 3, 4, 5\}$

The notation "$[A_{i,j} \geq q.] \Longrightarrow l$" means that " if $A_{i,j}(x_i) \geq q$ then **x** is from class l". Thus, for a given data point **x**, Rule 1 can be interpreted as "If membership value x_1 (i.e., value of the first feature F_1) to the fuzzy set 2 (3rd fuzzy set on the domain of F_1) is greater than or equal to 0.181818, then **x** belongs to class 3".

The values associated with the descriptors in the rules are called threshold values. To satisfy a rule, the membership value to each descriptor (fuzzy set) in the rule should be greater than or equal to the threshold value for that descriptor; for a negated descriptor, the membership value should be less than the threshold value. All conditions on the descriptors in a rule should be satisfied to draw any inference from a rule.

Next we follow step 3 to build descriptor pattern Tables 11.6 and 11.7.

Table 11.3 Initial DP table for the 18 - point data set

Descriptors	Class 1		Class 2		Class 3	
	L^1	M^1	L^2	M^2	L^3	M^3
$A_{0,0}$	0	0.181818	6	0.699301		
	1	0.699301				
	2	0.461538				
	3	0.741259				
	4	0.979021				
	5	0.699301				
$A_{0,1}$			7	0.58042	12	0.58042
			8	0.86014		
			9	0.86014		
			10	0.58042		
			11	0.86014		
$A_{0,2}$					13	0.699301
					14	0.979021
					15	0.741259
					16	0.461538
					17	0.181818
$A_{1,0}$	0	0.181818	6	0.606061	12	0.181818
	1	0.484848			13	0.484848
	2	0.787879			14	0.787879
	3	0.606061			15	0.909091
	4	0.909091			16	0.606061
	5	0.909091			17	0.181818
$A_{1,1}$			7	0.69697		
			8	1		
$A_{1,2}$			9	0.181818		
			10	0.787879		
			11	0.909091		
$A_{2,0}$			6	0.909091	12	0.181818
			7	0.409091	13	0.409091
			8	0.181818	14	0.636364
			9	0.636364	15	0.863636
			10	0.863636	16	0.909091
			11	0.636364	17	0.909091
$A_{2,1}$	0	1				
	1	1				
$A_{2,2}$	2	0.909091				
	3	0.409091				
	4	0.863636				
	5	0.181818				

Table 11.4 First level distinct descriptor pattern table for the 18 - point data set

Descriptors	Class 1		Class 2		Class 3	
$A_{0,2}$					13,14,	0.181818
					15,16,17	0.181818
$A_{1,1}$			7,8	0.69697		
$A_{1,2}$			9,10,11	0.181818		
$A_{2,1}$	0,1	1				
$A_{2,2}$	2,3,4,5	0.181818				

Table 11.5 Common descriptor pattern table for the 18 - point data set

Descriptors	Class 1		Class 2		Class 3	
$A_{0,0}$	0,1,2, 3,4,5	0.181818	6	0.699301		
$A_{0,1}$			7,8,9, 10,11	0.58042	12	0.58042
$A_{1,0}$	0,1,2, 3,4,5	0.181818	6	0.606061	12,13,14 15,16,17	0.181818
$A_{2,0}$			6,7,8,9, 10,11	0.181818	12,13,14 15,16,17	0.181818

Table 11.6 is computed by one CD and negation of one first level DD while Table 11.7 is obtained by one CD and negation of two first level DDs. But those 2 tables fail to generate any rule. So we proceed to follow step 4 and build two more tables, Table 11.8 and Table 11.9. Note that in Table 11.6 and others we show only the valid combinations of descriptors.

Table 11.8 is composed of 2 common descriptors while Table 11.9 uses 3 common descriptors. Each of these two tables generates two rules.

Rule 6: $[A_{0,0} \geq 0.699301 \;\&\; A_{2,0} \geq 0.181818] \Longrightarrow 2$. This rule *identifies* pattern 6 only

Rule 7: $[A_{0,1} \geq 0.58042 \;\&\; A_{1,0} \geq 0.181818] \Longrightarrow 3$. This rule can classify pattern 12

Rule 8: $[A_{0,0} \geq 0.699301 \;\&\; A_{1,0} \geq 0.181818 \;\&\; A_{2,0} \geq 0.181818] \Longrightarrow 2$. Like rule 6, rule 8 recognizes only pattern 6.

Table 11.6 DP Table with conjunction of one CD and one negated first level DD

Descriptors	Class 1	Class 2	Class 3
$A_{0,0}\&\neg A_{1,1}$	0,1,2,3,4,5	6	
$A_{0,0}\&\neg A_{1,2}$	0,1,2,3,4,5	6	
$A_{0,0}\&\neg A_{2,1}$	2,3,4,5	6	
$A_{0,0}\&\neg A_{2,2}$	0,1	6	
$A_{0,1}\&\neg A_{1,1}$		9,10,11	12
$A_{0,1}\&\neg A_{1,2}$		7,8	12
$A_{0,1}\&\neg A_{2,1}$		7,8,9,10,11	12
$A_{0,1}\&\neg A_{2,2}$		7,8,9,10,11	12
$A_{1,0}\&\neg A_{2,1}$	2,3,4. 5	6	12,13,14,15,16,17
$A_{1,0}\&\neg A_{2,2}$	0,1	6	12,13,14,15,16,17
$A_{1,0}\&\neg A_{0,2}$	0,1,2,3,4,5	6	12,13,14,15,16,17
$A_{2,0}\&\neg A_{0,2}$		6,7,8,9,10,11	12
$A_{2,0}\&\neg A_{1,1}$		6,9,10,11	12,13,14,15,16,17
$A_{2,0}\&\neg A_{1,2}$		6,7,8,9,10,11	12,13,14,15,16,17

Rule 9: $[A_{0,1} \geq 0.58042 \ \& \ A_{1,0} \geq 0.181818 \ \& \ A_{2,0} \geq 0.181818] \implies 3$.
This rule also can classify only pattern 12.

All data points are classified by these 9 rules. So we may not proceed to generate additional rules.

11.6 Some Issues Relating to the Rule Generation Scheme

Several questions may arise pertaining to the rule generation schemes just described.

11.6.1 What Sequence of Rule Generation to Follow ?

How to create the subsequent tables after partitioning of the initial table? In the model that we have followed, first we find out rules containing only one DD and then the rules that contain one CD and negation of one or more first level DDs. Next we extract rules that contain 2 or more CDs. After that we determine the rules in which the descriptors are negation of 2 or more first level DDs. There may be other possibilities as well. For

Table 11.7 DP table with conjunction of one CD and two negated first level DDs

Descriptors	Class 1	Class 2	Class 3
$A_{0,0} \& \neg A_{1,1} \& \neg A_{2,1}$	2,3,4,5	6	
$A_{0,0} \& \neg A_{1,1} \& \neg A_{2,2}$	0,1	6	
$A_{0,0} \& \neg A_{1,2} \& \neg A_{2,1}$	2,3,4,5	6	
$A_{0,0} \& \neg A_{1,2} \& \neg A_{2,2}$	0,1	6	
$A_{0,1} \& \neg A_{1,1} \& \neg A_{2,1}$		9,10,11	12
$A_{0,1} \& \neg A_{1,1} \& \neg A_{2,2}$		9,10,11	12
$A_{0,1} \& \neg A_{1,2} \& \neg A_{2,1}$		7,8	12
$A_{0,1} \& \neg A_{1,2} \& \neg A_{2,2}$		7,8	12
$A_{1,0} \& \neg A_{0,2} \& \neg A_{2,1}$	2,3,4,5	6	12,13,14,15,16,17
$A_{1,0} \& \neg A_{0,2} \& \neg A_{2,2}$	0,1	6	12,13,14,15,16,17
$A_{2,0} \& \neg A_{0,2} \& \neg A_{1,1}$		6,9,10,11	12
$A_{2,0} \& \neg A_{0,2} \& \neg A_{1,2}$		6,7,8	12

Table 11.8 DP table with conjunction of 2 CDs

Descriptors	Class 1	Class 2	Class 3
$A_{0,0} \& A_{1,0}$	0,1,2,3,4,5	6	
$A_{0,0} \& A_{2,0}$		6	
$A_{0,1} \& A_{1,0}$			12
$A_{0,1} \& A_{2,0}$		7,8,9,10,11	12
$A_{1,0} \& A_{2,0}$		6	12,13,14,15,16,17

Table 11.9 DP table with conjunction of 3 CDs

Descriptors	Class 1	Class 2	Class 3
$A_{0,0} \& A_{1,0} \& A_{2,0}$		6	
$A_{0,1} \& A_{1,0} \& A_{2,0}$			12

example, first find all rules consisting of only 2 descriptors. Then find all rules consisting of 3 descriptors and so on. The rule set generated this way may, usually will, be different. Moreover, the same data point may be classified by more than one rule.

How long should the rule generation be continued? The technique may vary. The basic idea is that all the training patterns which are used to build the descriptor pattern table should be classified by the rules that we generate. Once all training data points are classified we can stop. In this case the extracted rule base will depend on the order in which different low level descriptors are combined to form higher level descriptors. Moreover, one can reduce the data set after some points are classified by some rule. But continuing to find all the rules may have some advantage also which we discuss next.

11.6.2 Rule Minimization

It may so happen that number of rules that have been generated are very high and may even exceed the number of patterns that have been used to generate the rules. It is possible that a subset of rules classifies the entire set of patterns, or that a subset of rules classifies a specific subset of patterns which are again classified by a different subset of rules. Consider a data set with 4 points. To illustrate the various possibilities, consider the following cases.

Case 1: Let us consider a situation in which 4 rules a, b, c and d have been generated where rule a classifies patterns 1 and 2, rule b classifies patterns 3 and 4, rule c classifies patterns 1 and 3, rule d classifies patterns 2 and 4. In such a situation either rules a and b or rules c and d will be sufficient.

Case 2: Let there be 3 generated rules, a, b and c, where rule a classifies patterns 1, 2 and 4; rule b classifies patterns 3; and rule c classifies patterns 1 and 3. In this case rule a and any one of the rest will be enough.

In such a scenario, we go for minimization over the original set of rules that have been generated. But to do this, we need to know which rules classify which patterns. Then we select the smallest set of rules which classifies all the training patterns. This means finding the minimum cover of a finite set which is computationally very expensive. So we use an approximate but effective technique to get a reasonably small set of rules.

11.6.2.1 Algorithm for Rule Minimization

We first sort the set of rules in descending order of the number of patterns that each rule classifies. Let $R = \{R_1, R_2, \cdots, R_K\}$ be the list of rules after sorting and P_i be set of patterns classified by rule R_i such that $\mid P_i \mid \geq$

$\mid P_{i+1} \mid$. We now proceed as follows:

Step 1. Remove R_1 from the list and put it in the list of minimized rules.
Step 2. For all other rules remaining in the set, perform the set operation $P_i - P_1 (i \neq 1)$.
Step 3. Remove all rules R_i from the set for which the new $\mid P_i \mid = 0$.
Step 4. Sort the remaining set in descending order of the new $\mid P_i \mid$.
Step 5. Renumber all the rules with R_1 at the head.
Step 6. Perform steps 1 to 5 until the list is empty.

Such a procedure will retain rules that classify more points. This is very reasonable as for example, if a rule classifies just one point, then that rule is not expected to have much generalization capability.

11.6.3 Ambiguous Data and Unclassified Points

In the process of rule generation it may not always be possible to classify all the training patterns though the rules themselves are generated from the training data. This may not be obvious from the example that has been used for illustration of computation of the descriptor pattern table and subsequent rule generation. In the first sight it may appear unacceptable but this is a distinct possibility and has some merit. The entire concept of classification is based on an implicit assumption that patterns belonging to different classes occupy distinct regions in the feature space. So the greater the distance between the classes, the better is the chance of successful classification. But there might be cases in which there is significant overlap among different class boundaries for one or more features. If there are 2 similar patterns from different classes, then these patterns should not be classified and should be termed as ambiguous or unclassified patterns. The chief distinguishing feature of the proposed classifier from those already known is its ability to pinpoint the patterns that are ambiguous. This is not only applicable to training patterns but to the test patterns as well.

Consider for example 2 training data points $\mathbf{x} \in R^p$, $\mathbf{y} \in R^p$ such that $x_i = y_i, \forall\, i \neq k$ and $x_k = y_k + \epsilon$, where ϵ is a very small quantity. Suppose $\mathbf{x}$ is from class i and $\mathbf{y}$ from class j. This means that two patterns belonging to different classes fall in the same fuzzy sets for all features, so they are ambiguous. For test data, an unclassified point means that none of rules has been able to conclude about its class, i.e., no rule is satisfied. When a test data point is quite far from the training data, usually it will be declared as unclassified. This is not to be confused with misclassification when the rules suggest that the pattern belongs to a particular class whereas it actually belongs to some other class.

It is, however, possible to reduce the number of unclassified points by increasing the number of fuzzy sets on the input feature space, but this will increase the number of rules and generalization ability of the rule base may be reduced. The capability of the proposed classifier to find unclassified points is a distinct advantage.

Some classifiers (like RID3 [6]) perform feature analysis to find the most distinguishing features and assign more weights to them during classification. The proposed method, however, requires no such feature ranking but the rules which have been generated, themselves provide such information. For example, the features used in the rules generated from first level distinct descriptors are the most distinguishable features. Then the features contained in rules generated from second level distinct descriptors form the next subset of important features. This way the proposed classifier does an implicit feature analysis.

11.7 Classification of Test Data Using the Generated Rules

While classifying an unknown data point, we may find that different rules are suggesting different classes. Thus, in general there may be situations where different rules indicate different classes. To resolve this, we suggest 2 approaches.

i) Voting Approach: In this approach, whichever class gets the maximum number of votes is considered the class of the pattern. Ties can be broken arbitrarily.

ii) Conservative Approach: Here the minimum of all membership values in different descriptors involved in the rule is taken as firing strength of the rule. After considering the firing strength of all rules which can classify the pattern, the view of the rule with the maximum strength is taken. The membership value of a negated descriptor, for the purpose of computing firing strength, is found by subtracting the membership value from 1, e.g., if for a descriptor $A_{i,j}$, the membership value is t for a class, then the membership value for firing strength calculation of the negated descriptor is $(1-t)$. For example, the firing strength of a rule $A_{i,j} \wedge \neg A_{l,m}$ is taken as $min\{A_{i,j}(x_i), 1 - A_{l,m}(x_l)\}$. Note that, this will be computed only for the rules that can classify the data point under consideration.

11.8 Tuning With Genetic Algorithms

While building the rulebase, we try to keep the number of unclassified training patterns as well as the number of rules to as minimum as possible. If we go for more number of fuzzy sets, the number of unclassified training patterns may come down, but it is more likely that the number of rules will go up. So instead of going for more number of fuzzy sets, if we tune rule base we might be able to improve its performance. With this hope in mind we use genetic algorithms (GAs) [14] to tune the rulebase.

To tune the rule base, here we tune only the membership functions of the fuzzy sets. If the DP table has been created with k fuzzy sets per feature, then the total number of fuzzy sets in the system is equal to $T = p*k$. If the DP table has been created with k fuzzy sets per class per feature basis then $T = n*c*k$. Each string (chromosome) comprises the binary representation of all the triangle parameters. For equispaced symmetric triangles, the parameters are the base width and x co-ordinate of the peak whereas for triangles created with FCM, left width, peak and right width constitute the parameters. The fitness function or the objective function is defined by the total number of unclassified and misclassified data points.

We take each string from the population, then with the set of thresholds obtained during creation of the initial rules, we test the classifier with the training set and evaluate the fitness function, i.e., compute the sum of the number of unclassified and incorrectly classified data points. Then depending on the fitness values strings are copied into the mating pool and the usual operations like crossover and mutation are performed.

11.9 Results

To evaluate the performance of the proposed classifier, we have used several data sets but here we reports results only on Anderson's IRIS data [13]. IRIS is a 4-Dimensional data consisting of 150 points divided into three classes of equal size 50. The four features are Sepal Length, Sepal Width, Petal Length and Petal Width. IRIS has been used in many research investigation related to pattern recognition and has become a sort of benchmark-data.

We divide the data set randomly into two equal halves and then treat one set as test set while the other as the design(training) set and vice

versa. To elaborate further, we have $X = X_1 \cup X_2 \cup \cdots \cup X_c$. We randomly partitioned X into X^D and X^T such that
$X = X^D \cup X^T$,
$X^D \cap X^T = \phi$,
$X^D = X_1^D \cup X_2^D \cup \cdots \cup X_c^D$,
$X^T = X_1^T \cup X_2^T \cup \cdots \cup X_c^T$,
$X_i = X_i^D \cup X_i^T$ and $X_i^D \cap X_i^T = \phi$
If $\mid X_i \mid = n_i$, then $\mid X_i^D \mid = n_i/2$ and $\mid X_i^T \mid = n_i/2$.

We report the results obtained using all three types of membership functions: equispaced triangles, asymmetric triangular MFs created with the centroids obtained by FCM on the whole training data set, and asymmetric triangular MFs created with centroids obtained by FCM on each X_i^D, $i = 1, 2, \cdots c$. The results are shown with and without tuning by genetic algorithms and in all cases we used the conservative approach.

Table 11.10 Results of classification on IRIS using MFs generated from equispaced symmetric triangles

LVs/feat	3			4				5			
Total No of LVs	12			16				20			
Rules	47			39				73			
Reduced Rules	5			11				10			
Genetic Tuning	not done		done		not done		done		not done		done	
Data	TR	TE	TR	TE	TR	TE	TR	TE	TR	TE	TR	TE
No. of Patterns	75	75	75	75	75	75	75	75	75	75	75	75
Classified	69	61	73	70	71	65	74	73	72	64	74	65
Mis-Cla	-	3	1	1	-	2	1	2	-	6	1	7
Un-Cla	6	11	1	4	4	8	0	0	3	5	0	3
Error %	-	19	3	7	-	13	1	3	-	15	1	13

Row 1 of Table 11.10 indicates the number of Linguistic Values used for each feature (LVs/feat) while the 3rd row shows the total number of rules initially generated. In Table 11.10 and in subsequent tables we use TR to denote the training data and TE to indicate the test data. The number of rules is dramatically reduced after the rule minimization. In case of equispaced symmetric triangles, as we increase the number of fuzzy sets the number of unclassified training data, as expected, comes down. The number of unclassified (Un-Cla) test data points also decreases. The performance is better when the fuzzy sets have been tuned using genetic algorithms.

Table 11.11 Results of classification on IRIS using asymmetric triangular MFs generated with centroids obtained by FCM on the entire training data set

LVs/feat	3				4				5			
Total No of LVs	12				16				20			
No. rules	32				34				62			
Reduced Rules	8				10				12			
Genetic Tuning	not done		done		not done		done		not done		done	
Data	TR	TE	TR	TE	TR	TE	TR	TE	TR	TE	TR	TE
No. of Patterns	75	75	75	75	75	75	75	75	75	75	75	75
Classified	61	58	75	71	68	66	75	71	72	70	74	71
Mis-Cla	-	2	0	4	-	4	0	4	-	2	1	4
Un-Cla	14	15	0	0	7	5	0	0	3	3	0	0
Error %	-	23	0	5	-	12	0	5	-	7	1	5

Table 11.11 shows that as we create more number of fuzzy sets, the number of unclassified points, both in training and in test sets decreases while the number of rules goes up. Though nothing definite can be said about the number of mis-classifications (Mis-Cla) in the test data with increase in the number of fuzzy sets, the overall performance improves considerably. Like the previous case, the performance with tuning is better than without tuning.

Genetic tuning is carried out with the sole objective of reducing the number of unclassified and misclassified training data points, if there is any. For the case reported in Table 11.12, since there is no misclassified or unclassified points for the training data, the genetic tuning has not been done. Thus we see that when class information is used, the initial membership functions are quite good, at least for the IRIS data.

To summarize, with increase in the number of partitions in the feature

Table 11.12 Results of classification on IRIS using asymmetric triangular MFs generated with centroids obtained by FCM on each X_i, $i = 1, 2, \cdots c$

LVs/feat	1			2			3			
Total No. of LVs	12			24			36			
No. rules	51			104			111			
Reduced Rules	7			14			14			
Genetic Tuning	not done		done		not done		done		not done	done
Data	TR	TE	TR	TE	TR	TE	TR	TE	TR	TE
No. of Patterns	75	75	-	-	75	75	-	-	75	75	-	-
Classified	75	65	-	-	75	67	-	-	75	65	-	-
Mis-Cla	-	6	-	-	-	2	-	-	-	2	-	-
Un-Cla	0	4	-	-	0	6	-	-	0	8	-	-
Error %	-	13	-	-	-	11	-	-	-	13	-	-

space, on an average the number of unclassified training data reduces and the number of rules generated goes up. In this case, performance on training data improves at the cost of more rules. But that does not necessarily reduce the classification error on the test data because more rules usually reduce generalization ability. We also find that there has been a considerable improvement of the performance when genetic tuning was applied.

11.10 Conclusion and Discussion

Pao-Hu method (PHM) has limited use as it can handle only categorical data. Our proposed fuzzy generalization scheme is able to extract fuzzy rules to produce crisp class labels with real data. One feature of the proposed scheme, which separates it from majority of the classifiers is that it introduces the concept of unclassified test data. It has the capability of finding ambiguous data and declare them as unclassified. The proposed method does an implicit feature analysis. It can also deal with fuzzy test data which we explain next.

Handling of Fuzzy Test Data

If the test data are fuzzy, i.e., expressed by membership functions such as, x_{ij} is HIGH or x_{ij} is MEDIUM and so on, then to apply the proposed method we need a mechanism to find the extent to which a fuzzy input, characterized by a membership function (not just a value), satisfies the relevant antecedent clause of a rule. Suppose one of the antecedent clauses of a rule is "If x_1 is $A_{1,j}$", here x_1 is the first component of $\mathbf{x}$. Let the first feature of a test data point be described by "$x_{i1} = B_1$" where B_1 is a fuzzy set. The question is, to what extent B_1 satisfies $A_{1,j}$? One solution could be to use any measure of subsethood [5] $0 \leq S(A_{1,j}, B_1) \leq 1$. The rest of the procedure remains the same, i.e., in place of $\mu_{1,j}$ we use $S(A_{1,j}, B_1)$.

However, as with any other algorithm, there is some scope for improvement. The rule minimization method that we have chosen may not be the most ideal one. Significant improvement may be obtained if we do not go for any removal of rules that we considered redundant. The inherent weakness of the rule minimization technique lies in the fact that it takes into account only the number of data points that a rule classifies while ignoring the confidence with which they make the decisions. As a result, many rules which classify fewer data points with high confidence gets eliminated, while rules with low confidence may find place in the rule base, which in turn may degrade the performance of the rule base. So the rule minimization algorithm can be modified to take into account this factor. We have used very simple definitions MFs and their tuning can improve the performance of the classifier.

References

[1] Y. H. Pao, "Adaptive Pattern-Recognition and Neural Network," Addition-Wesley, New York, 1989.

[2] Y. H. Pao and C. H. Hu, "Processing of pattern based information, Part I : Inductive methods suitable for use in pattern recognition and artificial intelligence," In J. T. Tou (Ed.), Advances in Information Systems Science, Vol. 9, Plenum Press, NY, 1985.

[3] I. Hayashi and J. Ozawa, "A proposal of Fuzzy ID3 with ability of learning for AND/OR operators," Proc. 1996 Asian Fuzzy System Symp, (AFSS'96), Taiwan, pp 24-29, 1996.

[4] I. Hayashi, "Acquisition of fuzzy rules using fuzzy ID3 with ability of learning," Proc. of ANZIIS, 1996.

[5] B. Kosko, "Neural networks and fuzzy systems," Prentice Hall , Englewood Cliff,NJ, 1992.

[6] N. R. Pal, S. Chakraborty and A. Bagchi, "RID3:An ID3-Like Algorithm for Real Data," Information Sciences, 96, pp 271-290, 1997

[7] Gerrid P. M. , and R. J. Lantz, "Chemical Analysis of 75 crude oil samples from pliocence sand units," Elk oil fields, California , U. S. Geological Survey Open-File Report, 1969

[8] J. C. Bezdek, "Pattern Recognition With Fuzzy Objective Function Algorithms," Plenum Press, New York, 1981

[9] J. C. Bezdek, J. M. Keller, R. Krishnapuram and N. R. Pal, "Fuzzy Models and Algorithms for Pattern recognition and Image Processing", Kluwer Academic Publishers, 1999.

[10] R.O. Duda and P.E. Hart, "Pattern Classification and Scene Analysis", Wiley, New York, 1973.

[11] S. Haykin, "Neural Networks - a Comprehensive foundation", Macmillan College Proc. Inc. NY, 1994.

[12] S. L. Chiu, "Fuzzy model identification based on cluster estimation", Jour. Intell. Fuzzy Systs., 2, 267-278, 1994.

[13] E. Anderson, "The irises of the gaspe peninsula", Bull. American Iris Society, 1935.

[14] D.E.Goldberg, "Genetic Algorithms in Search, Optimization, and Machine Learning", Addison-Wesley,1989.

Chapter 12
Genetic Programming based Texture Filtering Framework

Mario Köppen,   Bertram Nickolay

Fraunhofer IPK Berlin
Department Pattern Recognition
Pascalstr. 8–9, 10587 Berlin, Germany

Abstract

A framework is presented, which allows for the automated generation of texture filters by exploiting the 2D-Lookup algorithm and its optimization by evolutionary algorithms. To use the framework, the user has to give an original image, containing the structural property-of-interest (e.g. a surface fault), and a binary image (goal image), wherein each position of the structural property-of-interest is labeled with the foreground color. Doing so, the framework becomes capable of evolving the configuration of the 2D-Lookup algorithm towards a texture filter for the structural property-of-interest. Genetic programming (GP) is used as the evolutionary algorithm. For this GP approach, a filter generator derives two operations based on formal superoperators from the tree, which represents an individual of the evolving population. The specification of the 2D-Lookup matrix is performed by a relaxation technique. The approach will be demonstrated on texture fault examples.

Keywords : pattern recognition, scene analysis, image processing, texture analysis, texture filtering, mathematical morphology, 2D-Lookup algorithm, evolutionary algorithms, genetic algorithms, genetic programming, fitness function, relaxation, convolution, ordered weighted averaging, texture numbers, ordered weighted minimum, multilayer backpropagation neural network, crossover, mutation, document preprocessing, visual inspection of surfaces, handwriting extraction, image processing framework

12.1 Introduction

Textures are homogeneous visual patterns that we find in natural or synthetic scenes. They are made of local micropatterns, repeated somehow.

producing the sensation of uniformity. Texture perception plays an important role in human vision. It is used to detect and distinguish objects, to infer surface orientation and perspective, and to determine shape in 3D scenes. An interesting psychological observation is the fact that human beings are not able to describe textures clearly and objectively, but only subjectively by using a fuzzy characterization of them [8].

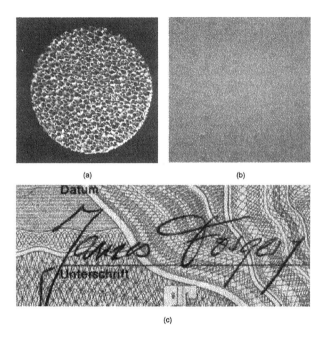

Fig. 12.1 Textures: ceramic filter (a), textile fault (b) and handwriting on bankcheck background texture (c).

Texture analysis is a subfield of image processing, which is concerned with the exploitation of pictorial textures for various image inspection tasks (see fig. 12.1). Such tasks, typically handled by methods of texture analysis, are texture segmentation, texture fault detection, texture synthesis and texture removal.

The purpose of texture filtering is to find image processing operations based on pixel information, which assign a texture class to a subregion of the image. Usually, the pixels, whose grayvalues or color values are used for these computations*, are taken from the image region, which has to be classified. Typical regions are: local neighborhoods (i.e., a pixel and its direct neighbours); regions-of-interest (connected subsets of the set of all pixels); windows (rectangularily bounded subsets); or the whole image. Means for computations are based on a rich variability of mathematical or information theoretical concepts, as, e.g., statistical approaches, structural approaches, fractal approaches or spectral approaches [3].

A given texture filtering approach can be considered a framework. This means, that some components of the processing chain and the relations between them remain open for adaptation, i.e. the texture filter has to be *configured* (by numerical or structural parameters, by operator selection and so forth) in order to fulfill its task. In some cases, the configuration might become too complex to be supplied by an user of the superposed system, of which the framework is a part. Adaptive techniques are needed in this case.

Since the early days of computer vision, the feature based classification approach has become the primary texture analysis technique for the treatment of images of textured surfaces. The key steps of the feature classification approach are: image acquisition, image preprocessing, feature extraction, feature selection and feature classification [4], [5]. The feature classification approach can be employed as a texture filter as well. Its main disadvantage is the underlying concept of a single processing chain, which is "as strong as its weakest part." In order to improve reliability and robustness of the texture filters, backtracking in the processing chain may be used. However, this is impractical, since the effect of modification of a part of the chain at its end can hardly be predicted, and since the number of alternative settings to explore in order to find better ones grows exponentially with the number of alternatives for each part. A better idea is to decompose the processing flow into several parallel parts with a knowledge of what has to be acquired by these subparts at its ends (for example that an edge image should be the result). Finally, the subparts are fused by a fixed algorithm. An example for this is the fusion of an edge image and a pre-classified image by the watershed transformation [7]. If there are exactly two subparts, the approach is referred to as 2D framework [10].

This paper presents a special 2D texture filtering framework based on the so-called 2D-Lookup, and its configuration by means of evolutionary

---

*These values are referred to as pixel values in the following.

algorithms. The 2D-Lookup framework allows, by its configuration, to represent a very large number of texture filters. By genetic programming (GP), framework configurations are evolved, which meet the user-given filtering goal as good as possible. This paper is organized as follows: in section 12.2, the framework LUCIFER2[†] is described. Its subsections detail the 2D-Lookup algorithm, recall evolutionary algorithms, give the fitness measure used and the relaxation procedure for deriving a 2D-Lookup matrix from two operation images and detail the structure of a tree, which represents an individual of a GP. Then, in section 12.3, this framework is applied to a set of texture fault detection tasks. The paper ends with the summary, an acknowledgment and the reference.

12.2 The LUCIFER2 Framework

The purpose of the presented framework is to design texture filters. Trained by user-provided examples, the adapted filters are able to separate a textured background from a foreground structure. Possible applications for these texture filters are: texture fault detection, texture border detection or handwriting extraction (on a bankcheck with textured background). These problems typically arise in fields like visual surface inspection on fabrics or optical document preprocessing.

The framework (see fig. 12.2) is composed of (user- supplied) original image, filter generator, operation images 1 and 2, result image, (user-supplied) goal image, 2D-Lookup matrix, comparing unit and filter generation signal.

The framework can be thought of as being composed of three (overlapping) layers.

(1) The instruction layer, which consists of the user-supplied parts of the framework: original image and goal image. The user may also supply other components (operation 1, operation 2, 2D-Lookup matrix), for maintenance purposes.
(2) The algorithm layer performs the actual 2D-Lookup, once all of its components (original image, operation 1, operation 2 and 2D-Lookup matrix) are given.
(3) The adaptation layer contains all adaptable components of the frame-

---

[†]This is an acronym for Lookup Compositional Inference System. Number 2 indicates that there was a genetic algorithm based version 1 [9].

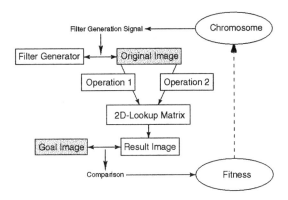

Fig. 12.2 The Framework for 2D-Lookup based texture filter generation.

work (operation 1, operation 2, 2D-Lookup matrix) and additional components for performing the adaptation (comparison unit, filter generator).

For the instruction layer, the user interface has been designed as simple as possible. The user instructs LUCIFER2 by manually drawing a (binary) goal image from the original image (by a photo retouching program as Photoshop). In this image, texture background is set to White and texture foreground (e.g. the texture fault, handwriting on a textured bankcheck background) to Black (see Fig.12.3 for an example). Rest of the approach is data-driven. No special texture model has to be known by the user. There are no further requirements for the goal image.

The algorithm layer performs the 2D-Lookup algorithm, which will be described in the next subsection. The algorithm decomposes the filter operation into a set of partial steps, each of which might be adapted to meet the user's instruction.

Adaptation is considered an optimization problem, and evolutionary algorithms are used for performing this adaptation. The fitness function is computed with the degree of resemblance between result image of an individual-specified 2D-Lookup and the goal image.

12.2.1 *2D-Lookup Algorithm*

The 2D-Lookup algorithm stems from mathematical morphology [13], [14]. It was primarily intended for the segmentation of color images. However,

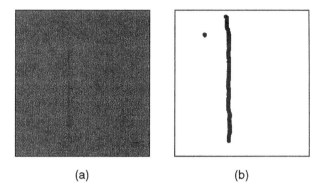

Fig. 12.3 Example for texture image containing fault (a) and goal image, as given by the user (b).

the algorithm can be generalized to use for grayvalue images as well.

For starting off the 2D-Lookup algorithm, the two operation images 1 and 2, which are of equal size, need to be provided. This is achieved by the filter generation signal, which is under the control of the individuals of the evolving population. The filter generation signal causes the filter generator to determine two image processing operations, which are applied to the original image. The 2D-Lookup algorithm goes over all common positions of the two operation images. For each position, the two pixel values at this position in operation images 1 and 2 are used as indices for looking-up the 2D-Lookup matrix. The matrix element, which is found there, is used as pixel value for this position of the result image. If the matrix is bi-valued (as for the goal image), the resultant image is a binary image.

Let I_1 and I_2 be two grayvalue images, defined by their image functions g_1 and g_2 over their common domain $P \subseteq \mathcal{N} \times \mathcal{N}$:

$$g_1 : \quad P \to \{0, \ldots, g_{max}\}$$
$$g_2 : \quad P \to \{0, \ldots, g_{max}\} \qquad (1)$$

The 2D-Lookup matrix is also given as an image function l, but its domain is not the set of all image positions but the set of tupels of possible grayvalue pairs $\{0, \ldots, g_{max}\} \times \{0, \ldots, g_{max}\}$,

$$l : \quad \{0, \ldots, g_{max}\} \times \{0, \ldots, g_{max}\} \to S \subseteq \{0, \ldots, g_{max}\}. \qquad (2)$$

Then, the resultant image function is given by:

$$r : P \to S$$
$$r(x,y) = l(g_1(x,y), g_2(x,y)). \tag{3}$$

In standard applications, every grayvalue is coded by eight bit, resulting in a maximum grayvalue of 255. Also, the domain of the image function is a rectangle. In this case, the 2D-Lookup is performed by the following (object-oriented) pseudo-code:

```
for x=0 to img width -1 do
begin
    for y=0 to img height-1 do
    begin
        g1 = g1(x,y)
        g2 = g2(x,y)
        out(x,y) = l(g1,g2)
    end y
end x
```

To give a simple example for the 2D-Lookup procedure, $g_{max} = 3$ is assumed in the following. Let

$$g_1 : \begin{array}{|c|c|c|} \hline 0 & 1 & 2 \\ \hline 0 & 3 & 3 \\ \hline \end{array} \quad \text{and} \quad g_2 : \begin{array}{|c|c|c|} \hline 2 & 3 & 1 \\ \hline 2 & 3 & 2 \\ \hline \end{array}$$

be the two input images and the 2D-Lookup matrix be given by

$$l : \begin{array}{|c||c|c|c|c|} \hline \frac{g_1}{g_2} & 0 & 1 & 2 & 3 \\ \hline\hline 0 & 0 & 0 & 1 & 1 \\ \hline 1 & 0 & 1 & 2 & 2 \\ \hline 2 & 1 & 2 & 3 & 3 \\ \hline 3 & 2 & 3 & 3 & 2 \\ \hline \end{array}$$

Then, the resultant image is

$$r : \begin{array}{|c|c|c|} \hline l(0,2) & l(1,3) & l(2,1) \\ \hline l(0,2) & l(3,3) & l(3,2) \\ \hline \end{array} = \begin{array}{|c|c|c|} \hline 1 & 3 & 2 \\ \hline 1 & 2 & 3 \\ \hline \end{array}$$

Since the goal image is supplied as a binary one and in order to keep user instruction as simple as possible, in the following the 2D-Lookup matrix contains only binary entries Black (0) and White (1).

12.2.2 Genetic Algorithms and Genetic Programming

Evolutionary algorithms are a family of computer models based on the mechanics of natural selection and natural genetics. Among them are genetic algorithms (GA) [6] and genetic programming (GP) [11]. Genetic algorithms were introduced and investigated by John Holland [6]. Later, they became popular by the book of David Goldberg [2]. Also, consider the GA tutorial of David Whitley [15] as a very good introduction to the field.

GAs and GPs are typically used for optimization problems. An optimization problem is given by a mapping $F : X \to Y$. The task is to find an element $x \in X$ for which $y = f(x), y \in Y$ is optimal in some sense. Genetic algorithms encodes a potential solution on a simple chromosome-like data structure, and apply genetic operators such as crossover or mutation to these structures. Then, the potential solution is decoded to the value x in the search space X, and $y = f(x)$ is computed. The obtained value y is considered as a quality measure, i.e. the fitness for this data structure. Some genetic operators, such as the mating selection, are under control of these fitness values, some other, like the mutation, are not related to fitness at all.

An implementation of a GA begins with a population of "chromosomes" (generation 1). For standard GA, each chromosome (also referred to as individual) is represented as a bitstring of a fixed length (e.g. 0101101 as a bitstring of length 7). Then, the genetic operators are applied onto all bitstrings iteratively in a fixed order, going from one generation to the next until a given goal (e.g. fitness value exceeds a given threshold or a predefined number of generations was completed) is met. Finally, the individual (or chromosome) with the best fitness value in the final generation is taken as the evolved solution of the optimization problem.

Figure 12.4 illustrates the iteration of a GA from generation n to generation $(n+1)$. At first, $2m$ bitstrings are selected out of the k individuals of generation n for mating. Usually, this is done by fitness-proportionate selection, i.e., the relative probability for an individual to be selected is proportional to its fitness value. The better the fitness, the better is the chance to spread out its "genetic material" (i.e., some of its bits) over the next generation.

Once the $2m$ individuals are chosen, they are paired. In the two bitstrings of each pair, a common splitting point is randomly selected, and a new bitstring is constructed by combining a half of the first bitstring with

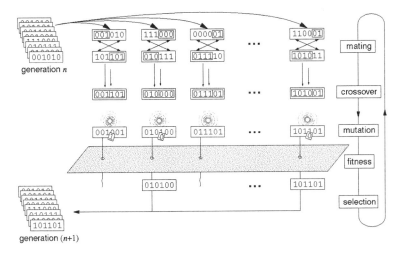

Fig. 12.4 General flow of a genetic algorithm: from generation n, individuals are selected for mating, according to their fitness. By crossover, new individuals are generated from the selected ones. Further, these new individuals are mutated, and its fitness function is computed. Only the individuals with the highest fitness values constitute the next generation $(n+1)$.

the other half of the other bitstring. Then, the new individuals are mutated, i.e. some of its bits are reversed with a given (usually small) probability. This gives the so-called *m children* of parent generation n.

Now, the fitness values of the children are evaluated by decoding them into x values and computing the $f(x)$. Some of the children might have a better fitness than its parents. From the k individuals of generation n and the m children, the best k individuals constitute the next generation $(n+1)$.

While randomized, GAs are no simple random walks. For the standard GA, John Holland has derived the well-known Schemata Theorem, which models a GA by means of the so-called schematas (or similarity templates). A schema is an incomplete bitstring in the sense that it contains unspecified bits. An example for a schema is 10*110, which leaves position 3 unspecified. 101110 is a realization of this schema. Generation n contains each possible schema to some extent. It can be said, that such a schema is tested by the GA, or that trials are allocated to it by the GA. Now, one measure for a schema is the average fitness of all of its realizations. A second measure is the ratio of this avarage to the "average average" of all schemata present in the generation n, i.e. its *above-averageness*. The Schemata Theorem relates the rate of a schema within a population with this measure. It says, that the rate of a schema within a population grows exponentially with its above-averageness. The most important point here is that all schematas are tested in parallel.

Strongly related to the application of a GA is the encoding problem. In general, GAs are applied to highly non-linear, complex problems, where it is hard to find a model which provides an approach to the solution. In these applications, they are the most simple approach. However, a GA is not guaranteed to find the global optimum of a problem. It only ensures, by the Schemata Theorem, to find better solutions than the random initialized ones. GAs find evolved solutions.

Genetic programming, as introduced by John Koza [11], is in some essential points very similar to a GA: there are generations, genetic operators as crossover and mutation, and there is a fitness function. However, the GP does not evolve bitstrings or other fixed data structures but it evolves *computer programs*. The computer programs are represented by its grammatical trees (shortly: trees). Each tree is composed of the available simple programming ingredients (nodes and terminals). The fitness of a tree is obtained by *performing* the tree as a computer program. GP then proceeds with iteratively applying the standard genetic operations, selection and crossover. For crossover, two individuals are chosen randomly, but according to their fitness. Then, randomly chosen subtrees are swapped. This gives two new children individuals from its two parent individuals. Based on the fitness values of the newly created children, they may become members of the next generation.

For applying GP, there is no encoding problem. However, the specification of suitable node and terminal functions might be as complicated as the specification of an encoding procedure. The question, whether the Schemata Theorem applies to GP search as well, is still discussed. The problem here are redundancies within the trees, leading to solutions with equal fitness, but different structure. It was shown by William Langdon and Riccardo Poli [12], that this growth in redundancy is caused by the fitness pressure itself (the effect is referred to as fitness-bloating). From this, there are two hints for succesfully applying GP: don't use simple node functions, and keep the trees small in its depth.

Since the upcoming of Soft Computing, there has been a huge amount of proposals about variations and modifications of GAs and GPs. Also, many hybrid systems, combining evolutionary algorithms with neural networks and/or fuzzy logic, has been proposed. Some new families of evolutionary algorithms appeared, too (as cultural algorithms, ant algorithms, scout algorithms, immune algorithms). Also, modified GAs were succesfully applied to hard-to-handle problem fields like multiobjective optimization problems. It is far beyond the scope of this paper, to give even an overview of these proposals. The inspiration from nature and from living systems has helped to produce this new challenge in the design of powerful and versatile search algorithms.

In the following, GP is just regarded as search technique for 2D-Lookup algorithm configuration. A recently presented GA approach [9] was proven to be outperformed by the GP approach, which is detailed here. In the following subsections it is described, how the fitness of a binary result image and the goal image is computed, how this fitness measure is reused for deriving an optimal 2D-Lookup matrix from two operation images, and how the trees of a GP population are built up.

12.2.3 Fitness Function

In order to compare the output image of the 2D- Lookup with the goal image, a quality function has to be designed for the comparison of two binary images. First, the definition of this fitness function will be given, then it will be discussed.

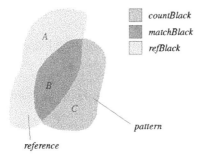

Fig. 12.5 Terms for fitness evaluation.

Consider figure 12.5, where two sets are shown, the reference set of the goal image and the pattern set of the result image.

Therein, *countBlack* is the number of black pixels in the result image

$(B+C)$, $matchBlack$ is the number of black pixels of the result image, which are also black in the goal image (B), and $refBlack$ is the number of black pixels of the goal image $(A+B)$. Then, the following ratios can be computed:

$$r_1 = \frac{matchBlack}{refBlack} \qquad (4)$$

is the amount of reference pixels matched by the pattern,

$$r_2 = 1.0 - \frac{countBlack - matchBlack}{N - refBlack} \qquad (5)$$

is the amount of correct white pixels set in the result image (N is the total number of image pixels), and

$$r_3 = \frac{matchBlack}{countBlack} \qquad (6)$$

is the amount of matching pixels of the result image. The multiple objective here is to increase these measures simultaneously. After performing some experiments with the framework, it was decided to use the following weighted sum of these three objectives as fitness measure:

$$f = 0.1r_1 + 0.5r_2 + 0.4r_3 \qquad (7)$$

This fitness measure has the following properties:

(1) It counts better for subsets of the reference. Subsets obtain a fitness value of at least 0.9, since r_2 and r_3 are 1 in this case.
(2) It counts better for subsets of the reference, which are supersets of other subsets of the reference.
(3) A white image gives a fitness of 0.5, therewith refusing to assign a good fitness value to the empty subset of the reference.

These properties make this fitness measure useful for genetic search. A genetic search evolves its population towards the higher weighted objective first. In our case this means, that measure r_2, weighted with 0.5, is evolved first. In other words, the first subgoal of the genetic search is to allocate as many correct white positions as possible. Due to the weighting of 0.4 for the r_3-part, the search then tries to allocate correct black positions of the reference, while the correct white allocations persist in the pattern. Once the pattern is reduced to a subset of the reference, the only way to increase the fitness is to expand the subset towards the whole reference set. This begins, when the fitness exceeds a value of about 0.9.

12.2.4 Deriving a 2D-Lookup matrix

In the following, it is assumed, that the two operation images and the goal image are given. The question is how to derive a suitable 2D-Lookup matrix, which gives the best match between goal image and result image by the fitness measure given in the last subsection. The interesting point here is, that this derivation can be done be reusing this fitness measure. To prove this, assume a 2D-Lookup matrix, where all but one positions are set to White (1), and only a single position (g_1, g_2) is set to Black (0). Then, the 2D-Lookup will give a resultant image with all positions (x, y) set to Black, for which operation 1 yielded pixel value g_1 and operation 2 yielded pixel value g_2. Usually, there will be only a few black pixels within the result image. Now, as it was remarked in the last subsection, the fitness measure will give values above 0.9, if the set of black pixels lies completely within the reference, no matter, how many pixels are there. So, a criterion can be given for setting a pixel to Black or White in the 2D-Lookup matrix.

Let $l_{(x,y)}$ be a 2D-Lookup matrix constituted by setting only the pixel at (x, y) to Black, and $r_{(x,y)}$ be the result of the 2D-Lookup with the operation images 1 and 2 and this 2D-Lookup matrix. Then

$$l(x,y) = \begin{cases} \text{Black,} & \text{if } f(r_{(x,y)}) > 0.88 \\ \text{White} & \text{otherwise.} \end{cases}$$

In case there are no black pixels in $r_{(x,y)}$ at all, $l(x, y)$ is set to Gray, which stands for positions within the 2D-Lookup matrix, whose pixel value pairs do never occur within the operation images 1 and 2 at the same location. The value 0.88 has been chosen instead of 0.9 to give the adaptation some tolerance.

Figure 12.6 shows the result of this derivation for two example images. This procedure, which resembles a relaxation procedure, gives a quasi-optimal 2D-Lookup matrix for given operation images 1 and 2. The following subsection describes the manner, by which the two operations needed are derived by an individual of a GP.

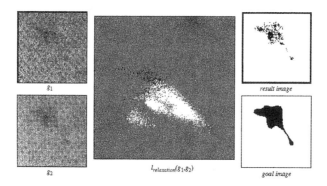

Fig. 12.6 The relaxation procedure for deriving the optimal 2D-Lookup matrix $l_{relaxation}(g_1, g_2)$, once the operation images g_1 and g_2 are given.

12.2.5 Building up a GP individual

In the following the structure of an individual of the GP population is described. On its base, there are formal superoperators, acting on an input image $o(x, y)$ and giving the result image $g(x, y)$. These superoperators make use of a common parameter structure PS, which contains the following entries:

- A mask $\mathcal{M} = \{(i, j)\}$ as a set of offset positions. The element k of $\mathcal{M}$ is assigned by $\mathcal{M}_k = (i_k, j_k)$. Applying a mask onto a pixel with position (x, y) gives a set of pixel positions $\mathcal{M} \circ (x, y) = \{(u, v) \mid u = x + i, v = y + j, (i, j) \in \mathcal{M}\}$, the "neighborhood" of (x, y). The cardinality of $\mathcal{M}$ is $|\mathcal{M}| = m$. Masks used in a PS are restricted to 3×3 symmetric masks.

- A weighted mask $\mathcal{M}_w$ is a tupel $(\mathcal{M}, f)$ of a mask $\mathcal{M}$ and a function $f : \mathcal{M} \to \mathcal{R}$, which assigns a weight value to each mask offset (i, j) of the mask $\mathcal{M}$. For convenience, mask and its weightings are pictured by a scheme as for a 3×3 mask:

$$\mathcal{M}_w = \begin{array}{|c|c|c|} \hline w_{(-1,-1)} & w_{(0,-1)} & w_{(1,-1)} \\ \hline w_{(-1,0)} & w_{(0,0)} & w_{(1,0)} \\ \hline w_{(-1,1)} & w_{(0,1)} & w_{(1,1)} \\ \hline \end{array}$$

Weight values are restricted to the range $[-5, 5]$. If only $\mathcal{M}_w$ is given, $\mathcal{M}$ can be found as set of all offset positions (i, j) with $f_w(i, j) \neq 0$.

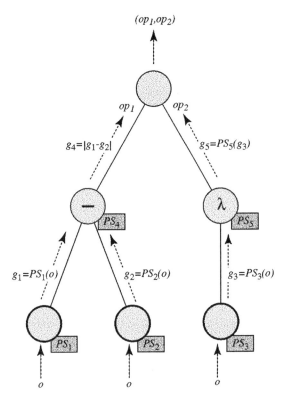

Fig. 12.7 Example for an individual GP tree, representing two image processing operations (for details, see text).

- A single offset vector $\vec{p} = (\delta_x, \delta_y)$. The magnitude of the components of the offset vector does not exceed 2.
- A BOOLEAN operation f_{bit} from $\{0,1\} \times \{0,1\}$ onto $\{0,1\}$ with number $N_{f_{bit}}$[‡]. The notation $f_{bit}(n,m)$ means applying f_{bit} bitwise, i.e. if $bit_i(n)$ extracts bit i of the number n in dual representation, then $bit_i(f_{bit}(n,m)) = f_{bit}(bit_i(n), bit_i(m))$.
- A permutation Π of the first m integers with Π_k the position of number k in the permutation.
- A ranking vector $\vec{v} = (v_1, v_2, \ldots, v_m)$, which assigns weights to a set of m sorted values. In the following, $rank_i^{max}(\mathcal{A})$ is the i-th

---

[‡]There are 16 such operations, and N refers to a given ordering of them, e.g. by lexicographical ordering of the two bit operands.

largest value of the value set $\mathcal{A}$, $rank_i^{min}(x,y)$ is the i-th smallest value. The components of $\vec{v}$ are restricted to the set $\{-1, 0, 1\}$.
- A symbolic mode value *mode*, which specifies which kind of superoperator is applied, using some of the parameters defined above. The mode symbols and their meaning are explained below.

Hence, a *PS* is a 6-tupel $(\mathcal{M}_w, \vec{p}, N_{f_{bit}}, \Pi, \vec{v}, mode)$.

In the following, all operations are to be restricted within the given image boundaries. Then, the following formal superoperators are introduced:

(1) Logical translation **TRANS**. It uses the vector $\vec{p}$ and the bit operation number $N_{f_{bit}}$. The operated image at position (x, y) is given by

$$g(x,y) = f_{bit}\left(o(x - \delta_x, y - \delta_y), o(x, y)\right).$$

(2) Convolution **CONVOL**. It uses the weighted mask $\mathcal{M}_w$. The convolved image is given by

$$g(x,y) = \sum_{(i,j) \in \mathcal{M}} f(i,j)\, o(x+i, y+j)$$

The weighted mask is zero-biased before operating with it, i.e., a value δ is chosen so that $\sum (f_w(\mathcal{M}_k) + \delta) = 0$.

(3) Ordered Weighted Averaging **OWA** [16]. This operation is used in fuzzy inference systems for defuzzification. It uses the ranking vector $\vec{v}$. Applying it as an image processing operation goes on as follows: the pixel values of the image function o of the original image in the neighborhood $\mathcal{M} \circ (x, y)$ are sorted in descending order, and the sorted value at position k is multiplied with the weight v_k. All prodcuts are summed up.

$$g(x,y) = \sum_{k=1}^{|\mathcal{M}|} v_k\, rank_k^{max}(o \circ (\mathcal{M} \circ (x,y)))$$

Some OWA weights represent well-known image processing operations. For example $(1, 0, \ldots, 0)$ as the dilation, $(0, \ldots, 0, 1)$ as the erosion, $(1, \ldots, -1)$ as the morphological gradient, $(0, 0, \ldots, 0, 1, 0, \ldots, 0)$ as a ranking operator and $(1/n, 1/n, \ldots, 1/n)$ as the averaging operation. OWA allows for formalizing these operations within a single expression.

(4) Texture Numbers **TN**. Here, the per Π is used. At position (x, y), the operation derives a bit vector b with elements from $\{0,1\}$ of the same size as $\mathcal{M}$, from the input image o. The element b_k of b is obtained by

$$b_k = \begin{cases} 1 & \text{if } (o \circ (\mathcal{M} \circ (x, y)))_k \geq o(x, y), \\ 0 & otherwise. \end{cases}$$

Now, a number n is constructed from b as follows: bit k of n is given by the element l of the sequence b, with l being the index of k in the permutation Π: $bit_k(n) = b_{\Pi_k}$. Then, $g(x,y) = n$. The resultant values n are automatically rescaled to the grayvalue range $\{0, \ldots, g_{max}\}$.

(5) Ordered Weighted Minimum **OWM** [1]. This operation uses the weighted mask $\mathcal{M}_w$. The mask weights are sorted in descending order, the pixel values in the neighborhood of (x, y) are sorted in ascending order. Then, the minmax of these two value sequences is computed as value of the result image at position (x, y):

$$g(x,y) = \min_{k=1}^{|\mathcal{M}|} \left[\max \left[rank_k^{max}(f_w \circ \mathcal{M}), rank_k^{min}(o \circ (\mathcal{M} \circ (x, y))] \right] \right.$$

From this, an image operation is fully specified by means of a PS. The GP individual trees are constructed according to the following rules:

(1) At the root level, every tree has two branches (in order to have two operations for the 2D-Lookup).
(2) At each level, each function node branches into a set of function nodes and terminals of the next lower level.
(3) To each function node and terminal, a randomly initialized PS is assigned.

To each function node, an image operation out of the following set is assigned (here, g_1, g_2 are the operands, g is the result of the operation):

(1) Pixelwise Subtraction –. $g(x,y) = |g_1(x,y) - g_2(x,y)|$.
(2) Pixelwise Squaring **sq**. $g(x,y) = g_1^2(x,y)/g_{max}$.
(3) Pixelwise Minimum **min**. $g(x,y) = \min\{g_1(x,y), g_2(x,y)\}$.
(4) Pixelwise Maximum **max**. $g(x,y) = \max\{g_1(x,y), g_2(x,y)\}$.
(5) Performing PS λ. $g = PS \circ g_1$.

A tree T generates the two operation images needed for 2D-Lookup from the original image in the following bottom-up manner. The original image o is given to all terminals. Each terminal applies its PS onto o. Then, the processed images are given as operands to the nodes at the next upper level, processed, given to the next upper level and so forth. The root node collects its both operand images, performs the relaxation procedure, which was described in the last subsection, and computes the fitness measure f for the now fully specified 2D-Lookup algorithm. In this manner, a fitness f is assigned to a tree T.

As an example, consider the six-node GP individual in Fig. 12.7. Five random initialized $PS = \{\mathcal{M}_w, \vec{p}, N_{f_{bit}}, \Pi, \vec{v}, mode\}$ are given:

$$PS_1 = \left\{ \begin{array}{|c|c|c|} \hline 0 & 2 & 0 \\ \hline 0 & 2 & 0 \\ \hline 0 & 3 & 0 \\ \hline \end{array}, (1,1), 11, \Pi_{213}, (1,0,0), \text{TRANS} \right\}$$

$$PS_2 = \left\{ \begin{array}{|c|c|c|} \hline 0 & 0 & 0 \\ \hline 1 & 2 & 2 \\ \hline 0 & 0 & 0 \\ \hline \end{array}, (1,2), 7, \Pi_{132}, (1,0,0), \text{OWA} \right\}$$

$$PS_3 = \left\{ \begin{array}{|c|c|c|} \hline 0 & 1 & 0 \\ \hline 1 & 2 & 1 \\ \hline 0 & 1 & 0 \\ \hline \end{array}, (-1,0), 3, \Pi_{12354}, (0,0,1), \text{OWA} \right\}$$

$$PS_4 = \left\{ \begin{array}{|c|c|c|} \hline 0 & 0 & 0 \\ \hline 3 & 5 & 2 \\ \hline 0 & 0 & 0 \\ \hline \end{array}, (-1,-2), 5, \Pi_{312}, (1,0,-1), \text{TN} \right\}$$

$$PS_5 = \left\{ \begin{array}{|c|c|c|} \hline 0 & 1 & 0 \\ \hline 1 & 2 & 1 \\ \hline 0 & 1 & 0 \\ \hline \end{array}, (2,0), 5, \Pi_{51243}, (1,0,0), \text{OWA} \right\}$$

Note, that PS_4 is never applied onto an image, and PS_3 and PS_5 share the same mask. Bit operation 7 is assumed to be the XOR operation. From this, operation 1 of the tree is specified as absolute difference of the original image translated and XOR-ed by the offset (1,1) (PS_1), and the original image dilated by a horizontal line-mask (PS_2). Operation 2 is given as morphological opening of the original image by a cross-mask (PS_3 and PS_5). Fig. 12.8 shows the intermediate and operation images of this tree structure.

The structuring of image processing operations by the trees has been chosen in this rather complicated manner for the following reasons:

- The operations, which are represented by such trees, resemble well-known image processing operations. A tree is likely to represent operations as dilation, erosion, closing, opening, morphological gradients, SOBEL operator, statistical operators, GAUSSIAN filtering, shadow images and so forth.
- The represented operations are unlikely to give unwanted operation images, which are completely white or black.
- They preserve image locations.
- The maximum arity of a node is two. Also, maximum tree depth was restricted to five. This was set in order to allow for the maintenance of the obtained trees, e.g. for manually improving the designed filters by removing redundant branches. Processing time is kept low, too (but processing time does not go into the fitness function itself!).

Finally, figure 12.9 gives some operation images obtained from the same original image by different randomly constructed and configured trees. These images demonstrate the variabilty of the generated operations, each of which enhances or surpresses different image substructures, and none of which gives a trivial image operation.

12.3 Results

To learn about the framework's abilities, textile images were used which were taken from the "Textilfehler-Katalog" of the IPK Berlin (TFK). Four examples will be given here. At first, a conventional feature classification approach was applied. Co-occurrence features of 10 8×8 texture windows for each class (background texture and fault) were computed. Then, for each type of texture a multilayer backpropagation neural network (MBPN) with 14 input neurons (for the 14 co-occurrence features), 16 hidden neurons and 2 output neurons (for the two classes) for each sample was trained over 1000 cycles. The trained MBPNs were recalled on the original images. The

294 *M. Köppen & B. Nickolay*

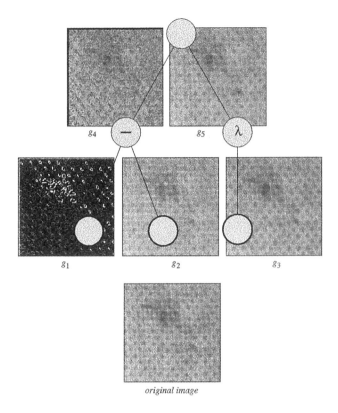

Fig. 12.8 Intermediate images, as generated by the tree in Fig. 12.7.

results are shown in Fig. 12.10. In general, the resolution of the method is not very high, since it is restricted to the texture window size of 8×8. The results for TFK 1-fr8 and TFK 1-st11 are good. The result for TFK 3-st23b contains many errors. This is due to the varying grayvalue appearance of the fault region. The MBPN can not generalize good in this case. The result for TFK 3-fr1a is inacceptable. The fault is very small and of low contrast. Too many conflicting grayvalue constellations appear within the image. They can't be classified by a MBPN.

Of course, these results will not prove, that the feature classification approach in general is not able to perform better. The approach may be adapted for each sample. But it has to be noted, that there is no other way for improving the recall results in this case than by either supplying more training samples, training the MBPN longer or changing the feature

Genetic Programming based Texture Filtering Framework 295

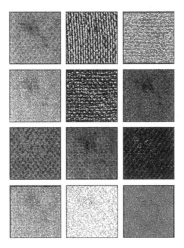

Fig. 12.9 Some operation images, as generated from the upper left image by randomly generated trees.

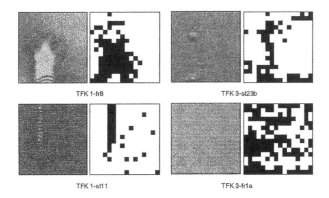

Fig. 12.10 Results for applying the conventional texture classification approach to four examples of the TFK (details see text).

calculation method.

For instructing the LUCIFER2 frameworking approach, subimages were cut from the whole images, containing the fault and its neighboring texture. Goal images were drawn by using a photo retouching program. Then, the framework is started for each of the four samples. The results, including both operation images and the relaxed 2D-Lookup matrix, are given in the figures 12.11 to 12.14. For each problem, a population of 30 individuals.

with 80 children in each generation, were used. The run went on until the genetic diversity of the population vanished (all individuals have the same fitness). Usually, this was the case after performing about ten generations.

As can be seen from the figures, the framework fulfills its task and designs appropriate texture filters. The performance is usually good and sometimes very good. It is to be noted, that *exact* resemblance will not be possible, and it would not be of any merit. The visual appearance of the fault border is a subjective one, and the user might give a slightly modified goal image as well. The goal image contains *virtual* borders.

Also, the framework will never find the (globally) optimal texture filter, since the searchspace is much too large to be covered by the genetic search. The most important aspect here is that there are many good solutions for a given task. The framework randomly evolves the initialized solutions towards better ones.

The generalization ability of the designed texture filters was checked on a larger test suite, also taken from the TFK. For 24 texture fault problems, small reference images were cut out and goal images were drawn. For each fault, the framework was run exactly once. The evolved filter was applied to the whole image. The number of black pixels out of the reference image part was counted, as well as the number of gray pixels. The first value gives a measure for the error rate ("false alarms") of the texture filter, the second a measure for the compatibility of reference image and total image. The results are given in Table 12.1. The average error rate is 1.9% and the average incompatibility is 2.2%. These are good results, too. However, the variations of the error rate are comparatively large (between 2 and 17278 pixels out of 262144 pixels, with one out-layer of 57774 pixels).

A consideration of the 2D-Lookup matrices helps to explain this fact. The following can be said:

- Some matrices seems to be separable, i.e. the textured background is represented by a group of compact white regions. The fault appearance (the black dots) surrounds these regions. In this case, the filter is expected to have a good generalization ability.
- There are regions, where black and white dots are hoplessly intermingled. The more such regions are found within a matrix, the more the evolutionary adaptation features random grayvalue constellations within the two operation images. In this case, the filter will perform bad on other images with the same texture and fault

categories.

Compactness within the 2D-Lookup matrices is considered as main provision for filter's higher generalization ability. If the matrices are manipulated in a manner, which enhances compactness of its black and white regions, the filter will perform better on newly presented images (possibly for the price of a slightly lower performance on the input image, from which the filter was designed). Future work will focus on this.

Table 12.1 Generalization ability of the LUCIFER2 framework for 24 texture fault examples taken from "Textilfehler-Katalog." All images contains 262144 pixels. On an average, there are 1.9% of the black pixels wrong, and 2.2% of the pixels gray.

TFK No.	No. of Wrong Blacks	No. of Grays
1-fr13a	407	12832
1-fr13b	11	33030
1-fr13c	2	2908
1-fr13d	18	1343
1-fr19	15	1322
1-st47a	1017	2276
2-i53	75	6
2-lau11b	70	2098
2-lau19	280	862
2-lau2	524	3804
2-lau6	498	495
2-lau24	614	283
3-fr4c	2325	16301
3-fr8	57774	5552
3-st18b	5717	10352
3-st20	2142	3367
3-fr19	15044	6216
3-st47a	17278	17680
4-fr1a	88	2004
4-st14	2355	3882
4-fr19	67	1854
4-st22a	536	2280
4-st27a	5	2555
4-st29	12135	6450

12.4 Conclusions

A framework was presented, which allows for the design of texture filters for fault detection (two class problem). The framework is based on the 2D-Lookup algorithm, where two filter output images are used as input.

The approach was applied to four texture problems and the performance of the framework was discussed. The results, obtained without "human intervention," are ready-to-use texture filters. Also, they can be tuned in order to obtain even more better results, or combined in a superposed inspection system. The following are our experiences during the test runs:

- The framework was able to design texture filters with good or very good performance.
- The goal image matched the fault region quite satisfactorily.
- Bordering regions should be neglected for fitness evaluation.
- The framework was able to design filters for the detection of non-compact fault regions and fault regions with varying appearance.
- The designed filters may be subjected to further improvements by the user.

Current work focuses on several improvements of the whole architecture, especially on the inclusion of rescaling and rescanning into the designed filter operations, and on an evaluation of the 2D-Lookup matrix by neural networks in order to get a comprehensive solution for a given texture filtering problem.

Acknowledgment

This research is supported by the Deutsche Forschungsgemeinschaft (DFG), Schwerpunktprogramm "Automatische Sichtprüfung technischer Objekte", EPISTO, Ni 473/1-2. The authors wish to thank Dr. B. Schneider to make the "Textilfehler-Katalog" accessible to this research (the "Textilfehler-Katalog" is accessible via *http://vision.fhg.de/ipk/tfk*) and to A. Zentner for implementing an on-line version of the LUCIFER2 framework (URL http://vision.fhg.de/ipk/demo/lucifer2).

Genetic Programming based Texture Filtering Framework 299

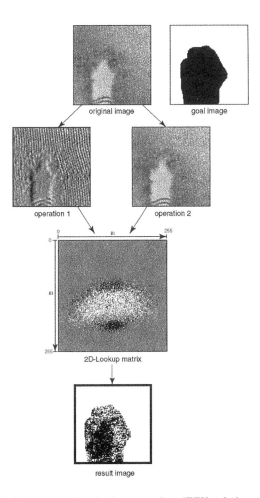

Fig. 12.11 Results for example 1 (TFK 1-fr8).

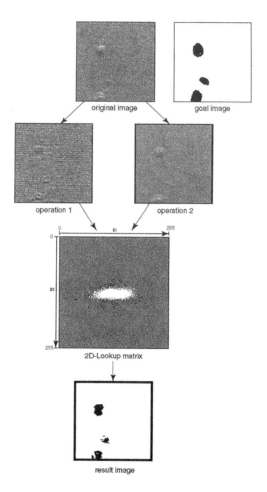

Fig. 12.12 Results for example 2 (TFK 3-st23b).

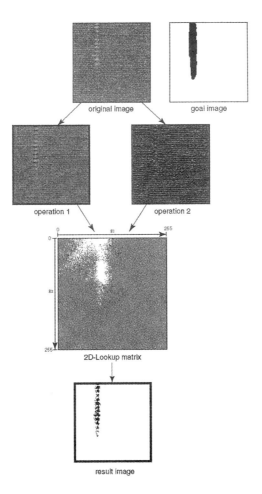

Fig. 12.13 Results for example 3 (TFK 1-st11).

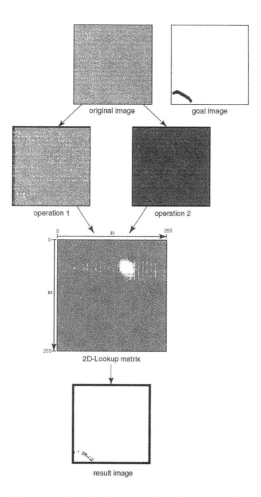

Fig. 12.14 Results for example 4 (TFK 3-fr1a).

References

[1] Dubois, D., Fargier, H., Prade, H., "Beyond min aggregation in multicriteria decision: (ordered) weighted min, discri-min, lexmin", in: Yager, R. R., Kacprzyk, J. (eds.), "The ordered weighted averaging operators — Theory and applications", Kluwer Academic Publishers, Dordrecht a.o., 1997.

[2] Goldberg, D. E., "Genetic algorithms in search, optimization & machine learning", Addison-Wesley, Reading, MA, 1989.

[3] Gonzales, R. C., Woods, R. E., "Digital Image Processing", Addison-Wesley, Reading MA, 1993.

[4] Haralick, R., Shanmugam, K., Dinstein, I., "Textural features for image calssification", IEEE Trans. SMC, 3, (6), pp.610-621, 1973.

[5] Haralick, R., Shapiro, L., "Image segmentation techniques", Computer Vision, Graphics and Image Processing, 29, pp.100-132, 1985.

[6] Holland, J. A., "Adaptation in natural and artificial systems", MIT Press, Cambridge MA, 1975.

[7] Köppen, M., Ruiz-del-Solar, J., Soille, P., "Texture segmentation by biologically-inspired use of neural networks and mathematical morphology", Proc. NC'98, Vienna, Austria, pp.267-272, 1998.

[8] Köppen, M., Ruiz-del-Solar, J., "Fuzzy-based texture retrieval", Proc. FUZZ-IEEE'97, Barcelona, Spain, pp.471-475, 1997.

[9] Köppen, M., Teunis, M., Nickolay, B., "A framework for the evolutionary generation of 2D-Lookup based texture filters", Proc. IIZUKA'98, Iizuka, Japan, pp.965-970, 1998.

[10] Köppen, M., Soille, P., "Two-dimensional frameworks for the application of soft computing to image processing", Proc. IWSCI'99, Muroran, Japan, pp.204-209, 1999.

[11] Koza, J., "Genetic programming — On the programming of computers by means of natural selection", MIT Press, Cambridge, MA, 1992.

[12] Langdon, W. B., Poli, R., "Fitness Causes Bloat", Proc. of the 2nd On-line World Conference on Soft Computing in Engineering Design and Manufacturing (WSC2), 1997.

[13] Serra, J., "Image analysis and mathematical morphology", Academic Press, London, 1982.

[14] Serra, J., "Image analysis and mathematical morphology. Vol. 2: Theoretical advances", Academic Press, London, 1988.

[15] Whitley, D., "A genetic algorithm tutorial", Statistics and Computing, 4, pp.65-85, 1994.

[16] Yager, R. R., "On ordered weighted averaging aggregation operators in multi-criteria decision making", IEEE Trans. SMC, 18, pp.183-190, 1988.

Chapter 13
A Texture Image Segmentation Method Using Neural Networks and Binary Features

Jing Zhang[1] and Shunichiro Oe[2]

[1] *Harbin Institute of Technology, China*
[2] *University of Tokushima, Japan*

Abstract

Texture image segmentation is the first essential and important step of low level vision. The extraction of texture features is a most fundamental problem to texture image segmentation. Many methods for extracting texture features of the image have been proposed, such as statistical features, co-occurrence features, two-dimensional AR features, and fractal based features etc. In this paper, a new method for extracting texture features of the image is proposed. In this method, the gray scale image is first decomposed into a series of binary images by variable thresholds, and then topological features of all of these binary images are computed. Using these topological features as texture features, we apply a pyramid linking with band-pass filter neural networks to segment the texture image into some homogeneous areas. Several experiments on synthetic texture images have been carried out to verify the efficacy of the new method.

Keywords : texture image segmentation, multi-resolution image processing, entropy, anisotropy coefficient, threshold, Euler number, binary image, connected components, bit quads, band-pass filter neural networks, pyramid structure, pyramid linking, similarity

13.1 Introduction

The process of identifying regions with similar texture and classifying regions with different texture is one of the early steps towards identifying surfaces and objects. This process is called texture image segmentation. It is the first essential and important step of low level vision. Its importance has been shown in various application areas such as analysis of remote sensing images, micrography images and scene images etc. Among them, segmenting a random texture image into different texture regions is a relative difficult problem.

In general, the image segmentation can be implemented into two steps. The first step is to extract the texture features of the image, and the second step is to segment the image into homogeneous texture areas according to the texture features.

Texture feature can be defined as a set of local neighborhood properties of the gray levels of the image. It is a very important low-level vision surface characteristic. The use of texture feature was suggested for image region segmentation and classification etc. The ability to effectively classify and segment image based on textural features is of key importance in scene analysis, medical image analysis, remote sensing and many other application areas. Texture is often qualitatively described by its coarseness in the sense that a patch of wool cloth is coarser than a patch of silk cloth under the same viewing conditions. The coarseness index is related to the spatial repetition period of the local structure. A large period implies a coarse texture and a small period, a fine texture.

In mathematics, the description of texture features can be divided into statistical and structural methods. On the statistical level, a texture is defined by a set of statistics extracted from a large ensemble of local picture properties. Now many computational methods have been proposed and applied to extract texture feature. Commonly used texture features include Fourier domain energy, co-occurrence matrix, second-order gray level statistics, two-dimensional autoregressive model and fractal dimension etc. [1; 2; 3]. To describe textures of more complex structures, structural analysis methods are often more useful. Structural methods describe textures in terms of texture primitives and spatial relationship among them. In this paper, the topological features of the texture image that are extracted from a series of binary images are used in the segmentation process. The basic idea of this method is first to decompose a gray-scale image into a series of binary images by using multiple thresholds, thus the information of different gray scale in the image are picked out. Then several shape features of binary image are extracted from the binary image series.

For texture image segmentation methods, up to now, many kinds of segmentation methods have been proposed [4; 5; 6; 7]. But there are still some problems for these segmentation methods. And it is more difficult in case of many different kinds of texture features are used simultaneously, because the multi-thresholding techniques must be considered. Neural network based segmentation approaches have been made to solve these problems. These methods have improved the segmentation result a lot, but the robustness to the noisy images and some texture images with unstationary texture areas are not still enough.

The multi-resolution image processing method has a good evaluation criteria such as image data compression, edge detection and matching [8; 9]. The basic idea of this method is the use of a multi-resolution image representation and pyramid linking algorithm. For image segmentation method by using pyramid linking, it is essential and very difficult to define the discriminant function which can determine the similarities between nodes of two adjacent levels, especially when several different kinds of texture features are used simultaneously in image segmentation process. In this paper, a new segmentation method by using band-pass neural networks during pyramid linking process is proposed.

The organization of the paper is as follow. In section 2, we will present the texture feature extraction method. In section 3, we will explain the construction of the neural networks. The conventional pyramid linking method for image segentation will be introduced in section 4. And the proposed segmentation method by using pyramid linking and neural networks is presented in section 5. To verify our method, several experiments have been carried out and the results will be shown in section 6. Finally, the paper will be concluded in section 7.

13.2 Texture Feature Extraction

From a statistical point of view, texture images are complicated pictorial patterns, on which, sets of statistics can be obtained to characterize these patterns. Stochastic models consider texture as realizations of a random process, but the structural and geometrical features appearing in textures are largely ignored. In this research, we propose a novel texture feature extraction method based on the geometrical properties of connected regions in a sequence of binary images. The first step of the approach is to decompose a texture image into a series of binary images. This decomposition has been proven to have the advantage of causing no information loss, and resulting in binary images that are easier to deal with geometrically. For each binary image, geometrical attributes such as the Euler number and the compactness or circularity of the connected region in binary image are considered. The detail algorithms are described in the next.

13.2.1 Decompose the texture image into a series of binary images

This approach of texture feature extraction consists of two-step: (1) decomposing a gray scale image into a series of binary images by using multiple thresholds, (2) computing the features of all these binary images.

Here, we use an automatic threshold selection method to get multiple thresholds [10]. The basic concept is the definition of an anisotropy coefficient, which is related to the asymmetry of the gray level histogram. Let us consider a histogram with $n+1$ possible gray levels. The probability of occurrence of each of these levels is denoted by $p(i)$, we obviously have:

$$p[0] + p[1] + p[2] + \ldots + p[n] = 1. \tag{1}$$

The entropy H (in the Shannon sense) is:

$$H = -\sum_{i=0}^{n} p[i] \cdot \ln(p[i]), \tag{2}$$

where $n+1$ is the number of gray levels, $p[i]$ is the probability of occurrence of level i.

The anisotropy coefficient α is defined by:

$$\alpha = \frac{\sum_{i=0}^{na} p[i] \cdot \ln(p[i])}{\sum_{i=0}^{n} p[i] \cdot \ln(p[i])}. \tag{3}$$

Let na denote the first level which satisfies:

$$p[0] + p[1] + \ldots + p[na] \geq \frac{1}{2}. \tag{4}$$

If na is the threshold, after thresholding, the image has two levels, white (w) and black (b). The probability and the entropy of the image becomes:

$$H' = -p'[w] \cdot \ln(p'[w]) - p'[b] \cdot \ln(p'[b]) = H'[w] + H'[b], \qquad (5)$$

where the $'$ denotes the two-level image.

If equality holds, na can divide the histogram into two parts containing the same number of points. In this case, we would have

$$p'[w] = p'[b],\ H' = 1,\ \text{and}\ \alpha = H[w]/H.$$

If k thresholds have to be selected, we have to find k levels $t[1], t[2], \ldots t[k]$ dividing the histogram into $k+1$ equal parts. Then we define k anisotropy coefficients $\alpha_1, \alpha_2, \ldots \alpha_k$ as follows:

$$\alpha_1 = \frac{\sum_{i=0}^{t[1]} p[i] \cdot \ln(p[i])}{\sum_{i=0}^{n} p[i] \cdot \ln(p[i])}. \qquad (6)$$

$$\alpha_k = \frac{\sum_{i=t[k-1]+1}^{t[k]} p[i] \cdot \ln(p[i])}{\sum_{i=0}^{n} p[i] \cdot \ln(p[i])}. \qquad (7)$$

A possible k thresholds $s[1], \ldots s[k]$ should satisfying

$$\sum_{i=0}^{s[1]} p[i] = \left\{ \sum_{i=0}^{t[1]} p[i] + \text{abs}\left(\sum_{i=0}^{t[1]} p[i] - \alpha_1 \right) \right\}. \qquad (8)$$

$$\sum_{i=0}^{s[k]} p[i] = \left\{ \sum_{i=0}^{t[k]} p[i] + \text{abs}\left(\sum_{i=t[k-1]+1}^{t[k]} p[i] - \alpha_k \right) \right\}. \qquad (9)$$

Fig.13.1 shows an example for decomposing a texture image into a series of binary images.

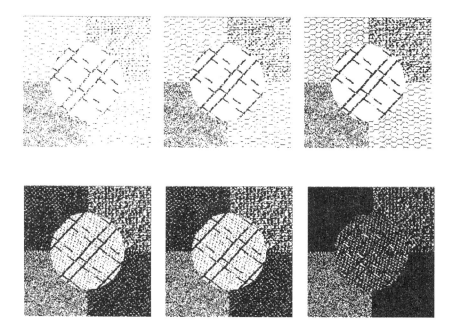

Fig. 13.1 An example of decomposing a texture image into a series of binary images

13.2.2 *The computation of the Euler number*

After decomposing the gray scale image into a series of binary images, the next step is to extract the features of these binary images. Several qualitative and quantitative techniques have been developed for characterizing the shape of objects within an image. These techniques are useful for classifying objects in a pattern recognition system and for symbolically describing objects in an image understanding system. Some of the techniques apply only to binary valued images, while others can be extended to gray level images. In this research, we use the Euler number [2; 3] of these binary images as the features of the original texture image.

The shape of an object refers to its profile and physical structure. These characteristics can be represented by the boundary, region, moment, structural representations and connectivity. Irregularly shaped objects can be described by their topological constituents. Here we first introduce the conception of connectivity that is a topological attribute of the image. For each binary image, we group all 1-valued (or 0-valued) pixels into a set of connected pixel groups termed connected components. Connected components

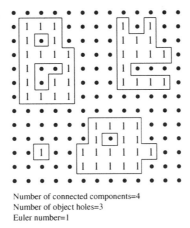

Number of connected components=4
Number of object holes=3
Euler number=1

Fig. 13.2 Connected components and Euler number

of an object may contain holes (the 0-valued or 1-valued pixels included in the connected components called as holes). Connected components of an object and the number of object holes are the topological properties. Fig.13.2 shows a binary valued image contained four connected objects and three holes (here the black points represent the 0-valued pixels).

There is a fundamental relationship between the number of connected object components N_C and the number of object holes N_H in an image called the Euler number, which is defined as:

$$E = N_C - N_H. \tag{10}$$

The Euler number is also a topological property because N_C and N_H are topological attributes.

Now consider the following set of 2×2 pixel patterns called bit quads defined in Fig.13.3. Let $n\{Q\}$ represent the count of the number of 1-valued pixels included in the image. Bit quad counting provides a very simple means of determining the Euler number of an image. Under the definition of four-connectivity, the Euler number can be computed as

$$E = n\{Q\} - n\{Q_1\} + n\{Q_3\}. \tag{11}$$

and for eight-connectivity

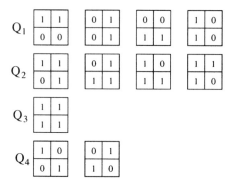

Fig. 13.3 Bit quad patterns

$$E = n\{Q\} - n\{Q_1\} - n\{Q_4\} + n\{Q_2\} - n\{Q_3\}. \tag{12}$$

It should be noted that while it is possible to compute the Euler number E of an image by local neighborhood computation, neither the number of connected components N_c nor the number of holes N_H, for which $E = N_C - N_H$, can be separately computed by local neighborhood computation.

13.3 Band-Pass Filter Neural Networks

Recently neural networks have been successfully applied to pattern recognition. Most conventional neural networks used in image segmentation belong to a pattern classification type. These neural networks can classify input patterns by complex nonlinear decision surfaces. However the problem is that the output values of most conventional neural networks do not correspond to candidate likelihoods. In this paper, the band-pass filter neural networks [13] (we call it as BPFN in short) was used in the segmentation process. The band-pass filter network is a feed-forward multi-layer supervised neural networks. It can pass patterns from only one category with no or little distortion and has a nonlinear filtering ability. Its output values represent the distances between the target pattern and the candidates of pattern categories. It has two advantages: The first one is that it is possible to recognize the pattern by comparing the similarities between the input and the output. The second is that it is independent of other category

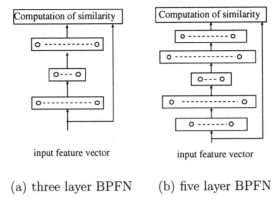

(a) three layer BPFN   (b) five layer BPFN

Fig. 13.4 The structure of BPFN

neural networks, because one such neural networks is trained only for one pattern. From the results of experiment we can see that due to the using of band-pass neural networks, the abilities of noise resistant in the segmentation process are enhanced, even though some unstationary texture areas are included in the original texture image. So the robustness of the system is improved a lot

In this section, the construction of the BPFN and the basic training process are introduced.

Fig.13.4 shows the configuration of the BPFN. In this kind of neural network, the number of hidden layers can be one or three. In the three-layer BPFN, the hidden layer has fewer units than those of the input layer and the unit number of output layer are equal to those of the input layer, as shown in Fig.13.4(a). In the five-layer BPFN the upper and lower hidden layers have more units than those of the input and output layers and the middle hidden layer has fewer units than those of the input units as shown in Fig.13.4(b). The relationship between two layers of the neural network is characterized by the following dynamic equations:

$$U_j^k = \sum W_{ij}^{k-1,k} \cdot H_j^{k-1} + \theta_j^k. \tag{13}$$

$$H_j^k = f(U_j^k). \tag{14}$$

where H_j^k is the output of unit j of layer k, $W_{ij}^{k-1,k}$ is the weights that dictate the effect of the ith unit of layer $k-1$ on the jth unit of layer k of the neural networks, U_j^k is the input of unit j of layer k and θ_j^k is the input offset of unit j of layer k.

In order to imitate the continuous input-output relationship of the real neurons and to simulate the integrative time delay due to the capacitance of real neurons, the output value of the networks will be immediately transformed by a nonlinear activation function of the neuron. For example, the most common activation functions are *step, ramp, sigmoid*, and *Gaussian function*. In particular the following nonlinear sigmoid activation function $f(U_i)$ is very often used:

$$f(U_i) = \frac{1}{1 + e^{-U_i/\sigma}}. \tag{15}$$

In this paper, we use the nonlinear sigmoid function as the activation function of the networks, and the sigmoid function is used only to the hidden layers of the networks.

Generally, two phases are included in a supervised learning networks: learning phase and retrieving phase. In the learning phase of the BPFN, the objective is to train the weights and offsets of the neural networks so that the output patterns of the BPFN are close to the inputs patterns which are the teacher patterns of the BPFN. Thus each BPFN is trained as the mapping of an identity patterns which belong to one pattern categories. Therefore the training will benefit from the assistance of the teacher. In this paper, the back-propagation algorithm was used to train the networks and the least-squares-error between the teacher pattern and output pattern was used as the discriminant function of the neural networks. The least-squares-error is calculated by the following formula:

$$E_p = \frac{1}{2} \sum_{k=1}^{k=M} [T_k - O_k]^2, \tag{16}$$

where E_p is the least-squares-error, M is the dimension of output pattern, T_k is the teacher pattern and O_k is the output pattern of the neural networks.

The purpose to update the weight $W_{ij}^{k-1,k}$ of the BPFN is to minimize the least-squares-error E_p, so that the output pattern of the BPFN is close to the input one. So the changes of weight $\triangle W_{ij}^{k-1,k}$ and E_p have following relationship:

$$\triangle W_{ij}^{k-1,k} \propto -\partial E_p / \partial W_{ij}^{k-1,k}. \tag{17}$$

According to this relationship, we can get the formula to update the weight vector $W_{ij}^{k-1,k}$ as following[12]:

$$W_{ij}^{k-1,k}(m+1) = W_{ij}^{k-1,k}(m) + \triangle W_{ij}^{k-1,k}(m). \tag{18}$$

As the training succeeds, each BPFN becomes a nonlinear band-pass filter, in other words, each BPFN passes patterns that belong to only one category with no or little distortion.

13.4 Pyramid Linking Method for Image Segmentation

Among the multi-resolution image processing methods, the pyramid segmentation algorithms have been reported to be successful in a large number of fields [9]. In this section, the process for constructing the pyramid structure and the basic pyramid linking method is presented.

13.4.1 Pyramid structure of the feature vectors

The generation of a pyramid structure for a given image can be viewed as the application of a series of low-pass filters with successively narrower bandwidths. The input image is fed through this series of filters, and the output of each stage corresponds to the reduced-resolution image at each level of the pyramid. It is very important to find an efficient and effective way to perform such filtering operations. Convolution with limited-size kernels represents fast implementations of low-pass filters.

In the traditional pyramid algorithms, the pyramid structure is constructed by the pixels itself. But for texture image, its properties are not meaningful for single pixel. So in this research, the pyramid structure based on the texture feature is constructed.

We begin to construct the pyramid structure with a fixed partition of the image into a number of small, equally sized windows and compute the AR-model and fractal features for each window. After the edge-preserve

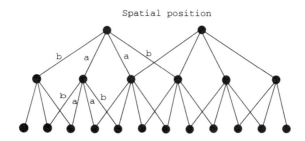

Fig. 13.5   An example of a 1-D overlapped pyramid

smoothing process, an exponentially tapering "pyramid" of the feature vectors are constructed. If the size of the original image is $2^n \times 2^n$ and the size of small region is 16 by 16, then the size of level 0 of the feature vector pyramid is $2^{n-3} \times 2^{n-3}$, the sizes of the successive level of the pyramid are $2^{n-4} \times 2^{n-4}$, $2^{n-5} \times 2^{n-5}$, ... 2×2, respectively. The reason for choosing the small region size as 16×16 is that the texture feature of the image can be extracted out correctly. If the size of the small region is too small, it is difficulty to get the texture feature correctly.

The approach to construct the pyramid structure is to calculate the feature vectors by the weighting average of 4×4 neighborhoods feature vectors in its preceding level. In our approach, the neighborhoods were overlapped 50% in the x and the y directions respectively. Fig.13.5 is an example for making 1-D overlapped pyramid structure. Here the parent-child relationship was defined between nodes in adjacent levels (The level $k-1$ nodes in the pyramid corresponding to a given node at level k is called children, and the level k to nodes obtained by 4×4 block at level $k-1$ is called parents). Because the pyramid is 50% overlapping, two adjacent parents has 50% of their possible children in common. So each node in the pyramid had four parents at the next level, and 16 children at the previous level. The level $1, 2, ..., L$ are generated by repeatedly applying a low-pass filter that generates reduced version of the original feature vectors. The low-pass filter is implemented by convolution of a kernel with the image. Using a kernel of size $K \times K$, each feature value in level k is a weighted sum of the feature values in a $K \times K$ neighborhood on level $k-1$ centered around that feature value point. In this paper, we use following Gaussian-like kernel $a = 0.37$ and $b = 0.13$ as the filter. The pyramid structure is shown as Fig.13.6.

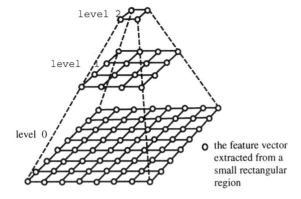

Fig. 13.6 The pyramid structure of feature vector of the image

$$\begin{bmatrix} 0.0169 & 0.0481 & 0.0481 & 0.0169 \\ 0.0481 & 0.1369 & 0.1369 & 0.0481 \\ 0.0481 & 0.1369 & 0.1369 & 0.0481 \\ 0.0169 & 0.0481 & 0.0481 & 0.0169 \end{bmatrix}$$

The process for constructing the pyramid structure is as follows.

Each node in the pyramid is indexed by a triple $[i, j, l]$, where l is its level of pyramid, and i and j are its row and column numbers within that level. Columns are numbered from 0 to $2^{(N-1)} - 1$ starting at the left, and rows are numbered in a similar manner starting at the bottom.

We defined four values with each node:

$c[i, j, l][t]$: the value of feature vector of the local image;
$a[i, j, l][t]$: the area over which the property was computed;
$p[i, j, l][t]$: a pointer to the feature node's parent in the next higher level;
$s[i, j, l][t]$: the segment property, the average value for the entire segment containing the feature node.

Here t is the iteration number, a positive integer.

The c values of the lowest level are the feature vectors extracted from the original texture image. Each node $[i, j, l]$ is considered to have a position $(x[i, l], y[j, l])$ relative to the image. The position of level $l = 0$ nodes are just the coordinates for the image sample points. If the sample interval is D then

$$x[i, 0] = (i + 1/2)D, \tag{19}$$

$$y[j, 0] = (j + 1/2)D, \tag{20}$$

Nodes spacing doubles with each higher level;

$$x[i, l] = (i + 1/2)2^l D, \tag{21}$$

$$y[j, l] = (j + 1/2)2^l D. \tag{22}$$

Note that, in this convention, node $[i, j, l]$ is located midway between its four nearest neighbors at level $l - 1$, nodes $[2i, 2j, l-1]$, $[2i+1, 2j, l-1]$, $[2i, 2j+1, l-1]$, $[2i+1, 2j+1, l-1]$.

For each node $[i, j, l]$ above the image level $(l > 0)$, there is a 4×4 subarray of candidate child nodes at level $l - 1$. This subarray is centered at the same (x, y) location as node $[i, j, l]$, so includes nodes $[i', j', l-1]$, where

$$i' = 2i - 1, 2i, 2i + 1, or\ 2i + 2, \tag{23}$$

$$j' = 2j - 1, 2j, 2j + 1, or\ 2j + 2. \tag{24}$$

Conversely, each node below the top level $(l < N)$ is a potential child of four level $l + 1$ candidate parent nodes, $[i'', j'', l+1]$, where

$$i'' = (i - 1)/2, or\ (i + 1)/2, \tag{25}$$

$$j'' = (j - 1)/2, or\ (j + 1)/2. \tag{26}$$

All pyramid computation are local in the sense that the values of c, a, p and s for each node are computed from the corresponding values of that node's parent and child. Pyramid computations are distributed in that the same evaluation functions are applied to all nodes. In the following definitions "bottom up" computation to level L will mean that the local computation is performed first at each node of the level array, then at each node of the level 1, then level 2 array, and so on until level L is computed.

Only c is computed in the initial iteration, $t = 0$, and computation is bottom up. The initial c value assigned to each node through this local, bottom up procedure is equivalent to a weighted average of image values using a Gaussian-like weighting function described in 13.4.1.

For $l = 0$,
$$c[i,j,0][0] = I(x[i,0], y[j,0]),$$
and for $0 < l \leq L$
$$c[i,j,l][0] = (1/16) \sum w_{uv} c[i',j',l-1][0], \qquad (27)$$
where w_{uv} is the Gaussian-like kernel.

13.4.2 The calculation of the similarity between child and its parents

The similarities between parents and child are computed by following performance index:

$$S = (X, X')/(||X|| \cdot ||X'||), \qquad (28)$$

where X is the feature vector of the parent, X' is the feature vector of child, (X, X') is the inner product of X and X', and $||X||$ is the norm of X.

13.4.3 Texture segmentation method by using pyramid linking

After the entire pyramid of the feature vectors are constructed, the pyramid linking (PL) algorithm was used to segment an image into several homogeneous areas. Here we just simply introduce the basic iterative pyramid linking process.

Step1 : Child-parent links are established for all nodes below the top of the pyramid. Let $d[n]$ be the similarity between value c of node $[i,j,l]$ and its nth candidate parent (25) and (26) (this value represent the similarity between parent and child, it is computed by equation (28)). There are four such candidates for each child, so $n = 1, 2, 3, 4$. If one d value is greater than those of other three, then node $[i,j,l]$ is linked to the corresponding "most similar" parent, that is:

$$d[m] < d[n], \quad for\ all\ n \neq m, \tag{29}$$

then

$$p[i,j,l][t] = m. \tag{30}$$

On the other hand, if two or more of the similarity are equally, then either of two assignments may be made. If one candidate for which d is maximal is the parent of the previous iteration, then this is retained as the updated parent. Otherwise one of the equally near candidate is selected at random. Special consideration must be given to boundary nodes since these nodes have one or two candidate parents as defined in equation (25) and (26). The 2×2 subarray of candidate parents for a level l boundary node is shifted by one row and/or one column so that it falls within the $l+1$ array. This adjustment is equivalent to augmenting each array with an additional row or column on each side. The values assigned to these nodes are reflected from the row or column one from the edge.

Step2 : The c and a values are recomputed bottom up on the basis of the new child-parent links.

For $l = 0$

$$a[i,j,0][t] = 1,$$

$$c[i,j,0][t] = I(x[i,0], y[j,0]).$$

For $0 < l \leq N$

$$a[i,j,l][t] = \sum a[i',j',l-1][t]. \tag{31}$$

Here the sum is over those children of node $[i,j,l]$ as indicated by the links p, assigned in $Step1$.

If $a[i,j,l][t] > 0$ then

$$c[i,j,l][t] = \frac{\sum (a[i',j',l-1][t])(c[i',j',l-1][t])}{a[i,j,l][t]}. \tag{32}$$

But if $a[i,j,l][t] = 0$ so the node has no child, $c[i,j,l][t]$ is set to the value of one of its candidate child selected at random.

Step3 : Segment values are assigned top down. At level L the segment value of each node is set equal to its local property value

$$s[i,j,L][t] = c[i,j,L][t].$$

For lower levels $l < L$, each node's value is just that of its parent

$$s[i,j,l][t] = s[i'',j'',l+1][t].$$

Here node $[i'',j'',l+1]$ is the parent of $[i,j,l]$ as established in $Step1$

At the end of $Step3$, the level 0 segment values represent the current state of smoothing-segmentation process. Any changes in pointers in given iteration will result in changes in the values of local image properties associated with pyramid nodes. These changes may alter the nearest parent relationship and need a further adjustment to pointers in the next iteration. Changes always shift the boundaries of segments in a direction which make their contents more homogeneous, so convergence is reached finally. The iteration process is continued until no changes occur from one iteration to the next. And at any stage of this process, the links defines a set of trees rooted at the top level of the pyramid. We can map segmentation result of the top level to the original texture image according to the relationship of the links between two adjacent levels of the pyramid. Here we summarize the iterative pyramid linking process as follows:

(1) Divide the input image into a number of small regions with same size, and compute the texture features of each small region.
(2) Construct the pyramid structure of feature vectors of the texture image.
(3) Link each feature node to one of its four parents of previous level whose values are closest to its own.
(4) Recompute feature vector values of the parents by averaging the values of only those children that are linked to the node.
(5) Change the links in accordance with these new values.
(6) Repeat steps (4) to (5) as many times as desired or there is no change between two iterations.

At any stage of this process, the links defines a set of trees rooted at the top level of the pyramid. We can map segmentation result of the top level to the original texture image according to the relationship of the links between two adjacent levels of the pyramid.

13.5 Image Segmentation by Using Pyramid Linking and Neural Networks

In pyramid linking process, the most important thing is whether the child can be linked to its parent which is closest to itself in values. Traditional pyramid linking method sometimes fails to find out this relationship. In this paper, while linking parent and child between two adjacent levels, the BPFN was used to determine to which parent node the child should be linked, according to the similarities between child and its four parents.

In order to avoid the result of segmentation to be too coarse at the edges between different texture areas because of large size of the small region, here we use the overlapped small region during computing the texture feature of the image. That means we move the small region to let the neighbor small region overlap each other, as shown in Fig.13.7, then we compute the texture feature of these small regions. Because we use the overlapped small regions, the processing time is longer than that of no overlapping regions.

13.5.1 *The training of the band-pass filter neural networks*

When the pyramid structure is constructed, we then construct the BPFN for all nodes except the nodes of the first level. Fig.13.8 show the linking method of the pyramid. The training and retrieving processes of the BPFN is as follows:

(1) Construct the BPFN for all parents respectively from level 1 of the feature vectors pyramid to the top level of the pyramid (the level 0 correspond to the feature vectors of the original image).
(2) Input the feature vectors of the parent to the input layer of their-self BPFN respectively, and compute the outputs according to equation (13) and (14) for every hidden layers and output layers of all the BPFN (but we did not use the sigmoid function to output layer of the BPFN).
(3) Update the weight vectors of all BPFN according to equation (18).
(4) Repeat steps (2) and (3) until the output vector of the networks are closest to their input one.

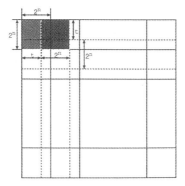

Fig. 13.7 The overlapped small region in calculating the feature vectors

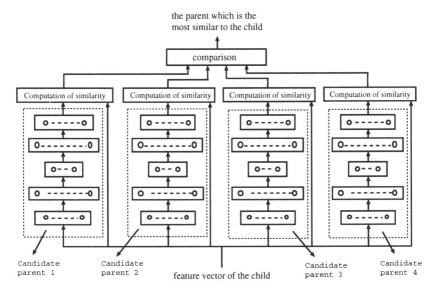

Fig. 13.8 Pyramid linking according to the similarity between parents and child

After the training process, the feature vector of the child is inputed into its four parents' BPFN (as shown in Fig.13.8) and the similarities between the input and outputs of the four parents' neural networks are computed respectively. We compare the values of these similarities and find out the maximum. And the parent which has maximum is the most similar parent of the child. Then the linking is done between the child and its most similar parent. This process is performed for all points from level 0 to the top level of the pyramid and repeated until there is no changes on linking. Finally, we map the result of segmentation to the original image.

The similarities between parents and children are computed by following performance index:

$$S = (X, X')/(||X|| \cdot ||X'||) \qquad (33)$$

where X is the feature vector of the parent, X' is the output vector of BPFN (the input of BPFN is the feature vector of the son), (X, X') is the inner product of X and X', and $||X||$ is the norm of X.

13.5.2 Texture segmentation by using pyramid linking and neural networks

In summary, the algorithm of texture segmentation method by using pyramid linking and neural networks is:

(1) Decompose the gray scale image into a series of binary images by using multiple threshold.
(2) Divide each binary image into a series of small windows of the same size and extract the feature vectors of small regions on each binary image. Since the feature vectors extracted from small regions have a wide variance in values, we smooth the feature vectors by applying the edge preserving smoothing method.
(3) Construct the feature vectors pyramid of texture image (but the top level of the pyramid is 2×2).
(4) Construct the neural networks for all parents and train them so that the outputs of neural networks is as close as inputs.
(5) Link each node to one of its four parents whose value is closest to its own by comparing the similarities between child and its parents using performance index (33).
(6) Recompute the node values by averaging the values of only those children that are linked to the node.
(7) Train the neural networks again and change the links in according to the revised neural networks.
(8) Repeat steps 6 - 7 until there are no changes between two iterations.

(a) Original texture image   (b) Segmentation result

Fig. 13.9 Original texture image and the segmentation result

(9) Map the clustering result to the original image.

13.6 Experiments

In this section, to verify the efficacy of the proposed method, segmentation experiments on several synthetic texture images have been carried out.

The experiments have been done by using 3-layer BPFN, 5-layer neural networks and 7-layer neural networks respectively in pyramid linking process. From the results of experiments, it has been proved that the segmentation ability by using pyramid linking and the three-layer BPFN could not be superior to that of the pyramid linking method only. And the segmentation results by using pyramid linking and 7-layer neural networks were almost same as that of 5-layer BPFN, and the learning time of networks is considerably longer than that of 5-layer networks. So in this paper, the 5-layer BPFN are used. The unit configuration of the networks is 7-12-5-12-7. Because the unit numbers of input and output layer is same as that of the dimension of the feature vector, which is 7 here (the number of the texture features), so the unit number of input and output is 7. The unit numbers of hidden layer was determined by experiments. The results of experiment shows that the segmentation performance is best in the construction.

The images, shown in Fig.13.9(a), Fig.13.10(a) and Fig.13.11(a), were constructed from real scene pictures in Brodatz's book [19]. For each

(a) Original texture image   (b) Segmentation result

Fig. 13.10   Original texture image and the segmentation result

original image, seven binary images were obtained using multi-threshold method, and the textural features were extracted by computing Euler numbers of every 16 × 16 window in the binary images. The pyramid linking method and BPFN were then implemented to the texture segmentation according to the extracted textural features. The segmentation results are shown in Fig.13.9(b), Fig.13.10(b) and Fig.13.11(b). Fig.13.11(c) is the segmentation result by using texture feature of two-dimensional AR model and fractal dimension. From the segmentation results we can see that a better segmentation results could be obtained by using the proposed method.

13.7   Conclusion and future works

In this research, a new method has been proposed for extracting textural features. In this method, a gray scale image is decomposed into a series of binary images and textural features are extracted by calculating the topological features of the binary images; then a segmentation method by using pyramid linking and neural networks is applied to the segmentation process. Efficacy and reliability of the proposed method of extracting texture features and segmentation were verified through several experiments.

But in this paper, only Euler numbers have been computed as the topological features. There are still some problems for segmenting the texture images which involve some unstationary areas. Therefore, our future works will involve in considering other shape features to improve the texture seg-

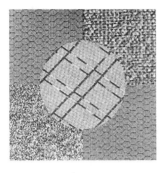

(a) Original texture image

(b) Segmentation result by using proposed features

(c) Segmentation result by using AR model and fractal dimension features

Fig. 13.11 Original texture image and the segmentation result

mentation performance for images in which textural elements have significant shape characteristics.

References

[1] Mikio Takagi, Haruhisa Shimoda, Handbook of Image Analysis, University of Tokyo Press, 1991.

[2] Anil K. Jain, Fundamental of Digital Image Processing, Prentice Hall Information and System Science Series, Englewood Cliffs, 1989.

[3] William K. Praff, Digital Image Processing, A Wiley-Interscience Publication, John Wiley & Sons, Inc. 1991.

[4] Shunichiro Oe, Yasunori Shinohara and Mikio Doi, "Segmentation method of texture image using two-dimensional AR model and pyramid linking," The Transactions of the Institute of Electronics, Information and Communication Engineers D-II, Vol. J75-D-II, pp.1132-1142, 1992.

[5] S.Oe, M.Enokihara, M. Hashida and Y.Shinohara, "Texture Segmentation Method Using Decision-Based Neural Networks," Proceedings of International Conference Modeling, Simulation & Identification, Vol. 9, pp.228-231, 1994.

[6] Nikhil P. Pal and Sankar K. Pal, "A review on image segmentation techniques," Pattern Recognition, Vol. 26, No. 9, pp.1277-1294, 1993.

[7] H. Greenspan, R. Goodman, and R. Chellappa, "Texture analysis via unsupervised and supervised learning," Proceedings of International Joint Conference on Neural networks, Vol. 1, pp.639-644, 1991.

[8] Jean-Michel Jolion and Azriel Rosenfeld, A Pyramid Framework for Early Vision, Kluwer Academic Publishers, 1994.

[9] M. Bister and J. Cornelis, "A critical view of pyramid segmentation algorithms," Pattern Recognition Letters, 11, pp.605-617, 1990.

[10] T. Pun, "Entropic thresholding, a new approach," Computer Graphics and Image Processing, No. 16, pp.210-239, 1981.

[11] Yan Qiu Chen, Mark S.Nixon and David W.Thomas, "Statistical geometrical features for texture classification," Pattern Recognition, Vol. 28, No. 4, pp.537-552, 1995.

[12] S.Y.Kung, Digital neural networks, PTR Prentice Hall Englewood Cluffs, New Jersey, 1993.

[13] M. Nakamura and S. Tamura, "Vowel recognition by phoneme filter neural networks," ICSLP-90 (International Conference on Spoken Language Proceeding), Proceedings, pp.669-672, 1990.

[14] C.H. Chen, Neural Networks in Pattern Recognition and Their Applications, World Scientific, 1991.

[15] Jianchang Mao and A. K. Jain, "Texture classification and segmentation using multi-resolution simultaneous autoregressive model," Pattern Recognition, Vol. 25 No. 2, pp.173-188, 1992.

[16] J.M.H.Du Buf, M.Kardan and M.Spann, "Texture feature performance for image segmentation," Pattern Recognition, Vol. 23, No. 3/4, pp.291-309, 1990.

[17] Matti Pietikainen, Azriel Rosenfeld, "Image segmentation by texture using pyramid node linking," IEEE Transactions on system, man, and cybernetics, Vol. SMC-11, No.12, 1981.

[18] Michael Hild and Yoshiaki Shirai, "Extraction of Texture Elements from Image of Shaded Scenes," Pattern Recognition, Vol. 26, No. 8, pp.1177-1191, 1993.

[19] PhilBrodatz, Textures: A photographic album for artists and designers, Dover Publications, Inc.New York, 1966.

[20] R. M. Haralick, K. Shanmugan, and I. Dinstein, "Texture feature for Image Classification," IEEE Trans. Systems, Man, and Cybernetics, SMC-3, pp.610-621, 1992.

[21] Timo Ojala, Matti Pietikäinen and David Harwood, "A Comparative Study of Texture Measures with Classification Based on Feature Distributions," Pattern Recognition, Vol. 29, No. 1, pp.51-59, 1996.

Chapter 14
Image Retrieval System based on Subjective Information

Kaori Yoshida[1], Toshikazu Kato[23], and Torao Yanaru[1]

[1] Kyushu Institute of Technology
[2] Chuo University
[3] Electrotechnical Laboratory

Abstract

These days, development of computer device leads to computer user explosion. On the other hand, conventional technology cannot handle user's diversity, because the computer cannot treat each user's subjectivity. It is important to materialize techniques which can answer user's subjective requests flexibly for the coming new media epoch. This research focuses on studying how subjective impressions are grounded in physical perceptions, especially in visual perception. In this paper, we propose a model for subjectivity and physical perceptions, and give an example in an image database system.

ART MUSEUM is our prototype system which can treat each user's subjective interpretation for advanced image database. It allows users to retrieve images from a database of impressionist paintings (e.g. Monet's works) by using adjective words. The system learns the correlation between the feature of sample paintings and user's descriptions, and provides interactive and progressive learning mechanisms. We show the interesting experimental results on ART MUSEUM (Multimedia Database with Sense of Color and Construction upon the Matter of ART) system.

Keywords : Kansei, multimedia database, visual perception, human computer interaction, image retrieval, impression, adjective, painting, subjectivity, user model, learning mechanism, canonical correlation analysis, subjective feature space, graphical feature space, unified feature space, perception model, human cognitive process

14.1 Introduction

In the current computer-centered information environment, even a novice user is obliged to be proficient in the computer systems and the information services available on them. With respect to database services, a user has been enforced unadaptable operation manners upon which to interact with database systems, that is a user's requests has been restricted by using prepared keywords. A user has to build his queries only by some keywords which the database systems can accept, even when he wishes to retrieve multimedia data by their contents. Although every user has his own criteria to evaluate and to describe information, according to his personal background, current database services only follow fixed criteria provided by their database managers. These are common problems in the current multimedia information technology.

Human media technology, which is a new concept for the global information infrastructure in the twenty first century, takes a user-centered approach in designing a multimedia information system as an advanced cyber space and provides a user friendly information environment for every person who has different personal backgrounds [1]. Here, "user-centered approach" has the following characteristics. Even a novice can perform smooth human-computer interaction with multimedia representation as a natural extension of human sense. A user can interact with the system according to his personal knowledge and knowledge level which may differ with each individual because of his experience, education, profession and personal interest. A user can also interact with the system according to his psychological state and cognitive process which may differ with each individual by his personal character, taste and feelings.

We have carried out a feasibility study on human media technology. This paper describes our ideas on user friendly system and our current implementation of human media technology for a cyber space database.

14.2 Overview of the Visual Perception Model

In order to provide a user friendly system for multimedia database retrieval with satisfying individual user's subjective criteria, we model human cognitive processes on pictorial information (Figure 14.1).

- Physical Level Interaction: A picture may often remind us of similar images or related pictures. This process is a kind of similarity based associative retrieval of pictorial data by physical level interaction with a pictorial database.
- Physiological Level Interaction: Early stage of mammal vision mechanism extracts graphical features such as intensity levels, edge, contrast, correlation, spatial frequency, and so on. Visual perception may depend on such graphical features.
- Psychological Level Interaction: Although human beings have anatomically the common organs, each person may show different interpretation in classification and similarity measure. This means that each person has his own weighting factors on graphical features. Graphical features are mapped into subjective features by the weighting factors.
- Mental Feeling Level Interaction: Each person may also differently give a unique interpretation after viewing the same picture. It seems each person has his own correlation between concepts and graphical features and/or subjective features.

In Figure 14.1, we also describe a particular implementation dedicated to image retrieval based on user's subjective requests. A top-down control of the user's subjectivity by translating the user's request or complex subjective impression is in relation to a collection words reflecting the impression of the person (we call such words as "impression words") and physical low-level features. A bottom-up control of a user's subjectivity is available physical observations and past experience, because it is synthesized by the system on the basis of the user's intervention. The model is used either to answer subjective requests formulated by the user and to provide the user with views on the currently established model. Therefore, it allows users to intervene in the process in order to increase (i) the system's performance and (ii) the user's knowledge of the system.

14.3 Requirements for Multimedia Database

Current image processing technology enables the recognition of objects in a restricted manner. Some equipments which can evaluate similarity using a specific graphical feature are provided [2] [6]. On the other hand, textual

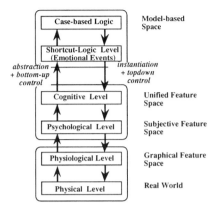

Fig. 14.1 Overview of a model of human cognitive processes

study focuses on the analysis of relations between words. We want to develop a system which can relate pictorial domain data with textual domain data.

Some recent research in this area includes a special neural network model, called Learning based on Experiences and Perspectives (LEP)[3], Type Abstraction Hierarchies (TAHs) for knowledge-based query processing[4], a technique of integrating color information with spatial knowledge[5], and Query By Image Content system which includes color, texture, shape, position, and dominant edges of image objects and regions[6]. These techniques are applied to advanced image database system such as face image retrieval system (CAFIIR)[3], a trademark archival and registration system (STAR)[3], a knowledge-based Spatial Image Model (KSIM) on X-ray images of tumors, magnetic resonance images, CT images[4], a prototype image retrieval system on a wide variety of categories[5], and well known huge image database system QBIC[6]. But these applications are limited to similarity based retrieval. There are a few image retrieval system which can obtain an overall impression of the images. This research focuses on not only similarity retrieval on shape or color but also retrieval on impression.

We can summarize the requirements of such a system according to each user's subjective interpretation as follows.

(1) We need an appropriate algorithm which can evaluate the values of multiple domains, such as pictorial domain and textual domain,

according to each user's subjective interpretation.
(2) We need an accurate modeling facility of each user's subjective interpretation through human-computer interaction without giving heavy load to the users [7].
(3) We want to draw an analogy between users or groups categorized by personal backgrounds, i.e., education, profession, interest and so on [8].

In conventional database systems, keyword indices are used for image retrieval. A user describes his request with a combination of keywords which are associated to images through an index. Even though a keyword thesaurus is available, this approach has the following problems:

(1) The index has to assign several keywords to each image in the database, which is a laborious work.
(2) While a keyword thesaurus is useful for enlarging the vocabulary of the user's query, the operations can be defined only on the textual domain data.

Our approach aims to unify textual domain data and pictorial domain data to describe the contents of an image. Thus, we have to model how a person feels, his impressions, while viewing a painting. We suggest that there is a reasonable correlation between pictorial domain data and textual domain data, and the adjustable method to individual variation using ART MUSEUM (Multimedia Database with Sense of Color and Construction upon the Matter of ART) system as an example.

At first, we show the overview of ART MUSEUM and explain how to unify the multiple domain data. And next, we show how to adjust operations to suit to each user's interpretation. Finally, we show some experimental results on image retrieval by impression words. We also demonstrate the learning effect and differences of each user's subjective interpretation. In our subsequent discussion we use the term "sense retrieval" to indicate retrieval based on impression words.

14.4 Experimental Framework

14.4.1 Overview of ART MUSEUM

ART MUSEUM system is an art gallery which treats full color paintings and its artistic impressions. The system has the personal index on unified feature (UF) space, which are derived from graphical feature (GF) space on color and construction and subjective feature (SF) space on words which express artistic impression (see Fig. 14.2). Each function in the Fig. 14.2 is explained in the following subsections.

The ART MUSEUM has 200 full color paintings in its image database now. We chose 50 paintings as a learning set from an image database by cluster analysis. A user gives his artistic impression about each painting from the learning set as the weight vector of adjective words. We can construct an UF space by canonical correlation analysis. It can be considered that neighboring paintings on the UF space give the similar impressions. Besides, the words which represent similar impression distribute neighboring points. Sense retrieval describes the neighboring paintings of a mapped weight vector according to the words presented by a user on UF space. We show details on each space and the retrieval mechanism in following subsections.

14.4.2 Textual Domain Data

Let us explain how to select textual domain data in ART MUSEUM system. Usually, art critics view paintings from several viewpoints, such as motif, touch, composition and coloring of paintings. Chijiwa [10] reported that the dominant impression derived from paintings is coloring. This report suggests that there is a reasonable correlation between coloring and impression. Thus, we selected the 30 adjective words which represent the impression from coloring of the paintings [7]. Some users answered their artistic impression on 50 paintings (learning set) using 30 adjective words.

We wanted to decrease the number of adjectives because the query should not give heavy load to users. Therefore, we removed 20 adjective words which were not used frequently and not learned properly. Currently, the ART MUSEUM system uses 10 adjective words as a textual domain data. In the same way, some users answered their artistic impression on 50 paintings (learning set) using the above mentioned 10 adjective words (Fig.

14.3) as the weight of the adjectives $\vec{a}_k$ to each painting $k \in$ the learning set (see Fig. 14.2).

14.4.3 Pictorial Domain Data

Next, let us explain what is meant by pictorial domain data. The system has the coloring feature of each painting in the database. The coloring feature is parametrized by the distribution and autocorrelation of the RGB values. In short, we can parameterize the coloring of a painting as follows:

(1) Divide a painting (Fig. 14.4) into 32 × 32 sub-pictures (Fig. 14.5) to approximate the combination and the arrangement of colors.
(2) Calculate the distribution of the RGB intensity value in the sub-pictures.
(3) Calculate the local autocorrelation [11] of RGB intensity as the GF vector $\vec{p}_i$.

The local autocorrelation features are obtained by scanning the image with the local masks and by computing the sums of the products of the corresponding sub-pictures. In a way, the features computed from the image show not only coloring but also something like touch of paintings. Because the features include very local and detail information.

14.4.4 Unified Feature Space

Let us show the algorithm for constructing an UF space. We cannot directly compare the subjective words in a query and the graphical features of a painting, since they are on the different domains.

We may expect that there is a reasonable correlation between the set of words and the parametrized graphical feature. The ART MUSEUM system can analyse the correlation between the different domains. We will regard the correlation as the personal view model for the user. We can construct a UF space on this model to compare the subjective words and graphical feature. The algorithm to construct a UF space is represented by following equations:

(1) Answer his artistic impression of the paintings (learning set) using a set of impression words.

(2) Apply the canonical correlation analysis to the result of the enquiry by the user. The linear mappings F and G make their correlation maximum: $\vec{f}_k = F\vec{a}_k, \vec{g}_k = G\vec{p}_k$.
(3) Calculate the UF vectors of paintings in the database from the following formula, $\vec{g}_i = G\vec{p}_i$.

It can be considered that the neighboring paintings have similar impressions and similar graphical features on the UF space. We will refer to the UF space of $\vec{g}_i$ as the personal index of the user model. Note that we do not have to assign the adjectives $\vec{a}_i$ to every painting in the database. Once the system has learned the linear mappings F and G, it can automatically construct the UF space only from the GF vectors. Accordingly, whenever we put new paintings into the existing image database, it is not necessary to construct the UF space.

14.4.5 Adaptable Method to Each User's Subjectivity

We want to adjust the operations to suit each user. In other words, a mapping function in Fig. 14.2 should dynamically suit to a specific user's subjective interpretation. We present the technique used to adjust to a specific user without giving heavy load. Note that the data set which represents graphical feature is invariant.

(1) Calculate the average personal view model according to a certain group of users' answers.
(2) Retrieve once using the average model.
(3) If the retrieval results don't fit his subjective interpretation, the user can give his interpretation on the target painting j using the set of impression words.
(4) Interpolate the weight vector $\vec{a}_j$ corresponding to the target painting j.
(5) Calculate the mapping function F and G using the changed weight vector $\vec{a}_j$.

After the user adjusts his personal view model using above-mentioned method, the following applications are possible among the users.

(1) We can compare the retrieval candidates by the same keywords represented by the weight vector $\vec{a}_0$ among the users because the

system provides the retrieval candidates of each user which have delicate differences. The system's interpretation will be close to each of the user's interpretation as a result of learning.

(2) We can observe each user's interpretation of any paintings which is retrieved using each user's personal view model. Because the system infers the suitable impression words for simulating the user's personal view using the inverse mapping function F^{-1} and Λ^{-1}, as follows, $\vec{a}_0 = F^{-1}\Lambda^{-1}G\vec{p}_0$.

14.5 Experimental Results

14.5.1 *Sense Retrieval*

Sense retrieval is retrieval using impression words. We may expect that the neighboring paintings in UF space will give similar impressions of coloring to the user. The system evaluates the most suitable coloring for the words according to the personal view model. Then the system can provide the paintings. The algorithm for sense retrieval is as follows.

(1) Apply the linear mappings F and Λ to the adjective vector $\vec{a}_0$ of a subjective description in the user's query.
(2) Choose neighboring paintings of the image $\vec{g}_i$ on the UF space as candidates for sense retrieval.

The UF space enables us to operate a multimedia query which has multimedia data of different domains in its parts. Therefore, this algorithm corresponds to a multimedia join on textual domain data and pictorial domain data. Note that the sense retrieval algorithm evaluates the visual impression in UF space. Therefore, we can retrieve paintings without assigning keywords to every paintings.

In this experiment, we used the UF space according to the average model of 20 men. Fig. 14.6 shows an example of sense retrieval. This figure shows the best 8 candidates for the adjectives; "very soft", "slightly elegant" and "not gorgeous". These paintings roughly satisfied the personal view of the subjects. We may conclude that the UF space reflects a personal sense.

An user retrieves an image using the average model. Then the user can express his impression on the retrieved image. This way one can do revision of sense. Fig. 14.7 shows how an user revises his impression about a retrieved image.

14.5.2 Differences of Each User's Subjectivity in Image Retrieval

In this experiment, we compare the retrieval candidates using each personal view model which is learnt for a specific user. Here, we show the results simulated by the model for a certain man in his thirties and the model for a certain woman in her twenties.

At first, Fig. 14.8 shows the retrieval candidates using the personal view model which is learnt for a certain man, and Fig. 14.9 shows the retrieval candidates using the personal view model which is learnt for a particular woman. The impression words (keywords) are "very natural", "slightly clear" and "not gorgeous". We can observe the different results in spite of the retrieval by the same keywords. These results tell us that if the user repeats his revision according to the above-mentioned learning method, the system's interpretation will be close to each of the user's interpretation.

Next, we show the results of inferred impression words from each user's view model of the same painting. The inferencing is done according to the method mentioned in the previous section. Table 14.1 shows the inferred weight vectors $\vec{a}_{0\ for\ a\ man}$ and $\vec{a}_{0\ for\ a\ woman}$ for the same painting showed in Fig. 14.10 as an example. The weight vectors give us the each user's subjective interpretation represented by impression words.

Table 14.1 shows that the system inferred "very warm", "not elegant" and "not chic" as impression words for the man and "very warm", "slightly natural", "not clear entirely", "not elegant entirely", "slightly gorgeous" and "very dynamic" for the women. The system can infer the suitable impression words for simulating each of the user's personal view model. We expect that in the future the results of such a simulation will give us a trend classified by personal backgrounds.

14.6 Concluding Remarks and Future Perspectives

In this chapter, we demonstrated the feasibility of a system for image retrieval that can handle each user's subjectivity based on the perception model. This enables computer users to use information system more easily.

We introduced the image database system which can answer user's sub-

Table 14.1 Inference of each user's subjective interpretation for monet-straw.jpg

adjective words	age:30-39, man	age:20-29, women
warm	2.00	2.00
soft	-0.24	0.55
natural	0.01	1.02
clear	-0.01	-1.98
elegant	-1.16	-2.33
chic	-0.85	-0.28
authentic	0.29	-0.08
classic	-0.13	-0.31
gorgeous	0.33	1.36
dynamic	-0.11	1.71

jective requests based on the visual perception model. It may be possible to apply a system which can suit each user's characteristic and increase the user friendliness of the system even more. As we introduced in this paper, the human media technology will give the principle to the user-centered information environment. We consider further extensions as follows; (i) dynamic and flexible modeling of a user, and (ii) database agent.

At first, we note the dynamic and flexible modeling of a user. We are now giving a dynamic and flexible modeling facility of a user to our pictorial database system prototypes. If the system can be designed to accept any term as thought appropriate by the user, then this will enable to learn each user's subjective interpretation which in turn can help in a more accurate retrieval. Similar to the recommended words, a user can re-describe his subjective interpretations to the set of sample pictures giving some weight values to the new words. In this case, we need to re-analyze the correlation between the subjective feature domain, i.e., word vector, and the graphical feature domain, i.e., GF vector. As an alternative way, a user can define the new word in relation with existing words. A user can also choose some of the sample pictures as the typical instances, i.e., positive instances, for the new word. By this definition, a new word can also be defined as a linear summation of existing words, because each sample picture has been given the subjective description with the combination of existing words. Therefore, we do not need to re-analyze on the multimedia domain for the latter cases.

Next, a note about database agents. There are huge number of digitized pictures uploaded on the world wide web, and the size is enormously increasing day by day. Therefore, collecting and storing the whole pictorial data into a single database is not practical at all. A reasonable solution is to manage, in a database system, only the GF vectors and UF vectors as well as the URLs to locate the original pictorial data on WWW. By this mechanism, we can provide a picture search engine without managing huge keyword indexes nor huge number of pictorial data. We are giving HTML analysis and image analysis facilities to a database agent mechanism to automatically find pictorial data on WWW and to distinguish the contents as well as their file formats. Through image analysis, we can classify wide variation of pictorial data into the following categories; full color picture, reduced color diagram, monochrome picture, and binary image.

Acknowledgment

This research is supported by Japan Society for the Promotion of Science, Promotion of Scientific Research and Human Media Project, Research and Development of Industrial Technology, New Energy and Industrial Technology Development Organization.

References

[1] Laboratories of Image Information Science and Technology: "Feasibility Study on Human Media Technology", Mar. 1995.

[2] T.Kato: "TRADEMARK: Multimedia Database with Abstracted Representation on Knowledge Base", Proc. of 2nd International Symposium on Interoperable Information Systems, Nov.1998.

[3] Jian-Kang Wu, "Content-Based Indexing of Multimedia Databases," IEEE Tran.on Knowledge and Data Engineering 9(6), pp.978–98, Nov./Dec.1997

[4] Chih-Cheng Hsu, Wesley W. Chu, Ricky K. Taira, "A Knowledge-Based Approach for Retrieving Images by Content," IEEE Tran.on Knowledge and Data Engineering 8(4), pp.522–532, Aug.1996

[5] Wynne Hsu, Chua T. S. and Pung H. K., "An Integrated Color-Spatial Approach to Content-based Image Retrieval," ACM Multimedia '95, pp.305–313

[6] Christos Faloutsos, Ron Barber, Myron Flickner, Jim Hafner, Wayne Niblack, Dragutin Petkovic, William Equitz, "Efficient and Effective Querying by Image Content," Journal of Intelligent Information Systems 3(3/4), pp.231–262 1994.

[7] K.Yoshida, T.Sakamoto, T.Sota and T.Kato: "An Image Retrieval System considering Users' Backgrounds", PRMU-IEICE, Jul.1997.

[8] T.Kato, T.Sota, N.Bianchi and K.Yoshida: "Supporting Human-Human Interaction beyond Cultural Backgrounds", CHI97, Mar.1997.

[9] T.Kato: "Multimedia Interaction with Image Database Systems", Proc. of Advanced Database System Symposium 89, Dec.1989.

[10] H.Chijiwa: "Chromatics", Fukumura Printing Co., Chap.5, 1983.

[11] J.A.Mclaughlin and J.Raviv: "Nth-order autocorrelations in pattern recognition", Information and Control, Vol.12, pp.121–142, 1968.

Image Retrieval System based on Subjective Information 343

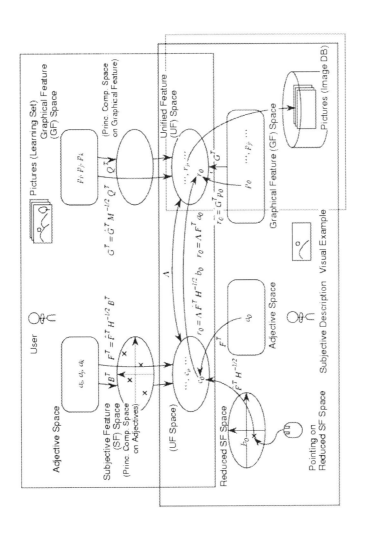

Fig. 14.2 Overview of ART MUSEUM system

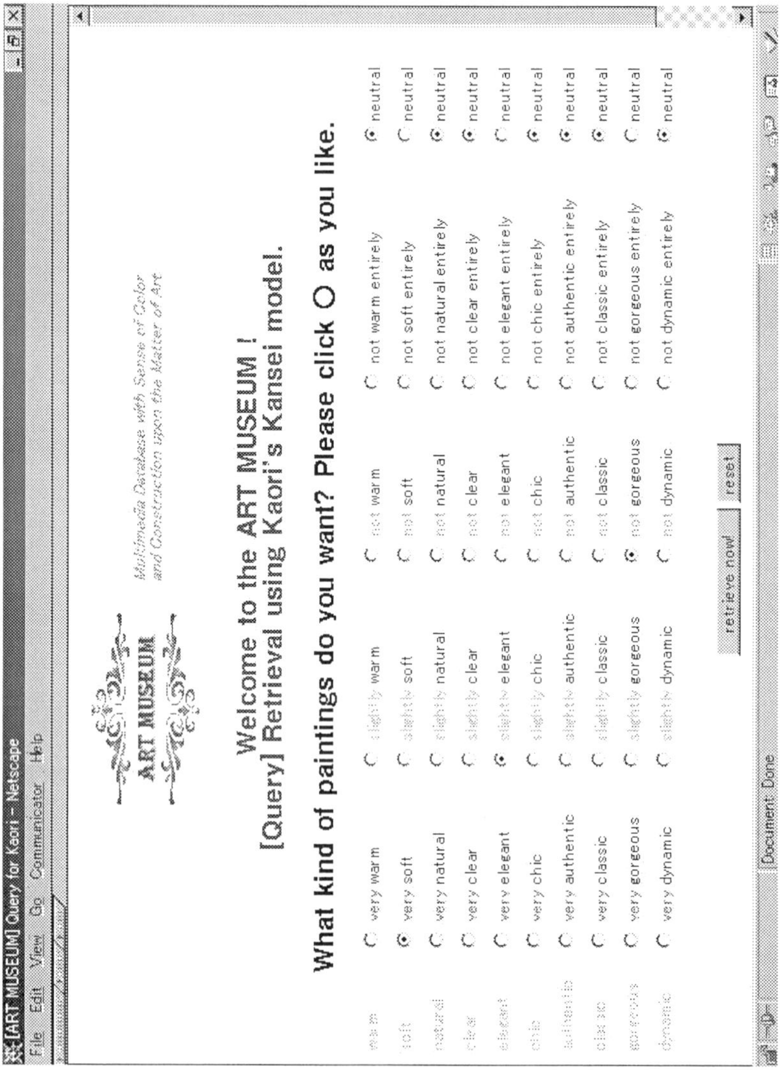

Fig. 14.3   A scene of query

Fig. 14.4 Sample image

Fig. 14.5 Image into 32×32 partition

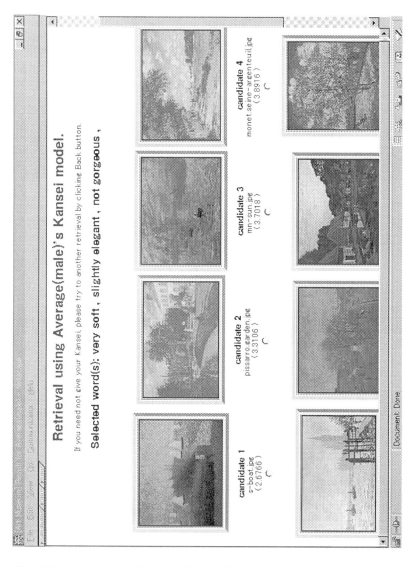

Fig. 14.6 An example of sense retrieval using the average personal view model

Image Retrieval System based on Subjective Information 347

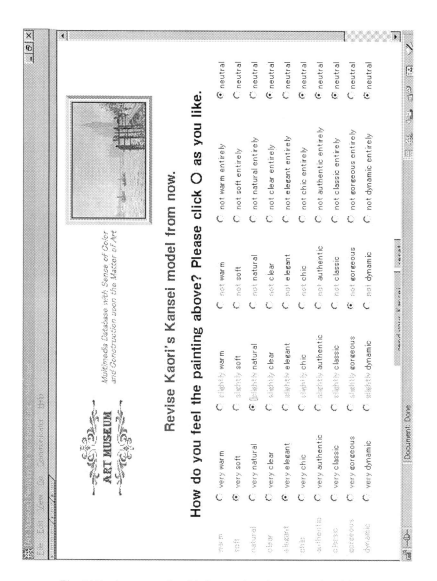

Fig. 14.7 An user revises his impression about a retrieved image

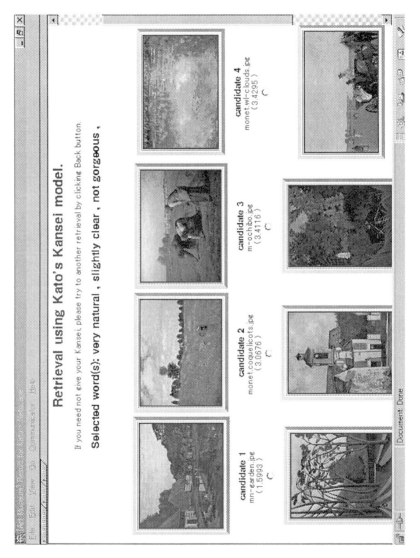

Fig. 14.8 Retrieval candidates by "very natural", "slightly clear" and "not gorgeous" (age:30-39, man)

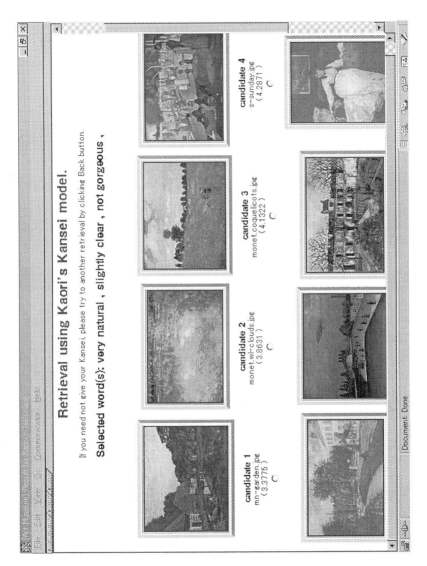

Fig. 14.9 Retrieval candidates by "very natural", "slightly clear" and "not gorgeous" (age:20-29, woman)

Fig. 14.10 A sample image for each user's subjective interpretation (monet-straw.jpg)

About the Authors

Jussi Ahola

Helsinki University of Technology
Laboratory of Computer and Information Science
P.O. Box 5400, FIN-02015 HUT, Finland

E-mail : jussi.ahola@hut.fi
Fax   : +358 9 451 3277

Jussi Ahola is currently preparing his M.Sc. (Tech.) thesis on explorative data analysis in hot rolling at the Laboratory of Computer and Information Science in Helsinki University of Technology.

Ewa J. Ainsworth

NASA Goddard Space Flight Center
Code 970.2
Greenbelt, MD 20771-5000, USA

E-mail : ewa@waw.gsfc.nasa.gov
Phone : +1 301 286 2980
Fax : +1 301 286 0268

Ewa J. Ainsworth has an engineering degree and M. Sc. in Applied Mathematics from Warsaw University of Technology and M. Phil. and Ph. D. degrees in Computing from the University of Bradford, Great Britain. For two years she was a research fellow at the Earth Observation Research Center of National Space Development Agency of Japan in Tokyo. Currently, she is working with General Sciences Corporation at NASA Goddard Space Flight Center. She is primarily engaged in designing of Artificial Intelligence applications to knowledge extraction from remotely sensed imagery. Her main interests lie in subjects of pattern recognition, signal processing, knowledge representation, machine learning, and mathematical and numerical methods leading to the automation of image understanding.

Esa Alhoniemi

Helsinki University of Technology
Laboratory of Computer and Information Science
P.O. Box 5400, FIN-02015 HUT, Finland

E-mail : esa.alhoniemi@hut.fi
Fax   : +358 9 451 3277

Esa Alhoniemi received the M.Sc. (Tech.) and Lic.Sc. (Tech.) degrees in computer science and engineering from Helsinki University of Technology in 1995 and 1998, respectively. Since 1994, he has been working as researcher in the Laboratory of Computer and Information Science in the Helsinki University of Technology. He is currently preparing his Ph.D. thesis on applications of neural networks in the analysis of industrial processes.

Basabi Chakraborty

Faculty of Software and Information Science
Iwate Prefectural University
Takizawamura, Iwate 020-0193
Japan

E-mail : basabi@soft.iwate-pu.ac.jp
Phone : +81-19-694-2580
Fax   : +81-19-694-2573
URL   : http://www.soft.iwate-pu.ac.jp/

Basabi Chkraborty received B. Tech., M. Tech. and Ph. D. degrees in Radio Physics and Electronics from Calcutta University, India. She was engaged in research work in the Electronics and Communication Sciences Unit and worked as a computer engineer in the National Center for Knowledge Based Computing Systems and Technology in Indian Statistical Institute, Calcutta, India until 1990.

From 1991 to 1993 she worked as a part time researcher in Advanced Intelligent Communication Systems Laboratory in Sendai, Japan. In March 1996 she received another Ph. D. degree in Information Science from Tohoku university, Sendai, Japan.

At present she is working as a faculty in Software and Information Science department of Iwate Prefectural University, Japan. Her main research interests are in the area of Pattern Recognition, Fuzzy Logic, Artificial Intelligence, Artificial Neural Network, Soft Computing Techniques and Computer Network Management Systems.

Pradip K Das

Department of Computer Science & Engineering
Faculty of Engineering & Technology
Jadavpur University
Calcutta 700 032, India

E-mail : pkdas@ieee.org
Phone : +91-33-472-0353

Pradip K Das received the Bachelor of Engineering degree in Electronics & Tele-communication in 1968 from Jadavpur University, Calcutta and the Master of Engineering degree in Electronics & Tele-communication in 1970 from Jadavpur University, Calcutta, India. He received the Ph.D. (Engg.) degree in 1978 also from Jadavpur University, India.

From 1970 to 1973, he was engaged in the development of a distributed computer system for an air-defence system for the Indian Air Force as a Scientific Officer at the Tata Institute of Fundamental Research, Bombay, India. From 1973 to 1984 he served as a Lecturer and then as a Reader in the Department of Electronics & Tele-communication Engineering at Jadavpur University. From 1984 to 1986 he was a Visiting Professor in the Department of Computer Science at the Queen's University of Belfast, UK. He then joined the faculty of Computer Science & Engineering, (CSE) Jadavpur University, Calcutta, India where he received a full professorship in April 1986. He also served as the coordinator of an Appropriate Automation Promotion Program Laboratory, established with funds from the United Nations Development Program and the Department of Electronics, Govt. of India. He is currently the head and a professor of CSE at Jadavpur University, Calcutta, India.

His main research interest lies in application of fuzzy concepts in character recognition and also the design of fault-tolerant hardware and software systems and operating systems. Pradip K Das has active interest in photography and is an avid listener of Indian Classical music and likes literature and driving.

Yutaka Hata

Department of computer Engineering
Faculty of Engineering
Himeji Institute of Technology
2167 Shosha, Himeji, Hyogo 671-2201, Japan

E-mail : hata@comp.eng.himeji-tech.ac.jp
Phone : +81-792-67-4986
Fax : +81-792-66-8868

Yutaka Hata was born in Hyogo on May 30, 1961. He received the BE degree (Electronics) in 1984, the ME degree in 1986 and the DE degree in 1989 from Himeji Institute of Technology. He is currently an associate professor in the Department of Computer Engineering, Himeji Institute of Technology. He was a visiting scholar from 1995 to 1996 and is now a visiting professor, in Computer Science Division, University of California at Berkeley, CA USA. His research interests include soft computing especially its application to medical imaging, and multiple-valued logic. He has served as the chairman of BISC special interesting group on medical imaging and an editor of an International Journal, Multiple-Valued Logic. He is a member of The Institute of Electronics, Information and Communication Engineers, Japan Society for Fuzzy Theory and Systems, Japan Society of Medical Electronics and Biological Engineering and the IEEE.

Johan Himberg

Helsinki University of Technology
Laboratory of Computer and Information Science
P.O. Box 5400, FIN-02015 HUT, Finland

E-mail : johan.himberg@hut.fi
Fax   : +358 9 451 3277

Johan Himberg received the M.Sc. (Tech.) degree in technical physics from Helsinki University of Technology in 1997. He is a graduate student and researcher at the Laboratory of Computer and Science in Helsinki University of Technology. He is currently preparing his Lic.Sc. (Tech.) thesis on explorative data analysis and data visualization applied to continuous casting of steel.

Miwako Hirakawa

Fukuoka International University
Dazaifu-city,
Fukuoka
Japan

Miwako Hirakawa received master degree in Computer Science and Systems Engineering from the Kyushu Institute of Technology, Japan, in 1993. Currently he is working as a Research Associate at Fukuoka International University, Dazaifu-city, Japan.

Katsuki Imai

Department of computer Engineering
Himeji Institute of Technology
2167 Shosha, Himeji, Hyogo 671-2201, Japan

E-mail : imai@cspc.ptdg.sharp.co.jp
Phone : +81-743-65-2559

Katsuki Imai was born in 1974 in Osaka, Japan. He received the B. Eng. degree in computer engineering in 1997 and the M. Eng. degree in computer engineering in 1999 from Himeji institute of Technology in Japan. He is an employee of SHARP Corporation in Japan from 1999.

His main research interests in the college were genetic algorithms, fuzzy clustering, and data mining. Now, he works on the development of design systems at SHARP Corporation.

Masami Ishibashi

Just System Inc.
Tokushima-city
Tokushima, Japan

Masami Ishibashi received the bachelor degree in Computer Science and Systems Engineering from Kyushu Institute of Technology, Japan, in 1999. Currently she is a Researcher at the Fuji Soft ABC, Inc., Japan

Hisao Ishibuchi

Department of Industrial Engineering
Osaka Prefecture University
Gakuen-cho 1-1, Sakai, Osaka 599-8531, Japan

E-mail : hisaoi@ie.osakafu-u.ac.jp
Phone : +81-722-54-9350
Fax : +81-722-54-9915
URL : http://www.ie.osakafu-u.ac.jp/~hisaoi/
ci_lab_e/index.html

Hisao Ishibuchi received the B. S. and M. S. degrees in precision mechanics from Kyoto University, Kyoto, Japan, in 1985 and 1987, respectively, and the Ph.D. degree from Osaka Prefecture University, Osaka, Japan, in 1992. Since 1987, he has been with Department of Industrial Engineering at Osaka Prefecture University, where he is currently a Professor from 1999. He was a Visiting Research Associate at University of Toronto from August 1994 to March 1995 and from July 1997 to March 1998. His research interests include fuzzy rule-based systems, fuzzified neural networks, genetic algorithms, fuzzy scheduling, and evolutionary games.

Naotake Kamiura

Department of computer Engineering
Faculty of Engineering
Himeji Institute of Technology
2167 Shosha, Himeji, Hyogo 671-2201, Japan

E-mail : kamiura@comp.eng.himeji-tech.ac.jp
Phone : +81-792-67-4918
Fax   : +81-792-66-8868

Naotake Kamiura received the BE degree in 1990, the ME degree in 1992 and the DE degree in 1995 from Himeji Institute of Technology. He is currently a research associate in the Department of Computer Engineering, Himeji Institute of Technology. His current research interests include multiple-valued logic and fault tolerance. He is a member of the Information Processing Society of Japan, of the Institute of Electronics and Communication Engineers of Japan, and of the IEEE.

Akihiro Kanagawa

Department of Communication Engineering
Faculty of Computer Science & System Engineering
Okayama Prefectural University
Soja, Okayama 719-1197, Japan

E-mail : kanagawa@c.oka-pu.ac.jp
Phone : +81-866-94-2096
Fax : +81-866-94-2199
URL : http://zeus.c.oka-pu.ac.jp/HomePage.html

Akihiro Kanagawa received the B. Eng. degree in 1983 in Systems Engineering from Kobe University, and the Ph.D. degree in 1991 from Osaka Prefecture University. From 1984 to 1988, he was a teacher at Osaka Prefectural Fujiidera Technical High School. From 1988 to 1993, he was a Research Associate in the Department of Industrial Engineering of Osaka Prefecture University. Since 1993, he is an Associate Professor at the Faculty of Computer Science and System Engineering of Okayama Prefectural University, and concurrently as an associate professor at Okayama Prefectural University Graduate School of Master and Doctor courses. He is also an Organizer of the fifth China-Japan International Symposium on Industrial Management (ISIM'2000). His representative studies related to fuzzy theory are applications of fuzzy sets theory to statistical quality control methods, such as sampling inspection, control charts and life testing. His current research interests are classification problems and application of neural networks. He is a member of SOFT, IEICE, IPSJ, JIMA, ORSJ, and ISCIE.

Toshikazu Kato

Electrotechnical Laboratory
Intelligent Systems Div. MBOX.1704
1-1-4, Umezono, Tsukuba Science city,
Ibaraki 305-8568 JAPAN

E-mail : kato@etl.go.jp
Phone : +81-298-54-5987
Fax   : +81-298-54-5989
URL : http://www.etl.go.jp/~kato/

Toshikazu KATO received the M.S. degree in information engineering from Kyoto University in 1980, and the Dr. degree of engineering in 1986. He has worked as a professor of industrial and systems engineering, Chuo University since 1997. He worked as a senior researcher of intelligent systems division, Electrotechnical Laboratory from 1986 to 1997. He is a chief researcher of Human Media Laboratory, ETL, and a supervisor of Kansei Factory group of Human Media Project. His research interests include multimedia database, and human interface. Dr. KATO is a member of IPSJ and IEICE.

Takanori Katsuki

Just System Inc.
Tokushima-city
Tokushima, Japan

Takanori Katsuki received bachelor degree in Computer Science and Systems Engineering from Kyushu Institute of Technology, Japan, in 1997. Currently he is a Researcher at the Just System Inc., Japan.

Noriaki Kinoshita

Hitachi Software Engineering Inc.
Yokohama-city
Kanagawa
Japan

Noriaki Kinoshita received master degree in Computer Science and Systems Engineering from Kyushu Institute of Technology, Japan, in 1998. Currently he is a Researcher at the Hitachi Software Engineering Inc., Japan.

Andreas König

Chair of Electronic Devices and Integrated Circuits
Faculty of Electrical Engineering, IEE
Dresden University of Technology
Mommsenstr. 13
D-01062 Dresden

E-Mail : koenig@iee.et.tu-dresden.de
Phone : +49 351 463 2805
Fax.   : +49 351 463 7260
URL   : http://www.iee.et.tu-dresden.de/~koeniga/

Andreas König received the diploma degree in electrical engineering from Darmstadt University of Technology in 1990. From 1990 to 1995 he worked as Research Assistant at Darmstadt University of Technology in the domain of neural network implementation and applications. In 1995 he obtained a Ph.D. degree from the same university. His doctoral thesis focused on neural structures for visual surface inspection in industrial manufacturing and related neural network VLSI-implementations. After completion of his Ph.D., he joined Fraunhofer Institute IITB in Karlsruhe and did research in visual inspection and aerial image evaluation. In 1996 he was appointed as an Assistant Professor (Hochschuldozent) for Electronic Devices at Dresden University of Technology. His main research interest lies in design, application, and microelectronic implementation of neural networks and bio-inspired systems for vision and cognition.

Mario Köppen

Fraunhofer IPK Berlin
Department of Pattern Recognition
Pascalstr. 8-9, 10587 Berlin
Germany

E-mail : mario.koeppen@ipk.fhg.de
Phone : +49 (0) 30 39006 200
Fax : +49 (0) 30 391 7517
URL : http://vision.fhg.de/ipk/koeppen

Mario Köppen was born in 1964. He studied physics at the Humboldt-University of Berlin and received his master degree in solid state physics in 1991. Afterwards, he worked as scientific assistant at the Central Institute for Cybernetics and Information Processing in Berlin and changed his main research interests to image processing and soft computing. Since 1992, he is with the Fraunhofer-Institute for Production Systems and Design Technology. He is finishing his Ph.D. thesis on the application of soft computing for image processing.

Takashi Koshimizu

Biometry
Product Development Division
Bayer Yakuhin, Ltd.
5-36 Miyahara 3-chome Yodogawa-ku, Osaka
532-8577, Japan

E-mail : takashi.koshimizu.tk@bayer.co.jp
Phone : +81-6-6398-1083
Fax   : +81-6-6398-1089

Takashi Koshimizu received the bachelor degree in arts and sciences in 1984 from Hiroshima University. He had studied at the division of Information and Computer Sciences, the graduate school of Engineering in Osaka-Electro Communication University, and received the Ph.D. degree for his studies on non-linear multivariate statistical models in 1999 from Osaka-Electro Communication University, Japan.

He joined Bayer Yakuhin, Ltd., Osaka, Japan in 1984, and he has been engaged in statistical evaluation for pharmaceutical development of new drugs.

His main research interest lies on multivariate categorical data analysis in biopharmaceutical research, and application of non-linear models such as feed-forward neural network models in biomedical field.

Tetsuya Miyazaki

Just System Inc.
Tokushima-city
Tokushima, Japan

Tetsuya Miyazaki received master degree in Computer Science and Systems Engineering from Kyushu Institute of Technology, Japan, in 1995. Currently he is a Researcher at the Just System Inc., Japan.

Bertram Nickolay

Fraunhofer IPK Berlin
Department of Pattern Recognition
Pascalstr. 8-9, 10587 Berlin
Germany

E-mail : nickolay@ipk.fhg.de
Phone : +49 (0) 30 39006 201
Fax   : +49 (0) 30 391 7517
URL   : http://vision.fhg.de/ipk/nickolay

Bertram Nickolay was born in 1953. He studied communication engineering at the Technical College Saarland and electronics at the Technical University of Berlin. Since 1981, he has been working as a scientist with the Fraunhofer IPK Berlin.

In 1990 he received his Ph. D. degree from the Department for Construction and Processing at the Technical University of Berlin. Since 1991 he is the head of the Department of Pattern Recognition at the IPK. In 1992, in honor for his work on applied research, he received the Joseph von Fraunhofer prize.

Manabu Nii

Department of Industrial Engineering
Osaka Prefecture University
Gakuen-cho 1-1, Sakai, Osaka 599-8531, Japan

E-mail : manabu@ie.osakafu-u.ac.jp
Phone : +81-722-54-9350
Fax   : +81-722-54-9915
URL : http://www.ie.osakafu-u.ac.jp/~hisaoi/
        ci_lab_e/index.html

Manabu Nii received the B. S. and M. S. degrees from Osaka Prefecture University, Osaka, Japan, in 1996 and 1998, respectively. He is currently a doctoral course student. His research interests include fuzzy rule-based systems, fuzzified neural networks, and genetic algorithms.

Shunichiro Oe

Department of Information Science &
 Intelligent Systems
Faculty of Engineering
University of Tokushima
2-1 Minami-josanjima-cho
Tokushima, 770-8506, Japan

E-mail : oe@is.tokushima-u.ac.jp
Phone : +81-88-656-7500
Fax : +81-88-656-7500

Shunichiro OE was born in Shiga Prefecture in 1943. He received the B. Eng and M. Eng. degrees from the University of Tokushima in 1967 and 1969, respectively, and the Ph. D degree from the University of Osaka Prefecture in 1980. From 1969 to 1974 he was a research assistant at the computer center of the University of Tokushima. Now he is a professor at the Department of Information Science and Intelligent System, Faculty of Engineering, University of Tokushima, Japan.

His current research interests include time series analysis, pattern recognition, neural networks, genetic algorithms, and image processing, especially texture segmentation, industrial image processing, three dimensional image processing and remote sensing.

Masahiro Okamoto

Dept. of Biochemical Engineering and Science
Kyushu Institute of Technology, Iizuka
Fukuoka 820-8502,
Japan

E-mail : okahon@bse.kyutech.ac.jp
Phone : +81-948-29-7821
Fax   : +81-948-29-7801

Masahiro Okamoto received a Ph.D. in Agriculture (Agricultural Chemistry) from Kyushu University, Japan, in 1981. Currently he is working as an Associate Professor at the Dept. of Biochemical Engineering and Science, Kyushu Institute of Technology, Japan.

Nikhil R. Pal

Electronics & Communication Sciences Unit
Indian Statistical Institute
203 B. T. Road
Calcutta 700035
INDIA

E-mail : nikhil@isical.ac.in
Phone : +91-33-577-8085
Fax   : +91-33-577-6680

Nikhil R. Pal obtained his B. Sc. (Physics) and Master of Business Management (Operations Research) degrees from the University of Calcutta, and M. Tech. and Ph. D. degrees in Computer Science from the Indian Statistical Institute, Calcutta. He is currently a professor in the Electronics and Communication Sciences Unit of the Indian Statistical Institute, Calcutta. He was a guest lecturer of the University of Calcutta also. He has co-authored a book titled "Fuzzy Models and Algorithms for Pattern Recognition and Image Processing", Kluwer Academic Publishers, 1999 and also co-edited "Advances in Pattern Recognition and Digital Techniques", ICAPRDT'99, Narosa Publishing Co., 1999. His research interest includes fuzzy logic, neural networks, pattern recognition, image processing and quantification of uncertainty. He is an associate editor of *International Journal of Approximate Reasoning, International Journal of Fuzzy Systems, IEEE Transactions of Fuzzy Systems,* and *IEEE Transactions on Systems, Man and Cybernetics – B (Electronic).*

Anujit Sarkar

Macmet Interactive Technologies Pvt. Ltd.
69, Park Street
Calcutta - 700 016

E-mail : anujit@vsnl.com
Phone : +91-33-246-3245

Anujit Sarkar obtained his Bachelor of Mechanical Engineering from the Jadavpur University, Calcutta in 1993 and the Master of Engineering in Computer Applications from Birla Institute of Technology, Meshra in 1999. Currently he is working as a Senior Engineer at Macmet Interactive Technologies Pvt. Ltd., Calcutta. Prior to this he worked as a Software Design Engineer with Vedika International Pvt. Ltd., Calcutta.

His research interest includes distributed computing, artificial intelligence, fuzzy logic, and networking, He enjoys listening to Tagore's songs, western classical music, and folk songs.

Olli Simula

Helsinki University of Technology
Laboratory of Computer and Information Science
P.O. Box 5400, FIN-02015 HUT, Finland

E-mail : olli.simula@hut.fi
Phone : +358 9 451 3271
Fax   : +358 9 451 3277
URL   : http://www.cis.hut.fi/ollis/

Olli Simula received the Dr. Tech. degree in computer science from Helsinki University of Technology, Finland, in 1979. He is currently a Professor of Computer Science and Engineering at the Laboratory of Computer and Information Science, Helsinki University of Technology, Finland. Dr. Simula is the author of a number of journal and conference papers and book chapters on digital signal processing, image analysis and artificial neural networks and their applications in data exploration, including process monitoring, modeling, and analysis, and intelligent methods in telecommunications.

Shamik Sural

NIIT Limited
6B Pretoria Street
Calcutta 700 071, India

E-mail : shamik_s@hotmail.com
Phone : +91-33-430-1867

Shamik Sural received the Bachelor of Engineering degree in Electronics & Telecommunication engineering in 1990 from Jadavpur University, Calcutta and the Master of Engineering degree in electrical communication engineering in 1992 from the Indian Institute of Science, Bangalore, India. He obtained his Ph. D. (Engg.) degree from the Jadavpur University in 2000.

From 1992 to 1993, Shamik was engaged in the design of a VLSI DRAM chip at Texas Instruments as an IC Design Engineer. From 1993 to 1998 he worked as a software professional at CMC Limited in Calcutta, developing and managing projects. He subsequently joined NIIT Limited as a consultant engaged in software project management using SEI-CMM Level 5 compliant software quality processes.

His main research interest is soft computing techniques for character recognition and application of computational intelligence in project management and software engineering problems. Shamik has active interest in traveling and listening to Indian music.

Hiromitsu Takahashi

Department of Comunication Engineering
Faculty of Computer Science & System Engineering
Okayama Prefectural University
Soja, Okayama 719-1197, Japan

E-mail : tak@c.oka-pu.ac.jp
Phone : +81-866-94-2095
Fax : +81-866-94-2199
URL : http://zeus.c.oka-pu.ac.jp/HomePage.html

Hiromitsu Takahashi received the B. Eng., M. Eng. and Ph.D. degrees from Osaka University in 1965, 1968 and 1971, respectively. From 1971 to 1994, he was with the Department of Mathematical Sciences of Osaka Prefecture University. Since 1994, he is a Professor at the Faculty of Computer Science and System Engineering of Okayama Prefectural University. His research interests include graph theory and computer algorithms. He is a member of IEEE, the Mathematical Society of Japan and Information Processing Society of Japan.

Masaaki Tsujitani

Department of Engineering Informatics
Faculty of Information Science & Technology
Osaka Electro-Communication University
18-8 Hatsu-cho, Neyagawa, Osaka 572-8530
Japan

E-mail : tujitani@isc.osakac.ac.jp
Phone : +81-720-25-4685
Fax   : +81-720-24-0014

Masaaki Tsujitani received the B. Ed. degree in 1972 from Osaka Kyoiku University, and the M. Eng. degree in 1977 from University of Osaka Prefecture. He received the Ph.D. degree for his studies in 1980 from University of Osaka Prefecture, Japan.

From 1972 to 1975, he had worked for Kajima Corporation, Tokyo. Since 1995, he is a professor of Engineering Informatics at the faculty of Information Science and Technology, Osaka Electro-Communication University, Neyagawa, Japan.

His main research interest lies on multivariate categorical data analysis, and non-linear multivariate analysis using feed-forward neural networks.

Juha Vesanto

Helsinki University of Technology
Laboratory of Computer and Information Science
P.O. Box 5400, FIN-02015 HUT, Finland

E-mail : juha.vesanto@hut.fi
Fax   : +358 9 451 3277

Juha Vesanto received the M.Sc. (Tech.) degree in technical physics from Helsinki University of Technology, Finland, in 1997. He is currently a researcher and a Ph.D. student at the Laboratory of Computer and Science, Helsinki University of Technology, Finland. His research interests focus on data mining, especially visualization and analysis of multivariate data.

Torao Yanaru

Department of Electric, Electronic &
Computer Engineering
Faculty of Engineering
Kyushu Institute of Technology
1-1, Sensui, Tobata, Kitakyushu city
Fukuoka 804-8550 JAPAN

E-mail : yanaru@comp.kyutech.ac.jp
Phone : +81-93-884-3245
Fax : +81-93-884-3245
URL : http://human1.soft.comp.kyutech.ac.jp/

Torao YANARU received the M.S. Degree in electrical engineering from Kyushu Institute of Technology, Kitakyushu in 1967, and the Dr. degree of engineering in 1982. From 1975 to 1988 he worked as an associate professor in the information scientific center at Kyutech, and from 1989 to 1991 he worked as a professor of artificial intelligence engineering at Kyutech. At present he is a professor of electrical engineering, faculty of engineering at Kyutech. His present research interests include development of the emotion processing system based on the theory for subjective observation model. Dr. YANARU is a member of BMFSA, Society for Fuzzy Theory and Systems, and so on.

Kaori Yoshida

Department of Computer Science & Electronics
Faculty of Computer Science & Systems Engineering
Kyushu Institute of Technology
680-4 Kawazu, Iizuka city
Fukuoka 820-8502, Japan

E-mail : kaori@cse.kyutech.ac.jp
Phone : +81-948-29-7686
Fax : +81-948-29-7651
URL : http://www.iizuka.kyutech.ac.jp/

Kaori YOSHIDA received her M.S. degree in computer engineering from Kyushu Institute of Technology, Kitakyushu, Japan in 1996, and the Dr. degree of engineering in 1999. She has worked as an intern of intelligent systems division, Electrotechnical Laboratory AIST MITI since 1996. She is now a research associate of Computer Science and Systems Engineering in Kyushu Institute of Technology, Iizuka. Her research interests include development of the emotional information processing system and Kansei information processing. Dr. YOSHIDA is a member of BMFSA and JSAI.

Jing Zhang

Department of Computer Science & Engineering
Harbin Institute of Technology
92 West Dazhi   Street Harbin
China

E-mail : cq@public.hr.hl.cn
Phone : +86-451-6416485
Fax   : +86-451-6413309

Jing ZHANG received the B. Eng. and M. Eng. Degrees in Electrical Engineering from the Harbin University of Science and Technology, China. She received the Ph.D degree for her study on Systems Engineering in 1999 from the University of Tokushima, Japan.

She is currently working at the Department of Computer Science and Engineering, Harbin Institute of Technology, China. Her main research interests include image processing, neural networks, and pattern recognition especially image segmentation.

Keyword Index

A

activation 100
aerosols 69, 70, 77
AIC 198, 209, 211, 214, 217, 222
alpha-cuts 127
ambiguous data 266, 271
anisotropy coefficient 308, 309
appendicitis data 236
artificial neural network 182
aspect angles 105
assessment of feature 28
association 165, 166, 168, 170, 171, 172, 174, 176, 177
associative classification 165, 168, 172, 175, 177
associative memory 164, 166, 168, 173
- device 170
associatron memory 177
atmospheric correction 69,70,71,77,91
atmospheric path radiance 69
augmented error function 97
automated classification system 95
automatic diagnosis 170
automatic feature selection 4
autoregressive model 306
average connectivity 99, 100
average recognition rate 104

B

backpropagation 101, 197, 205, 314
- network 6, 16
backward step-wise procedure 235
band-pass filter network 312, 313
band-pass neural network 307
belongingness 147
binary images 307, 308, 310, 324, 326
biological reality 107

C

CAD like functionality 19
canonical correlation analysis 337
canonical frame 192
categorical value 250
cellular neural network 164, 168
cerebral neural network 165
characteristic value 172, 173
chlorophyll 67, 68, 69, 70, 71, 72, 75, 79, 86, 88, 91, 92
circle extraction 121
class affiliation 21
classifiability 229, 235, 246
classification 2, 15, 66, 70, 72, 73, 74, 76, 77, 79, 80, 81, 84, 85, 86, 87, 92, 103, 111, 250
- accuracy 101

- errors 28
- performance 173
- rate 101
classifier failure 127
cluster analysis 40
cluster number 143
clustering 250
- techniques 29
coarseness index 306
cognitive tasks 96
color code 58
combined features 103
common descriptor 251, 252, 254, 255
- table 254
compactness 3, 307
complete rule 254, 255
complexity of computation 96
component planes 21, 43
connected components 310, 311
connection links 99
connection strength 100
connectionist model 97
conservative approach 267
convolution 290
co-occurrence matrix 306
correlation 22
  - coefficient 78
  - detection 40
credit approval data 236
cross-entropy 197, 200, 201, 202, 205, 207, 222
crossover 282, 284
crude oil data 130
curse of dimensionality 2

D

data 2, 27, 39, 40, 81, 192
  - analysis
  - exploration 39
  - fusion 81
  - glove 192
  - mining 2
database mining 27

database navigation tasks 34
Delaunay grid 23
descriptor pattern table 253, 258, 260, 266
design of recognition systems 28
deviance 197, 208, 209, 217, 222
diagnosis 175
diagnosis sensitivity 176
diagnostic ability 175
dimensionality reduction 1, 19, 34
discriminance 3, 11, 18
  - analysis 18
discriminant function 164
discriminatory power 96
distance preservation 6, 15, 30
distance preserving 9
distinct descriptor 251, 252, 254, 255
  - table 254
document defect model 113

E

electromagnetic spectrum 68
embedded pattern 165, 166, 169, 171
enhanced NLM 32
entropy 308
Euclidean distance 99
Euler number 307, 310, 312, 326
evolutionary algorithms 277, 282, 285
excess widths 238, 239, 240, 241, 244, 246
explicit selection 4

F

feature 1, 2, 3, 19, 21, 27, 41, 70, 72, 73, 77, 79, 83, 92, 95, 96, 111, 112, 127, 225, 247, 250, 267, 271
  - analysis 3, 70, 72, 77, 79, 83, 92, 250, 267, 271
  - based classification 111
  - computation 2
  - evaluation criteria 97
  - extraction 1, 2, 41, 112

- quality index 127
- saliency 21
- selection 2, 95, 112, 127, 225, 247
- space 19, 27, 73
- subset 96
- visualization 3

feed-forward network 196, 197, 198, 204, 205, 207, 210, 216, 222, 227, 228, 231, 235

firing strength 267

fitness function 268, 285, 293

fixed global pivot points 12

flexible objects 184

forward step-wise procedure 235

fractal 98, 99, 100, 102, 306, 326
- connection set 98
- connection structure 98, 99
- dimension 99, 100, 306, 326
- network configuration 102

full connections 100

fully connected network 98

fuzzy 111, 118, 119, 120, 123, 125, 143, 177, 250, 253, 254, 256
- c-Means 143, 256
- descriptor 254
- expert system 177
- feature 250, 253
- feature extraction 119
- Hough transform 118, 120
- MLP 118
- neural networks 123
- pattern class 12, 125
- perceptron 123
- rule 17
- sets 111, 118
- systems 177

G

Gaussian GRBF 182

generalization ability 271

generalized radial basis function 182

genetic algorithm 127, 128, 143, 268, 282

genetic tuning 270, 271

geometrical attributes 307

geometrical features 307

gestalt theory 29

global mapping quality 33

graphical feature 332, 335

ground truth 69, 70, 74, 75, 76, 90, 92

H

Hamming distance 171, 173, 174

hand shape change 184

handwriting extraction 278

hard clustering 142

hardware implementation 107

hepatitis 169

hidden layer 98, 101

hierarchical clustering and mapping 29

hierarchical mapping 25, 27, 29
- and visualization 25

hierarchical network 18

hierarchical subdivision 243, 244, 246, 247

Hinton diagrams 21

histogram 81, 82, 83, 88

Hopfield network 164

hot rolling 55

Hough transform 112

human media technology 331, 340

I

ID3 251

identical vectors 24

if-then rules 164

image processing 280, 290, 293

image retrieval 334, 339

image segmentation 306, 312, 315, 322

impression words 338, 339

inclusion monotonicity 232, 242

incomplete vector 230, 233

industrial processes 39

information compression 197, 220
initialization 84, 85
interactive analysis 1
interactive navigation 24
interactive visual data analysis 1
interactive visualization 2
interpolation 184
interval input 230, 231, 232, 233, 234, 239, 240, 241, 242, 243, 244, 245, 246
interval representation 230
interval vector 227, 230, 236, 240, 242, 243, 246
interval-arithmetic-based approach 226, 227, 241
intra/inter-cluster distance 6
intrinsic dimension 9, 19
intrinsic dimensionality 29
intuitive man-machine-interface 19
inverse power law 98
IRIS data 103, 130, 174, 236, 238
irrelevant features 101

K

knowledge 2, 72, 74, 76, 83, 84, 89, 92
  - discovery 2
Kohonen's self-organizing map 6
Kullback-Leibler measure 197, 202, 207, 208, 222

L

labeling 75, 83, 90
land cover classification 72
lattice 168
least-squares minimum difference 74
likelihood-ratio 198, 208, 209, 213, 218, 219, 222
line detection 119
linear discriminant analysis 13
linguistic fuzzy sets 124
linguistic values 269
liver disease 175, 177

local autocorrelation 336
local mapping quality 29, 33
local neighbourhood display 25
lookup algorithm 278, 279, 280, 285, 292, 298
low-pass filter 315

M

machine learning 2
Mahalanobis generalized distance 164
mapping 9, 25, 27, 29, 182
  - error 25,29
  - faults 25, 27
  - reliability 27
Markov chain 113, 130
mathematical morphology 279
matlab 48
maximum likelihood estimators 197, 201
measurement cost 227, 228, 229, 234, 235, 236, 238, 247
medical classification 222
medical data analysis 34
medical image analysis 306
membership degree 143
membership function 146, 252, 255, 256, 258, 268, 269, 270, 272
membership value 260
memory matrix 172
minimal-spanning-tree 11
minimum allowable output error 102
misclassification 127
motion capture 191
multilayer neural networks 164
multilayer perceptron 97, 111, 115, 196
multimedia 331, 332
  - database 332
  - information technology 331
multivariate data projection 1
multivariate data visualization 20
multivariate normal 164
mutation 282, 284

N

natural clusters 256
natural interval extension 240, 242
neighbor cells 168
neighbourhoods 73, 81
neural networks 39, 66, 72, 75, 76, 77, 81, 90, 92, 312, 322
neuron 73, 74, 75, 78, 81, 82, 83, 84, 85, 90
NLM recall algorithm 9
noise 68, 78, 90
nonlinear discriminant analysis 197
nonparametric measures 96
nonparametric scattermatrix 13
normal density curve 143
normal distribution 143
novelty detection 40

O

objective function 143
occluded vectors 24
ocean colour 67, 68, 69, 70, 71, 72, 77, 79, 80, 86, 87, 92
operation monitoring 40
optical character recognition 111
optimization 29
optimum efficiency 101
optimum salient characteristics 95
optimum sparseness 106
outliers 23, 28

P

Pao-Hu method 251, 252, 271
parameter optimization 28
parametric measures 96
partial information 226, 232
partial rule 252, 254
partially localized 99
pattern recognition 2, 19, 24
 - system design 24
performance 177
personal view model 339
perspective view 182
pictorial domain data 334, 336
piecewise linear continuous 172
plural embedded patterns 166
power spectral envelope 105
pre-assigned limit 102
preprocessing 105
principal component analysis 4
probability 143
pruning 197, 209, 218, 219, 222, 225, 247
pulp digester 51
pulping 51
pyramid linking 307, 315, 319, 322, 325, 326
pyramid structure 315, 316, 317, 321

Q

quality of feature 96
Quick Cog 20, 29, 34

R

radial basis function 18
radiance 68, 69, 70, 72, 73, 74, 75, 76, 77, 78, 80, 81, 82, 83, 84, 85, 86, 88, 90
radiative transfer model 69, 70, 75, 76, 92
random number 100
real-time processing 71
recognition 29, 181
 - system design 29
reference point 11, 29, 33
regularity detector 74, 75
rejected training patterns 235
relaxation 278, 287, 292
research software 42
response time 27
RGB colour cube 81
RID3 267

rough set 164
rule based classifier 251
rule based system 250
rule induction 252

S

saliency metric 96
Sammon's non-linear-mapping 7
Sammon's projection 42
satellite images 72
scatter matrices 13, 14
scatter plot 19
sea surface temperature 69
search functions 27
self similar scale invariant 98
self-organizing feature maps 66, 72, 73, 74, 75, 77, 78, 80, 81, 84, 85, 87, 89, 90, 92
self-organizing map 39
sense retrieval 335, 338
separability 11, 15
similarity dimension 98, 99
simple subdivision 241, 242
single winner 231
singular value decomposition 169
sketch of the class borders 21
small sample size 96
snow flakes 22
soft computing 19
softmax activation function 207, 208
SOM lattice 23
SOM visualization techniques 20
SONAR data set 103
sparse neural network 100
sparsely connected 98
spatial location 99
stacking mechanism 24
standard deviation 143
standard view 184
statistical measures 96
statistically fractal 99
steel 55
structural learning 185

structure preservation 5, 33
structured GA 143
subjective feature 335
subjective interpretation 334, 337
supervised learning 112
synapse connection 165
synaptic connection distribution 99

T

teacher flag 183
template matching 111
template matrix 168
test set 101
testing 75, 80, 81, 87
textual domain data 334, 335
texture 22, 277, 298, 305, 306, 307, 308, 319, 321, 322, 326
- features 306, 307, 308, 321, 322, 326
- filtering 279, 298
- image segmentation 305
- like pattern 22
- segmentation 319, 326
- similarity 22
three-dimensional 73, 80, 81, 82, 84, 85, 87, 89
time series 50
topological attribute 310
topological fault 30
topological features 306, 326
topological properties 311
topology 6, 30
- measure 30
- preservation 30
- preserving mapping 6
training 73, 74, 75, 76, 80, 81, 84, 101
- data 101
triangulation 11, 12
- mapping 12
- method 11
trouble shooting 24, 28, 29

U

UC Irvine database 236
unclassified points 266
underwater target recognition 103
unfolding 29
unified distance matrix 7, 43
united extension 240
unmeasured attributes 227, 229, 236, 247
unsupervised clustering 143
user interface 49
user-centered approach 331

V

validation set 101
validity measure 156
variance 149
visual patterns 275
visual perception model 331, 340
visualization 1, 39
Voronoi cell 7, 23
Voronoi tessellation 23
voting approach 267

W

weight icons 22
weight watcher 20
wire frame model 184